SMART DECARCERATION

Smart Decarceration

ACHIEVING CRIMINAL JUSTICE TRANSFORMATION
IN THE 21ST CENTURY

Edited by

Matthew W. Epperson

and

Carrie Pettus-Davis

OXFORD
UNIVERSITY PRESS

OXFORD
UNIVERSITY PRESS

Oxford University Press is a department of the University of Oxford. It furthers
the University's objective of excellence in research, scholarship, and education
by publishing worldwide. Oxford is a registered trade mark of Oxford University
Press in the UK and certain other countries.

Published in the United States of America by Oxford University Press
198 Madison Avenue, New York, NY 10016, United States of America.

Library of Congress Cataloging-in-Publication Data
Names: Epperson, Matthew W., editor. | Pettus-Davis, Carrie, editor.
Title: Smart decarceration : achieving criminal justice transformation in the
21st century / edited by Matthew W. Epperson and Carrie Pettus-Davis.
Description: Cambridge ; New York : Oxford University Press, [2017] | Includes index.
Identifiers: LCCN 2017009332 (print) | LCCN 2017019901 (ebook) |
ISBN 9780190653101 (updf) | ISBN 9780190653118 (epub) |
ISBN 9780190653095 (alk. paper)
Subjects: LCSH: Alternatives to imprisonment—United States. |
Imprisonment—United States. | Criminals—Rehabilitation—United States. |
Criminal justice, Administration of—United States.
Classification: LCC HV9304 (ebook) | LCC HV9304 .S559 2017 (print) |
DDC 364.6/80973—dc23
LC record available at https://lccn.loc.gov/2017009332

9 8 7 6 5 4 3 2 1
Printed by Sheridan Books, Inc., United States of America

Contents

Foreword vii
    by Michael Sherraden
Contributors xi
Introduction xvii
    by Matthew W. Epperson and Carrie Pettus-Davis

PART I │ SETTING THE CONTEXT FOR DECARCERATION
*1. Smart Decarceration: Guiding Concepts for an Era of Criminal Justice
    Transformation* 3
    by Matthew W. Epperson and Carrie Pettus-Davis

*2. Reflections on a Locked Door: Lessons from History and the Failed Promise
    of Penal Incarceration* 29
    by Rebecca Ginsburg

*3. From Moment to Movement: The Urgency for Formerly Incarcerated Individuals
    to Lead Decarceration Efforts* 44
    by Glenn E. Martin

PART II │ ADVANCING JUSTICE AND COMMUNITY REFORMS
*4. From the Inside Out: A Perspective on Decarceration from a Formerly
    Incarcerated Individual* 55
    by Ronald Simpson-Bey

*5. The Prosecutor's Role in Promoting Decarceration: Lessons Learned
    from Milwaukee County* 71
    by John Chisholm and Jeffery Altenburg

6. Learning to Lead in the Decarceration Movement 90
    by Vivian D. Nixon

7. Prisoner Reentry in an Era of Smart Decarceration 101
   by Reuben Jonathan Miller

8. Community and Decarceration: Developing Localized Solutions 115
   by Kathryn Bocanegra

PART III | RETHINKING POLICY AND PRACTICE

9. Minimizing the Maximum: The Case for Shortening All Prison Sentences 137
   by Nazgol Ghandnoosh

*10. Reforming Civil Disability Policy to Facilitate Effective
   and Sustainable Decarceration* 160
   by Carrie Pettus-Davis, Matthew W. Epperson, and Annie Grier

*11. A Public Health Approach to Decarceration: Strategies to Reduce the Prison
   and Jail Population and Support Reentry* 179
   by Ernest Drucker

*12. Community Interventions for Justice-Involved Individuals: Assessing Gaps
   in Programming to Promote Decarceration* 193
   by Faye S. Taxman and Amy Murphy

*13. Empirical Means to Decarcerative Ends? Advancing the Science and Practice
   of Risk Assessment* 210
   *by Julian Adler, Sarah Picard-Fritsche, Michael Rempel,
   and Jennifer A. Tallon*

PART IV | MOVING FROM CONCEPTS TO STRATEGIES

*14. Imagining the Future of Justice: Advancing Decarceration through
   Multisector Social Innovations* 231
   by Margaret E. Severson

*15. Guideposts for the Smart Decarceration Era: Recommended Strategies
   from Researchers, Practitioners, and Formerly Incarcerated Leaders* 250
   *by Carrie Pettus-Davis, Matthew W. Epperson, Samuel Taylor,
   and Annie Grier*

INDEX 271

Foreword

Michael Sherraden

I AM HONORED to have the opportunity to comment on the contributions and meaning of this excellent book, *Smart Decarceration: Achieving Criminal Justice Transformation in the 21st Century*, edited by my colleagues Drs. Matthew W. Epperson and Carrie Pettus-Davis.

In 2014, the Smart Decarceration Initiative (SDI) originated at the Center for Social Development as a partnership between the George Warren Brown School of Social Work at Washington University in St. Louis and the University of Chicago School of Social Service Administration. Both schools have notable track records in defining and testing social innovations and using evidence to inform social policies and programs since the early 20th century. Working very much in this tradition, SDI holds an outlook that is pragmatic (in the philosophical sense of American Pragmatism), theoretical (in the sense of specifying relationships to be tested), and empirical (by using research evidence to inform change)—the hallmarks of effective applied social science, in my view. In September of 2015, Drs. Epperson and Pettus-Davis planned and led the conference From Mass Incarceration to Effective and Sustainable Decarceration at Washington University in St. Louis. This volume is the culmination of that inaugural conference.

This book is motivated by an ambitious goal: criminal justice transformation. As a reader, you may ask whether this is actually feasible. In this regard, allow me to set the stage with a big-picture view—because our vision is too often unnecessarily limited by current realities.

Humans are highly social—and enormously innovative—animals. Social innovations have shaped and defined what we think of as civilization. Such innovations did not arise spontaneously or by chance; they had to be conceived and implemented by people. Most have been remarkably positive. But, as we are not a perfect species, humans have also imagined and implemented highly problematic social innovations: imperialism, destructive wars, torture and genocide, slavery, economic exploitation, and incarceration.

A bizarre social aberration and practical failure, mass incarceration in the U.S. criminal justice system is by any standard excessive, racially biased, ineffective, and unaffordable. We humans created mass incarceration and it is in our power to uncreate and replace it. Effective change will require strong political commitment and effective applied research, followed by the implementation of program and policy innovations. Though this task is daunting, the editors and authors of *Smart Decarceration* are uniquely qualified to take this challenge.

Drs. Epperson and Pettus-Davis know that smart decarceration must not be viewed simply as getting people out of jails and prisons. Rather, they are aware that it should involve changing imperfect social institutions—in housing, social services, schooling, policing, and adjudicating—that feed and support mass incarceration. For example, SDI has recently launched a 2-year research project to advance "deferred prosecution" programs. Deferred prosecution is an innovative but understudied intervention: People charged with certain criminal offenses can be diverted from traditional court proceedings and avoid not only incarceration but also the burdens of a criminal record. Drs. Epperson and Pettus-Davis will study how existing deferred prosecution programs were implemented in Milwaukee County, Wisconsin, and Cook County, Illinois. They also will engage stakeholders in the City of St. Louis in planning for a similar program. The study will lead to the design of a multisite randomized control trial for these three urban Midwestern regions. The project has the potential to shape and expand deferred prosecution programs across the country by generating clear evidence. Widespread use of effective deferred prosecution programs would then serve to funnel individuals out of the criminal justice system. Many other such innovations are waiting to be tested, refined, and put in place.

It is fitting that Drs. Epperson and Pettus-Davis are social workers. Social work has a long history of getting people out of incarceration in America, dating back to the 1909 White House Conference on Children, where Jane Addams, Florence Kelly, and other leading social workers decided young people should not be incarcerated for reasons of economic dependency. This very purposeful decision marked the peak of orphanage care in the United States and the beginning of "outdoor relief" in the form of Mother's Aid Laws, which later became Aid to Families with Dependent Children (AFDC), and now Temporary Assistance to Needy Families (TANF)—the programs often called simply "welfare." Though "welfare" has since come under criticism and political pressure, this has been a vast improvement over the bleak incarceration of hundreds of thousands of children. Later, U.S. social workers also played a leadership role in decarceration of people with mental illness during the 1960s and 1970s. This change too has not been free of problems—because adequate community-based care was never established—but anyone who knew the dreadful conditions in many large-scale mental health institutions would never want to reestablish them. In general, incarcerations for any purpose, no matter how idealistic the original intentions, have a long history of not turning out well. And Drs. Epperson and Pettus-Davis understand the importance of learning from history.

Social work continues to blaze the path of decarceration to this day. Under the Grand Challenges for Social Work initiative led by the American Academy of Social Work and Social Welfare, *Promoting Smart Decarceration* is one of 12 grand challenges for social work to address in the coming decade.

In closing, allow me to say that despite the recent popularity of (and unprecedented bipartisan support for) the issue, Drs. Epperson and Pettus-Davis have been dedicated to lessening incarceration through criminal justice reform for almost 20 years. For most of that time, the topic was unpopular. Still, they immersed themselves in the field and in applied scholarship and worked while most of us were not paying much attention. However, their foundational efforts are now paying off, and no one is better positioned to lead this effort than they are.

My sincere thanks to the two editors and all the chapter authors for undertaking the scholarship and critical thinking to lay out the challenge of *Smart Decarceration* for the nation, and for giving us this visionary, informative, determined, and useful book.

Michael Sherraden
George Warren Brown Distinguished University Professor
Director, Center for Social Development
Washington University in St. Louis
August 22, 2016

Contributors

Julian Adler is the director of Research-Practice Strategies at the Center for Court Innovation, which synergizes the agency's three primary areas of work: research, operating programs, and expert assistance. Mr. Adler directs the Center's work on the MacArthur Foundation's Safety and Justice Challenge, an initiative to reduce overincarceration by changing the way America thinks about and uses jails. He also works on the development of holistic evidence-based and evidence-generating practices, including assessment instruments and short-term interventions.

Jeffery Altenburg is a Milwaukee County Assistant District Attorney. Prior to becoming a community prosecutor, he served as a prosecutor in the Milwaukee County District Attorney's Gun Enforcement Unit, where he helped develop Milwaukee County's Gun Court and helped coordinate the office's participation in Project Ceasefire, later known as Project Safe Neighborhoods. Mr. Altenburg has also served in the Drug, Domestic Violence, and General Misdemeanor Units. In May 2002, he became one of the first assistant district attorneys to serve in the district attorney's community prosecution unit.

Kathryn Bocanegra, AM, MA, LCSW, is a doctoral student at the University of Chicago and has been appointed to several criminal justice reform initiatives: the Illinois Sentencing Policy Advisory Council and the Governor's Commission on Criminal Justice and Sentencing Reform. Ms. Bocanegra has led various community-based public safety initiatives and serves as a consultant for national policy initiatives focused on local strategies for decarceration, such as the Alliance for Safety and Justice.

John Chisholm is an American prosecutor and the district attorney of Milwaukee County, Wisconsin, serving since 2007.

Ernest Drucker, PhD, is research scientist and professor of public health at NYU's College of Global Public Health; Professor Emeritus of Family and Social Medicine at Montefiore Medical Center/Albert Einstein College of Medicine; and adjunct professor and scholar in residence at John Jay College of Criminal Justice of The City University of New York. He is licensed as a clinical psychologist; conducts research in AIDS, drug policy, and prisons; and is active in public health programs and human rights advocacy in the United States and abroad.

Matthew W. Epperson, PhD, is an associate professor at the University of Chicago School of Social Service Administration. His research centers on developing, implementing, and evaluating interventions to reduce disparities in the criminal justice system. His primary area of focus is understanding and addressing person- and place-level risk factors for criminal involvement among persons with mental illnesses. Professor Epperson's interests also include developing conceptual, evidence-based frameworks for effective and sustainable decarceration. His scholarship and teaching aim to build and advance the capacity of the social work profession to address these challenges and opportunities for criminal justice transformation.

Nazgol Ghandnoosh, PhD, is a research analyst at The Sentencing Project, a nonprofit organization engaged in research and advocacy for criminal justice reform. She has written about racial disparities in the justice system, public opinion about punishment, and the scope of reform efforts. Dr. Ghandnoosh earned a bachelor of science in economics at the University of Pennsylvania (2001) and a PhD in sociology at the University of California, Los Angeles (2013). Her dissertation examined a South Los Angeles–based group's challenges to prolonged life sentences.

Rebecca Ginsburg is the director of the Education Justice Project, a comprehensive college-in-prison program based at the University of Illinois at Urbana-Champaign that provides academic programs to incarcerated individuals and outreach services to the families of incarcerated people and returning citizens. The Education Justice Project programs operate in Danville, Champaign, and Chicago, Illinois.

Annie Grier, MSW, is a project manager at the Center for Social Development, where her work focuses on reversing mass incarceration in the United States. Ms. Grier has developed and managed programs in North Carolina and Pennsylvania for women reentering society after incarceration. As a graduate student at the George Warren Brown School of Social Work, she contributed to research focused on the interaction of trauma and substance abuse in criminal offending and the impact of social supports on male recidivism.

Glenn E. Martin is the founder and president of JustLeadershipUSA, an organization that aims to cut the U.S. correctional population in half by 2030 by empowering those affected by incarceration to drive policy reform. Mr. Martin is cofounder of the Education Inside Out Coalition and the David Rothenberg Center for Public Policy. He is a 2014 Echoing Green Fellow, a 2012 America's Leaders of Change National Urban Fellow, and a member of the Boards of The College and Community Fellowship, Million Hoodies, and the California Partnership for Safe Communities. Mr. Martin was appointed in 2016 to the Independent Commission on New York City Criminal Justice and Incarceration Reform at the invitation of New York State Chief Judge Jonathan Lippman to look at the possibility of closing Rikers Island. He regularly contributes his expertise to national news outlets such as MSNBC, Fox News, CNN, and C-SPAN.

Reuben Jonathan Miller, PhD, AM, is a 2016–17 Member of the Institute for Advanced Study in Princeton, NJ in the School of Social Science and an Assistant Professor at the University of Chicago School of Social Service Administration. His research, writing, and advocacy focuses on the lives of prisoners and former prisoners and how carceral expansion has transformed the urban landscape.

Amy Murphy, MPP, is a research associate at the Center for Advancing Correctional Excellence. Her experience includes working as a research specialist with the Center for Evidence-Based Corrections at the University of California, Irvine, as well as work in the consulting field in Washington, DC, and with the Criminal Justice Research Division of the San Diego Association of Governments.

The Reverend Vivian D. Nixon is the executive director of College and Community Fellowship (CCF), an organization committed to removing individual and structural barriers to higher education for women with criminal record histories and their families. As a formerly incarcerated woman and prior CCF program participant, Reverend Nixon is uniquely positioned to lead the charge to help justice-involved women and their families have a better future. While incarcerated, Reverend Nixon spent time as a peer educator for the adult basic education program at Albion State Correctional Facility in New York. Following her release, she was ordained by the African Methodist Episcopal Church (AMEC) and currently serves as an associate minister at Mt. Zion AMEC in New York City. She is a Columbia University Community Scholar and a recipient of the John Jay Medal for Justice, the Ascend Fellowship at the Aspen Institute, the Soros Justice Fellowship, and the Petra Foundation Fellowship. She is a cofounder of the Education from the Inside Out Coalition, a collaborative effort to increase access to higher education for justice-involved students and serves on the advisory board of JustLeadershipUSA.

Carrie Pettus-Davis, PhD, is founding director of the Institute for Advancing Justice Research and Innovation and cofounder and codirector of the Smart Decarceration Initiative. Professor Pettus-Davis oversees research to better understand factors and disseminate practices that will dramatically reduce incarceration rates. She has served as assistant professor at the Brown School at Washington University since 2011. Prior to joining academia, she spent more than a decade designing and delivering programs in criminal justice and community settings. Building on her social work practice experience, Professor Pettus-Davis focuses her research on the development and implementation of innovative services and policies impacting adults in the criminal justice system and their loved ones. She aims to advance science and practice in ways that will redress racial, economic, and behavioral health disparities among justice-involved populations. She is helping to lead public-private-academic partnerships committed to accelerating the research-to practice-to policy engagement feedback loop.

Sarah Picard-Fritsche is the associate director of research and deputy director of research-practice at the Center for Court Innovation. She currently coleads the Center's research and technical assistance effort to reduce the use of jail incarceration nationally, funded by the MacArthur Foundation. She is also the principal investigator on several federally funded studies, including a quasi-experimental evaluation of "neighborhood-oriented" probation funded by the National Institute for Justice, and several studies examining the use of actuarial risk assessment in justice system settings.

Michael Rempel is the research director at the Center for Court Innovation, overseeing all research conducted at the agency. He is currently directing a statewide evaluation of specialized drug courts in New York; a randomized trial of evidence-based assessment tools; a national study of the commercial sexual exploitation of children; and a multisite formative study of initiatives to address children's exposure to violence.

Margaret E. Severson, JD, teaches graduate students of social work in the MSW and PhD programs at the University of Kansas School of Social Welfare. Her research involves jail and prison mental health and suicide prevention programs, reentry services, social justice and human rights as related to prisoners and their families, and correctional systems organization and management. She provides consultation to the U.S. Department of Justice and to jails and prisons across the United States.

Ronald Simpson-Bey is an Alumni Associate for JustLeadershipUSA (JLUSA) and a 2015 LwC Fellow with JLUSA. He serves on the steering team of the Michigan Collaborative to End Mass Incarceration. He is a former Program Associate with American Friends Service Committee and Research Assistant at the University of Michigan School of Social Work. Ronald served 27 years in the Michigan prison system as an engaged, thoughtful, and creative leader, founding many enrichment programs rooted in transformation, redemption, and self-accountability. Mr. Simpson-Bey was a paralegal and jailhouse lawyer who got his conviction reversed by the courts and was subsequently released from prison.

Jennifer A. Tallon, PhD, is a senior research associate at the Center for Court Innovation. Dr. Tallon is presently leading a National Institute of Corrections–funded project to develop and pilot-test a set of Risk-Need-Responsivity-based assessment tools for justice-involved military veterans. She is also providing technical assistance regarding strategies to reduce the use of jail as part of the MacArthur Foundation's Safety and Justice Challenge. Additionally, she is the lead researcher on several federally funded studies examining topics such as violence prevention and police-led diversion programs.

Faye S. Taxman, PhD, is a university professor in the Criminology, Law and Society Department and Director of the Center for Advancing Correctional Excellence at George Mason University. Dr. Taxman is recognized for her work in the development of the seamless systems of care models that link criminal justice with other service delivery systems as well as reengineering probation and parole supervision services, and organizational change models. Her work covers the breadth of the correctional system from jails and prisons to community corrections and adult and juvenile offenders, including all types of interventions and system improvement factors.

Samuel Taylor, MSW, serves as project manager at the Center for Social Development and the Envolve Center for Health Behavior Change at Washington University in St. Louis. In his work at the Center for Social Development, Taylor assists with design, data analysis, and manuscript preparation and dissemination for the national tax-time saving intervention, the Refund to Savings initiative.

Introduction

THE UNITED STATES is on the cusp of something historic—a nascent era of decarceration. Simply saying the word "decarceration" would likely have drawn perplexed looks just a few years ago, and the term may still be unfamiliar to many. What is all too familiar, though, are the deleterious effects of the exceptionally American phenomenon of mass incarceration. Previously easily ignored by all save for the individuals and communities most affected, mass incarceration has become so unsustainable that it has forced its way into the national consciousness. It is a shameful reminder of how America has overused such a blunt instrument for too long on far too many people, especially already marginalized and oppressed people. Countless books, articles, reports, and all variety of news media, art, and music have documented the atrocities of mass incarceration and inspired active debate in classrooms, meeting rooms, and living rooms. There is little disagreement that mass incarceration must end.

But if the United States is to move away from mass incarceration, we must begin by asking one critical question: What is it to do instead?

That question was the driving motivation behind the creation of the Smart Decarceration Initiative. Before cofounding this initiative, we both worked for years in jails and prisons and saw firsthand the toll mass incarceration takes on individuals and their families. As we transitioned into academic careers, we synthesized our practice experience with the immense body of research on the ills and ineffectiveness of mass incarceration. We noticed how conversations about incarceration were starting to shift in social and political circles, becoming more critical of the War on Drugs and other tough-on-crime policies, in addition to the billions of dollars spent on incarceration every year. In essence, we recognized what was becoming a perfect storm for mass incarceration to be reversed.

But something as complex and societally entrenched as mass incarceration cannot be easily undone. The challenge of decarceration is far greater than simply not incarcerating. The real challenge and opportunity involves building an array of policy and practice innovations that, whenever possible, replace incarceration. It is too limiting to think of decarceration as a reaction to mass incarceration. Decarceration must catalyze a paradigm shift in justice, punishment, rehabilitation, and safety. It must change the thinking that led to mass incarceration in the first place. Such a task will take time and concerted effort.

It is for this reason that we declare this the *era* of decarceration. It is not a moment, but a movement. Rather than a quick fix, it must be a well-planned, thoughtful, and comprehensive approach. Decarceration efforts must not aim to just reduce jail and prison populations; they must do so in ways that reverse long-standing race, class, and health disparities in the U.S. criminal justice system. And it must do so in ways that uphold public safety and well-being. Decarceration must be effective, sustainable, and socially just—it must be *smart decarceration.*

Recognizing the innumerable challenges of entering an era of decarceration, we extended our focus beyond our own expertise to include a diverse, multidisciplinary, and coordinated effort. To help shape such a field, we convened the first national conference on decarceration—From Mass Incarceration to Effective and Sustainable Decarceration—in September 2015 at Washington University in St. Louis. We intentionally invited presenters and attendees who represented a vast range of critical perspectives and areas of expertise, including formerly incarcerated leaders, researchers from diverse disciplines, practitioners, policymakers, and advocates. Our goal was to create an event that was interactive, one that generated both concrete strategies and challenges to existing narratives. We hoped to provoke meaningful debate between people with diverse perspectives who are not often at the same table working toward a shared goal. What we experienced, and what we have heard from conference attendees, was that it was a unique and challenging convening, one that inspired new ideas and momentum for advancing smart decarceration. The conference was everything we hoped it would be, due mostly to the dedication, hard work, and creativity of all those in attendance.

This book is our attempt to capture and synthesize the ideas generated at the conference. Reflecting the conference structure, this book is organized into four parts. In the first, "Setting the Context for Decarceration," we offer guiding concepts to inform future efforts at the beginning of this era. Rebecca Ginsburg discusses the challenges of incarceration through a historical lens, and Glenn E. Martin emphasizes the essential component of leadership among formerly incarcerated individuals in building a smart decarceration movement. In Part I and throughout the book, you will hear directly from individuals who have lived through the realities of incarceration and have committed to transform that experience into active leadership in decarceration work.

Part II, "Advancing Justice and Community Reforms," offers unique perspectives on specific examples of reforms that could support smart decarceration. The important but often overlooked role of prosecutors and the necessity for prosecutorial reform is discussed from two drastically different but complementary perspectives: that of John Chisolm, a district attorney in a large urban county, and that of Ronald Simpson-Bey, who unnecessarily spent over 20 years in prison due to prosecutorial misconduct. The social institution of prisoner reentry is examined by Vivian Nixon and illuminated by Rueben Miller in respective chapters as a means to sustain decarceration in the context of racism and other structural barriers, social service delivery, and individual-focused interventions. The concluding chapter of this section by Kathryn Bocanegra builds on these themes by underscoring the importance of centering community in the development of decarceration efforts.

Part III, "Rethinking Policy and Practice," takes up questions about how current policies and practices must be reimagined to realize effective and sustainable decarceration. Two major areas of policy are addressed: Nazgol Ghandnoosh tackles prison sentencing reform for all types of crime, including violent crime, and we address the compendium of civil disability policies that undermine rehabilitative practices, community participation, and, ultimately, decarceration. Ernest Drucker offers an alternative lens to decarceration by mobilizing concepts of prevention to reconceptualize decarceration as a public health outcome. The landscape of community-based interventions for people with criminal justice involvement, as well as intervention quality and capacity, are illustrated by Faye Taxman and Amy Murphy. Julian Adler and colleagues conclude Part III by exploring the science and practice of risk assessment and its potential role in decarceration.

The book's final part, "Moving from Concepts to Strategies," is a look forward. First, Margaret Severson challenges us to take on a futurist's perspective on decarceration and to consider innovations across traditionally bound sectors and disciplines. In the concluding chapter, we summarize work that was done in small group sessions at the conference to operationalize guiding concepts into clear guideposts and strategies for decarceration efforts. In all sections of the book, authors pose important questions and recommendations that will help to shape the era of decarceration in meaningful ways.

The real work of decarceration is just beginning. In the same way, we recognize that this book signifies not an ending, but a launching of ideas and solutions. We hope that something in this volume challenges your thinking or inspires a new idea or action. Truly the work of smart decarceration requires all to be involved. Your voice, your ideas, and your work are needed to build a sustained effort and an era of smart decarceration.

Matthew W. Epperson and Carrie Pettus-Davis
Editors and Cofounders of the Smart Decarceration Initiative

PART I

Setting the Context for Decarceration

1

Smart Decarceration

GUIDING CONCEPTS FOR AN ERA
OF CRIMINAL JUSTICE TRANSFORMATION

Matthew W. Epperson and Carrie Pettus-Davis

BACKGROUND

The United States is at a unique moment in history. After nearly 40 years of exponential growth in the numbers of people incarcerated in jail and prison, it has become increasingly apparent that the era of mass incarceration is nearing its end. During this time, the criminal justice system evolved into a highly punitive system designed to distance people from society. It neglects the strengths of individuals and communities and generally leaves individuals worse off than before they entered the system. The consequences of this era are staggering: The United States is the world leader in incarceration, with 2.3 million adults in jail or prison on any given day and an incarceration rate of more than 700 per 100,000 citizens (Pew Center on the States, 2008). Mass incarceration disproportionately affects vulnerable segments of the country's population. People of color, those in poverty, and those with behavioral health disorders are grossly overrepresented in U.S. jails and prisons. As a result, a ripple effect of mass incarceration has crippled poor and minority communities. Mass incarceration has become financially unsustainable and politically unpopular, and a broad spectrum of public figures is now motivated to reduce incarceration rates.

What will follow the era of mass incarceration? Growing evidence suggests it will be an era of decarceration—a range of approaches to lessen the use of incarceration (Jacobson, 2005; Petersilia & Cullen, 2014; Pettus-Davis & Epperson, 2015). Like its predecessor, this era will likely involve a lengthy and sustained process. Protracted processes and complex racial, economic, and political histories led to mass incarceration; therefore, the decarceration approach must not seek quick and simplistic methods to cut incarceration rates if it hopes to maintain durable reductions. Instead, to ensure effective and sustainable decarceration, it must plan and do the difficult work of developing a "smart" approach—one that is evidence driven and grounded in a social justice orientation.

SMART DECARCERATION OUTCOMES AND GUIDING CONCEPTS

For the country to achieve effective, sustainable, and socially just decarceration—hereafter referred to as *smart decarceration*—the following three outcomes must be accomplished:

1. Substantially reduce the incarcerated population in jails and prisons.
2. Redress the existing social disparities among the incarcerated.
3. Maximize public safety and well-being.

In this chapter, we first review the era of mass incarceration, its ripple effects, and the evidence that it is coming to a close. We then discuss what it means to be at the beginning of an era of decarceration, the challenges and opportunities of a criminal justice system in flux, and the importance of articulating the aforementioned outcomes and key strategies to achieve smart decarceration. We then present the following guiding concepts for how to guide efforts to achieve those outcomes and transform the criminal justice system, and ask key questions for each concept:

1. *Changing the narrative on incarceration and the incarcerated.* The smart decarceration approach must critically examine the utility and function of incarceration, challenge the existing view of currently and formerly incarcerated individuals, and actively welcome those individuals as leaders in decarceration efforts.
2. *Making criminal justice system-wide innovations.* Criminal justice transformation that leads to smart decarceration will require advances in all sectors of the criminal justice system, including law enforcement, court systems, jails and prisons, and community supervision.
3. *Implementing transdisciplinary policy and practice interventions.* Smart decarceration will be complex and comprehensive and will require integrating perspectives from multiple disciplines to produce substantive policy reforms and practice innovations.
4. *Employing evidence-driven strategies.* The smart decarceration approach must both generate new evidence for optimal reforms and use existing evidence to guide decision-making and program development. Methods must be integrated to continuously examine and assess the effects of policy and practice interventions, thus developing further evidence from which to act.

Applying these core concepts at the onset of the decarceration era will result in fundamental shifts in the criminal justice system and inform the postdecarceration era. We conclude by offering some possibilities for what the postdecarceration era could include, depending on the transformation of the criminal justice system.

THE ERA OF MASS INCARCERATION

For nearly 40 years, the theme for the U.S. criminal justice system had been "growth." Beginning in 1972, the annual prison and jail population increased dramatically and without exception for 37 years (Glaze & Parks, 2012). In that time, incarceration rates increased sevenfold, making the United States the world leader in incarceration, both in numbers of incarcerated individuals and in proportion of the incarcerated population (Travis, Western, & Redburn, 2014). The United States makes up just 5% of the world's population, but it houses a staggering 25% of its incarcerated individuals (Alexander, 2012). At the peak of incarceration in 2008, 2.3 million adults were incarcerated in U.S. prisons or jails on any given day, at a cost of over $50 billion annually (Schmitt, Warner, & Gupta, 2010). Though this rate of one in 100 adults incarcerated marks a historic benchmark, it captures only a cross-section of incarcerated individuals—the daily prison population remains stable at nearly 1.5 million, but the daily jail census of around 700,000 does not adequately represent the more than 11.5 million individuals cycling through local jails annually (Minton & Zeng, 2015; Subramanian, Delaney, Roberts, Fishman, & McGarry, 2015). Taking this into account, about 13 million American adults—a startling one in 20—experience some form of incarceration each year.

There is a growing body of research that more fully explores the origins and dramatic effects of mass incarceration in the United States. Notably, the National Research Council of the National Academies commissioned the comprehensive report *The Growth of Incarceration in the United States: Exploring Causes and Consequences* (Travis et al., 2014). The report assesses the evidence pertaining to mass incarceration and its effects, notes that the exponential growth in incarceration is due to the concentration of poverty and unemployment in U.S. cities, and indicates sentencing policy changes as a reaction to rising crime rates in the 1960s through the 1980s, which led to a more punitive political and social climate. Travis et al. (2014) also provide an in-depth account of the consequences of incarceration, including the individual effects of confinement; damaged health and mental health; diminished employment and earnings; and detrimental effects for children, families, communities, and society. Contrasting these multilayered ripple effects of incarceration with the uneven impact of incarceration on crime and public safety, the report's findings demonstrate that

Given the available evidence regarding the causes and consequences of high incarceration rates, and guided by fundamental normative principles regarding the appropriate use of imprisonment as punishment, we believe that the policies lead-ing to high incarceration rates are not serving the country well. We are concerned that the United States has gone past the point where the numbers of people in prison can be justified by social benefits. Indeed, we believe that the high rates of incarceration themselves constitute a source of injustice and, possibly, social harm. A criminal justice system that made less use of incarceration might better achieve its aims than a harsher, more punitive system (Travis et al., 2014, p. 9).

Social Disparities of Mass Incarceration

Incarceration in the United States is a problem not only because of the numbers of per-sons incarcerated but also because of who is most affected. Incarceration overwhelmingly affects people of color, people in poverty and other forms of social disadvantage, and people with behavioral health disorders.

Racial Disparities

Arrest rates for African Americans are double the national average, and African Americans face more severe charges and longer sentences than others with similar characteristics (Mauer, 2011; Snyder, 2012). Although African Americans make up only 13% of the general popula-tion, they constitute 40% of all incarcerated individuals (Pew Center on the States, 2008).

Economic Disparities

Over half of incarcerated individuals were in poverty the year before their arrest and have little chance of rising out of poverty after incarceration (Wheelock & Uggen, 2005). Having a history of incarceration reduces men's annual income by 40% (Western, 2002; Western & Pettit, 2010). Homelessness among formerly incarcerated individuals is four to six times the rate of the general population (Greenberg & Rosenheck, 2008). Two-thirds of state incarcerated individuals do not have a high school diploma upon entering prison, and 44% of those incarcerated in jails have less than a high school education (Harlow, 2003).

Behavioral Health Disorder Disparities

Given the role of the War on Drugs in the growth of incarceration, it is not surprising that people with substance abuse disorders are disproportionately incarcerated. Nearly 1.5 million individuals incarcerated in prisons and jails (65%) meet the criteria for sub-stance use disorders, and an estimated 75% of incarcerated individuals are in need of substance abuse intervention; meanwhile, only about 11% receive any type of treatment while behind bars (National Center on Addiction and Substance Abuse at Columbia University, 2010).

The estimated prevalence of serious mental illnesses (e.g., schizophrenia, bipolar disorder, major depression) in U.S. prisons and jails is approximately 14%, which is more than double the rate of serious mental illness in the general adult population (Fazel & Danesh, 2002; Steadman, Osher, Robbins, Case, & Samuels, 2009). This equates to more than 375,000 people with serious mental illnesses incarcerated on any given day, rather than living in community or therapeutic settings (Epperson, et al., 2014). It is clear that the era of mass incarceration has ushered in the criminalization of behavioral health disorders.

These trends have led some to suggest that the term "hyperincarceration" better describes disproportionate impacts of incarceration based on class and race, as opposed to "mass incarceration," which implies that incarceration affects the population equally and uniformly (Wacquant, 2010).

Ripple Effects of Mass Incarceration

The historically high levels of incarceration are problematic for many reasons. Once a person has been incarcerated, his or her access to the conventional means of citizenry that promote desistance from crime can be permanently disrupted (Hagan & Dinovitzer, 1999). Persons with histories of incarceration are barred access to education, employment, housing, and other social and health services available to the remaining general public (Legal Action Center, 2009). Instead of reforming incarcerated individuals, the overuse of incarceration causes a number of ripple effects (e.g., recidivism, health concerns, family-related consequences) that also affect families and communities in addition to following incarcerated individuals over the course of their lives (Clear, 2007; Travis & Waul, 2003).

Recidivism

Contrary to its purported deterrence and rehabilitative aims, incarceration is not effective at reducing criminal behavior for most. Nearly 77% of individuals released from prisons are rearrested for a new crime within 5 years (Durose, Cooper, & Snyder, 2014). Research demonstrates that even short-term incarceration in jail is associated with increased rates of criminal activity; low-risk defendants held 2 to 3 days during the pretrial phase are almost 40% more likely to commit new crimes before trial than defendants held less than 24 hours (Lowenkamp, VanNostrand, & Holsinger, 2013). The evidence generated by decades of recidivism research is clear: For the vast majority of individuals, mass incarceration does not increase public safety by reducing criminal behavior. In fact, the disruptive factors associated with imprisonment fuel the likelihood of future offending, creating a system in which people are perpetually trapped.

Health Concerns

The process of incarceration has been shown to exacerbate health conditions and increase the likelihood of disease acquisition and transmission (Baillargeon & Bradshaw,

2003; Freudenberg, 2006). Incarcerated individuals have disproportionately high rates of chronic health conditions and communicable diseases such as tuberculosis, Hepatitis C, and HIV. Similarly, many studies report upward of 90% of people in jails and prisons have high rates of lifetime traumatic experiences (Teplin, Abram, & McClelland, 1996; Weeks & Spatz Widom, 1998; Wolff & Shi, 2012). Because imprisonment is a traumatic experience, incarceration can amplify the negative psychological symptoms of trauma and cause problems during and after incarceration. Few people receive adequate supports for health or mental health problems during or after incarceration.

Family-Related Consequences

Having a history of incarceration can affect whether an individual will be able to have a family. In many states, a person with any felony conviction is banned from fostering or adopting children—even their own relatives (Greenaway, 2002). Therefore, incarceration does not affect just the individual who is imprisoned; it also shapes the lives of people who have never engaged in crime.

Research shows that incarceration of a loved one can send a family into poverty; children of the incarcerated are thrust into a cycle of emotional, behavioral, and academic problems; and communities with high rates of incarceration suffer sustained economic and social deprivation (Clear, Rose, & Ryder, 2001; Mumola, 2000). Over half of incarcerated individuals are parents of minor children, and children with incarcerated parents are more likely to have behavioral and emotional problems and are at six times greater risk of later being incarcerated themselves (Glaze & Maruschak, 2008; Harrison & Beck, 2006). Poor and minority communities, where incarceration is often concentrated, suffer from indirect effects of incarceration (e.g., weakened family functioning, disrupted labor force attachments, reduced collective efficacy, stigma) that further destabilizes communities already struggling with limited resources (Clear, 2007; Lynch & Sabol, 2004; Pattillo, Weiman, & Western, 2004).

The End of an Era

Though mass incarceration has often appeared as an intractable phenomenon, data indicate that, similar to the housing and dot-com bubbles, the incarceration bubble may be beginning to burst. Table 1.1 lists the numbers of individuals incarcerated in federal prisons, state prisons, and local jails, and the total incarcerated population per year from 2008 to 2014. Beginning in 2009, the total incarcerated population declined slightly after several years of plateau, and the decline has continued for 6 consecutive years (Carson, 2015; Minton & Zeng, 2015). Though this is a historic development, the setting-specific data tell a less consistent story. For example, the state prison population was reduced in 2010, 2011, and 2012, but the number of state incarcerated individuals increased in 2013, before decreasing again in 2014 and 2015. Average daily jail populations have fluctuated similarly, 3 consecutive years of reductions followed by years of increase, reduction, and

TABLE I.I

Numbers of Individuals Incarcerated in the United States by Year, 2008–2014*

Year	Federal Prison	State Prison	Total Prison	Jail (Avg. daily pop.)	Total Incarcerated
2008	201,280 +	1,407,002 +	1,608,282 +	776,573 +	2,384,855 +
2009	208,118 +	1,407,369 +	1,615,487 +	**768,135 −**	**2,383,622 −**
2010	209,771 +	**1,404,032 −**	**1,613,803 −**	**748,553 −**	**2,362,356 −**
2011	216,362 +	**1,382,606 −**	**1,598,968 −**	**735,565 −**	**2,334,533 −**
2012	217,815 +	**1,352,582 −**	**1,570,397 −**	737,369 +	**2,307,766 −**
2013	**215,866 −**	1,361,084 +	1,574,741 +	**731,352 −**	**2,306,093 −**
2014	**210,567 −**	**1350,958 −**	**1,561,525 −**	738,975 +	**2,300,500 −**
2015	**196,455 −**	**1,330,337 −**	**1,526,792 −**	**728,200 −**	**2,254,992 −**

* + or − indicates an increase or decrease from that same category in the prior year. Any year-to-year reductions are in bold (Carson, 2015; Minton & Zeng, 2015).

increase again. Reductions in the federal prison population were the most recent, not appearing until 2013. And 2015 marked the first year in which the federal prison, state prison, and jail population all decreased in the same year. Although the recent changes in jail and prison populations are not yet consistent and predictable, they signify variability in the incarcerated population for the first time in a generation. This variability marks both an opportunity and a warning sign. The opportunity to reduce incarceration rates exists, but limited, underconceptualized, and underresourced efforts cannot compete with a nearly 40-year trend of persistently high incarceration rates.

What has led to these reductions in incarceration over the past five years? More importantly, what evidence indicates that this incarceration system in flux marks the end of an era of mass incarceration? First, as a result of the ample evidence that indicates the financial instability of the continued growth of incarceration, many states are calling for reductions in prison expenditures, which will require significantly reducing prison populations and the likely closure of facilities (Gottschalk, 2009; Kyckelhahn, 2011; Spelman, 2009). Second, a growing body of research demonstrates that incarceration has few positive effects on individual change, community stability, or public safety (Durose et al., 2014; Pattillo et al., 2004; Travis et al., 2014; Wakefield & Uggen, 2010). Third, mass incarceration is increasingly viewed as socially unacceptable, as evidenced by now daily media reports criticizing the overuse of jails and prisons; the profit-seeking business of prison privatization; and the social justice implications of incarceration's effects on poor, vulnerable, and minority individuals and communities (Coates, 2014; Gopnik, 2012; Mauer & Cole, 2015). Last, these mounting factors seem to have culminated in the dwindling political will for "tough on crime" proincarceration policies and a new emphasis on criminal justice reform. On both sides of the political aisle and from those who once supported mass incarceration policies, there is growing consensus that reducing the incarceration population is needed and ultimately good for the country (Ford, 2015; Petersilia & Cullen, 2014). This unprecedented convergence of factors epitomizes a growing skepticism about the function and effectiveness of incarceration in the United States (Bosworth, 2011). Moreover, it signifies a unique period in history in which an era of decarceration is a distinct reality.

ARTICULATING OUTCOMES FOR SMART DECARCERATION

Reducing the overreliance on incarceration will require a substantial shift in how the entire U.S. criminal justice system operates. Articulating key outcomes for decarceration to realize this shift is an important early step. To achieve smart decarceration, the following outcomes must be accomplished.

Outcome 1: Substantially Reduce the Incarcerated Population in Jails and Prisons

The term "mass incarceration" is associated with the growth of state and federal prison populations. For example, recent incarceration research (Travis et al., 2014) focuses primarily on individuals who spend a year or more in prison. Though the effects of long-term imprisonment are substantial, ignoring the importance of local jails will severely hamper smart decarceration efforts. Originally designed as pretrial holding facilities, jails have increasingly become indistinguishable from prisons in many respects. Because of long pretrial periods (some longer than 2 years) and prison overcrowding, people are serving longer sentences in jails. Though most serve a relatively short time in jail, there are seven times the number of people incarcerated in local jails than in prisons (Minton & Zeng, 2015; Subramanian et al., 2015). Even short-term jail incarcerations can disrupt various aspects of an individual's life (e.g., employment, family relationships, positive peer networks, community supports), and jail incarceration of even a few days can lead to future recidivism (Lowenkamp et al., 2013). For these reasons, reducing the overreliance on incarceration requires attention to jails in addition to prisons. Doing so demands complementary strategies that both reduce the flow of individuals into the front end of the system, and reduce or eliminate lengths of stay for those who face incarceration (Jacobson, 2005; Subramanian et al., 2015).

A Lesson from Deinstitutionalization

Defining a "substantial" reduction in the jail and prison population is a difficult task. Since the 2010s, bold challenges have been made by multiple advocacy groups, some of which suggest that the prison population could be cut in half in the next 10 to 15 years.[1] Although this type of rapid reduction may be attractive to both prisoner advocates and states that wish to reduce correctional spending, a rapid and drastic reduction in the incarcerated population may prove to be unsustainable.

---

[1] See http://www.justleadershipusa.org, http://www.aclu.org; and http://www.cut50.org.

Lessons from history should be considered in this case. In 1963, President Kennedy issued a call to action to reduce the number of people with mental illnesses in psychiatric hospitals by 50% within a decade or two. Remarkably, with bipartisan support, the population of psychiatric hospitals and asylums dropped by 60%. Yet deinstitutionalization failed in many respects. Few mental health systems meet the needs of the communities they serve. Today, people with mental illnesses are more likely to be found in jails and prisons than in psychiatric hospitals, leading correctional facilities to be considered the "new asylums" (Torrey, Kennard, Eslinger, Lamb, & Pavle, 2010). Many would agree that rapid deinstitutionalization without full development of effective and sufficient community resources was a key contributor to the movement's failings. The decarceration approach must not repeat the mistakes of the past.

In the era of decarceration, periods of extreme declines may be likely, but steady and consistent decreases over time would be more favorable, similar to the steady and consistent rise in incarceration over a 4-decade period. Interestingly, the U.S. incarceration rate prior to the era of mass incarceration was very much in line with other industrialized western countries (Travis et al., 2014). It could be argued that an appropriate target for long-term decarceration efforts would be to return to the pre-mass-incarceration rate—roughly less than 200 per 100,000. Aiming for pre-mass-incarceration levels equates to a reduction in the total incarcerated population by one million individuals. But this marker could be misguided; if the United States overhauls its reliance on incarceration and the criminal justice system that fuels it, would even 200 per 100,000 people incarcerated be an acceptable rate, or would it be possible to downsize incarceration even further?

Outcome 2: Redress Existing Social Disparities Among the Incarcerated

Social disparities (e.g., racial, economic, behavioral) among incarcerated populations have become overwhelming in the era of mass incarceration. Such disparities stem from numerous causes, including systemic bias in court case processing (Kingsnorth, MacIntosh, & Sutherland, 2002), uneven policing in poor minority neighborhoods (Brunson & Miller, 2006), irregular sentencing practices (Bushway & Piehl, 2001), and, for some crimes, differential offending patterns (Sampson, Morenoff, & Raudenbush, 2005). To be socially just, the smart decarceration approach must not only reduce the number of incarcerated individuals but also redress the disproportionate burden of incarceration on vulnerable and oppressed populations. This will require attention to the unique factors that led to the overincarceration of people of color, people in poverty, and people with behavioral health disorders, and a commitment to remediate these factors. Articulating the reduction of disparities as a key outcome in decarceration efforts is critical to ensuring that future reductions in incarceration do not further exacerbate existing disparities by benefiting only those who already benefit from structural privileges and opportunities.

Outcome 3: Maximize Public Safety and Well-Being

For decarceration to be effective and sustainable, public safety must be maximized. Otherwise, retrenchment in incarceration policies would likely occur. Smart decarceration must involve more than just reducing incarceration; it must include the development of responses to crime and undesired behaviors to ultimately benefit all members of society. This is particularly the case for communities that have borne the burden of mass incarceration, resulting in exacerbated economic and social disadvantage (Clear, 2007).

Decarceration will only be effective, sustainable, and socially just if these three outcomes are simultaneously realized. It would be possible to substantially reduce the number of incarcerated persons, but maintain, or even increase, the disproportionate rates of imprisonment among people of color and people in poverty. Therefore, smart decarceration efforts must be held to an expectation to reduce disparities if the progress made in an era of decarceration is to be socially just. Clearly, if decarceration threatens public safety, the likelihood of regressing back to mass incarceration policies and practices is great. Strong attention to these three interrelated goals at the onset of the decarceration era is critical to its ultimate success.

GUIDING CONCEPTS FOR SMART DECARCERATION THROUGH CRIMINAL JUSTICE TRANSFORMATION

Launching an era of smart decarceration will require a paradigm shift on how the criminal justice system views, prevents, and responds to crime. Though there is social and political will to reduce incarceration, an applied, comprehensive approach to decarceration has not yet been developed. Also underdeveloped is the transformative work only possible through bringing together diverse disciplines, sectors, and levels of interventions. To bring about a transformative era of decarceration, a range of key stakeholders must first develop some consensus around foundational concepts and principles that would guide smart decarceration.

Recognizing this need, Travis et al. (2014) offered four principles to limit the scale of incarceration and point toward new approaches: (1) *Proportionality*—criminal sentences should respond to the seriousness of the crime; (2) *Parsimony*—length of confinement should not be greater than necessary to achieve the goals of sentencing policy; (3) *Citizenship*—effects of imprisonment should not violate a person's fundamental status as a member of society; and (4) *Social justice*—prisons' collective effect should promote a fair distribution of rights, resources, and opportunities. Petersilia and Cullen (2014) similarly highlighted five principles to downsize prisons: (1) *Set inmate population caps*—states should articulate specific limits to prison capacity; (2) *Take recidivism seriously*—use risk assessments and data to carefully monitor recidivism; (3) *Reaffirm rehabilitation*—community corrections must be adequately resourced to be a fully viable option; (4) *Provide expert technical assistance to states and communities willing to downsize*—build the technical capacity for the emerging field of downsizing; and (5) *Develop a criminology of downsizing*—build a full literature and evidence base on downsizing prisons.

These principles offer important points to consider, but they are also limited for developing a comprehensive guiding conceptual framework of smart decarceration. The principles Travis et al. (2014) put forth are quite broad and overarching, and the report does very little to suggest practical strategies for implementing these ideals. The principle of parsimony is aimed at avoiding unnecessarily long and ineffective incarceration sentences, but it presupposes a system that still relies primarily on imprisonment as a response to crime. On its surface, the parsimony principle accepts the notion that incarceration is an appropriate response to a broad swath of crime and is silent on the detrimental effects of even a short incarceration sentence on individuals, families, communities, and budgets. Petersilia and Cullen focus more squarely on specific policies to downsize prisons, but their principles do not fully acknowledge the need for a more robust set of effective replacements for incarceration. They suggest that the answers to reducing incarceration rest in the development of a field of criminology focused on prison downsizing. Although criminologists' expertise and institutional knowledge are vital to smart decarceration, a criminology of downsizing ignores the need for a multidisciplinary, comprehensive approach to overcome the complex problems of mass incarceration. Additionally, neither set of principles directly responds to the overwhelming problem of mass incarceration's disproportionate impact on people of color and vulnerable populations. In short, these principles have relevance and will likely help to moderately curtail incarceration in the short term, but they are not sufficient on their own to achieve the kind of transformation necessary to achieve the outcomes of smart decarceration.

Building on these principles, this section defines concepts to stimulate applied policy and behavioral intervention innovations that could ultimately transform the criminal justice system. These concepts are not intended to offer immediate, specific answers to the challenges of decarceration; rather, they lead to important questions whose answers will build a framework and strategy for smart decarceration. With an established framework, decarceration efforts can be tracked using a range of benchmarks of success. We propose four guiding concepts to achieve the outcomes of smart decarceration and to transform the criminal justice system into one that supports decarceration. We also ask key questions to consider as decarceration innovations are developed and implemented.

Guiding Concept 1: Changing the Narrative on Incarceration and the Incarcerated

In America's criminal justice system, the current default answer to crime is incarceration, which leaves incarcerated individuals disenfranchised. To change that narrative, two key steps are necessary: reconsidering the utility of incarceration, and amplifying the perspectives of currently and formerly incarcerated individuals.

Reconsidering the Utility of Incarceration

The prevailing approach to crime over the past 4 decades has been to rely first and foremost on incarceration. For both major and minor offenses, the initial response is to take a person into custody; although some states have expanded their use of "desk appearance tickets," booking into local jails is still the most common approach by law enforcement to most criminal offenses (Snyder, 2012). This practice illustrates a primary assumption—that incarceration increases public safety by removing the alleged offender from society. For persons charged with or convicted of violent crimes (e.g., murder, rape, robbery, assault), there may be some validity to the argument that incarceration is effective at incapacitation, or preventing those individuals from harming others. However, in 2010, violent offenses constituted about 4% of all arrests nationwide; by comparison, nearly 30% of arrests were for drug or property crimes (Snyder, 2012). In the same year, nearly 47% of state incarcerated individuals and over 90% of federal incarcerated individuals were serving time for nonviolent offenses (Snyder, 2012). In addition, nearly two-thirds of individuals held in local jails are unconvicted (Minton & Zeng, 2015), and the jail population is made up primarily of individuals with nonviolent charges (Subramanian et al., 2015). These statistics suggest that a large proportion of those incarcerated in U.S. jails and prisons do not pose an imminent risk for violence in their communities, and there is potentially little public safety value in incapacitating these individuals. Even for those convicted of violent offenses, the objective of incapacitation is not permanent; at least 95% of state incarcerated individuals will be released back into the community (Hughes & Wilson, 2002).

A second commonly held assumption about the utility of incarceration is that it reduces the likelihood of future illegal behavior. Whether by providing rehabilitative services or by administering deterrence to crime via punishment, the notion of the term "corrections" suggests that incarceration corrects or alleviates one's propensity toward criminal behavior. If this assumption held true for all or even most incarcerated individuals, it could be argued that incarceration serves a public safety purpose, even for those nonviolent offenders who do not require incapacitation, by serving to reduce future criminal offending. However, years of research and data actively refute this assumption. Multiple studies have highlighted the abysmal recidivism rates for formerly incarcerated individuals. For example, Durose et al. (2014) found that over three-fourths of formerly incarcerated individuals are rearrested for a new crime within 5 years. Other recent research demonstrates that even short-term incarceration in jail is associated with increased rates of criminal activity; spending 2 or 3 days in jail has been linked to increased likelihood of future offending compared with jail stays of less than 24 hours (Lowenkamp et al., 2013). This body of research underscores the fact that incarceration, at best, does not reduce recidivism and, at worst, actually increases the risk for future offending.

Assumptions associated with the efficacy of incarceration drove legislation and criminal justice policy and practice for the past 40 years, resulting in the era of mass incarceration. For an era of smart decarceration to occur, these assumptions must be tested and replaced with more evidence-based appraisals of incarceration's utility. The nation has embraced the notion that incarceration is *the* appropriate tool to make people behave in desired ways and follow the law. This reliance on incarceration has muted the nation's creativity to promote socially desirable behaviors and deafened its attention to the causal factors of addiction, debt, and crime. We suggest that the smart decarceration approach views incarceration as an effective tool only for incapacitation of individuals at high risk of violence who most threaten public safety.

Amplifying Perspectives of Currently and Formerly Incarcerated Individuals

Historically, currently and formerly incarcerated individuals have been systematically disenfranchised from criminal justice reform efforts. However, individuals with incarceration histories have firsthand knowledge of the complexities of criminal justice involvement; therefore, they have unique perspectives on what is necessary to reduce criminal activity. Peer-led and -informed interventions are widely accepted in other areas of rehabilitation, including substance abuse (Liddle, Rowe, Dakof, Ungaro, & Henderson, 2004); health and mental health (Davidson, Chinman, Sells, & Rowe, 2006; Dennis, 2003; Sells, Davidson, Jewell, Falzer, & Rowe, 2006); veterans, first responders, and other job classifications (Chinman, Shoai, & Cohen, 2010; Levenson & Dwyer, 2003); and persons with disabilities (Corrigan, 2006; Haring & Breen, 1992). The smart decarceration approach must view current and formerly incarcerated individuals not as merely objects for intervention but as key experts in crafting effective solutions. Indeed, as with the women's and civil rights movements, in order for this ideal moment for decarceration to develop into a sustained decarceration movement, those most directly affected by incarceration must be centered. This will require a philosophical shift about how "offenders" are viewed. Instead of a mark of failure and mistrust, experiences with the criminal justice system both inside and outside of incarceration settings should inform targeted social innovations.

Key Questions

The following questions begin to explore how smart decarceration can rethink incarceration and the incarcerated:

- How can the criminal justice system shift its thinking away from incarceration as the default response to crime? Even the language—"diversion" and "alternatives to incarceration" and "suspended sentence"—implies that incarceration is what is supposed to happen, but another approach will be tried out in its place. For what offenses (both misdemeanors and felonies) could incarceration not even be an option? What needs to change to relinquish the current beliefs about incarceration? What new terms and language can be developed to reflect a more sober view of incarceration?

- What if, as in medical and mental healthcare, we took a "level of care" approach to criminal justice responses, in which incarceration is the last resort—one that required justification? How could the criminal justice system develop a hybrid between determinate and indeterminate sentencing (neither of which has worked very well) wherein reassessment happens over time to determine optimal sentence length? How could it identify and avoid diminishing returns of incarceration?

- What can currently and formerly incarcerated persons contribute toward the development and implementation of social innovations aimed at criminal justice reform? What punishments would these individuals have chosen as the best response to their own offenses? How does the criminal justice system identify and develop peer-led strategies to reduce recidivism, increase community supports, and prevent crime? What policies and practices will acknowledge that the era of mass incarceration was misguided, and reduce levels of stigma for those who have been most affected?

Guiding Concept 2: Making Criminal Justice Systemwide Innovations

Much of the discourse on reversing mass incarceration has been focused on state and, to a lesser extent, federal prison systems. Although prisons do serve as the most visible and intensive manifestation of mass incarceration, they simply reflect the symptoms of an overall system of policies and practices that support mass incarceration. In addition to developing policy and legislative reforms, smart decarceration will require social innovation at all levels of the criminal justice system. The current criminal justice system tends to function in a siloed manner, with each governing sector operating independently without a thorough understanding of that sector's effects on other parts of the criminal justice system. Each sector of the criminal justice system has played a part in sustaining mass incarceration, and transforming aspects of each sector will be necessary to achieve smart decarceration.

Law Enforcement

Law enforcement represents the gateway into formal criminal justice involvement. For any person who ends up incarcerated in jail or prison, there was first some type of encounter or interaction with law enforcement, namely police. As such, police practices and policing policies play an important role not only in the number of persons arrested, but also the demographic and community characteristics of those individuals. Studies have shown that neighborhoods with similar crime levels may experience very different arrest and incarceration rates, driven mostly by the level of policing presence and monitoring of the neighborhood (Brunson & Miller, 2006; Weitzer, 2000). Police also employ a significant amount of discretion in their daily duties, regularly making decisions on what neighborhoods and blocks to patrol; whom to stop, question, and detain; and whether to charge an individual with a crime and, if so, the particular offense (Brown, 1988). Ultimately, in many cases, police are faced with the important decision of whether to formally arrest an individual, or to use another intervention, whether a standardized, planned alternative to incarceration or by using a case-driven substitute for arrest.

As the formal law enforcement arm of the judicial system, prosecutors are an equally key contributor to the era of mass incarceration, as well as potential change agents in the new era of decarceration. Prosecutors make decisions daily that have great impact on the use of incarceration, including whether and what charges to file on a defendant, types of sentences to recommend for those convicted of a crime, and what penalties (including possible jail or prison incarceration) will be included in plea agreements (Reinganum, 1988; Smith & Levinson, 2011). However, prosecutors are often viewed as an isolated arm of the judiciary, operating independently of other court offices, and perhaps with the intention of leveling the most severe penalties possible (Barkow, 2013). Prosecutorial decision-making and what drives the perceived culture of punishment is woefully understudied. However, there is a growing recognition of the critical role prosecutorial discretion plays in sustaining mass incarceration and the importance of reforming prosecutorial practices to advance decarceration (Henning, 2013; May, 2015; McLeod, 2012).

The Court System

The court system has played a major role in mass incarceration, and its role in advancing smart decarceration cannot be minimized. During the adjudication phase of criminal justice processing, multiple actors in the court system make key decisions on every criminal case—decisions that ultimately determine whether and to what extent incarceration is an option. Given that the court system has evolved into one in which 90% to 95% of cases reach a disposition by plea agreement, it is critical that judges, defense attorneys, and prosecutors, as well as a variety of court staff, begin to work together to intentionally reverse the hasty decision to incarcerate (Devers, 2011). Instead, they must develop and adopt a range of dispositional outcomes that do not include incarceration, and there must be a commitment within the court system to prioritize these alternatives unless the threat to public safety is so great that incarceration is warranted.

Perhaps the lowest hanging fruit in the court system that could have substantial impact on the jail population is the increasingly popular topic of bail reform. Over 60% of persons in jail are not convicted of their current charge, but are rather waiting in jail for their court hearing (or other disposition) because they cannot afford to pay expensive bail (Minton & Zeng, 2015). For many, this dilemma equates to individuals sitting in jail long enough to enter a guilty plea, with the agreement that the time that they have served will be a sufficient penalty (Subramanian et al., 2015). In effect, these individuals have paid the price for their alleged offense before ever being convicted of it. For others who are desperate to return to their homes and communities, predatory bail/bond agencies may be solicited, which further subjects the individual to financial hardship and targeted supervision and coercion by "bounty hunters" with very little training and oversight. For these reasons, substantially reforming bail policies and procedures is an important first step for the court system to take in a move toward decarceration (Hutchinson, 2015).

Prisons and Jails

In the era of mass incarceration, prisons and jails have become veritable warehouse facilities, brimming with millions of individuals who come into contact with the criminal justice system. As a result, the "correctional" intention of prisons and jails fall largely to priorities of institutional safety and social control. There simply are not adequate resources to provide incarcerated individuals needed rehabilitative treatment and interventions, because resources are being allocated primarily to support basic confinement needs (Henrichson & Delaney, 2012). Incarcerated individuals with drug problems are half as likely to receive treatment today in prison as they were in 1990 (National Center on Addiction and Substance Abuse at Columbia University, 2010). Those exiting jails and prisons are reentering communities with fewer individual skills and social supports than they had when they entered, which leads to high risk for recidivism and reincarceration (Hughes & Wilson, 2002).

In the coming era of decarceration, prison and jail sentences should be rendered only when it is determined that nothing less restrictive can be used without compromising public safety. When that goal is realized, the remaining incarcerated individuals will be those at the highest risk to public safety, but the population will be substantially smaller. This reduction will allow for incarceration to serve its ultimate function, incapacitation, alongside the facilitation of evidence-driven interventions that will aim to reduce criminal risks and potential threats to public safety. For those who would remain in incarceration settings, specific interventions could be tailored to their risk for violence and reoffending, thus improving public safety upon their release. Cost savings from a smaller incarcerated population would be reinvested in research and development of social innovations and community supports to prevent the likelihood of contact with the criminal justice system.

Community Supervision

Community supervision, namely probation and parole, are strategies used either to shorten the amount of time that an individual spends incarcerated or to replace an incarceration sentence altogether. In the era of mass incarceration, probation grew at a faster rate than any other segment, and of the approximately 7 million individuals currently involved in the criminal justice system, the vast majority, nearly 5 million, are on probation and parole (Glaze & Bonczar, 2007; Petersilia, 1997). Community supervision was originally meant to be an alternative to incarceration, and an opportunity to provide supportive, rehabilitative services to individuals and facilitate their positive contributions to their communities. Unfortunately, the exponential growth of community supervision, particularly probation, resulted in overwhelming caseloads (often more than 100 per officer), which renders the facilitation of individually tailored rehabilitative services nearly impossible (Maruschak & Parks, 2012; Petersilia, 1997). Additionally, the use of incarceration as a consequence for technical violations of probation and parole hastens the process to incarceration. In fact, about 16% of people exiting probation each year do so because of incarceration for a new offense or probation revocation (Maruschak & Parks, 2012), and nearly 40% of parole terminations are for unsatisfactory reasons, the bulk of which result in reincarceration (Glaze & Kaeble, 2014). For many, probation and parole have become nothing more than a waiting room for reincarceration (Epperson, Canada, Thompson, & Lurigio, 2014).

The smart decarceration approach must include an overhaul of community supervision to maximize its rehabilitative aims. Resources and incentives should be aimed at helping clients develop skills and supports that will increase prosocial community involvement and reduce their likelihood to reoffend. When clients struggle with community supervision, interventions other than incarceration must be made available, unless there is an imminent threat to public safety. Community supervision should occur in the individual's community, rather than office-based centralized departments, where there are logistical barriers to community supervision staff understanding neighborhood supports and resources.

Key Questions

The following questions can guide criminal justice professionals as they work to innovate toward the goal of decarceration:

- How can the criminal justice system develop a better understanding of what part each sector plays in contributing to mass incarceration? What changes can be made to the incentive structure that favors incarceration at nearly every sector?
- What practices can be articulated for each sector that reflect the goal of avoiding unnecessary incarceration? How can we create more exit points throughout the criminal justice system versus pipelines to jail or prison?
- What strategies will minimize baton passing from law enforcement to courts to incarceration with individual offenders and instead move toward integrated action for decarceration?

Guiding Concept 3: Implementing Transdisciplinary Policy and Practice Interventions

As the United States enters an era of decarceration, policymakers and practitioners from different disciplines must come together to implement interventions. Doing so requires first understanding the current policy and practice landscape affecting mass incarceration. Then transformation of those policies and practices can begin, followed by the development of transdisciplinary strategies.

The Landscape of Policy and Practices Affecting Mass Incarceration

Over time, both policy and practice developments affected the scope of mass incarceration. Legislative changes have clearly played a role in increasing the numbers of individuals eligible for incarceration and the length of their imprisonment. Mandatory minimum laws typically associated with the War on Drugs imposed harsh sentences on particular drug offenses such as possession of certain quantities of crack cocaine. Civil disability laws that mushroomed in the 1980s and 1990s had a drastic impact on those with felony convictions, governing where they could live, work, reside, and vote, and how they could build a family. The Violent Crime Control and Law Enforcement Act of 1994, the largest crime bill in the nation's history, had significant effects on states' sentencing policies. By the end of the 20th century, as a result of financial incentives in the bill, most states adopted truth-in-sentencing laws that required incarcerated individuals to serve 85% of their sentences behind bars regardless of good behavior or other mitigating circumstances (Sabol, Rosich, Mallik-Kane, Kirk, & Dubin, 2002; Turner, Greenwood, Chen, & Fain, 1999). "Three strikes" laws, which have been established by 28 of 50 states, require extended prison sentences, often life imprisonment, for persons with multiple felony convictions (Benekos & Merlo, 1995).

Unfortunately, as the net widened for those who came into contact with the law and went to jail or prison, there was not substantial development of coherent and effective practice interventions to address the needs of the expanding incarcerated population. Still affected by the rejection of rehabilitative practices in the 1970s, the bulk of fiscal and intellectual resources and efforts went toward punishment and so-called deterrence throughout the 1980s and 1990s (Garland, 2001; Martinson, 1975). At the same time, neighborhood- and school-focused drug and violence prevention efforts emerged to reduce the funnel to incarceration such as "just say no" programs, neighborhood watch groups, "weed and seed" campaigns, and community policing (Trojanowicz & Bucqueroux, 1990). Once people came into contact with the law, there was some effort to divert minor offenders away from courts and to engage in restorative justice efforts once incarcerated or nearing release. However, these efforts were not uniformly experienced, with those from vulnerable and marginalized groups being less likely to benefit (Rosenbaum, 1994).

Transforming Policies and Practices for Smart Decarceration

The policies and practices that contribute to mass incarceration have been an extremely costly experiment—40 years of over $50 billion per year, plus significant human and community resources (Spelman, 2009). To develop a transformative, smart decarceration approach, the same level of fiscal, political, human capital, and community investment that allowed mass incarceration to flourish is needed, at least initially (smart decarceration is likely to save money over time, but perhaps not in the short term). Smart decarceration requires much more than simply reducing the prison and jail populations. As evidenced by the deinstitutionalization of psychiatric hospitals, it is not necessarily difficult to empty out institutions. It is, however, a challenge to develop multiple systems to receive, assist, and support those who would have been previously institutionalized. To be successful, the smart decarceration approach must build capacity to respond to the devolving of jails and prisons by promoting behavioral and primary health, housing, education, employment, and civic opportunities. Developing the tools and approaches to achieve capacity-building will require the perspectives of those from many disciplines, sectors, and well beyond criminal justice and corrections. Additionally, the smart decarceration approach must develop an array of replacement interventions for incarceration. It would be insufficient to simply not incarcerate and hope that undesired behaviors will be discontinued.

Developing Transdisciplinary Strategies

The smart decarceration approach rejects the notion that criminologists, criminal justice, and corrections professionals should be solely responsible for reversing mass incarceration. Rather, it promotes transdisciplinary collaborations that combine perspectives from multiple disciplines not to just describe the current landscape, but also to generate a *futurescape* of public safety and well-being. Transdisciplinary perspectives are necessary to redefine and reconsider what constitutes truly criminal behaviors, what symptoms of public health crises are, what kinds of behaviors police and practice innovations can prevent, and when it is truly necessary to confine human beings. Finding these answers will require more than just identifying the key directions for change or success. The smart decarceration approach must be based in an understanding of the economic formulations for creating and supporting systems of care and change. When rehabilitation is needed, it is important to understand how to best move people through the criminal justice system with the least harm to individuals and communities upon release. Existing paradigms and small adjustments to existing approaches will not achieve these aims—new perspectives, transformed approaches, and transdisciplinary paradigms are needed to achieve smart decarceration.

Key Questions

These key questions can guide the criminal justice system as it works to implement transdisciplinary policy and practice interventions to achieve smart decarceration:

- How can policy and practice interventions move beyond an individual perspective to engage with social and environmental risk factors? What strategies will enhance synergies between policy and practice interventions? What does a continuum of "incarceration replacement" interventions look like? Who is best equipped to implement and facilitate them?

- How can transdisciplinary innovations be fostered and replicated? What disciplines have important contributions to make to smart decarceration, but may have been previously ignored? Are any areas of current practice immune from the need for transdisciplinary reforms?

Guiding Concept 4: Employing Evidence-Driven Strategies

Evidence-driven strategies are necessary to prevent repeating the mistakes of mass incarceration. Responding to and privileging evidence will help achieve this end.

The Problems with Not Responding to Evidence

Much of what led to mass incarceration was the enactment of policies and practices based on political motivations, reactionary approaches, and trendy (but not grounded) solutions. Despite the enormous financial and social costs of mass incarceration, and decades of research that demonstrate how the majority of individuals exiting prison will return, it is perplexing that a unified call to reduce incarceration rates has only recently occurred. What other social intervention has a cost of over $50 billion annually, a failure rate of 60% to 75%, and has been tolerated for nearly 4 decades? Moreover, the majority of policies and practices that fostered mass incarceration were implemented and sustained without proper evaluation, and were not discontinued despite years or even decades of poor outcomes.

Privileging Evidence in Smart Decarceration

In contrast, the smart decarceration approach must be evaluative in nature, continuously assessing the effects of interventions at multiple levels. Social innovations should be based on existing evidence from multiple disciplines about what works to prevent the initiation and recurrence of crime. In this sense, new solutions that emerge will be based on past evidence of risk and protective factors for criminal behaviors, the needs of people affected by incarceration, and the effectiveness of current intervention approaches.

However, relying on past evidence alone would be insufficient. Smart decarceration requires rigorous testing and timely incorporation of emerging evidence. New solutions should be continually evaluated over time with no true endpoint. Instead, built into any new intervention should be an expectation that people and systems evolve and therefore approaches must adapt and respond accordingly. Smart decarceration innovations should include mandated program, policy, and evaluation cycles. Interventions should be expected to undergo needs assessments and evaluations of theory, logic, process, outcomes, and efficiency. To uphold the evidence-driven principle, qualified and applied researchers should always be involved in intervention development and implementation. Interventions should strive to achieve the highest scientific standards. The perceived success and proliferation of social innovations should be based primarily on their effectiveness, not on extraneous motivators. In short, science must drive the process of smart decarceration.

Key Questions

The following key questions will ensure that smart decarceration approaches foster and uphold the evidence-driven strategies:

- How can decarceration evaluation support a range of outcomes that lead to smart decarceration outcomes? What are alternative definitions of success and failure beyond recidivism? How can evaluation best inform incremental modifications, tailoring and adapting interventions as opposed to using canned dissemination strategies or disregarding the intervention altogether? How can the approach develop and formalize the principle of responsivity in its research?
- What if decarceration interventions represented state-of-the-art research and evaluation instead of criminal justice's history of lagging behind? How can expectations for evaluation and responding to evidence be incentivized? What will bring the best scientific minds to study innovations in decarceration?

POSTDECARCERATION

What will follow the era of decarceration? If smart decarceration is able to simultaneously (1) substantially reduce the incarcerated population; (2) redress existing social disparities among the incarcerated; and (3) maximize public safety and public well-being using the aforementioned guiding principles, the postdecarceration era will be one that can move beyond the primary goals of undoing the damages of mass incarceration. A postdecarceration era would likely be one in which the criminal justice system is smaller, more nimble, and focused on building on strengths rather than a punishment-focused approach. The postdecarceration era could be one in which communities are well equipped and positioned to prevent crime and support the needs of their members. In short, the work we do in the decarceration era, if successful, will prepare us for an era focused on rehabilitation and prevention. Conversely, if the era of decarceration is not successful, the United States could enter a renewed era of hyperincarceration and a retrenchment of punishment-oriented approaches.

CONCLUSION

The emerging era of decarceration holds both great promise and considerable gravity. Our intention in this chapter is to note that the decarceration era is likely to be a prolonged one, in which the primary task is not only to reduce the use of incarceration but also to develop an effective, sustainable, and socially just set of policy and practice innovations that will promote public safety and well-being. In that spirit, the guiding concepts we offer are meant to spur discussion, questions, and innovation that will drive smart decarceration. Wrestling with how to operationalize these guiding concepts at the beginning of the decarceration era will increase the likelihood that social innovations will have sustained ability to meet the outcomes of smart decarceration.

The beginning of the era of decarceration marks a chance to transform the way criminal justice operates in the United States. To do anything less would be an unthinkable squandering of an historic opportunity.

REFERENCES

Alexander, M. (2012). *The new Jim Crow: Mass incarceration in the age of colorblindness*: New York, NY: New Press.

Baillargeon, J., & Bradshaw, P. (2003). The association of infectious disease diagnoses with incarceration-related factors among prison inmates. *Journal of Correctional Health Care, 10*(1), 15–33. doi:10.1177/107834580301000103

Barkow, R. E. (2013). Prosecutorial administration: Prosecutor bias and the Department of Justice. *Virginia Law Review, 99*(2), 271–342.

Benekos, P. J., & Merlo, A. V. (1995). Three strikes and you're out: The political sentencing game. *Federal Probation, 59*(1), 3–9.

Bosworth, M. (2011). Penal moderation in the United States? *Criminology and Public Policy, 10*(2), 335–343.

Brown, M. K. (1988). *Working the street: Police discretion and the dilemmas of reform.* New York, NY: Russell Sage Foundation.

Brunson, R. K., & Miller, J. (2006). Young black men and urban policing in the United States. *British Journal of Criminology, 46*(4), 613–640.

Bushway, S. D., & Piehl, A. M. (2001). Judging judicial discretion: Legal factors and racial discrimination in sentencing. *Law and Society Review, 35*(4), 733–764.

Carson, E.A. (2015). *Prisoners in 2014.* Washington, DC: Bureau of Justice Statistics.

Chinman, M., Shoai, R., & Cohen, A. (2010). Using organizational change strategies to guide peer support technician implementation in the Veterans Administration. *Psychiatric Rehabilitation Journal, 33*(4), 269–277. doi:10.2975/33.4.2010.269.277

Clear, T. R. (2007). *Imprisoning communities: How mass incarceration makes disadvantaged neighborhoods worse.* New York, NY: Oxford University Press.

Clear, T. R., Rose, D. R., & Ryder, J. A. (2001). Incarceration and the community: The problem of removing and returning offenders. *Crime and Delinquency, 47*(3), 335–351.

Coates, T.-N. (2014, October 17). Mapping the new Jim Crow. *The Atlantic.* Retrieved from http://www.theatlantic.com/politics/archive/2014/10/mapping-the-new-jim-crow/381617/

Corrigan, P. W. (2006). Impact of consumer-operated services on empowerment and recovery of people with psychiatric disabilities. *Psychiatric Services, 57*(10), 1493–1496.

Davidson, L., Chinman, M., Sells, D., & Rowe, M. (2006). Peer support among adults with serious mental illness: A report from the field. *Schizophrenia Bulletin, 32*(3), 443–450. doi:10.1093/schbul/sbj043

Dennis, C.-L. (2003). Peer support within a health care context: A concept analysis. *International Journal of Nursing Studies, 40*(3), 321–332.

Devers, L. (2011). *Plea and charge bargaining.* Washington DC: Bureau of Justice Statistics.

Durose, M. R., Cooper, A. D., & Snyder, H. N. (2014). *Recidivism of prisoners released in 30 dates in 2005: Patterns from 2005 to 2010.* Washington, DC: Bureau of Justice Statistics.

Epperson, M. W., Canada, K. E., Thompson, J. G., & Lurigio, A. (2014). Walking the line: Specialized and standard probation officer perspectives on supervising probationers with serious mental illnesses. *International Journal of Law and Psychiatry, 37,* 473–483.

Epperson, M. W., Wolff, N., Morgan, R. D., Fisher, W. H., Frueh, B. C., & Huening, J. (2014). Envisioning the next generation of behavioral health and criminal justice interventions. *International Journal of Law and Psychiatry, 37*(5), 427–438.

Fazel, S., & Danesh, J. (2002). Serious mental disorder in 23,000 prisoners: A systematic review of 62 surveys. *Lancet, 359,* 545–550.

Ford, M. (2015, February 25). Can bipartisanship end mass incarceration? *The Atlantic.* Retrieved from http://www.theatlantic.com/politics/archive/2015/02/can-bipartisanship-end-mass-incarceration/386012/

Freudenberg, N. (2006). *Coming home from jail: A review of health and social problems facing US jail populations and of opportunities for reentry interventions.* Washington, DC: Jail Reentry Roundtable Initiative, Urban Institute. Retrieved from http://www.urban.org/sites/default/files/inmate_challenges.pdf

Garland, D. (2001). *Mass imprisonment: Social causes and consequences.* Thousand Oaks, CA: Sage Publications.

Glaze, L., & Kaeble, D. (2014). *Correctional populations in the United States, 2013.* Washington, DC: Bureau of Justice Statistics.

Glaze, L. E., & Bonczar, T. P. (2007). *Probation and parole in the United States, 2006.* Washington, DC: U.S. Department of Justice, Office of Justice Programs.

Glaze, L. E., & Maruschak, L. M. (2008). *Parents in prison and their minor children.* Washington, DC: Bureau of Justice Statistics.

Glaze, L. E., & Parks, E. (2012). *Correctional populations in the United States*: U.S. Department of Justice, Office of Justice Programs.

Gopnik, A. (2012, January 30). The caging of America. *The New Yorker.* Retrieved from http://www.newyorker.com/magazine/2012/01/30/the-caging-of-america

Gottschalk, M. (2009). Money and mass incarceration: The bad, the mad, and penal reform. *Criminology and Public Policy, 8*(1), 97–109.

Greenaway, A. (2002). When neutral policies aren't so neutral: Increasing incarceration rates and the effect of the Adoption and Safe Families Act of 1997 on the parental rights of African-American women. *National Black Law Journal, 17,* 247.

Greenberg, G. A., & Rosenheck, R. A. (2008). Jail incarceration, homelessness, and mental health: A national study. *Psychiatric Services, 59*(2), 170–177. doi:10.1176/appi.ps.59.2.170

Hagan, J., & Dinovitzer, R. (1999). Collateral consequences of imprisonment for children, communities, and prisoners. *Crime and Justice, 26,* 121–162.

Haring, T. G., & Breen, C. G. (1992). A peer-mediated social network intervention to enhance the social integration of persons with moderate and severe disabilities. *Journal of Applied Behavior Analysis, 25*(2), 319–333. doi:10.1901/jaba.1992.25-319

Harlow, C. W. (2003). *Education and correctional populations*. Washington, DC: Bureau of Justice Statistics.

Harrison, P., & Beck, A. (2006). Prison and jail inmates at midyear 2005. *Bureau of Justice Statistics Bulletin*. Retrieved from https://www.bjs.gov/content/pub/pdf/pjim05.pdf

Henning, K. N. (2013). Criminalizing normal adolescent behavior in communities of color: The role of prosecutors in juvenile justice reform. *Cornell Law Review, 98,* 383–462.

Henrichson, C., & Delaney, R. (2012). The price of prisons: What incarceration costs taxpayers. *Federal Sentencing Reporter, 25*(1), 68–80.

Hughes, T., & Wilson, D. J. (2002). *Reentry trends in the United States*. Washington DC: Bureau of Justice Statistics.

Hutchinson, D. (2015, July 20). There's never been a better time for bail reform. *The Washington Post*. Retrieved from https://www.washingtonpost.com/posteverything/wp/2015/07/20/theres-never-been-a-better-time-for-bail-reform/

Jacobson, M. (2005). *Downsizing prisons: How to reduce crime and end mass incarceration*. New York, NY: NYU Press.

Kingsnorth, R. F., MacIntosh, R. C., & Sutherland, S. (2002). Criminal charge or probation violation? Prosecutorial discretion and implications for research in criminal court processing. *Criminology, 40*(3), 553–578.

Kyckelhahn, T. (2011). *Justice expenditures and employment*. Washington, DC: Bureau of Justice Statistics.

Legal Action Center. (2009). *After prison—roadblocks to reentry: A report on state legal barriers facing people with criminal records*. New York, NY: Legal Action Center

Levenson, R. L., & Dwyer, L. A. (2003). Peer support in law enforcement: Past, present, and future. *International Journal of Emergency Mental Health, 5*(33), 147–152.

Liddle, H. A., Rowe, C. L., Dakof, G. A., Ungaro, R. A., & Henderson, C. E. (2004). Early intervention for adolescent substance abuse: Pretreatment to posttreatment outcomes of a randomized clinical trial comparing multidimensional family therapy and peer group treatment. *Journal of Psychoactive Drugs, 36*(1), 49–63.

Lowenkamp, C. T., VanNostrand, M., & Holsinger, A. M. (2013). *The hidden costs of pretrial detention*. Laura and John Arnold Foundation. Retrieved from http://www.arnoldfoundation.org/wp-content/uploads/2014/02/LJAF_Report_hidden-costs_FNL.pdf

Lynch, J. P., & Sabol, W. J. (2004). Assessing the effects of mass incarceration on informal social control in communities. *Criminology and Public Policy, 3*(2), 267–294.

Martinson, R. (1975). What works? Questions and answers about prison reform. In J. A. Gardner & M. A. Mulkey (Eds.), *Crime and criminal justice*. Lexington, MA: Health.

Maruschak, L. M., & Parks, E. (2012). *Probation and parole in the United States, 2011*. Washington DC: Government Printing Office.

Mauer, M. (2011). Addressing racial disparities in incarceration. *Prison Journal, 91*(3 suppl), 87S–101S.

Mauer, M., & Cole, D. (2015, May 23). How to lock up fewer people. *The New York Times*. Retrieved from http://www.nytimes.com/2015/05/24/opinion/sunday/how-to-lock-up-fewer-people.html?_r=0

May, A. (2015, August 12). It's time to examine the role prosecutors play in driving mass incarceration. *The Huffington Post*. Retrieved from http://www.huffingtonpost.com/art-way/prosecutors-mass-incarceration_b_7978076.html

McLeod, A. M. (2012). Decarceration courts: Possibilities and perils of a shifting criminal law. *Georgetown Law Journal, 100*(1587), 1587–1674.

Minton, T. D., & Zeng, Z. (2015). *Jail inmates at midyear 2014*. Washington, DC: Bureau of Justice Statistics.

Mumola, C. J. (2000). *Incarcerated parents and their children*. Washington, DC: Bureau of Justice Statistics.

National Center on Addiction and Substance Abuse at Columbia University. (2010). *Behind bars II: Substance abuse and America's prison population*. New York, NY: The National Center on Addiction and Substance Abuse at Columbia University.

Pattillo, M., Weiman, D., & Western, B. (2004). *Imprisoning America: The social effects of mass incarceration*. New York, NY: Russel Sage Foundation.

Petersilia, J. (1997). Probation in the United States. *Crime and Justice, 22*, 149–200.

Petersilia, J., & Cullen, F. T. (2014). Liberal but not stupid: Meeting the promise of downsizing prisons. *Stanford Journal of Criminal Law and Policy, 2*, 1–42.

Pettus-Davis, C., & Epperson, M. W. (2015). *From mass incarceration to smart decarceration*. American Academy of Social Work & Social Welfare. Retrieved from http://aaswsw.org/wp-content/uploads/2015/03/From-Mass-Incarceration-to-Decarceration-3.24.15.pdf

Pew Center on the States. (2008). *One in 100: Behind bars in America, 2008*. Washington DC: The Pew Center on the States: Public Safety Performance Project.

Reinganum, J. F. (1988). Plea bargaining and prosecutorial discretion. *American Economic Review, 78*(4), 713–728.

Rosenbaum, D. P. (1994). *The challenge of community policing: Testing the promises*. Thousand Oaks, CA: Sage Publications.

Sabol, W. J., Rosich, K., Mallik-Kane, K., Kirk, D. P., & Dubin, G. (2002). *The influences of truth-in-sentencing reforms on changes in states' sentencing practices and prison populations*. Urban Institute. Retrieved from http://www.urban.org/research/publication/influences-truth-sentencing-reforms-changes-states-sentencing-practices-and-prison-populations

Sampson, R. J., Morenoff, J. D., & Raudenbush, S. (2005). Social anatomy of racial and ethnic disparities in violence. *American Journal of Public Health, 95*(2), 224–232.

Schmitt, J., Warner, K., & Gupta, S. (2010). *The high budgetary cost of incarceration*. Washington, DC: Center for Economic and Policy Research.

Sells, D., Davidson, L., Jewell, C., Falzer, P., & Rowe, M. (2006). The treatment relationship in peer-based and regular case management for clients with severe mental illness. *Psychiatric Services, 57*(8), 1179–1184.

Smith, R. J., & Levinson, J. D. (2011). The impact of implicit racial bias on the exercise of prosecutorial discretion. *Seattle University Law Review, 35*, 795.

Snyder, H. N. (2012). *Arrests in the United States, 1990–2010*. Washington, DC: Bureau of Justice Statistics.

Spelman, W. (2009). Crime, cash, and limited options: Explaining the prison boom. *Criminology and Public Policy, 8*(1), 29–77.

Steadman, H. J., Osher, F. C., Robbins, P. C., Case, B., & Samuels, S. (2009). Prevalence of serious mental illness among jail inmates. *Psychiatric Services, 60*(6), 761–765.

Subramanian, R., Delaney, R., Roberts, S., Fishman, N., & McGarry, P. (2015). *Incarceration's front door*. Vera Institute of Justice. Retrieved from http://www.vera.org/sites/default/files/resources/downloads/incarcerations-front-door-report_02.pdf

Teplin, L. A., Abram, K. M., & McClelland, G. M. (1996). Prevalence of psychiatric disorders among incarcerated women. I. Pretrial jail detainees. *Archives of General Psychiatry, 53*(6), 505–512.

Torrey E. F., Kennard, A. D., Eslinger, D., Lamb, R., & Pavle, L. (2010). *More mentally ill persons are in jails and prisons than hospitals: A survey of the states*. Arlington, VA: Treatment Advocacy Center.

Travis, J., & Waul, M. (2003). *Prisoners once removed: The impact of incarceration and reentry on children, families, and communities*. Washington, DC: Urban Institute.

Travis, J., Western, B., & Redburn, S. (2014). *The growth of incarceration in the United States: Exploring causes and consequences*. Washington, DC: National Academies Press.

Trojanowicz, R. C., & Bucqueroux, B. (1990). *Community policing: A contemporary perspective*. Cincinnati, OH: Anderson.

Turner, S., Greenwood, P. W., Chen, E., & Fain, T. (1999). The impact of truth-in-sentencing and three strikes legislation: Prison populations, state budgets, and crime rates. *Stanford Leland and Policy Review, 11*, 75.

Wacquant, L. (2010). Class, race and hyperincarceration in revanchist America. *Daedalus, 139*(3), 74–90.

Wakefield, S., & Uggen, C. (2010). Incarceration and stratification. *Annual Review of Sociology, 36*, 387–406.

Weeks, R., & Spatz Widom, C. (1998). Self-reports of early childhood victimization among incarcerated adult male felons. *Journal of Interpersonal Violence, 13*(3), 346–361.

Weitzer, R. (2000). Racialized policing: Residents' perceptions in three neighborhoods. *Law and Society Review, 34*(1), 129–155. doi:10.2307/3115118

Western, B. (2002). The impact of incarceration on wage mobility and inequality. *American Sociological Review, 67*(4), 526–546.

Western, B., & Pettit, B. (2010). *Collateral costs: Incarceration's effect on economic mobility*. Washington, DC: Pew Charitable Trusts.

Wheelock, D., & Uggen, C. (2005). *Race, poverty and punishment: The impact of criminal sanctions on racial, ethnic, and socioeconomic inequality*. National Poverty Center at the University of Michigan, Ann Arbor, September, 15–16.

Wolff, N., & Shi, J. (2012). Childhood and adult trauma experiences of incarcerated persons and their relationship to adult behavioral health problems and treatment. *International Journal of Environmental Research and Public Health, 9*, 1908–1926.

2

Reflections on a Locked Door

LESSONS FROM HISTORY AND THE FAILED PROMISE OF PENAL INCARCERATION

Rebecca Ginsburg

BACKGROUND

What can we learn from a locked door?

I must pass through seven heavy, locked doors during my walk from the prison parking lot to the education building. At each, I am forced to halt and wait until a correctional officer buzzes me through. The constant stops are frustrating, but they are a fact of prison life. Locked doors and heavy surveillance are ubiquitous in American prisons, and their primary purpose is clear—controlling people's movement through prison grounds.

This is a key feature of the American prison landscape, and it is one that speaks to the failure of penal incarceration.

In seeking to control movement, prison administrators are trying to accomplish a number of goals. The locked doors, cameras, sally ports, and other devices designed to slow down and regulate travel in prisons prevent people from entering and leaving at will; monitor their actions and locations; instill incarcerated individuals' dependence on prison authorities for even the simplest of tasks, like opening a door; and keep people contained, as desired, in particular sections of the prison. Their use supports in multiple ways the fundamental objectives of penal incarceration—to control, isolate, and separate individuals in an effort to remake them. This has been the purpose of the penitentiary since it was first invented, and continues to be the vision that, theoretically, animates incarceration today.

Unfortunately, history tells us that those objectives are unachievable. Indeed, as early as the mid-19th century, contemporaries observed that the recently introduced system of penal incarceration, with its insistence on keeping incarcerated people apart from society, was a failure.

The fact that our society clings to an institutional regime that is not working should disturb us, and make us curious. Why do we continue to rely on penal incarceration despite its being discredited by many over 150 years ago? Why do we still build prisons according to standards that were considered innovative in the early 1800s?

This chapter considers why the effort to control, isolate, and separate has had such persistence, and poses some questions about what we might do instead.

LEARNING FROM HISTORY

The decades-long efforts of prison activists, journalists, and scholars have finally placed the issue of incarceration in the national spotlight. It is now relatively well known that the U.S. incarceration rate began to rise sharply in the early 1970s, that since the early 1990s we have been the world's most energetic jailer, and that states spend more than they can afford to lock their residents up.

Those facts not withstanding, the weakness of the U.S. prison system lies deeper than in numbers. The problem is not that we lead the world in individuals cycling in and out of our jails and prisons each year, but that prisons, as they currently operate, are an insufficient and ineffective response to crime and violence. This is no secret. The evidence lies in our high recidivism rates and the levels of violence in American society, especially as compared with similar nations. It is apparent by the fact that there is a whole area of criminology devoted to calculating the criminogenic effects of prisons—that is, the extent to which incarceration itself generates crime. Thankfully, we finally have consensus among informed policymakers and wide swaths of the public of the need for significant reform.

The smart decarceration movement is a product of the current moment. Anticipating that many more states will follow the leads of California, New Jersey, and others that have already taken steps to reduce their reliance on imprisonment, the movement aims to provide critical guidance to such efforts. Smart decarceration involves more than opening up cell doors and releasing people. Efforts to decrease the prison and jail population in a given jurisdiction ideally form part of transformative policy and procedural changes (Pettus-Davis & Epperson, 2015). The era of decarceration is already provoking the necessary critical conversations about such basic matters as why we incarcerate in the first place and whether we should continue to do so.

This, then, is a hopeful—if cautious—time.

As we move thoughtfully and critically toward implementing criminal justice systems that will ensure a more just and humane future, it is important to do two things. First, we must look back squarely at the decisions that created the current situation and learn from them. Second, we must keep people in the equation, especially the on-the-ground experiences of those most affected by incarceration. In this chapter, I aim to do both. I reflect on the lessons of prison history for today, with emphasis on the ordinary people who have been caught up in that history and currently live it.

My perspective is informed in part by my work as an architectural historian who specializes in landscapes marked by violence and racial inequality. It is also shaped by the many hours I spend inside prisons. For almost 20 years I have been in and out of state facilities as director of the University of Illinois at Urbana-Champaign's prison education program, the Education Justice Project, and before that as an instructor in a prison education program at San Quentin State Prison in California. My engagement with currently and formerly incarcerated individuals, their family members, prison administrators, prison staff, and increasingly with victims of crime as well, informs the way I understand prisons past and present. On an almost daily basis, inside and outside of prisons, I am reminded of the failure of penal incarceration to live up to the ambitions of its original promoters. That strengthens my commitment to the struggle to reverse course on America's well-meaning but ultimately failed experiment with penal imprisonment.

BEFORE THE PRISON

The primary response to crime in the United States is to place individuals convicted of wrongdoing into small, locked cells. We group those cells together into complexes called "prisons," and set those structures off from their surrounding communities with tall walls and fences. People held in prisons have minimal access to community resources, family members, and even to one another. In most prisons, there is little to do besides work at menial jobs, socialize, and exercise. People are confined to these facilities for years at a time, sometimes for their entire lives.

Anyone from the year 1750 who read the above description would be shocked.

Prisons are a relatively recent invention, dating from the late 18th century. Before then, *penal incarceration*—the confinement of individuals who had been convicted of criminal wrongdoing—was very rare. Societies in western Europe had other ways of dealing with crime. (Because the modern prison evolved from western tradition and was exported through colonialism and like mechanisms throughout the world, this chapter focuses on western punishment histories.) One of the most common approaches was for people to treat wrongdoing against themselves and their kin as a private matter. For those that sought the formality of external authorities, there were several options.

Blood Sanctions and Early Jails

Criminal courts commonly sentenced individuals found guilty of crime or misdemeanors to "blood sanctions," punishments that involve infringement to bodily integrity, in some cases resulting in the drawing of blood. Common examples are branding, whippings, pillory, and execution (for accounts of the administration of blood sanctions in the early modern era, see Foucault, 1975; Spierenburg, 1995).

Individuals awaiting trial were confined in jails, which were administered at the local level. If they were found guilty, the court ordered them to return to jail to await the administration of punishment. The period of internment before and after trial was considered a practical necessity, meant to provide flight, and was not part of the punishment.

Because jail simply served the purpose of holding a person fast, there was no perceived need to secure the social separation of jailed individuals, whether to achieve punishment or rehabilitation. Accordingly, there was little effort to keep visitors or outside influences from jails. In 18th-century jails, there was considerable coming and going. Individuals who were held in the debtors' prison section of county jails, for instance, could even leave during the day to conduct business and visit their creditors. How else could they manage to lift themselves out of debt? In the rest of the jail, there were coming and goings by attorneys, family members and friends, and prostitutes and other vendors. One of the most common businesses were suppliers of liquor. In fact, innkeepers sometimes applied for the coveted jailkeeper's licenses, because the two businesses were so complementary. They could set up a taproom right inside the jail and add charges to a person's account throughout his or her stay. As all this suggests, a jailkeeper's license could be quite lucrative, with no external constraint on the fee structure, no enforceable standards of care, and only indifferent local magistrates to report to.

Blood sanctions themselves had been in use throughout Europe for centuries. Such punishments were held to have deterrent effects—deterring the individual wrongdoer from committing such an act again (i.e., *individual deterrence*) and deterring others, especially those who witnessed the public administration of justice, from committing it (i.e., *collective deterrence*). For minor matters, European jurisdictions employed workhouses, bridewells, and houses of correction. There are subtle differences between the three, but they all worked more or less in the same way. A man, woman, or child could be sent by a court to these places on the basis of a mere complaint—no trial was required. In practice, that meant that these institutions often functioned as relatively unchecked ways of controlling those considered a threat to the social order—frequently that meant outsiders and the poor. Their supposed purpose was to provide "training" to their residents to make them fit for productive employment on release. In reality, they functioned as factories. The institutions that controlled them exploited the workers, who had no bargaining power, entering into contracts with private companies to provide inmate-produced goods (e.g., rope and lace) at prices below market, and enforcing compliance through threats and corporal punishment. They were dreaded, awful places, that nonetheless enjoyed the support of philanthropists and the church for centuries (for accounts of bridewells, workhouses, and houses of correction, see Evans, 1982; Ignatieff, 1978; McGowen, 1995).

The Ecclesiastical Court System

Alongside the government's criminal justice system lay the church's. During the medieval period, as many as 10% of the population could have been members of religious communities (e.g., nuns, monks, or priests living in convents or monasteries). When they violated the rules of their orders, religious individuals would find themselves caught up in the ecclesiastical court system. Transgressions could range from minor misdeeds (e.g., talking back to a superior) to major offenses such as assaults and killings. The death sentence was disallowed within monasteries and convents as being contrary to ecclesiastical laws. Violators of their social order, then, had to be dealt with in other ways. Corporal punishment was used, especially imposed fasting and flagellation. Another common practice was to compel confinement of offenders either to one's monastery cell or to a cell specific for the purpose (Johnson, Dobrzabska, & Palla, 2005). The avowed objective of internment within the monasteries was to provide opportunity for self-reflection that would lead to rehabilitation (Lehner, 2013).

In some instances, entire monastic buildings were given over for the purpose of confining monks who had been sentenced to such punishment. Life sentences were not uncommon, though the emphasis was on reconciliation with the wrongdoer and his or her eventual reentry back into the community after being rehabilitated.

Banishment and Hulks

The final form of western punishment that existed before the prison was banishment. An ancient practice, it underwent resurgence in early modern England, as urban unemployment rose and the colonies sought labor. Individuals brought before English courts could be ordered "transported" to English colonies in North America for a fixed length of years. Transported individuals—the vast majority of them men—were sometimes shipped to the Americas on the same ships that on other occasions hosted Africans bound for slavery, the shipping companies making good profits on both forms of cargo (Christianson, 1998). In the Americas, they could find themselves laboring alongside enslaved workers and indentured servants.

The English halted transportation during the American Revolution. British jurists, like many others, believed the disruption would not last long and that, once order was reimposed on the colonies, commerce and trade could resume as usual, including the shipment of individuals. For the time being, though, the accumulation of individuals who were being sentenced to transportation produced a challenge. The English jails holding them quickly became full.

The solution was to store them instead on old, worn warships, or *hulks*. These vessels were not sufficiently seaworthy to make them useful in the war effort but were solid enough that they could be retrofitted to hold cells, each of which held many men much in the manner as jails on land. Those awaiting transportation slept on the ships, and during the day were sent ashore to build and repair roads and perform other labor.

THE DREAM OF THE PENITENTIARY

Scholars are still trying to unravel the various threads that led to the invention of the prison in the late 18th century. In England, one factor was the legislature's interest in responding to mounting public complaints about hulks. The ships were moored in rivers throughout the country, and their neighbors complained about the noise, stench, and danger. There was also rising concern about the condition of English jails, which had become the subject of a best-selling book that exposed them as disease-infested, corrupt institutions in need of reform (West, 2011).

Around this time, there was also a shift in sentiment away from the spectacle of blood sanctions, which were often administered publicly and attracted boisterous crowds of callous spectators. To be sure, the purposes of blood sanctions had always been deep and spiritual. The point had never been to provide displays of gore to the populace or to engage in sadistic spectacle. Instead, the infliction of pain was widely understood to promote spiritual hearing and social reconciliation. Even in instances where the accused was to be killed, the process and ritual of his death was understood to create the sort of suffering that opened the way for both individual and social redemption (Olson, 2005). However, this aspect of blood sanctions was often overshadowed by the drunken parties that accumulated on execution grounds and the disrespectful behavior displayed by the mobs who attended, at least, to the minds of the elite classes who now sought to change long-standing practices of punishment.

The legislature acted boldly. In 1779, it passed the Penitentiary Act, which approved the construction, for the first time, of state penitentiaries. This solution to the problems of overcrowded hulks, unhealthy and corrupt county jails, and chaos-inducing corporal punishments represented a new vision of criminal justice. The word "penitentiary" itself came from ecclesiastical law. Like monastic cells and workhouses, the aim of state penitentiaries would be to rehabilitate the individuals held within. Furthermore, like hulks, they would harness and exploit labor. And, even better than jails, they would confine individuals and protect society from dangerous men and women. However, the essence of the penitentiary would be more than the sum of its parts. The penitentiary was an experiment that spoke to the hopefulness of society and its belief in the resilience of individuals and their capacity to be repaired. It would be something like a machine that manufactured virtue (Evans, 1982). Reformers claimed that the penitentiary was "a remedy for all the evils in society" (Rothman, 1971, p. 118).

It is difficult for us today to absorb just how revolutionary the idea of the penitentiary was to contemporaries. The heart of the idea was that confinement in the penitentiary would be, in itself, the punishment. Unlike a jail, the penitentiary was not meant to be a holding pen that kept prisoners until the "real" punishment could be meted out. Being sentenced to the penitentiary *was* the punishment. Certainly, it had sometimes happened in the past that courts would determine that someone had spent so much time in jail awaiting trial, or so much time confined after trial, awaiting punishment, that the court vacated the actual sentence and freed the person. Some courts occasionally even sentenced an individual for a fixed term of limited confinement in a jail. But the penitentiary undertook this on a whole new scale, and envisaged confinement taking place in an altogether different environment than what the jail offered. The penitentiary was much more than a large jail, an expanded workhouse, or a "land-hulk."

First, penitentiaries would not accommodate individuals in large common rooms, as had been the case in all those settings (with the exception of cells for condemned people). Instead, each person would be assigned to his or her own individual cell. Second, prisons would not allow easy commerce and communication between prisoners or between prisoners and the free world, as jails, workhouses, and hulks did. Isolation, in order to promote self-knowledge and rehabilitation, would be the order of the day.

Labor played a central role. All incarcerated people would be expected to work on productive tasks such as weaving, carpentry, or breaking stones. The idea was for individuals to cultivate healthy habits and shed their former lives through the discipline and rigors of labor, isolation, and separation from the influences of the environments from which they came. This was not an attempt to deter individuals, but a project with a higher aim—rehabilitation. The penitentiary would be a pathway to a new life. It allowed those who served their sentences to reenter the world newly born in spirit and character, with the added benefit of being equipped with skills that would help them get employment.

THE UNITED STATES TAKES THE LEAD

The Penitentiary Act of 1779 established two national penitentiaries in England, one for men and the other women, and in that lay its downfall (for the legislative history of the Act, see Devereaux, 1999). Until this time, criminal justice had been a local concern, as were workhouses and hulks. The Act anticipated more oversight at the national level, and the associated loss of parochial avenues of enrichment. There would still be a need for local jails to house individuals awaiting trial, but the Act promised, or threatened, national-level oversight over their operations, as wardens would be forced to coordinate with penitentiary authorities, and an overall professionalization of the entire business of dealing with prisoners. Many recoiled from that prospect.

In another respect, too, the vision of two national institutions, large enough to house the entire prisoner population of England, led to downfall of the Act, with its grand ambitions and intentions. Land was required to build the penitentiaries, and a suitable architectural plan was necessary to bring the vision to life. There followed literally decades of arguments, negotiations, construction (in one case, only to have it discovered that the Crown had built the new facility on marsh lands), demolition, and the drawing up of new plans. Lawsuits, of course, followed. By the late 18th century, while the English were still thrashing out details such as the siting of the buildings, the first penitentiary had been built—in the United States.

Within the new nation was a spirit of innovation and forward thinking. Elites sought to distinguish the United States from its colonial past, and this effort was reflected in a range of fields, from architecture to banking to prisons. The Walnut Street Jail in Philadelphia was in need of expansion, and its board, its eye on developments in England, decided to follow a penitentiary-like design that would allow for confinement in individual cells, the example set by the Penitentiary Act. Eventually, the political and legal struggles around the penitentiary would be resolved in England. Then, that nation would finally move ahead with its own prison-modernizing project. However, by that time, the United States had become the acknowledged global leader in penitentiary building, a distinction it has, rather problematically, kept until today. (For adaptation of the penitentiary in the early United States, see Barnes, 1921; Rothman, 1971.)

THE DREAM TURNS INTO A NIGHTMARE

American states and territories, each in turn, took up the question of whether to abandon use of jails and blood sanctions in favor of sentencing individuals to long-term incarceration in prisons. The main sticking points were typically the loss of local control over punishment and the cost of building large, secure structures to house people. However, the idea of the penitentiary gradually found widespread support. By the outbreak of the Civil War, most states had at least started to implement penal incarceration, including New York, Pennsylvania, Vermont, Kentucky, Ohio, Illinois, Georgia, Missouri, and Tennessee, to name only some. Contemporaries were self-conscious that they were forging a new path: "an experiment," one called it (Rothman, 1971, p. 120), in the realm of criminal justice and public safety.

American prisons became famous worldwide, and an object of fascination. They were notoriously spartan, and individuals were sentenced for longer periods of time than was usual in other countries. Highly regimented routines prevailed, as prison administrators sought to create a radical egalitarianism among prisoners. The idea was not to make imprisonment itself a form of torture, but neither to make conditions so attractive that people would consider committing crimes as a means to get three steady meals and a safe place to sleep. The term of imprisonment was to be a time of severe reflection that led to spiritual rebirth.

On one count, though, the early prisons did create extraordinary pain and suffering, and that was through their insistence on isolation. No interaction whatsoever was allowed with one's fellow prisoners or guards. Communications with family on the outside was also sharply circumscribed, in some cases limited to one letter a year and no visits. In most American prisons, women and men left their cells during the day to labor in the prison work yard. In others, people were not allowed to leave their cells, ever. Everything was provided for them within. Food was delivered by guards. Toilet facilities were contained within the cell, and so was a small, private courtyard in which they could stretch their legs and feel the sky. Cells held their workplace materials, as prisoners were expected to labor in their isolation and meet production quotas.

Facilities that followed the more common model, called *Auburn-style prisons* because they were based on an early prison in Auburn, New York, allowed prisoners to come into regular contact with one another through work. However, rules forbade them to talk or even to make eye contact. The challenge of working and eating next to others and being unable to extend one's self to them or be recognized by them was great. Indeed, simply being efficient in their jobs would require the prisoners to occasionally communicate with the person working beside them about supplies or workflow. Communications did occur, of course, and the punishments meted out for this behavior were prompt and severe. It was this—the regime of violence required to suppress the most natural of urges—that gave Auburn prisons a reputation for being notoriously brutal.

For some time, early American prisons were the pride of their communities. The new institutions created jobs and brought in tourism. They demonstrated in highly visible fashion the forward-thinking attitudes of local inhabitants and community leaders. Some prisons even generated revenue by charging visitors or through work contracts.

However, the shine did not remain long. Thoughtful people could see that prisons did not realize their goals of rehabilitation and created further problems of their own. The most biting articulation of that opinion came from the author Charles Dickens, who, prior to his visit to the United States in 1842, had expressed enthusiasm for the American prison system. For many idealistic and humane people, the idea of seeking to rehabilitate those who committed crimes, rather than making examples of them, had initial appeal. But after Dickens visited Eastern State Penitentiary, which was built on the Pennsylvania model, he changed his mind. In scathing words, he described the penitentiary as a distinct form of hell. Its regime of isolation struck at the core of a person's humanity and unraveled it. "I hold this slow and daily tampering with the mysteries of the brain to be immeasurably worse than any torture of the body" (Dickens, 1842).

People read Charles Dickens. They read critical accounts of others who visited the new prisons, including Alexis de Tocqueville in 1833 (de Tocqueville, 1969). There were also news reports, which cautioned that holding people in extreme isolation in individual cells without access to visitors could lead to abuse, as in the case of the woman in a New York prison who became pregnant after her incarceration and was later beaten to death in her cell. Because these sites were tourist attractions, many individuals had the opportunity to see for themselves their strange, mournful environments and to ponder the implications of complete isolation for healthy rehabilitation.

A person did not even have to enter a prison to become dubious about the efficacy of this approach to crime. Dickens reported that many prisoners, when they were being processed after completion of their sentences, were physically unable to hold a pen to sign their names and staggered away from the facility, as if drunk (Dickens, 1842). This must have been a common sight for those who lived in prison towns. Those with family members or close friends who had served prison sentences would know the truth as well. People often returned home unable to navigate the world and needing to relearn the habits of human interaction. Some never did, and required special care and attention for the rest of their lives. This was a far cry from engaging the productive, reformed lives that early boosters of the penitentiary had imagined for them. The final blow was that the use of prisons did not even appreciably reduce crime.

FORWARD, BACKWARD

The idea of locking people up as punishment for crime had been controversial from the start. Within decades, its critics felt they had been proven right. Not only did the use of prisons fail to decrease crime or to reduce recidivism, but imprisonment also created new problems for those sentenced to serve time within the facilities. However, despite all the evidence, jurisdictions lacked the courage to abandon their use of prisons.

There were many reasons for this. Prisons had become part of the fabric of communities. They accomplished for local economies what whipping, hanging, fines—all earlier responses to criminal wrongdoing—had never been able to do. They brought in tourists, provided many jobs, and become local points of pride. In addition, prisons were typically purpose-built structures. Unlike jails, which were sometimes located on the second floors or basements of commercial structures or in spare rooms in civic buildings, prisons were built as prisons, to serve that particular use. Dismantling them would be an expensive job and a conspicuous declaration of failure.

To be sure, many observed and criticized the racist nature of prisons. African Americans had been overrepresented in prisons, according to contemporary public authorities, since the early 19th century (Upton, 2008). Throughout the 19th century, prisons also held increasing numbers of immigrants, especially Irish Americans. Some critics of incarceration argued that prisons had not been effective in reducing crime because members of immigrant groups and nonwhites were less susceptible to their reha-bilitative effects. Criminality was less an environmental "disease" among them, one that could be cured if the person were placed in the proper conditions, as it was an inherent part of their character (Upton, 2008). Some argued that it made little sense to invest in expensive systems designed to reform these populations if such reform were not possible.

Still, imprisonment continued to satisfy the racist interests of the majority when it came to detaining and incapacitating minority populations. Not only that, prisons provided employment, mostly to native-born white men, while supporting local economies. In the end, the advantages of locking up disproportionate numbers of African Americans and foreign-born individuals appeared to outweigh arguments against doing so.

The prison was, anyway, still cloaked in the "mantle of legitimacy," according to the prison historian David Rothman (Rothman, 1971, p. 125). For all these reasons, instead of abandoning course, American states and territories continued to invest in penitentiaries and to make penal incarceration the centerpiece of their approaches to criminal justice. Thankfully, by the end of the 19th century, the regime of isolation had softened. There were simply too many people being sentenced by the courts to continue offering separate cells to each prisoner. The system was not sustainable. As it also was not working, administrators simply and quietly abandoned the effort to provide extreme isolation. Rothman argues that they convinced themselves that simply holding individuals behind bars, in and of itself, did some good (Rothman, 1971), even when the evidence pointed to other conclusions.

PRISONS TODAY

In my years teaching and running an educational program inside an Illinois state prison, I have seen firsthand how incarceration fails those we lock up. Though our criminal justice system has, at this point, effectively abandoned the ideal of rehabilitation, the discipline of isolation (except, troublingly, as a punishment for certain behaviors within prison), and the pretense that hard labor builds character, we have kept the penitentiary itself. Incarceration today is no longer the project of reforming the soul and cleansing the individual who had supposedly been polluted by his or her former environment, as misguided as that agenda might have been. Many states designate their prisons as "correctional centers." However, the job of penitentiaries today is to simply lock up and secure offending bodies.

What remains, now that the ideology of reform has been jettisoned, is the long sentence of confinement, the separation from family, and the degradation and stigma of incarceration. What remains is the building, the solid prison edifice. And it is still good, if for nothing else, for incapacitating and hiding those we define as criminals. At this point, penal incarceration has truly turned into the warehousing of human beings.

In each state, it is possible to identify half a dozen census tracts from which a plurality or majority of its incarcerated people come. We can think of penitentiaries as extensions of those neighborhoods, and the criminal justice system as cycling predominantly black and brown people back and forth between the marginalized, underresourced, interconnected communities located on either side of the fence (Wacquant, 2002). The problem does not lie with the individuals who are trapped in what has been called the "revolving door" of incarceration, but with the lack of investment in institutions, like public education or healthcare that would allow them to tackle head-on the challenges that they and their communities face.

Because prisons have become places for simply storing individuals for years and decades at a time, the prisoners' prospects on release are not much improved since Dickens's time. When they return home without vocational certification that could help them find jobs, educational qualifications that open doors and instill confidence, or the ability to engage comfortably with people in the free world, their chances for successful reentry diminish. Moreover, parole boards impose additional restrictions that frustrate their efforts to thrive and render them a burden to their families. For instance, they may be obligated to report regularly to the parole office and have to depend on unreliable public transportation to get there, or be subject to unannounced visits by their parole officer, throwing the entire household into turmoil. It is no wonder that most return to prison within 5 years.

Most Education Justice Project students resist those odds. They emerge from prison shaken up, but ready to engage the world. They do a better than average job of finding decent jobs and staying employed. Some enroll in college and work to complete their undergraduate degrees. The lesson is not that college-in-prison programs are the solution to what ails prisons. We will serve incarcerated people and the larger society ill if we simply replace the 19th-century program of spiritual reawakening with a 21st-century plan for intellectual reawakening, without digging deeper and considering the larger contexts that support poverty, crime, and political marginalization. Any approach to incarceration that simply seeks to fix individuals will miss the mark.

The lesson, instead, is that this is a struggle worth fighting. Our prisons hold tens of thousands of individuals whom our society has effectively thrown away. Many of them are smart, compassionate, and well loved by their families and friends. They are neither lost causes nor expendable. Rather, they are full-fledged human beings who often startle me with their resilience and hopefulness. They are leaders, too, and in the best position to move us forward in the next chapter of the history of the prison.

LESSONS FOR DECARCERATION

It has been only about 200 years since the prison was invented, and about 150 years since contemporaries declared it to be a failure.

It is comforting to believe that our basic institutions, the ones that define us and that we rely on the most, are reasoned, optimal solutions to our social needs. That is not always the case, and certainly not what has happened with respect to the prison. Its widespread use is a consequence of historical accident and lack of political courage, not the result of thoughtful weighing of evidence about its efficacy.

Had 19th-century arguments about the obvious deficiencies of penal incarceration won the day, we might have seen a return to older approaches to punishment, such as blood sanctions, or continued innovation, including efforts to explore interventions that might truly support personal rehabilitation or to better understand the ways in which environmental conditions such as poverty and economic opportunity contribute to crime. We continue to incarcerate today not because moral imperatives or public safety demand it, but, in the words of a Norwegian observer of the American system, a warden who runs an open prison that has a much lower recidivism rate than is common in the United States, because we are lazy (Dreisinger, 2016).

The history of the prison in the United States also has more hopeful notes, and some lessons for today. First, awareness of how we came to adopt a system of penal incarceration, and why we persisted in using it even after it failed to live up to its promise, liberates us from any misguided belief that the use of the prison has proven the test of time, been with us always, or is in any way natural or inevitable. America is not tied to the prison, any more than we were ever tied to public hangings or the stocks. There are particular and historically bound reasons that we incarcerate, and we have the freedom to turn away from it and consider other ways of thinking about criminal punishment, public safety, and social health. As we move forward, how can we best ensure an inclusive, clear-eyed exploration of the many options available? How can we avoid the mistake of closing ourselves off from innovative ideas, or of clinging to worn approaches out of prejudice or fear?

We adopted the prison out of an idealistic conviction that what had existed previously was not good enough for our new nation, and that we could do better. Today, we can also do better, and we must. We can no longer afford the financial costs of incarceration, the collateral damage to families and communities, and the harm our reputation sustains due to our being the world's largest jailer. Fortunately, history reflects our openness to look abroad for ideas, and our willingness to learn and borrow from supposed friends and enemies both. We can use such openness today, especially when so many other nations appear to be doing a better job of containing crime and caring for those who commit crime and their victims. How can we learn from other nations' experiences with criminal justice? How can we create a climate of openness to borrowing from others?

Our avowed abandonment of harsh forms of corporal punishment in the 18th century was based on a rejection of imposing pain and suffering in favor of more peaceful ways of addressing crime. The intention was humane and admirable. This inclination away from punishment and toward gentleness—as misguided as it was in practice—speaks to a goodness that we should call on again. Our history also speaks to American optimism and energy, useful things to tap into now, as we gather the courage to change direction and explore alternative approaches to crime and the harms that it reveals. How can we create a movement to decarcerate that is humane, critical, compassionate, and inclusive? How can we support respectful dialogue and dissent among ourselves? And how can we ensure that those who have been most affected by incarceration have seats at the table?

This all suggests that simply seeking to reduce recidivism or promote public safety will be an overly low bar as we go forward. Our goal should not be fewer people in prison or a smaller proportion returning. As we contemplate a major shift in approach to crime and punishment, we should seek to build institutions that are consistent with our values and help us build the society we wish to become. That will require us facing head-on the most damaging aspects of past practices.

First, we must be highly attentive to the roles that racism and anti-immigration bias have played in shaping our current penal system and that, in so many respects, continue to infect American society today. Can alternatives to incarceration not only avoid embroiling disproportionate numbers of marginalized groups but also be part of the solution of addressing historic injustices and fostering more openness toward others?

Second, our insistence on tinkering with the psyche and souls of those in early American prisons was part of a larger and long-standing bias toward understanding crime as a matter of individual deviance. An overly sharp focus on those convicted of crime has blinded us to other matters that ought to be of concern. As we develop institutions to take the place of prisons, how can we be less insistent about fixing people, and more curious about the contexts and conditions that contribute to their making choices to commit crimes? Related to that, how can we take better care of victims of crime, and honor research that demonstrates that allowing them to play larger roles in the criminal justice system can be healing for them and produce more confidence in the fairness of any remedy imposed?

Finally, it bears repeating that our approach to decarceration, and to whatever institutions we develop to replace our overreliance upon penal incarceration, if not penal incarceration itself, should be guided by the values of humanity, equity, reason, and compassion. Those are what guided the early American pioneers of the penitentiary and, of all lessons we can take from them, to submit our own efforts to these concerns is the most important. It is human to sometimes miss in our attempts to realize solutions that are consistent with what we most care about. Fortunately, history is equally clear that we are more than capable of doggedly continuing the fight to get things right.

REFERENCES

Barnes, H. E. (1921). Historical origin of the prison system in America. *Journal of Criminal Law and Criminology, 12*(1), 35–60.

Christianson, S. (1998). *With liberty for some: 500 years of imprisonment in America.* Boston, MA: Northeastern University Press.

Devereaux, S. (1999). The making of the Penitentiary Act, 1775–1779. *Historical Journal, 42*(4), 405–433.

Dickens, C. (1842). *American notes for general circulation.* London, UK: Chapman & Hall.

Dreisinger, B. (2016). *Incarceration nations: A journey to justice in prisons around the world.* New York, NY: Other Press.

Evans, R. (1982). *The fabrication of virtue: English prison architecture, 1750–1840.* New York, NY: Cambridge University Press.

Foucault, M. (1975). *Discipline and punish: The birth of the prison.* New York, NY: Vintage Books.

Johnson, R., Dobrzanska, A., & Palla, S. (2005). The American prison in historical perspective: Race, gender, and adjustment. In J. M. Pollack (Ed.), *Prisons today and tomorrow* (pp. 22–42). Burlington, MA: Jones & Bartlett Learning.

Lehner, U. L. (2013). *Monastic prisons and torture chambers: Crime and punishment in central European monasteries, 1600–1800.* Eugene, OR: Cascade Books.

McGowen, R. (1995). The well-ordered prison. In N. Morris, & D. J. Rothman (Eds.), *The Oxford history of the prison: The practice of punishment in western society* (pp. 79–101). New York, NY: Oxford University Press.

Olson, T. (2005). The medieval blood sanction and the divine beneficence of pain: 1100–1450. *Journal of Law and Religion, 22,* 63–129.

Pettus-Davis, C., & Epperson, M. W. (2015). From mass incarceration to smart decarceration. American Academy of Social Work and Social Welfare. Retrieved from http://aaswsw.org/wp-content/uploads/2015/03/From-Mass-Incarceration-to-Decarceration-3.24.15.pdf

Rothman, D. J. (1971). *The discovery of the asylum: Social order and disorder in the new republic.* New Brunswick, NJ: AldineTransaction.

Spierenburg, P. (1995). The body and the state: Early modern Europe. In N. Morris, & D. J. Rothmans (Eds.), *The Oxford history of the prison: The practice of punishment in western society* (pp. 49–77). New York, NY: Oxford University Press.

de Tocqueville, A. (1969). Democracy in America. In J. P. Mayer (Ed.). New York, NY: HarperCollins.

Upton, D. (2008). *Another city: Urban life and urban spaces in the new American republic.* New Haven, CT: Yale University Press.

Wacquant, L. (2002). From slavery to mass incarceration. *New Left Review.* Retrieved from https://newleftreview.org/II/13/loic-wacquant-from-slavery-to-mass-incarceration

West, T. (2011). *The curious Mr. Howard: Legendary prison reformer.* Hook, UK: Waterside Press.

3

From Moment to Movement

THE URGENCY FOR FORMERLY INCARCERATED

INDIVIDUALS TO LEAD DECARCERATION EFFORTS

Glenn E. Martin

LEADING WITH CONVICTION: A PERSONAL TESTIMONY

Upon exiting prison in 2000, I was faced with the same bleak odds encountered by so many of our nation's formerly incarcerated. A severely limiting labor market was only the most glaring of the many hurdles that dotted my path to successful reentry. Determined to beat the odds, I set out on an earnest mission to obtain meaningful employment, achieve a decent standard of living, and further cultivate the voice I had begun to develop as an advocate during my incarceration.

Yet with brutal consistency, I was met with dozens of rejections in my quest for employment. I suffered no delusions about my chances in the job market, but the blows of rejection and continued punishment still landed with tremendous force. But in exceptional fashion, and regrettably so, I was soon offered a pathway out of the many cruelties of postimprisonment life.

As I gained notoriety in the advocacy world, my voice, once suffocated to a whisper, was growing to a resounding pitch. Not long ago, I failed to land a job moving boxes for $16,000 a year. I now run a bourgeoning nonprofit with a $23-million budget and a staff of 12. All the while, I remember that my exceptional story, of which I am reminded frequently, only serves to prove the wickedness of the rule. And it must be swallowed that that rule is a choice we have made. The upshot is clear: We can absolutely do otherwise.

It is a decision I am reminded of every time I reflect on my most difficult day in prison—the day of my exit. To be sure, I was excited to reacquaint myself with the texture of freedom, but was dispirited to be leaving behind some of America's best and brightest. In all cases, these voices to which I felt so viscerally and substantively connected spoke with an expertise and courage that I came to know as entirely the domain of those directly affected by the criminal justice system. It was the driving epiphany of my advocacy life.

And to them I say, never forfeit your right to dream. I came out of prison owing $100,000 in fines, fees, restitution, and child support. In 2015, I met with President Obama to discuss the importance of transforming our criminal justice system.

I am well aware that this trajectory is not everyone's. The odds are long and decidedly stacked against anyone who has come into contact with the criminal justice system. But Frederick Douglass's poignant wisdom still rings true: "Power concedes nothing without a demand" (1857).

BACKGROUND

The right to democratic participation—few principles in the history of America's constitutional republic enjoy such tremendous ceremonial devotion. The refrain appears time and time again in popular discourse, presented as inviolable American doctrine. It lies at the heart of the national narrative: The founding fathers rode populist waves of revolutionary zeal to war over the right to determine for themselves the course of their lives and their nation's arc. This was made possible in large part by accommodating popular colonial bigotry that precluded the extension of these rights to the nonwhite, nonmale, non-land-holding majority. The Unites States was conceived in contradiction—simultaneously championing and increasing self-determination for some while sabotaging it for others. Even as society gradually expands the recognition of rights inherent to human dignity—it continues to falter when the time comes to align doctrine with practice.

In no area of civic life is this gulf more apparent than in the growing national conversation around criminal justice reform. Many participating voices—from elected officials and popular pundits to academic and legacy institutions that have recently joined the long-standing fight for comprehensive criminal justice reform—are loud enough to be deafening. Certainly among these various voices there exists legitimate difference in terms of public policy prescriptions for treating our failed carceral system. Yet, as battle lines are drawn and ideological camps come into focus, so too does the glaring homogeneity of those participating in the conversation. The irony is hard to miss: Low-income people and people of color, though disproportionately affected by incarceration, are glaringly absent—or worse, omitted—from the conversation. Though there is ostensibly ample room to criminalize, detain, and imprison members of these communities, there is an apparent shortage of space within the ranks of the reform movement erected in their name. The movement's purported leaders and thinkers—at this moment composed largely of the elected officials, pundits, academics, and legacy institutions mentioned above—bear no resemblance to the communities ravaged by the past 4 decades of failed policy. No community wants, needs, or understands the urgency of sweeping reform more than the ones directly affected by a failed criminal justice system. Why, then, has the reform movement not sought their advice about what needs to change, where it can improve, and what strategies it needs to implement to manifest such change?

HEARING THE VOICES OF FORMERLY INCARCERATED INDIVIDUALS

People of color and low-income people are massively overrepresented among the incarcerated. In 2014, Latinos represented approximately one-fifth of people in state prisons, and one-quarter of people in federal prisons. Nearly half of people in both state and federal prison were black (Carson, 2015). In 2016, black males in their 30s made up one of every 10 in prison or jail any day of the week (The Sentencing Project, n.d.). There is no confusion about the demographic realities of incarceration.

Taken to its logical and strategic conclusion, the disproportionate representation of people of color within prisons should translate into movements with a similar constitution. After all, who understands the nature of a particular and specific harm better than the harmed?

Leading with Conviction: Empowering Formerly Incarcerated Individuals to Lead

Talk of strategy and representation recalls the nation's initial premise of self-determination. It is not enough that advocates for reform be genuine believers in the depravity and inhumanity of carceral policies. The conviction may be necessary, but alone is hardly sufficient. Leaders must acknowledge that the quest for meaningful change calls them to honor a principle so fundamental to self-determination that uttering it borders on redundancy: Everyone, regardless of station, has a right to participate in the decisions that have an impact on their lives. That oppressed peoples—a class that includes the incarcerated— cannot be, nor do they desire to be, delivered from their circumstances. Those freedoms, as well as the dignity of human life, are not things to be given.

This is not an abstract point. The idea of self-determination has a long pedigree in Western political thought—from the city-states of Greek antiquity to the American and French Revolutions, to Woodrow Wilson's Fourteen Points following World War I to the United Nations Charter of 1945. At first glance then, it remains a curiosity that liberals recoil at the insistence of oppressed peoples to lead the movements aimed at addressing and alleviating their collective grievances. Self-determination has been a bedrock of every movement for social transformation: from the black South African freedom struggle to the American and international movements for civil rights, women's rights, indigenous rights, LGBTQIA rights, and countless others.

IMPROVING THE CRIMINAL JUSTICE SYSTEM FROM WITHIN

History supports the notion that the space must be created for those injured by policy to shepherd their own struggles for justice. Yet the insistence of powerful forces within the Left to stand at the vanguard of such struggles is also knitted into the very fabric of this history. The South African freedom fighter Steven Biko wrote of the widely uncontroversial notion of injured parties organizing for themselves in the context of the black South African freedom struggle:

> When workers come together under the auspices of a trade union to strive for the betterment of their conditions, nobody expresses surprise in the Western world. It is the done thing. Nobody accuses them of separatist tendencies. Teachers fight their battles, garbagemen do the same, nobody acts as a trustee for another. Somehow, however, when blacks want to do their thing the liberal establishment seems to detect an anomaly. This is in fact a counter-anomaly. The anomaly was there in the first instance when the liberals were presumptuous enough to think that it behooved them to fight the battle for the blacks. (Biko & Stubbs, 2002, p. 25)

This riposte is an expression of the leader's shock at the incredulity of his white, liberal compatriots. For Biko, there was a glaring gulf between liberal thought and practice. He was determined to reveal the hypocrisy of South Africa's liberal establishment, which consistently labored to undermine indigenous leadership of the black freedom struggle. Yet, with great strategic acuity, he did so not by chastising his purported allies for their antidemocratic and paternalistic nature, but by making overtures to what he knew to be their philosophical and tactical sensibilities.

Let us be clear: One of the most corrupting features of the U.S. criminal justice system is that the criminalized have been historically barred from making decisions regarding their own lives. The agency and humanity of those the government claims to serve is diminished when politics are haunted by the shadow of paternalism, particularly those politics advocating for the freedom of those people. If freedom means anything, it must mean determination of self. The idea is simple enough: Policies will invariably reflect the interests of those that design them. The surest way to safeguard against the adoption of policies harmful to the interests of any group is to ensure that group is a part of the decision-making process. Identifying both the barriers and solutions to the shameful absence of formerly incarcerated leaders from mainstream criminal justice reform is actually easier than the breadth of the problem implies.

Currently, formerly incarcerated people involved in criminal justice reform are largely relegated to token roles as spokespeople, but seldom are they enabled to drive the policy agenda on criminal justice reform. Unsurprisingly, they are left with vanishingly little political power. With the exception of organizing opportunities at the local level, their participation is often peripheral and outside the bounds of key decision-making on both the policy and strategy level within reform initiatives. Formerly incarcerated leaders should be given substantive roles beyond the vital work of storytelling. Those of us with the access to amplify their expertise, visions of change, and presence are directly responsible for doing so. These groups' vastly superior knowledge of the criminal justice system is a woefully underused weapon in the fight against mass incarceration. This would be no small contribution. The formerly incarcerated are uniquely positioned to develop the advocacy and organizing strategies that will grow the base for the movement and ultimately lead us down the path of decarceration.

That examples of their pivotal role in this movement are rare is, in many ways, precisely the point. But they do exist. Take the incredible success of the Ban the Box campaign, which captures the decisive role directly affected people can take in effecting change. The campaign to remove the box on applications for employment, public assistance, and social services that applicants are required to check if they have ever been convicted of a crime was conceptualized by formerly incarcerated people from All of Us or None, a membership-based project of Legal Services for Prisoners with Children in the Bay Area. The campaign gained rapid and remarkable momentum and won policies in more than 100 local jurisdictions, 18 states, large corporations such as Target and Koch Industries, and federal employers under the Obama Administration. Of course, this type of policy campaign requires the skills of lawyers, policymakers, and advocates, but it was formerly incarcerated leaders who devised the strategy and laid the groundwork for success. Their brave and brilliantly orchestrated effort to shine an unforgiving spotlight on the moral bankruptcy of employment discrimination is a testament to the importance of leadership by those most affected by the issues.

Necessary Support

There is an appalling lack of support being devoted to improving the well-being of those with conviction histories, along with their families and communities. Akin to this concern is the abysmal level of funding and influence enjoyed by organizations led by the formerly incarcerated, and the transparent bias toward well-established legacy institutions with greater capacity to lead criminal reform campaigns. Formerly incarcerated leaders welcome and applaud the recent commitment of organizations such as the American Civil Liberties Union (ACLU) to the long-standing fight for comprehensive criminal justice reform. However, though such efforts have not gone unnoticed or unappreciated, for too long those who have directly faced the destructive power of the criminal justice system have labored tirelessly in the dark, demanding many of the same policy changes these institutions have now begun to offer as solutions. This provides as glaring an opportunity as any to amplify the vital work already being done by directly affected leaders. By supporting the community organizing efforts of organizations such as the Formerly Incarcerated and Convicted People and Families Movement—a national coalition led by directly affected people across the nation—the decarceration movement can begin the process of reforming the policies that affect their lives.

Indeed, the success of this campaign will require the support of organizations with deep institutional reach and influence, but nowhere should it be accepted that one's support for a campaign insulates one from criticism stemming from actions that jeopardize that campaign's success. Quite the opposite. It is precisely because the current battle is one with real and tremendous human consequences that such criticism is uniquely urgent. To abandon this principle would only serve to erode the transformative potential of this historic moment. This happens most conspicuously when the approach puts advocates in unintended collusion with the forces of power and oppression they rightfully advocate against. Thus, though it may seem anomalous for outsider groups to lead on behalf of others, the attempts to do so are consistent with history. The resulting disempowerment may not be intentional, but if society at large is to deal seriously with the consequences of its actions, it must be able to distinguish intent from impact, rhetoric from action, and remain objective from result. A declaration of noble intent matters little when measured against injury. Intentions must always accommodate impacts. Meaning well does not readily translate to doing well.

This is not to minimize the importance of outside advocacy. After all, every movement against systemic injustice (e.g., the abolition of slavery, civil rights, the Third World solidarity movements) has relied on the support of partners and sympathetic voices that stand closer to levers of power than they do. When such allies follow the directives of the affected people, their participation is most meaningful. This is as much about principle as it is strategy. Therefore, the remedy is obvious: Donors, advocates, and sympathizers of criminal justice reform ought to support organizations such as the Formerly Incarcerated and Convicted People and Families Movement and All of Us or None with the same measure of devotion and gusto that they do the megainstitutions that stand on their shoulders.

One of the most elementary moral truisms is the principle of universality: We must subject ourselves to the same standards of conduct that we apply to others. This is especially true for criminal justice reform, where the stakes for those targeted by the prison-industrial complex are alarmingly high. More specifically and to the point, we cannot with moral legitimacy lambaste a legal regime for failing to affirm the humanity of oppressed peoples as we refuse to do so in our own work.

THE MYTH OF THE VOICELESS: WORKING WITH FORMERLY INCARCERATED INDIVIDUALS TO IMPLEMENT REFORM STRATEGIES

Carving out greater paths to leadership and advocacy for the formerly incarcerated is only difficult to digest if one refuses to recognize the expertise cultivated and nurtured through lived experience. Where one studied, whom one studied under, and one's record of professional accomplishment all matter, to be sure, but are not preeminent or decisive in the context of this work. Scholars study as a science what multitudes have experienced as a matter of everyday toil. Given that such knowledge is secondhand, it is by definition, limited. Even decades of scholarship are no match for a lifetime spent navigating and mastering a life on the margins. It is worth mentioning here that within the realms of scholarship and advocacy—most noticeably criminology and social work—there exists a significant array of scholars and activists who have surfaced from those very margins. A stirring example of this is the provocative *Convict Criminology* (Ross & Richards, 2003)—an anthology of essays authored by criminologists, half of whom have incarceration histories, testifying to the absurdities of the American carceral state and the exacting toll imposed on the formerly incarcerated, their families, and communities. But again, it throws the rule into vivid relief that the lion's share of scholarship on this subject is conducted from a secondhand perspective. The failure is evident.

Hence, it is incumbent on progressive America to recognize that there are no "voiceless" individuals for whom they must speak. The notion that a faceless, suffering mass of people needs to be advocated for certainly comforts humans' ostensibly altruistic sensibilities, but it has no basis in reality. The formula is convenient but self-promoting, lazy, and reductive. Such reductionism obscures the reality of marginalized voices—namely that this manufactured voiceless mass is a contradiction in terms. Anyone who has experienced life on the margins knows well the rich legacy of outspoken resistance from within those communities; therefore, it is of paramount importance to distinguish between the silent and the silenced.

In the same way it did around the tough-on-crime agenda, a bipartisan consensus has begun to emerge around the need for a smarter, healthier approach to crime prevention and redress. Both historical moments share features beyond their consensus, namely a complete omission of the currently and formerly incarcerated within the discussion. Though these voices may not have been able to transform the cultural obsession with punishment that has pervaded the last 40 years of policymaking, their omission may spoil what ought to be the human-centered efforts of the future. This point should give pause to genuine reform advocates. The currently and formerly incarcerated must be given due reverence within the criminal justice reform movement. If we can effectively bar or refuse to listen to people on the issues that affect them most, then when will they ever be heard?

We begin by acknowledging what the historical record makes clear: The "voiceless" can be more aptly described as the "systematically silenced," with few deviations. The road ahead requires that reformers be deliberate and unequivocal in their language. They reinforce the tyranny of imposed silence every time they speak on behalf of, rather than with, people. If notions of true solidarity and ethical practice guide reform intentions, intention will align with impact.

More precisely, it is widely uncontroversial among criminal justice reform advocates that the U.S. criminal justice system has become an expensive and ineffective knee-jerk response to behaviors that are, by a wide margin, the predictable outcome of social catastrophes. Our combined tolerance for persistently high rates of unemployment and poverty as well as systems of second-class education and healthcare for some bears much of the blame. Institutions of punishment have long served as surrogates for access to community-based mental health and drug treatment, job training and placement, quality education, and affordable healthcare and follow-up. We can and must do otherwise. By raising the floor on human suffering in this context, we fulfill an elementary moral principle: We are all responsible for the consequences of our own actions.

CONCLUSION

In the context of criminal justice reform, such concepts do not require liberal allies to abandon their advocacy and silence themselves full stop. The meaningful course of action requires that those allies step aside, creating the space for those they serve to articulate their own humanity, as only they can. Optimally, they should serve as amplifiers for said voices when necessary or when called on. Under no circumstances can the voices of allies act as muzzles on the injured.

But in no way should this be interpreted as an argument for the wholesale withdrawal of advocates, elected officials, and policymakers from our current reform moment. It is important to remember that the criminal justice system exists as it does because of conscious, deliberate policy. It is not an accident of history. Structural accountability has to occur alongside self-determination. In fact, that same accountability is required for the realization of self-determination. There is no tension between the two. Insofar as access to freedom is prevented—freedom to work, freedom to democratic participation, freedom to live fully and determine one's destiny—the meaning of self-determination becomes severely limited and obsolete. That freedom is effectively blocked and trampled for multitudes of low-income people and people of color caught within the criminal justice system. Change requires that those who do the trampling cease and make amends. This is to say, the moral catastrophe that is our criminal justice system is entirely of human creation, and thus has human solutions.

The moment is urgent and the task significant. Those with the experience, wherewithal, and interrogative eye toward the prison-industrial complex must set and drive the agenda of the criminal justice reform movement, lest we reproduce the errors of the past. To avoid that abyss, criminal justice reformers will need to engage and employ the leadership of the world's most formidable experts on incarceration and criminal justice—the incarcerated themselves.

REFERENCES

Biko, S., & Stubbs, A. (2002). *I write what I like*. Chicago, IL: University of Chicago Press.
Carson, E. A. (2015). Prisoners in 2014. *Bureau of Justice Statistics*. Retrieved from http://www.bjs.gov/index.cfm?ty=pbdetail&iid=5387

Douglass, F. (1857, August 3). *West India Emancipation speech*. River Campus Libraries. Retrieved from http://rbscp.lib.rochester.edu/4398

Ross, J. I., & Richards, S. C. (Eds.). (2003). *Convict criminology*. Boston, MA: Cengage.

The Sentencing Project (n.d.). Racial disparity. *The Sentencing Project*. Retrieved from http://www.sentencingproject.org/issues/racial-disparity/

PART II

Advancing Justice and Community Reforms

We must change the way in which our laws work, change the way in which the system works, so that we can make a clear distinction between those who need to stay in prison to keep the public safe versus those who present little risk.

—HAWAII GOVERNOR NEIL ABERCROMBIE (D), January 23, 2012

4

From the Inside Out

A PERSPECTIVE ON DECARCERATION FROM A FORMERLY INCARCERATED INDIVIDUAL

Ronald Simpson-Bey

BACKGROUND

For the most part, the movement in America to end mass incarceration—*decarceration*—is driven primarily from the view, perspective, and theories of people who are far removed from the realities of prison; people who have only stood outside the criminal injustice system looking in; people who have never stood at the intersection of race and prosecution in America and experienced the abuse of the process; people who have not spent a single day inside the "belly of the beast" called prison; people who have not suffered the horrific impact of the draconian policies that govern every aspect of the lives of those in prison; people who have not suffered the dramatic dehumanizing effects and indignities intentionally inflicted on those in prison.

Though the intellect, effort, and concern of such well-meaning people make the decarceration movement possible, the perspective and input of those who have directly suffered the abuses of being incarcerated is vital in the discussion and formulation to decarcerate America. As stated in the oft-repeated mantra of JustLeadershipUSA, "Those closest to the problems are closest to the solutions" (Martin, 2015). In other words, the most compelling advocates of criminal and juvenile justice reform are those who have been directly affected by incarceration.

This chapter is from the perspective of someone who directly experienced and suffered the harms, inhumanity, and experience of prison.

In 1985, I found myself standing at the intersection of race and prosecution and did not see freedom until 2012, when the federal courts agreed that the state prosecutor's misconduct was egregious enough to be considered a violation of the constitution. I have always wondered why it took them so long to come to this obvious conclusion, especially because the facts of misconduct were the same for all those years. In the decision to reverse my conviction the court opined, "Given the prosecutor's deliberate and repeated 'foul blows' this Court has 'grave doubt' that such errors did not have a 'substantial and injurious effect or influence in determining the jury's verdict'. This Court grants Petitioner a conditional writ of habeas corpus" (*Simpson v. Warren*, 2009).

In this chapter, I discuss how my firsthand experience with the criminal justice system can help inform decarceration efforts through reforming prosecutorial misconduct, preparing incarcerated individuals for reentry, and restructuring parole practices. I conclude with a section on the need to include mercy, redemption, and second chances in the criminal justice system.

DECARCERATION'S ROLE IN REFORMING PROSECUTORIAL MISCONDUCT

It is apparent that tremendously complex societal issues—poverty, lack of employment, and racial and educational inequality—contribute to today's mass incarceration condition. These issues loom so large that it will take more than the decarceration movement to resolve them. However, decarceration can achieve a much more attainable yet equally monumental goal: prosecutorial practice reform. On the front end of the movement to decarcerate the United States, the office, function, and actions of the prosecutor's office must be addressed. Prosecutors are arguably the most powerful actors in the legal system. Their decisions have significant implications for how crime is defined, who is charged, and the sentence they receive.

The Commonplace Nature of Prosecutorial Misconduct

To be perfectly clear, not all prosecutors are inherently bad, corrupt, or unethical. Most of them are an honor to their profession. The bad ones, of which there are far too many, give the profession a black eye and condemn too many bodies to prison under questionable circumstances.

That said, *prosecutorial misconduct* is too ambiguous and vaguely defined by the courts. In *Berger v. United States* (1935), Justice Sutherland explained prosecutorial misconduct meant "overstepp[ing] the bounds of that propriety and fairness which should characterize the conduct of such an officer in the prosecution of a criminal offense." Ask yourself what that means, who makes that determination, and how is it enforced. Another definition is as follows:

> Prosecutorial misconduct is largely the result of three institutional conditions: vague ethics rules that provide ambiguous guidance to prosecutors; vast discretionary authority with little or no transparency; and inadequate remedies for prosecutorial misconduct, which create perverse incentives for prosecutors to engage in, rather than refrain from, prosecutorial misconduct. These three conditions converge to create uncertain norms and a general lack of accountability for how prosecutors view and carry out their ethical and institutional obligations. (Joy, 2006)

Despite its prevalence, prosecutorial misconduct remains an underaddressed problem in the U.S. criminal injustice system. Vast numbers of prosecutors across the country violate their oaths and snub the law with impunity (Hollway, 2016). Prosecutorial misconduct was a factor in 36% to 42% of the convictions in cases where the conviction was overturned based on new DNA evidence (California Innocence Project, n.d.). Even in the most serious of cases, prosecutors often commit the worst kinds of deception. For example, Cameron Todd Willingham was executed in 2004 for setting a fire that killed his three young daughters at their home. In 2015, the State Bar of Texas formally accused the lead prosecutor of misconduct after an investigation revealed that the prosecutor, John H. Jackson, knew about evidence that bolstered the case for Willingham's innocence and deliberately kept it from his attorney (Childress, 2015). In another case, former Texas prosecutor, Charles Sebesta, was stripped of his law license in June 2015 after a panel of the Texas State Bar determined he withheld evidence and used false testimony to win a capital murder conviction against Anthony Graves, a now-exonerated death row inmate (CBS Crimesider, 2015).

As of October 2015, the University of Michigan's National Registry of Exonerations report found that out of 1,633 exonerations recorded since 1989, 778 or 48% of the exonerations were based all or in part on "official misconduct," which I contend is a euphemism for misconduct by the prosecutor in most or all of these cases. However, these are only the known cases. Out of the millions of convictions since 1989, how many more are wrongful convictions? It should be noted that 115 of the reported 778 exonerations based on prosecutorial misconduct were people who had been placed on death row.

In many cases, prosecutors have often abandoned the "Blackstone" concept they learned in law school, which states, "All presumptive evidence of felony should be admitted cautiously; for the law holds it better that ten guilty persons escape, than that one innocent party suffer" (Commentaries on the Laws of England, 1760).

Reasons for Prosecutorial Misconduct

Why do prosecutors, who swear oaths to uphold the constitution and protect the integrity of the trial process, commit such egregious actions? Put simply, they do it to win. They do it to win at all costs. They do it because they rarely, if ever, get punished. Prosecutors in America are elected, and no prosecutor in the post–civil rights era wins elections by appearing to be soft on crime. This creates an inherent bias to be tough on crime, to prioritize conviction over all else, instead of being tough on results or fairness.

According to Neil Gordon of the Center for Public Integrity (2014),

> Prosecutors, like other attorneys, must adhere to the standards of professional conduct that exist in the state where they practice. Every state has a disciplinary system under which lawyers can be punished for violating ethical standards. Some acts of prosecutorial misconduct, apart from leading to reversals of convictions, can constitute ethical violations and thus subject the prosecutor to disciplinary action by the state bar authority.

However, most punishment, if any, meted out to offending prosecutors is woefully inadequate and does nothing to deter other prosecutors from committing misconduct. For example, the Center for Public Integrity (Gordon, 2014) studied 44 cases of prosecutorial misconduct and found discovery violations; improper contact with witnesses, defendants, judges, or jurors; improper behavior during hearings or trials; cases not supported by probable cause; harassment or threatening of defendants, lawyers, or witnesses; improper, false, or misleading evidence; a lack of diligence or thoroughness in prosecution; and improper public statements about a pending criminal matter. Out of 44 attorney disciplinary cases, seven were dismissed without punishment; 20 involved a public or private reprimand or censure; 12 prosecutors' licenses to practice law were suspended; two prosecutors were disbarred; one period of probation was imposed in lieu of a harsher punishment; 24 prosecutors were assessed the costs of the disciplinary proceedings; and three cases were remanded for further proceedings (Gordon, 2014).

Racial Disparities and Prosecutorial Misconduct

The elephant in the room regarding race and prosecution in America is one that nearly everyone except minorities seems to ignore: the interaction of race and white privilege. The most successful and long-standing prison diversion program in America is white skin. The country needs a criminal justice system built on social justice, parsimony, compassion, citizenship, and proportionality (National Academies of Science, 2014)—the same values afforded to some privileged (mostly wealthy white) Americans when they find themselves in handcuffs. But until this happens, policymakers have to do something realistically achievable instead of doing the same thing over and over and expecting a different result.

According to a study commissioned by the San Francisco–based Women Donors Network (Fandos, 2015; Wofford, 2015) and analyzed by the Center for Technology and Civic Life, a nonpartisan group that specializes in aggregating civic data sets, 95% of elected prosecutors in America are white, and two-thirds of the states that elect prosecutors have no black prosecutors. Yet, nationally, 40% of the incarcerated population is black and one in three black men will have spent time in prison during his lifetime. The deleterious collateral consequences on the black community and negative implications are astronomical. This is deliberate, not a coincidence. According to the University of Michigan's National Registry of Exonerations (2016), out of the 1,849 exonerates reports to date, 859, or 46% of them were Black. How can the U.S. criminal justice system be considered fair when such a huge racial disparity exists in that system's most powerful position?

Overcriminalization and "Lack of Intent" Laws

Overcriminalization is the act of imposing unbalanced penalties with no relation to the gravity of the offense committed or the culpability of the wrongdoer; it is the imposition of excessive punishment or sentences without adequate justification (U.S. Legal, n.d.). When considering overcriminalization, the avenues of abuse become amplified. According to the Manhattan Institute for Policy Research (2014), Michigan's dubious model of overcriminalization has at least 3,102 crimes—1,209 felonies and 1,893 misdemeanors. Over 26% of felonies and 59% of misdemeanors on the Michigan books do not explicitly require the state to make a showing of intent on the part of the accused, which decreases due process protections and increases the aggressiveness of overzealous prosecutors or prosecutors with racial proclivities. When this is multiplied by 49 other states, one begins to glimpse the immensity of the problem.

The worst example of the lack of intent in Michigan is the "Felony Murder" rule (Manhattan Institute for Policy Research, 2014). The rule of felony murder is a legal doctrine that broadens the crime of murder in two ways. First, when an offender kills (whether accidentally or with specific intent) in the commission of a dangerous or enumerated felony, he or she is automatically guilty of murder without the prosecutor having to prove the element of intent. Second, it makes any participant in such a felony criminally liable for any deaths that occur during or in furtherance of that felony. In Michigan, that liability comes with a "statutorily mandated" sentence of life without the possibility of parole (Box 4.1).

BOX 4.1
CASE STUDY: REGINALD HARDING

In 1983, Reginald Harding and his two codefendants robbed a man in Detroit, Michigan. During the robbery, while Reginald drove the getaway car, the victim was shot in the backseat by one of the codefendants. At some point, the victim was dumped out of the car and Reginald and his friends drove off. The victim survived. Because Reginald was not the principle, he was tried as an "aider and abettor." Reginald was eventually convicted of assault with intent to murder, for which he received a 20- to 60-year sentence. He was also convicted of armed robbery, for which he received a 7- to 20-year sentence and a 2-year sentence for the felony firearm conviction. He went off to prison and began his sentence, serving his debt to society.

However, more than 4 years later in the middle of summer, the victim defied the strict orders of his personal physician/cardiologist and decided to play basketball outdoors for over 90 minutes in 80° heat. The victim did so while wearing a heart pacemaker. The game was hard-fought and involved a monetary wager between the two teams. Immediately after the game, the victim got into a fistfight with several of the participants. During this altercation, the victim went into convulsions and later died at the hospital.

Although the victim died 4 years after Reginald's original conviction, the prosecutor decided to take Reginald back to court and arraigned him on the new charge of First Degree Felony Murder based on the theory that gunshot wounds inflicted by one of Reginald's codefendants 4 years earlier were the direct cause of the victim's death. Reginald was convicted and given a mandatory sentence of life without parole. He has now languished for 32 years in Michigan's prisons, his only hope currently for release is via commutation or in a body bag.

On Reginald's appeal, two Michigan Supreme Court Justices, Cavanaugh and Levin, dissented from the majority and sided with Reginald. They opined,

> the prosecutor failed to present sufficient evidence to prove beyond a reasonable doubt that the defendant proximately caused the victim's death. . . . Proximate cause requires a sufficient casual connection between the defendant's conduct and the result of the conduct (i.e., the death must have been the natural, direct, and necessary result of the defendant's unlawful act). In this case, intervening or superseding causes negate the proximate cause. The victim knew the limitations on his physical activities, yet he chose to ignore them. In doing so, he proximately caused his death.

Though truly tragic that the victim lost his life, it is unfair that the prosecutor was allowed to bring these "overcharges" at all. Such an example illustrates the need for solutions to prosecutorial overreaching and misconduct through the Smart Decarceration movement.

PREPARING INCARCERATED INDIVIDUALS FOR REENTRY

Another effort to end mass incarceration must include the issue of dealing with those who are currently incarcerated. The stated goal of several decarceration initiatives is to cut the prison population in half, which will lead to historically large numbers of individuals leaving prisons within a concentrated time frame (JustLeadershipUSA, n.d.).

From my 27 years of incarceration experience, I am well acquainted with Michigan's view on reentry. Its vision is that every offender released from prison will have the necessary tools and opportunities to be productive, self-sufficient, and successful citizens (Michigan Department of Corrections, n.d.). However, the reality is that access to programing in Michigan's prisons is based on how close a person is to his or her release date. This practice applies to reentry programs even more so. When reentry programs were first established in Michigan, they were provided 18 months prior to release. But with the crush of numbers of those eligible for parole, the reentry program time was cut to 6 months immediately prior to release. As a result, people who have served 20 or 30 years are expected to sufficiently adjust to the rigors of the free world in just 6 months.

Therefore, it is clear that not enough attention or effort is being put forth to prepare the incarcerated population for release. It is analogous to the release of slaves after the passage of the Emancipation Proclamation. Because the slaves had not been prepared for freedom, once the joy and euphoria of freedom subsided, many of them simply walked back to the plantations because they knew nothing else. Unless decarceration efforts are much more proactive in the area of prerelease preparation for those incarcerated, history will surely repeat itself.

Restoring Justice in the Prison Setting

Sending people to prison for over 20 years or for the rest of their lives is inhumane. It is critical that the decarceration movement change the discourse in this country from one steeped in retribution to one that understands and incorporates the wider parameters of redemption and the human ability to change into better people. One way to address this problem is through the adaptation and introduction of restorative justice principles into the prison setting. In traditional restorative justice, the emphasis is placed on the direct interaction between the actual victim and perpetrator. However, by expanding the definition of victim to include the community-at-large as secondary victims, decarceration efforts can implement a broader-based and farther-reaching restorative effort. As with direct victims, communities are also severely affected by crime. When given a voice, communities are empowered to directly affect the character of the incarcerated person returning to the community, instead of leaving it to the discretion of corrections officials, whose livelihoods are directly supported by the perpetuation of incarceration.

The Good Neighbor Project: A Proactive Program

The Good Neighbor Project, created and launched by the Michigan Criminal Justice Program of the American Friends Service Committee (AFSC), provides this avenue for community empowerment. The project applies restorative justice practices and principles by way of a one-on-one co-mentorship program between community members and those serving life and long indeterminate sentences in Michigan prisons. It focuses on the basic needs of the community before and after the harms caused by crime, while creating and promoting mutual obligations for all community members and those incarcerated to participate in the process of healing and redemption. The relationships built through this project are intended to shed light on the problem of using excessive long-term punishment to deal with deep harms caused in communities and to recognize the power of people working together toward transformation, redemption, and deep healing.

Though it is important for incarcerated citizens to be held accountable for the harms they have caused in their communities, it is equally necessary and important that Americans recognize the violence inherent within prison and work to create spaces of healing and transformation inside prison. As humans are creatures of habit, it makes sense to address these issues long before their release from prison instead of addressing them a few weeks or months before their release, as is the current practice for the most part. The creation of healing spaces and long-term programs such as the Good Neighbor Project must be a collaborative effort between the incarcerated citizens and the community-at-large, grassroots programs, and programs provided by the state. The Good Neighbor Project achieves these goals by getting community faith-based groups, organizations, and concerned citizens directly involved in the process of getting incarcerated citizens to understand how their actions have affected other people and to take responsibility for those actions.

POLICY RECOMMENDATIONS TO ACHIEVE DECARCERATION

Since time immemorial, the power elite has used fear to paralyze, distract, and divide. Fear paralyzes people into inaction, distracts their attention away from real problems and those who cause them, and divides people who have more in common than not into hierarchal groups. Those who control social, political, and economic institutions employ this debilitating fear to dehumanize individuals serving life sentences (i.e., *lifers*) and, thus, to justify racism, classism, xenophobia, genocide, and the reduction of human rights. They do so deliberately to maintain the status quo, expand control, and undermine organized efforts for accountability and decarceration. To challenge this paradigm and eventually triumph over such institutionalized oppression, decarceration efforts must consider the actionable steps of reforming prosecution practices and releasing lifers through mandatory parole reviews.

Reform Prosecution Practices

As discussed earlier, prosecutorial misconduct runs rampant in the U.S. criminal justice system. Decarceration can address this issue by advocating three potential policy recommendations: (1) allowing the wrongfully convicted to sue for monetary relief, (2) reducing prosecutorial immunity, and (3) eliminating the election of prosecutors.

Allow the Wrongfully Convicted to Sue for Monetary Relief

To motivate prosecutors not to commit misconduct, wrongfully convicted individuals should be allowed to sue for monetary relief, including from the prosecutor's office, if misconduct is established. As of 2016, the following 20 states do not have compensation statutes: Alaska, Arizona, Arkansas, Delaware, Georgia, Hawaii, Idaho, Indiana, Kansas, Kentucky, Michigan, Nevada, New Mexico, North Dakota, Oregon, Pennsylvania, Rhode Island, South Carolina, South Dakota, and Wyoming (The Innocence Project, 2016). Therefore, a federal compensation statute would help reform prosecution practices.

Reduce Prosecutorial Immunity to a Qualified Immunity

Rather than being absolute, prosecutorial immunity should be qualified. Being a prosecutor carries not only the authority to ruin lives but also in many cases the power to end them; it is also one of the positions most shielded from liability and accountability. Given the U.S. Supreme Court ruling on torts law and the 1976 case *Imbler v. Pachtman*, prosecutors enjoy absolute immunity from any lawsuit over any action undertaken as a prosecutor (Balko, 2013). Because such personal immunity was extended to cover supervisory prosecutors who fail to properly train their subordinates, even prosecutors who knowingly submit false evidence in a case that results in the wrongful conviction of an innocent person cannot be personally sued for damages (Balko, 2013).

Eliminate the Election of Prosecutors

The United States is the only country in the world that elects prosecutors via voting (Ellis, 2012), which distorts the prosecutors' incentives and has disastrous consequences for justice (Novak, 2015). Though prosecutors are supposed to balance the public's interest in prosecuting criminals with fairness, elections have adverse effects on their objectivity and behavior; for example, prosecutors often become aggressive when running for reelection and sacrifice fairness for winning at any cost (Novak, 2015). Therefore, eliminating the election of prosecutors is key to address the commonplace nature of prosecutorial misconduct.

Release "Lifers" Through Mandatory Parole Reviews
for Individuals Incarcerated for More Than 20 Years

Any discussion to decarcerate America without considering the release of long-term incarcerated individuals (i.e., lifers) would be disingenuous and unrealistic. Though lifers are the best behaved, most well adjusted segment of the prison population, they receive the least amount of consideration while the so-called nonviolent offenders, who are released back to communities after short prison stints, are generally the most problematic segment of the prison population.

Empirical evidence (Prison Legal News, 2013; Weisberg, Mukamal, & Segall, 2011) shows that lifers and those who have served long sentences have the lowest recidivism rates of any category of incarcerated people. California is always held up as the poster child for having the most problematic prison population in America. However, it should be noted that California has released over 1,400 lifers since 2011 (Associated Press, 2014). Those released lifers have the lowest recidivism rate of any group of parolees—much lower than even the so-called nonviolent offenders. Therefore, older previously incarcerated individuals are less prone to commit new crimes than younger ones. If this is the case, then why is so little being done to provide meaningful review of the cases of older incarcerated persons and granting relief where warranted?

When it comes to crime, the so-called nonviolent drug offender creates as much or more havoc in the community than does the murderer. According to the FBI 2014 crime statistics, police made an estimated 11,205,833 arrests during 2014—498,666 for violent crimes, and 1,553,980 for property crimes. The highest number of arrests was for drug abuse violations (1,561,231), followed by larceny-theft (1,238,190) and driving under the influence (1,117,852) (FBI, 2015). But because these and other offenders are classified as nonviolent, they are repeatedly released back into communities. Communities are not made safe by creating artificial lines between "victims" and "offenders," and neither is anything gained through artificial lines between those who commit crimes.

Generally, when it comes to traditional review considerations by parole boards, the practice has been to give more favorable consideration to those classified as nonviolent. Even the current national discussion on criminal justice reform focuses primarily on "nonviolent" offenses and offenders. However, recidivism rates remain unacceptably high at more than 50% within the first year of release (National Institute of Justice, 2014). And yet the criminal justice system continues to do the same thing over and over without changing its methods while expecting different results—the quintessential definition of insanity. Relying on outdated and factually false rhetoric to make artificial distinctions between offenders only perpetuates the insanity. General opinion and intuition suggests that violent offenders present the highest risk for release when in fact the opposite is true, especially for those who have served over 20 years.

I would argue that once an offender has served 20 years, especially if they are aged older than 50 years, a meaningful individual review and analysis should be made to determine whether he or she is suitable for release. As a reader, ask yourself whether you are the same person today as you were 20 years ago, whether you think the same way you thought 20 years ago, whether you act the same way you did 20 years ago. Of course you do not, and neither do those who have served over 20 years in prison. Though not all will be suitable for parole, the facts have consistently shown that a significant majority can be reasonably released and pose less of a public safety threat than other nonviolent parolees.

At some point in their sentences, lifers with the possibility of parole tend to realize the incentive of seeking personal redemption and growth. However, the national widespread decline in granting parole to lifers, and Michigan's adoption of the "life means life" premise (Citizens Alliance on Prisons and Public Spending, 2015) undermines or even eliminates the incentive for reform, even in cases of clearly demonstrated personal change. This sends an inconsistent message to incarcerated individuals on how to spend their years behind bars. To address this issue, states should create Lifer Review Boards that are separate and independent of the parole boards that consider other segments of the incarcerated.

Lifer Review Boards and Commutation Contracts

Other than in a body bag or casket, the only way for nonparolable lifers to be released from prison is by a commutation or pardon issued by a governor. Independent commutation legislation should be implemented to establish a Lifer Review Board that is separate and independent of the parole board that oversees parole reviews for nonlifers. This board should be composed of civil service members—not political appointees who are politically beholden to the dictates of their appointers. Such members need not fear losing their jobs for making unpopular yet pragmatic decisions.

Additionally, policymakers should develop a *commutation contract* to outline mandatory criteria for commutation review after an incarcerated citizen has served a predetermined number of years (e.g., 20 to 30 years). The criteria for automatic commutation consideration (not automatic release) should include overall institutional conduct, participation in self-improvement programs, institutional work ethic and performance, demonstrated examples of maturity, and other personal quantifiable achievements. Each incarcerated individual should receive a commutation contract upon his or her processing into the prison system. Institutional staff must be given a voice in this process. As it currently stands, the very people who manage every aspect and every minute of every day of an incarcerated person's life do not have any voice in the consideration process.

The statutes and laws that mandate sentences of life without parole should be amended to allow for at least a flat number of years to life (e.g., 20 to life). This will allow the Commutation Review Board to determine whether the incarcerated individual has sufficiently been rehabilitated to warrant meaningful review after having served the designated number of years.

If the incarcerated individual has met or exceeded the legislatively set criteria after serving the predetermined amount of time, the Commutation Review Board would recommend commuting the sentence to a parolable life sentence or a set number of years. At that point, it would be up to the governor to grant or deny the commutation recommendation. If granted, the incarcerated individual would be released directly by the governor or placed under the jurisdiction of the parole board and the dictates applied to parolable lifers.

Parole Requirements

Because those sentenced to the harshest sentences have committed the harshest crimes, they should naturally be subject to rigorous parole requirements. To assuage the "tough on crime" community, lifetime parole could be imposed instead of a set number of years. With current technology (e.g., GPS monitoring, body cameras), a real-time digital footprint can be maintained on every minute of a paroled lifer's day. Parole boards could also require other newly released nonparolable lifers to meet with public service workers (e.g., counselors) or to work a certain number of hours on public works programs.

To advance decarceration's goal of reducing the prison population in a manner that ensures public health, incarcerated individuals whom the statistics verify are the least likely to reoffend should be released: lifers.

CONCLUSION: REDEMPTION AND SECOND CHANCES TO RETURN TO HUMANITY

To help reform prosecution practices, the Smart Decarceration Initiative must learn from history, avoid past missteps, and rethink the way society views and "categorizes" offenders by race and class. It also must not make distinctions between violent and nonviolent offenders. Such distinctions are manufactured to play into the same narrative as society's obsession with the superficial separation by race. It promotes a form of polarization called *otherizing*, which pits one group against the other instead of fostering the inclusion necessary for real reform. It is the same plantation psychosis slave owners employed to divide and conquer the enslaved via artificial hierarchal structures.

Therefore, I wish to conclude by discussing the need for mercy, redemption, and second chances to promote decarceration and criminal justice reform. During his 2004 State of the Union Address, President George W. Bush stated, "America is the land of the second chance—and when the gates of the prison open, the path ahead should lead to a better life" (*New York Times* Editorial Board, 2014). At the 2003 American Bar Association, Associate Supreme Court Justice Anthony M. Kennedy went even further and stated, "A people confident in its laws and institutions should not be ashamed of mercy."

As the adage goes, "Hurt people, hurt people." Yet, the primary focus and result of the U.S. criminal justice system is the perpetuation of that hurt. Historically, prisons were created to punish the offender, protect society, deter others from committing similar acts, and rehabilitate the offender. Once these penological objectives are met, there is no need to keep citizens incarcerated except for purposes of punishment and revenge. Why does the criminal justice system continue to heap more unabated hurt and injury on people who have suffered untold, unaddressed harms instead of seeking ways to heal those hurts? I truly believe anyone who commits a crime should be held accountable, but the U.S. criminal justice system has become dysfunctionally punitive to the point of diminished returns. Any punishment that does not allow for redemption, rehabilitation, and a second chance is excessive.

Such an inherently unfair strategy is neither safe nor smart. It does not recognize human dignity. It does not recognize human fallibility. And it does not recognize human redemption. Completely ignored at every level of the criminal justice system, redemption is treated with disdain and viewed with cynicism for political reasons (especially by prosecutors). Lawmakers often use such concepts as ways to attack other lawmakers as "soft on crime," which, until recently, was a death knell for any politician.

Victim anger fuels this cynicism. Victims are totally justified to feel anger, many take a very long time to get over it and in some cases they never do. Exploiting this anger to block or eliminate any consideration of redemption and second chances into incarceration and rehabilitation is inhumane.

The United States professes to be a country founded on Christian values, and its citizens are quick to hurl Christian slogans. However, many Americans have become convenient Christians who only observe or espouse Christian beliefs as long as it advances their agenda. It is as hypocritical as it is shameful.

I speak not from a position of theory or assumption, but from the expertise born from the experience of being someone who is directly affected as a victim. While I was incarcerated, my only son and namesake, who was aged 21 years at the time, was murdered on Father's Day 2001 by a 14-year-old child. I advocated for the child to be adjudicated as a juvenile and not as an adult because I saw that it served no useful purpose for the child to be sentenced to life in an adult prison. I knew he would be better served in the juvenile system and have a chance at redemption and a second chance to become a productive member of society. I realized that it serves no useful purpose for our already distressed community to forever lose yet another potential precious resource to be ground to death in the gristmill called the prison system. This was my most personal contribution to the movement to decarcerate America.

I recognize that even though he committed a horrible crime, the boy who killed my son was still a child. Scientific research has proved what many parents already know: Children's brains are still developing and they possess tremendous capacity for change. We also know that children do not have the same capacity as adults to resist pressure from peers and adults, think through the long-term consequences of their actions, or remove themselves from dangerous situations. That courts and prosecutors selectively pick and choose when to recognize credible scientific evidence is reprehensible.

Even though the judge granted my wish to try and sentence the youth who killed my son as a juvenile, it did not come without some resistance from the prosecutor's office. I did not fit into the traditional image of a victim, and my wishes were ignored. As is often the case, the voices of low-income people and people of color are silenced on these issues. Prosecutors and others in the criminal- and juvenile-injustice systems are far more likely to prioritize the perspectives of individuals from wealthier, whiter communities. The only victims who are considered legitimate are those who are in lockstep with prosecutors looking to implement the harshest penalties possible. Victim services, financial resources, and other types of support are often meted out accordingly.

As evidenced by the growing national support for restorative-justice programs, my perspective is certainly not unique. The residents of the communities that are most affected by violence committed by young people and extreme sentences often recognize that communities are not made safe by creating artificial lines between "victims" and "offenders." It is clear that many of the children accused of crime have themselves been victims of violence, neglect, poverty, inadequate schools, and failing social services. In addition, many families are suffering after having lost some members to violent crime and others to jail.

So in conclusion, the War on Drugs and the ways in which the U.S. criminal justice system has addressed crime cannot even be considered a Pyrrhic victory. In the efforts to redefine justice in America and reduce the specter of mass incarceration, a more holistic plan with a more inclusive lens must be implemented. To establish the more perfect union espoused and envisioned by the founders of America, it is crucial to seriously redefine how to prosecute people, address the needs of the victims of crime, construct avenues of redemption for incarcerated citizens, and determine who is suitable to be released from prison. A society that sacrifices humanity for the purpose of safety will lose both and deserve neither.

REFERENCES

Associated Press. (2014, February 25). 1,400 "lifers" released from California prisons in last 3 years. *CBS News.* Retrieved from http://www.cbsnews.com/news/1400-lifers-released-from-california-prisons-in-last-3-years/

Balko, R. (2013, August 1). The untouchables: America's misbehaving prosecutors, and the system that protects them. *The Huffington Post.* Retrieved from http://www.huffingtonpost.com/entry/prosecutorial-misconduct-new-orleans-louisiana_n_3529891

Berger v. United States, 295 U.S. 78. (1935).

California Innocence Project. (n.d.). *Prosecutorial misconduct.* California Innocence Project. Retrieved from https://californiainnocenceproject.org/issues-we-face/prosecutorial-misconduct/

CBS Crimesider. (2015, June 12). DA disbarred for sending Texas man to death row. *CBS Crimesider.* Retrieved from http://www.cbsnews.com/news/charles-sebasta-prosecutor-of-wrongfully-convicted-man-anthony-graves-loses-law-license/

Childress, S. (2015, March 18). Texas bar charges Willingham prosecutor with misconduct. *Frontline*. Retrieved from http://www.pbs.org/wgbh/frontline/article/texas-bar-charges-willingham-prosecutor-with-misconduct/

Citizens Alliance on Prisons and Public Spending. (2015). *10,000 fewer Michigan prisoners*. Citizens Alliance on Prisons and Public Spending. Retrieved from http://2015capps.capps-mi.org/wp-content/uploads/2015/06/CAPPS-report-10000-fewer-prisoners.pdf

Commentaries on the Laws of England. (1760). Book IV, Chapter 27. Retrieved from http://avalon.law.yale.edu/18th_century/blackstone_bk1ch1.asp

Ellis, M. J. (2012). The origins of the elected prosecutor. *Yale Law Journal, 121*. Retrieved from http://www.yalelawjournal.org/note/the-origins-of-the-elected-prosecutor

Fandos, N. (2015, July 7). A study documents the paucity of black elected prosecutors: Zero in most states. *New York Times*. Retrieved from http://www.nytimes.com/2015/07/07/us/a-study-documents-the-paucity-of-black-elected-prosecutors-zero-in-most-states.html?_r=0

FBI. (2015, September 28). *2014 crime statistics*. Retrieved from https://www.fbi.gov/news/stories/latest-crime-stats-released/latest-crime-stats-released

Gordon, N. (2014, May 19). *Misconduct and punishment: State disciplinary authorities investigate prosecutors accused of misconduct*. The Center for Public Integrity. Retrieved from https://www.publicintegrity.org/2003/06/26/5532/misconduct-and-punishment

Hollway, J. (2016, July 4). Reining in prosecutorial misconduct. *Wall Street Journal*. Retrieved from http://www.wsj.com/articles/reining-in-prosecutorial-misconduct-1467673202

Innocence Project. (2016). *Compensating the wrongly convicted*. The Innocence Project. Retrieved from http://www.innocenceproject.org/compensating-wrongly-convicted

Joy, P. A. (2006). The relationship between prosecutorial misconduct and wrongful convictions: Shaping remedies for a broken system. *Wisconsin Law Review, 2006*, 399.

JustLeadershipUSA. (n.d.). *Dedicated to cutting the US correctional population in half by 2030, while reducing crime*. Retrieved from https://www.justleadershipusa.org/about-us/

Kennedy, A. M. (2003, August 9). *Speech at the American Bar Association annual meeting*. Retrieved from https://www.supremecourt.gov/publicinfo/speeches/sp_08-09-03.html

Manhattan Institute for Policy Research. (2014). *Overcriminalizing the Wolverine State: A primer and possible reforms for Michigan*. Manhattan Institute for Policy Research. Retrieved from https://www.manhattan-institute.org/html/overcriminalizing-wolverine-state-primer-and-possible-reforms-michigan-5724.html

Martin, G. E. (2015). *Elements of oppression*. Retrieved from http://elementsofoppression.blogspot.com/2015/07/glenn-e-martin.html

Michigan Department of Corrections. (n.d.). *Mission statement*. Michigan Department of Corrections. Retrieved from http://www.michigan.gov/corrections/0,4551,7-119-33218---,00.html

National Academies of Science. (2014, April 30). *U.S. should significantly reduce rate of incarceration*. National Academies of Science. Retrieved from http://www8.nationalacademies.org/onpinews/newsitem.aspx?recordid=18613

National Institute of Justice. (2014). *National statistics on recidivism*. National Institute of Justice. Retrieved from http://www.nij.gov/topics/corrections/recidivism/pages/welcome.aspx#statistics

New York Times Editorial Board. (2014, June 1). In search of second chances. *New York Times*. Retrieved from http://www.nytimes.com/2014/06/01/opinion/sunday/in-search-of-second-chances.html?_r=0

Novak, A. (2015, August 24). It's too dangerous to elect prosecutors. *The Daily Beast*. Retrieved from http://www.thedailybeast.com/articles/2015/08/24/it-s-too-dangerous-to-elect-prosecutors. html

Prison Legal News. (2013). *California: Stanford reports analyzes lifer paroles*. Prison Legal News. Retrieved from https://www.prisonlegalnews.org/news/2013/apr/15/california-stanford-report-analyzes-lifer-paroles/

Simpson v. Warren. 662 F. Supp.2d 835. (2009).

US Legal. (n.d.). *Over criminalization law and legal definition*. Retrieved from http://definitions. uslegal.com/o/over-criminalization/

Weisberg, R., Mukamal, D. A., & Segall, J. D. (2011). *Life in limbo: An examination of parole release for prisoners serving life sentences with the possibility of parole in California*. Stanford Criminal Justice Center. Retrieved from http://law.stanford.edu/wp-content/uploads/sites/default/files/child-page/164096/doc/slspublic/SCJC_report_Parole_Release_for_Lifers.pdf

Wofford, T. (2015, July 7). 95% of elected prosecutors are white. *Newsweek*. Retrieved from http://www.newsweek.com/95-percent-elected-prosecutors-white-study-finds-350922

5

The Prosecutor's Role in Promoting Decarceration

LESSONS LEARNED FROM MILWAUKEE COUNTY

John Chisholm and Jeffery Altenburg

BACKGROUND

Line prosecutors, those who are in the courtroom on a daily basis processing cases, give little thought to aggregate incarceration numbers outside the confines of their own caseloads. The cases (lots of cases) come from the police, and prosecutors review them and decide to charge based on the evidence and merits of each unique set of circumstances. The prosecutor's role largely ends with the final disposition in front of the judge. Win, lose, or draw, prosecutors move on and it becomes the State Department of Correction's or County House of Correction's problem.

As a line prosecutor, I certainly did not ask the questions prosecutors now routinely ask about risk, mental illness, drug addiction, trauma exposure, and the impact of the individual on their family and neighborhood. At that time early in my career, prosecutors did not have the capacity or the tools to effectively ask such questions. That is changing, and with the change comes the additional responsibilities and possibilities for reimagining the role of prosecution to address the persistent problems related to mass incarceration. Given their unique role in the system, prosecutors should closely examine their experience in light of some important emerging research.

This chapter does not explore the many factors that led to the current state of U.S. mass incarceration; rather, its purpose is to first illustrate how prosecutors are entrusted with significant discretionary authority to act as gatekeepers to the justice system, and how their role is being increasingly examined in that context. In this chapter, I introduce the four guiding principles to sentencing and highlight five ways prosecutors can use them to promote decarceration: (1) developing and applying new data sources and analytics, (2) creating community prosecution units, (3) collaborating for systemic change, (4) focusing on violent crimes as a public health issue, and (5) reinvesting in and revitalizing communities.

FOUR GUIDING PRINCIPLES OF SENTENCING

In its 2014 report *The Growth of Incarceration in The United States*, the National Research Council emphasizes four guiding normative principles to sentencing, particularly sentences involving incarceration: proportionality, parsimony, citizenship, and social justice (Travis, Western, & Redburn, 2014). Because elected prosecutors are responsible for values-based organizations and must direct their offices in accordance with those values, I contend that these four guiding principles reflect the ethical obligations imposed under the American Bar Association's model rules related to the functions and duties of the prosecutor.[1]

Specifically, the four principles of sentencing are that (1) criminal sentences should be *proportionate* to the seriousness of the offense; (2) the period of incarceration should be sufficient, but not greater than necessary, to achieve the goals of the desired sentence (*parsimony*); (3) the conditions and consequences should not be so severe or lasting as to violate one's *citizenship*; and (4) the criminal justice system should be reflected in the system of confinement; therefore, its effects should promote society's desire to have a fair distribution of rights, resources, and opportunities (*social justice*).

Similarly, the ethical rules under which prosecutors operate require a focus on problem solving and alternative ways to hold offenders accountable in ways that avoid criminal convictions and all of the alienating consequences that accompany it. Therefore, reflecting on the principles of proportionality, parsimony, citizenship, and social justice rather than falling into the practice of being reactive case processors, prosecutors have an obligation to focus on issues such as risk, substance abuse, and mental health in fashioning appropriate responses to violations of the law.

I believe rigorous examination directed specifically at the role prosecutors play in the growth of incarceration would help to develop national best practices and promote smart

---

[1] The American Bar Association has significantly modified two sections of the model code related to the role of the prosecutor under Section 3-1.2 paragraphs (e) and (f). It merits examination.

Standard 3-1.2 Functions and Duties of the Prosecutor

(e) The prosecutor should be knowledgeable about, consider, and where appropriate develop or assist in developing alternatives to prosecution or conviction that may be applicable in individual cases or classes of cases. The prosecutor's office should be available to assist community efforts addressing problems that lead to, or result from, criminal activity or perceived flaws in the criminal justice system.

(f) The prosecutor is not merely a case-processor but also a problem-solver responsible for considering broad goals of the criminal justice system. The prosecutor should seek to reform and improve the administration of criminal justice, and when inadequacies or injustices in the substantive or procedural law come to the prosecutor's attention, the prosecutor should stimulate and support efforts for remedial action.

decarceration. Front-end change is critical for long-term success in reversing incarceration trends. In this chapter, I detail the promising models that can guide decarceration efforts and explore, based on both my practical experience and what has been tried in other prosecutor's offices, some ways that prosecutors can help operationalize practices that meet their constitutional obligations to serve both the public safety and the civil liberty needs of their respective communities in ways that promote fairness, effectiveness, and trust in the system.

In this chapter, I focus on Milwaukee County's approaches to engage in proportionality, parsimony, citizenship, and social justice. I do so with full recognition that there is no construct that can be defined as *the* criminal justice system in the United States. Rather there are thousands of individual justice systems that vary in size and complexity; from urban to rural areas, and from offices that focus solely on felony offenses and others that handle a mixture of forfeitures, misdemeanor, and felonies, there are substantive differences in criminal justice processing. That said, based on my actual experience as a line prosecutor and an elected district attorney, and my knowledge of other district attorney offices, I submit that these categories—developing and applying new data sources and analytics, creating community prosecution units, collaborating for systemic change, focusing on violent crimes as a public health issue, and reinvesting in and revitalizing communities—could apply to the many diverse prosecutorial jurisdictions across the country as they work toward decarceration.

DEVELOPING AND APPLYING NEW DATA SOURCES AND ANALYTICS TO INFORM NEW INTERVENTION PROGRAMS

Because the criminal justice system serves the same population as other vital institutions (e.g., law enforcement, public health, social service, community resource and development fields), prosecution data could be meaningfully analyzed in relation to these institutions. If the decarceration movement can identify the issues and needs common to both those other fields and the criminal justice system, it can use the data to predict long-term system involvement and develop focused community-based prevention and intervention strategies. Doing so creates the opportunity to reserve traditional prosecution for those individuals that pose the biggest risk to the community.

The Milwaukee Homicide Review Commission

In 2004, the Milwaukee district attorney's office began to address this challenge by collaborating with a public health epidemiologist to inaugurate the Milwaukee Homicide Review Commission (MHRC), which strives to reduce homicides and nonfatal shootings through a multilevel, multidisciplinary, and multiagency homicide review process. Comprising law enforcement professionals, criminal justice professionals, and community service providers, the MHRC meets regularly to exchange information regarding the city's homicides and other violent crimes to identify methods of prevention from both public health and criminal justice perspectives. The MHRC makes recommendations—ranging from micro-level strategies to macro-level policy change—based on trends identified through the case review process. Many have been implemented, but the problems are never static. What works for a period of time may not work when other dynamics intervene or supersede. As crime adapts, so must the MHRC, which continues to provide a unique forum for addressing violence. This model provides a real example of using cross-system data to aid in decarceration efforts. By engaging in a cross-systems approach to analyzing data, criminal justice partners, including prosecutors, can develop innovative ways to proactively use non-law-enforcement community-based resources to address factors that lead to crime. This is the essence of the preferred sentencing principles outlined above.

The Vera Institute of Justice Collaboration

Shortly after the launch of the MHRC, the Vera Institute of Justice approached the Milwaukee County District Attorney's Office (MCDA) with the concept of analyzing prosecutorial data to determine whether policies or practices related to charging cases was associated with racial disparity in the jail and prison populations. This partnership came at an opportune time, as it preceded the release from The Sentencing Project, which showed that some of the greatest disparity in the country for incarcerated African Americans existed in Wisconsin. This research showed that, in 2005, Wisconsin had the second-highest rate of incarceration among the 50 states, trailing only South Dakota (Mauer & King, 2007). At the same time, the black-to-white ratio of incarceration in Wisconsin was greater than 10:1 placing it the fifth-worst state in this category (Mauer & King, 2007).

To determine why this was occurring, the MCDA collaborated with the Vera Institute of Justice to better understand its system, laws, and the community served by drawing meaningful insights from existing information systems. It was no small undertaking. The City of Milwaukee, like many densely populated urban areas, had pockets of deeply entrenched negative indices in relation to crime, poverty, segregation, poor health outcomes, unemployment, and poor educational outcomes. Also, the MCDA still used a primarily paper-based records system at the time. With the ethos "You can't effectively change what you don't effectively measure," Vera began tracking the measurable data.

What stands out in the data is that, overall, there was no significant disparity in the Milwaukee County charge, no-charge rate. But when focusing on the specific offense categories, a significant disparity in certain types of offense categories became apparent, particularly in the low-serious drug offenses. Specifically, the data showed that the MCDA chose not to prosecute 41% of whites charged with possession of drug paraphernalia compared to only 27% of nonwhites arrested for the same crime. After looking at the data, we staff considered a number of possible explanations for this disparity, which included policing practices, case-screening procedures, and unconscious bias based on the character of the drug paraphernalia involved. As a result of this review, we determined as an office that we would generally not issue the possession of drug paraphernalia charge. Reverse disparity also raised questions, such as "Why do we charge more white defendants with burglary?" and "Are we depreciating victims of property crime?"

The data from the Vera collaboration formed the basis of Milwaukee's application for and acceptance into the National Institute of Corrections (NIC) Evidence Based Decision Making framework. In turn, this led to the development of universal risk-based screening for arrestees, the creation of an early intervention and drug treatment path, expansion of deferred prosecution, and diversion from the system and a dosage-based probation program. As a result, there has been a dramatic reduction in admission to the Wisconsin prison system for drug-related offenses from Milwaukee.

As a result of the work with Vera and NIC, the MCDA solidified the importance of focusing on each decision point within the criminal justice process. This is especially true of the arrest and charging process and capturing data around each of these decision points to allow for all of the criminal justice stakeholders to understand and modify this process when appropriate. Specifically to Milwaukee, the work with Vera resulted in a move away from charging possession of drug paraphernalia in most cases because of the racial disparities the study revealed. Additionally, the study catalyzed a focus on postarrest, precharging diversion for low-risk offenders, which holds offenders accountable while still allowing them to become productive citizens of the community. By adopting these practices, jurisdictions across the United States can evaluate their respective systems and determine similar strategies for reform.

Early Intervention Programs

Milwaukee County offers the opportunity for some defendants, under appropriate circumstances, to participate in one of several early intervention programs.[2] The purpose of these early intervention programs is to maximize the opportunity to support and encourage prosocial attitudes and behaviors among those who become involved in the justice system, while minimizing the potential negative consequences that may accrue to an individual involved in the system, such as social stigma, exposure to higher risk offenders, and loss of prosocial supports (e.g., family, employment, educational activities).

One of the first things we developed was a working template that guided the decision-making for assistant district attorneys and is shared with the public defender's office.

---

[2] Though the primary purpose of this summary is to describe the Diversion and Deferred Prosecution Programs, eligibility for the Day Reporting Center, Drug Treatment Court, and the Veterans Treatment Initiative Programs are also summarized to provide a complete picture of the intervention options available in the County.

This template guides determinations concerning eligibility for the Early Intervention (EI) programs and clarifies that the District Attorney's Office retains complete discretion in making charging decisions. However, it sets forth parameters for the parties to consider in balancing the need to protect the community and hold offenders accountable with the importance of providing these same offenders with the opportunity to become prosocial and productive members of our community. In states like Wisconsin that have a court record system open to anyone with an Internet connection,[3] accountability for low-risk offenders that does not affect employment and housing opportunities helps ensure proportionality between the offense and the consequence and recognizes the importance of retaining productive citizens in one's community. Because these goals are often accomplished effectively with reduced charges, parties are encouraged to negotiate an appropriate charge at the outset of the action. This goal should be particularly taken into account when public protection can be accomplished while reducing long-term consequences to the offender.

Research demonstrates that the delivery of swift services and interventions (e.g., Burdon, Roll, Prendergast, & Rawson, 2001; Dayan & Abbott, 2001; Griffith, Rowan-Szal, Roark, & Simpson, 2000; Higgins & Silverman, 1999; Marlowe & Kirby, 1999; Murphy, Vuchinich, & Simpson, 2001; Rhine, 1993), commensurate with the possibility that an individual will continue criminal behavior—"level of re-offense risk" (e.g., Andrews, 2007; Andrews & Bonta, 2007; Andrews, Bonta, & Wormith, 2006; Andrews & Dowden, 2007; Andrews, Dowden, & Gendreau, 1999; Bonta, 2007; Dowden, 1998; Gendreau, Goggin, & Little, 1996; Lipsey & Cullen, 2007)—and the presence of risk factors that are indicators of criminal behavior—"criminogenic needs" (e.g., Andrews, 2007; Andrews et al., 1990)—offers the greatest opportunity for public safety. These strategies also provide for the best use of criminal justice dollars and resources, by reducing the costs of processing cases for those at lower risk to reoffend and instead investing those resources in those who pose the greatest risk to the community (e.g., Aos & Drake, 2010; Aos, Miller, & Drake, 2006; Johnson, Austin, & Davies, 2002; Pew Center on the States, 2009). Such programs use available data to guide decisions on where to concentrate the resources and prosecution efforts.

Milwaukee County's early intervention programs are based on these important research findings. The goal of all of these programs is to reduce the long-term recidivism risk of individuals involved in the justice system while ensuring public safety and the efficient allocation of limited criminal justice resources.

The Milwaukee County Diversion Program offers those who are determined to be at low risk for reoffense—based on the results of one or more scientifically validated criminal reoffense risk assessment scales—and who are not excluded by criteria,[4] the opportunity to be diverted from the justice system. Diversion requires that these individuals, after

---

[3] See Wisconsin Circuit Court Access Program, www.wcca.wicourts.gov.
[4] See Pretrial Diversion at http://milwaukee.gov/ImageLibrary/Groups/2014.10.31MilwaukeeCountyEarly.pdf.

being arrested for a crime that the MCDA determines can be proven beyond a reasonable doubt (hereafter referred to as the *provable charge*) and is not subject to legitimate 4th, 5th, or 6th amendment claims,[5] meet specific program expectations,[6] and remain crime-free for the term of the Diversion. All participants in the Diversion Program are required to have the assistance of legal counsel and complete and sign a written Diversion Agreement. Those who successfully meet these conditions are not subject to a criminal charge on their record. Those who fail to meet these conditions will be prosecuted for their provable charge.

This process has been refined in Milwaukee by the addition of the Arnold Foundation's Public Safety Assessment (PSA) risk-screening tool. By focusing on the data related to the of risk of future violence, the MCDA can make more compelling distinctions between those who should have a significant amount of traditional law enforcement and prosecutorial resources directed at them and those who can be diverted in different directions.

The Sentinel Event Review Process

To use data to address systemwide issues, the Bureau of Justice Assistance of the U.S. Department of Justice sponsored the Sentinel Event review process. Taking models from the worlds of healthcare and traffic safety, the Sentinel Event review process in Milwaukee focused on a significant homicide involving a juvenile suspect. A group of police, prosecutor, child protection, juvenile supervision (county and state), and school, public defender, and judiciary representatives convened to take a deeper dive into juvenile justice and mental health responses. The goal was to openly examine an event that all parties agreed had a poor outcome to develop prospective practices to avoid such problems in the future. Through their examination of the specific homicide, the parties identified a number of gaps within the juvenile justice system and the need for better collaboration among the parties working within that system. As a result of this process, a number of information-sharing mechanisms and processes were put into place.

The Evolution and Purpose of Data in the Decarceration Movement

In Milwaukee and elsewhere, a significant body of evolving work supports research-based, information-rich, and intelligence-led strategies. Through the use of data, these strategies can enable system actors to improve their response to criminal activity and related problems.

Because so many different criminal justice systems operate in this country, access to reliable and timely data is a challenge. Many systems have only rudimentary data-sharing

---

[5] Consistent with current practice, the Early Intervention Program is not be used for cases that are not provable or subject to legitimate 4th, 5th, or 6th amendment claims.

[6] The requirements are clearly set forth and agreed to by all parties.

capability between the four major actors—police, prosecutors, courts, and corrections—*within* their respective jurisdictions, and it is often a challenge to analyze the data even at the county level. Milwaukee's criminal justice system is currently exploring a cross-agency data repository, the Milwaukee Data Hub, to better understand the county's at risk population. The data hub is a highly flexible platform designed to integrate and synthesize complex data sets from public health, education, and community-development structures with criminal justice system information. Data are deidentified at the personal level but coded and linked at the individual level with the aim to integrate data sources to improve outcomes in both local and national community health environments. The creation of this collaborative data bank will allow practitioners to do more than recognize single data set connections (and) triangulate data from multiple, integrated data set systems. Meaningful information can be extracted from this data hub and used to inform policy and practice in each of the fields mentioned above. Maximizing the potential for data to impact decarceration will require this type of innovative approach to data sharing and analyses within and between multiple systems.

The normative imperatives still remain. Data must be used for two purposes: to improve what occurs within the current criminal justice system, and to improve efficiency, effectiveness, and fairness. The same data used by core criminal justice partners to improve the internal response can also be linked to other essential community institutions and their data to inform community-wide change in a focused, population-specific, geographic, and collaborative way.

Data collection and analysis allows for criminal justice actors to periodically examine the results of their practices and modify accordingly those areas that prevent important collaboration and information sharing. These are the practices that the public expects out of a just and fair criminal justice system that focuses on proportionality and protecting the rights of all citizens, including those who interact with the system when they commit a violation of the law. Moreover, by focusing on the risk of offenders to reoffend and the appropriate strategies to address the factors that drive criminal activity (e.g., addiction, mental health issues, poor decision-making), prosecutors and other criminal justice professionals can ensure that the sanction matches the seriousness of the offense while also maximizing the probability that reoffense will not occur.

CREATING COMMUNITY PROSECUTION UNITS

First initiated in Milwaukee in 2000 through a U.S. Department of Justice grant, *community prosecution*—the concept of placing a prosecutor in a neighborhood or entire police district and out of the courtroom—is an evidence-based strategy to prevent crime through early intervention in neighborhood-level disorder challenges. Employed in conjunction with community policing strategies, community prosecution can help redefine the broader role of community corrections and allow prosecutors to participate in solving problems at the neighborhood level instead of waiting for the drop-off at the jail. This requires a fundamental reorientation of traditional prosecutor offices and the adoption of a philosophy that makes prosecutors responsible for more than just case processing. This can and should be victim centered as well as offender centered, because data show that there is little distinction between victim and offender in terms of background and exposure to multiple layers of adversity.

The Milwaukee County District Attorney's Office Community Prosecution Unit

The MCDA Community Prosecution Unit (CPU) is a nationally recognized proactive crime prevention team focused on lowering crime, increasing quality of life in Milwaukee's neighborhoods, and engaging and educating the city's residents. Its CPU team consists of prosecutors, the Milwaukee Police Department, the Wisconsin Department of Corrections, City of Milwaukee Agencies, community-based organizations, citizens, landlords, and business owners. The community-driven model marks a move away from *response-driven prosecution*, which relies on the traditional practice of a prosecutor at the courthouse simply reviewing and charging individuals based on police reports and witness statements after the alleged crime has occurred with little context of neighborhood environment. Milwaukee's CPU is a *community-driven model*, which focuses on preventing crime and increasing quality of life based on specific knowledge of neighborhoods and the often unique factors affecting that specific community based on input from residents. In Milwaukee's CPU, community prosecutors (1) apply their legal knowledge in the field with police officers to effectively discern nuisance activity based on addiction, mental health, or youthful poor decision-making versus violent activity conducted by a much smaller percentage of those in a particular neighborhood; (2) effectively apply their communication skills to reach out to community members for their input and inclusion into the criminal justice system and its often complex processes; and (3) use their courtroom and trial skills to prosecute the most violent criminals and refer the nonviolent offenders to community-based alternatives.

The Milwaukee CPU model addresses neighborhood crime and nuisance problems by using the public and private resources available to abate quality-of-life issues. For example, by working with neighborhood residents, community prosecutors are able to identify areas of prostitution and drug-related activities and focus on places associated with the activity in addition to the specific people and implement environmental changes to properties such as lighting, fencing, or cameras to make the locations less attractive for this type of activity. At the same time, community prosecutors are able to proactively refer drug users to appropriate neighborhood treatment resources in lieu of arrest and court processing.

Given its effectiveness, the Milwaukee County District Attorney has placed prosecutors in a majority of the City of Milwaukee Police Districts. This neighborhood placement allows prosecutors, police, and residents to collaborate to strategically resolve community crime and nuisance issues. The model is flexible, designed to meet the specific needs of the neighborhoods served, but generally works to achieve the following goals.

Create Crime-Prevention Initiatives

A significant part of a community prosecutor's time is spent addressing the crime and quality-of-life issues facing neighborhoods. Prosecutors are most often thought of as trial attorneys. As community prosecutors, however, they become part of a Milwaukee community, learn that community's strengths and weaknesses, communicate daily with residents and neighborhood associations and the Milwaukee Police Department, and then formulate appropriate crime-prevention strategies. In every corner of the city of Milwaukee, community prosecutors have created plans to prevent prostitution, litter, burglaries, robberies, and violent crimes.

Increase Quality, Efficiency, and Priorities for Prosecution

Effective criminal justice requires thoughtful decisions on how to best use limited law enforcement and court resources. Community prosecutors are tasked with targeting each police district's most violent offenders, charging them with crimes, and prosecuting them to the fullest extent of the law. Prosecutors use search warrants, subpoenas, and criminal trials to convict violent offenders and remove them from communities based on their specific knowledge of places and people that are most directly affecting neighborhoods and their residents as opposed to the typical law enforcement model. In addition to prosecuting the City's most violent criminals, community prosecutors also work with the community and police to identify individuals who are a constant detriment to a neighborhood's quality of life. Community prosecutors can criminally charge these targets or find alternatives to criminal charges that will appropriately abate the issue. Noncriminal nuisances can significantly decrease a community's quality of life. Community prosecutors work with residents to identify a neighborhood's most problematic properties to create a positive change from homeowners, landlords, and businesses.

Community prosecutors work closely with the police department, courts, the Department of Corrections, community-based organizations, residents, the City, and the State to improve the criminal justice system by making it cost-effective, fair, evidence-based, and just for the community it serves. For example, community prosecutors participate in a review and evaluation of every homicide and shooting that occurs in the City in an effort to prevent violence in the future through the Milwaukee Homicide Incident Review Commission and provide specific information about the areas and individuals involved in the incident and any prior intervention and prevention efforts with the properties and their owners. Community prosecutors also work with Department of Corrections agents that are also located in the police district stations to directly supervise the most problematic offenders through numerous home visits and meetings with the district police officers. Finally, community prosecutors are at the forefront of community-based initiatives designed to direct offenders to direct treatment resources in the community instead of being subjected to ticketing, arrest, or prosecution. The best example of this is working with the police to surveil and refer individuals engaged in prostitution to a nearby treatment resource focusing on drug treatment, employment resources, and housing and child care in lieu of running undercover sting operations to identify and arrest offenders.

Engage and Share Information with Community-Based Organizations

One of the greatest difficulties facing the criminal justice system is the limited resources available to address the substantial amount of crime that is funneled through the courts. Community prosecutors form relationships with community organizations that can fill the gaps by providing resources for alcohol and drug abuse treatment, mental health treatment, drug testing, crime victim needs, after-school programming, veterans' needs, and counseling for victims of domestic violence.

Perhaps the most important role of community prosecutors is communicating with residents, businesses, associations, and community organizations that are unfamiliar with the criminal justice process and the role each professional plays. Connecting individuals with the correct person within the system and helping to break down the various stages of a criminal case helps reduce the barriers that exist between the community and various actors and processes within the criminal justice system. The information provided by the community is invaluable to appropriate and efficient law enforcement and also serves the purpose of empowering neighborhoods to take control of their streets, parks, and schools.

Provide Training and Education Programs

Community prosecutors can train police officers on best practices for investigations, constitutional search-and-seizure issues, report writing, and community relations. Community prosecutors' education and experience allows them to train community members on workings of the criminal justice system, crime prevention through environmental design, and target-hardening techniques.

Educating the public about the community prosecution model, prosecutors, and the criminal justice system is essential to a functioning democracy. Community prosecutors participate in a number of educational programs at colleges and universities across the State.

Connect Government Agencies to Community Groups

A challenge facing Milwaukee is the siloed nature of many resources, wherein there is a lack of communication between many important entities and the community. Community prosecutors work to open lines of communication between governmental agencies and the neighborhoods that they serve. Given their knowledge of both the government and private resources (e.g., housing code inspectors, homeless outreach specialists, public works officials, domestic violence shelters, the VA, other law enforcement professionals), community prosecutors are able to serve as a bridge between resident concerns and complaints and the appropriate resource to address those concerns and complaints. Equally important, community prosecutors and members of the CPU are then able to communicate back to the specific residents concerning what resources were brought to bear on a particular problem as a way to motivate the residents to continue to serve as eyes and ears in their neighborhoods.

The vast majority of incarcerated individuals return to the community. Community prosecutors work with community organizations, the Department of Corrections, and the Milwaukee Police Department to ensure individuals released from incarceration are closely monitored, held accountable for their actions, and have appropriate resources that make recidivism less likely.

The MCDA has a close working relationship with Milwaukee Public Schools and has, in the past, had a prosecutor assigned to the school system. The goal was to focus and train school administrators and staff on restorative principles and address safety issues unique to the school environment.

Be Available 24 Hours, 7 Days a Week

Crime never stops; therefore, community prosecutors must be on-call for law enforcement in their respective district or target area at all times. Whether it is answering a legal question, reviewing a search warrant, or being called to a crime scene, community prosecutors are always available.

Community Prosecution Units' Role in Decarceration

Community prosecutors, working in neighborhoods and district police stations every day, have a unique opportunity to identify resources within the neighborhood that are best qualified to deal with youthful offenders, individuals suffering from addiction and mental health issues, and those in need of housing and employment assistance. Though some of these individuals are identified through interactions with the police after violations of the law, community prosecutors are able to access the above-referenced types of resources as an alternative to a criminal charge for low-risk nonviolent offenders. This type of intervention enhances the communities' confidence in the criminal justice system by reducing the numbers of individuals that are charged and ultimately convicted, consistent with the principle of social justice. These alternatives also ensure proportionality and parsimony within the system while reducing the numbers of individuals that disenfranchise individuals from rights other citizens enjoy, such as voting and access to housing and employment.

COLLABORATING FOR SYSTEM CHANGE

To successfully decarcerate America, it is essential for all the stakeholders across the criminal justice spectrum—law enforcement, prosecutors, defense bar, courts, corrections, and neighborhoods—to collaborate in a consistent and structured way to allow for the most efficient, cost effective, and just system of criminal justice. Community Justice Councils are a means of accomplishing this goal.

The Milwaukee Community Justice Council

The Milwaukee Community Justice Council (CJC) commenced in 2007 to oversee numerous efforts to improve outcomes in the criminal justice system. With assistance from the National Institute of Corrections, the Milwaukee CJC focused on four critical decision points that spanned the spectrum from arrest to sentencing: (1) the expansion of Crisis Intervention Team (CIT) policing to more effectively respond and intervene with individuals in mental health crisis; (2) implementation of a 24/7 Universal Screening process in the jail to assess people's risk of not returning to court or committing new criminal violations during the pretrial period; (3) application of a longer-term risk assessment to make determinations about who is eligible for Early Intervention Program precharge diversions and preadjudication deferred prosecution agreements; and (4) a pilot project around determining the appropriate hours of supervision or "dosage" for individuals placed on probation based on their criminogenic risk and need. The structure of the CJC is based on collaborative discussions and decision-making, and is maintained through regular and meaningful engagement by all system partners.

Collaboration with Behavioral Health Specialists

The Milwaukee CJC's first project involved a dramatic expansion of the core CIT policing model to develop working teams of police and behavioral health specialists. This team focused on high-risk, high consumers of police and behavioral health resources. It also focused on identification of mental health resources and facilities as an alternative to arrest for the officers to access, especially in the middle of the night. Data played a critical role in identifying and responding to this population and helping the CIT team identify individuals in need of mental health resources. Data also helped identify where more resources were needed for the CIT trained officers to access instead of sending individuals to jail or emergency detention at the county's psychiatric hospital.

　　The Milwaukee CJC then dramatically increased its screening resources to make real the concept of *universal screening* for everyone arrested and processed into the county jail. The collaboration expanded resources in the public health sector and treatment providers to allow for accountable responses for low-risk offenders through precharge diversion. Creating a validated risk assessment tool specific to the Milwaukee population was essential to help determine an appropriate Early Intervention Program for offenders. It also enhanced the likelihood that offenders would not return to the criminal justice system if they received the treatment and therapy needed. Finally, the Milwaukee CJC addressed the high rate of supervision recidivism through the "dosage-based" probation model, with the goal of removing individuals from supervision as soon as they meet the specific goals and conditions deemed most relevant to their risk.

These projects collectively allowed for greater collaboration between the police, prosecutors, defense bar, and the courts. The benefits included reducing the number of low- and moderate-risk offenders incarcerated in jails and the creation of a systematic, cost-effective, and community model.

FOCUSING ON VIOLENT CRIME AS A PUBLIC HEALTH CRISIS

Violent crime and violent offenders should receive the vast share of the limited justice resources. Gun violence in particular poses the greatest threat to system improvement because it receives the most attention from the public and often drives a demand for harsher penalties across the spectrum, including nonviolent crimes, and this can be harmful to the aspirations of parsimony, proportionality, citizenship, and social justice. Applying a public health lens to violent crime means broadening the scope beyond the prosecution of individual cases to the ways in which violent crime affects communities and neighborhoods. By relying on prevention and intervention for those low- and moderate-risk nonviolent offenders (much as the U.S. public and private health system emphasized preventive care), prosecutors and other criminal justice system actors can focus the bulk of its suppression law enforcement, prosecutorial, and other court resources for the most violent of offenders.

Violent crime presents unique challenges to the administration of justice and the commitment to system reform. Though overall violent crime rates have plunged dramatically since 2005, the perception of violence and episodic increases in gun violence make the public discourse complicated. The work of the MHRC has demonstrated the close connection between the histories of victims and offenders in terms of their backgrounds.

Law enforcement's response to violent crime generally takes two forms: (1) general deterrence strategies as reflected in Computer Statistics (COMPSTAT) efforts that emphasize information sharing; responsibility and accountability; and improving effectiveness of intelligence, rapid deployment of resources, effective tactics, and frequent follow-up; and (2) specific deterrence, such as the Intelligence Led Prosecution initiative. General deterrence strategies and their largely unexamined and unintended consequences related to low-level intervention for public space and public disorder maintenance have come under close scrutiny since 2014. Though focused efforts to enforce low-level offenses are related, there has been a rise in municipal level fines and forfeitures among the population least capable of affording them.

Three Models to Address Violent Crime

Intelligence Led Prosecution acknowledges that a small percentage of individuals commit a disproportionate amount of high-risk harm and that those individuals are often well known within circles of law enforcement, prosecution, and corrections, but often the coordination of efforts allows those individuals to evade serious consequences until committing major harm. The model developed by the District Attorney's Office of New York (DANY) merges intelligence fusion efforts from the New York City Police with a similar capacity in the Manhattan DA's Office, creating a real-time link between police and prosecution to refine a list of offenders for close monitoring. This moves away from general deterrence to specific engagement based on risk, which reduces the number of individuals processed for lower risk offenses.

A longer term intervention strategy is exemplified in the Sojourner Family Peace Center (SFPC) model in Milwaukee. The SFPC is expressly linked to and colocated with Children's Hospital of Wisconsin because children exposed to violence are prosecutors' most predictable future clients. Addressing exposure to violence as a public health crisis reframes the role of criminal justice actors in the long-term remediation of the harm, violence, neglect, abuse, and sexual trauma causes. The goal of this model is to use system involvement as doctors would use an emergency room visit—as a red flag that intervention is needed to stop the progress of the disease.

The current system for helping victims of domestic violence can be confusing, complex, and difficult to access. Inefficiencies strain limited public and private resources and often force victims to recount their painful experiences to multiple providers. The SFPC's vision for Milwaukee is to be one of the first in the nation to house holistic services for domestic violence victims of all ages, under one roof.

The Family Justice Center model enables communities to transform their response to family violence, ultimately making Milwaukee and its surrounding communities a healthier, safer, more peaceful place to live. Sojourner, a domestic violence provider and shelter, and Children's Hospital of Wisconsin formed a unique partnership to create one of the first colocated child advocacy and family violence centers in the country, providing comprehensive services for victims and families affected by domestic violence. Partners include the Milwaukee Police Department Sensitive Crimes Unit, Milwaukee Public Schools, the Milwaukee County District Attorney's Domestic Violence Unit, Aurora Healthcare Abuse Response Services, and others. The key to its success is the colocation of multidisciplinary professionals focused on advocating for victims' safety and quality of life, surrounding the victim with the support and resources they need at a critical time.

Community Agency Involvement in Addressing Violent Crime

To address violent crime as a public health issue, more than just criminal justice involvement and intervention is needed. In collaboration with the Family Justice Center, a broad array of community organizations contribute to an overarching strategy for preventing, responding to, and healing from violence. Local hospitals provide an array of services, particularly for children who have experienced community violence or abuse.

A multidisciplinary collaboration of counseling agencies provide individual, family, and community level prevention and intervention strategies to reduce stress and conflict, enhance parenting skills and strengthen family ties. Specialized advocacy and forensic nursing services are targeted toward sexual assault victims, and other trauma-related services are available for individuals and families affected by violence. Child welfare organizations provide services to families in crisis to help ensure child safety in their home of origin, as well as in foster and adoptive family homes.

Legal and criminal justice entities collaborate with these community organizations. The Milwaukee Police Department Sensitive Crimes Division focuses on investigations involving domestic violence, crimes against children (child abuse and neglect), sexual assaults, child custody interference, missing persons, and other sensitive matters. A nonprofit law firm provides limited legal advice and representation for low-income individuals. The Marquette Law School provides healing circles and restorative justice programming for families impacted by violence.

This comprehensive approach illustrates how responding to violence as a public health issue requires a multilayered system with multiple agencies and community entities represented. The MCDA is positioned within this comprehensive community approach. The mission of the Office includes promoting public peace and safety, to seek and do impartial justice, to protect the health and welfare of children, and to promote citizens' participation in law enforcement. By collaborating with this community network, MCDA can better advance its mission and maximize its efforts.

REINVESTING IN AND REVITALIZING COMMUNITIES

The collective efforts to decarcerate America have to be directly tied to specific geographic community reinvestment and revitalization initiatives that explicitly tie criminal justice strategies into plans to create greater economic security and opportunity for the community. The most comprehensive example of this effort in Milwaukee is the Near West Side Partners (NWSP) initiative and its 3- to 5-year Promoting Assets and Reducing Crime (PARC) project.

The Near West Side Partners

The mission of the NWSP is to revitalize and sustain the Near West Side as a thriving business and residential corridor through collaborative efforts to promote economic development, improve housing, unify neighborhood identity and branding, and provide greater safety for residents and businesses. Recognizing the importance of collaboration between employers, education institutions, and government, the anchor institutions of Miller Coors, Harley Davidson, Aurora Healthcare, Forest County Potawatomi Indian Tribe Business Development Corporation, and Marquette University have formed NWSP to focus on public safety, workforce development, and neighborhood redevelopment within a specific geographic area in the Near West Side of Milwaukee. Representatives of these anchor institutions and members of the seven neighborhoods that constitute the target area for the NWSP serve on working teams focusing on safety and security, housing, commercial corridor development, and neighborhood identity and branding.

The PARC project sponsored by the NWSP and the five anchor institutions focuses on promoting assets to transform the negative perception of the neighborhood and reducing crime to address the reality of the neighborhood's challenges. The project supports the priorities established by NWSP Working Teams, working collaboratively with stakeholders to benefit Near West Side employers, employees, residents, students, and visitors and funds a full-time community prosecutor and a CPU coordinator working through a local crime prevention and advocacy organization, a community organizer, some police overtime, and private security guards that walk the commercial corridors and work with the CPU in identifying problem people and places, conduct security surveys, and provide neighborhood outreach. Through these efforts, NWSP and the PARC project recognize that by changing the underlying dynamics that lead to crime in neighborhoods, those same neighborhoods will be able to attract businesses and employees who want to live in the neighborhood, especially if they are able to improve the housing stock and strengthen residential organizations. This type of effort recognizes that reliance solely on law enforcement and other government agencies involved in the criminal justice system will not lead to true sustainable change within a neighborhood and will do little to empower the residents of the neighborhood or reduce the long-term rates of incarceration from that neighborhood. Most agree that sustainable reductions in criminal activity are tied to employment and education and that public-private partnerships like the NWSP provide a template for impactful long-term change.

CONCLUSION

Prosecutors are the gatekeepers of the criminal justice system. As such, they play an integral role in using research and best practices to ensure that those they bring into the system are appropriate for criminal prosecution and conviction. By focusing on the sentencing principles of proportionality, parsimony, citizenship, and social justice, prosecutors can act consistently with their ethical responsibility to be problem solvers who consider diversionary and deferred prosecution alternatives to the traditional charge-and-convict model that has dominated the criminal justice system for too long. In the MCDA, prosecutors have followed these principles to promote decarceration in five distinct ways: (1) developing and applying new data sources and analytics, (2) creating community prosecution units, (3) collaborating for systemic change, (4) focusing on violent crimes as a public health issue, and (5) reinvesting in and revitalizing communities.

REFERENCES

Andrews, D. A. (2007). Principles of effective correctional programs. In L. L. Motiuk & R. C. Serin (Eds.), *Compendium 2000 on effective correctional programming.* Ottawa, Canada: Correctional Service of Canada.

Andrews, D. A., & Bonta, J. (2007). *Risk-need-responsivity model for offender assessment and rehabilitation (2007–06).* Ottawa, Canada: Public Safety Canada.

Andrews, D. A., Bonta, J., & Wormith, J. S. (2006). The recent past and near future of risk and/or need assessment. *Crime and Delinquency, 52*(1), 7–27.

Andrews, D. A., & Dowden, C. (2007). The risk-need-responsivity model of assessment in human service and prevention and corrections crime prevention jurisprudence. *Canadian Journal of Criminology and Criminal Justice, 49*(4), 439–464.

Andrews, D. A., Dowden, C., & Gendreau, P. (1999). *Clinically relevant and psychologically informed approaches to reduced reoffending: A meta-analytic study of human service, risk, need, responsivity, and other concerns in justice contexts.* Unpublished manuscript. Ottawa, ON: Carleton University.

Andrews, D. A., Zinger, I., Hoge, R. D., Bonta, J., Gendreau, P., & Cullen, F. T. (1990). Does correctional treatment work? A clinically relevant and psychologically informed meta-analysis. *Criminology, 28,* 369–404.

Aos, S., & Drake, E. (2010). *WSIPP's benefit-cost tool for states: Examining policy options in sentencing and corrections.* Olympia, WA: Washington State Institute for Public Policy.

Aos, S., Miller, M., & Drake, E. (2006). *Evidence-based public policy options to reduce future prison construction, criminal justice costs, and crime rates.* Olympia: Washington State Institute for Public Policy.

Bonta, J. (2007). Offender assessment: General issues and considerations. In L. L. Motiuk & R. C. Serin (Eds.), *Compendium 2000 on effective correctional programming.* Ottawa, ON: Correctional Service Canada. Retrieved from: http://www.csc-scc.gc.ca/text/rsrch/compendium/2000/index-eng.shtml

Burdon, W. M., Roll, J. M., Prendergast, M. L., & Rawson, R. A. (2001). Drug courts and contingency management. *Journal of Drug Issues, 31,* 73–90.

Dayan, P., & Abbott, L. F. (2001). *Theoretical neuroscience: Computational and mathematical modeling of neural systems.* Cambridge, MA: MIT Press.

Dowden, C. (1998). *A meta-analytic examination of the risk, need and responsivity principles and their Importance within the rehabilitation debate.* Unpublished master's thesis. Ottawa, ON: Carleton University, Department of Psychology.

Gendreau, P., Goggin, C., & Little, T. (1996). *Predicting adult offender recidivism: What works! (1996–07).* Ottawa, ON: Solicitor General of Canada.

Griffith, J. D., Rowan-Szal, G. A., Roark, R. R., & Simpson, D. D. (2000). Contingency management in outpatient methadone treatment: A meta-analysis. *Drug and Alcohol Dependence, 58,* 55–66.

Higgins, H., & Silverman, K. (1999). *Motivating behavior change among illicit-drug abusers: Research on contingency management interventions.* Washington, DC: American Psychological Association.

Johnson, K. D., Austin, J., & Davies, G. (2002). *Banking low-risk offenders: Is it a good investment?* Washington, DC: George Washington University, Institute on Crime Justice and Corrections.

Lipsey, M. W., & Cullen, F. T. (2007). The effectiveness of correctional rehabilitation: A review of systematic reviews. *Annual Review of Law and Social Science, 3*, 297–320.

Mauer, M., & King, R. S. (2007). *Uneven justice: State rates of incarceration by race and ethnicity*. The Sentencing Project. Retrieved from http://www.sentencingproject.org/wp-content/uploads/2016/01/Uneven-Justice-State-Rates-of-Incarceration-by-Race-and-Ethnicity.pdf

Marlowe, D. B., & Kirby, K. C. (1999). Effective use of sanctions in drug courts: Lessons from behavioral research. *National Drug Court Institute Review, 2*(1), 11–29.

Murphy, J. G., Vuchinich, R. E., & Simpson, C. A. (2001). Delayed reward and cost discounting. *Psychological Record, 51*, 571–588.

Pew Center on the States. (2009). *One in 31: The long reach of American corrections*. Washington, DC: The Pew Charitable Trusts.

Rhine, E. (1993). *Reclaiming offender accountability: Intermediate sanctions for probation and parole violators*. Laurel, MD: American Correctional Association.

Travis, J., Western, B., & Redburn, S. (2014). The growth of incarceration in the United States: Exploring causes and consequences. *National Research Council*. Retrieved from http://www.nap.edu/catalog/18613/the-growth-of-incarceration-in-the-united-states-exploring-causes

6

Learning to Lead in the Decarceration Movement

Vivian D. Nixon

BACKGROUND

Training and education each play a critical role in preparing those directly affected by incarceration—currently and formerly incarcerated individuals—to lead the decarceration movement. For the purposes of this chapter, *directly affected people* are defined as individuals with criminal convictions, those among the 70 million adults in the United States with criminal history records on file (Rodriguez & Emsellem, 2011). The theory of change presented in this chapter draws on multiple experiences of imprisonment and reentry, focusing primarily on the opportunity that higher education provides for critical reflection on criminal justice policy and practice.

This chapter discusses the importance of educating and providing leadership opportunities for directly affected people and outlines the limits of current proposals for criminal justice reform. It does so through the lens of a population that experiences disproportionate percentages of incarceration—African Americans. More specifically, it examines reforms that take the reentry of the formerly incarcerated as their starting point.

In this chapter, I examine racial marginalization through the criminal justice system and analyze current criminal justice reforms using three assumptions outlined in a working group called Community Leadership and Education After Reentry and published in an article that I coauthored (Nixon et al., 2008): (1) reentry created a new phase of institutionalization of the criminal justice system that extends penal forms of control beyond prison walls; (2) people in reentry may be at the leading edge of a new politics of control given their capacity for development, creativity, and leadership; and (3) criminal justice reforms will only be minimal and, in the long run, susceptible to quick reversal until new practical and theoretical understandings of racial justice prevail. I begin the chapter by sharing how these assumptions affected me personally.

MY PERSONAL STORY

My personal story, though not typical, is indicative of both the need for leadership and the capacity to lead. I grew up in a very wealthy community, though my family was working class. Working-class families often lived in the same areas as wealthy families in the late 1800s and early 1900s, usually to serve as maids, gardeners, and nannies to their affluent neighbors. My great-great-grandmother was a midwife to the Rockefeller and Guggenheim families (Shodell, 1984). My parents were actively involved in the civil rights movement. Among many other African Americans who participated in that movement and then began to work in civil service and government, my parents believed that success meant a well-paying job with good benefits and a retirement plan.

The Bootstrapper Mentality

That generation, believing that the passage of the Civil Rights Act meant equality, developed the "bootstrapper" mentality. The rhetoric of the bootstrapper mentality is grounded in privilege, and it is devoid of contextual relationships to chattel slavery and the ideology of white supremacy. Even in my church, bootstrapping was embraced as the primary way to overcome all obstacles of race, gender, economic disadvantage, and health. Floyd Flake, one of the most popular and charismatic leaders in the African Methodist Episcopal Church, an international religious community with more than 2,510,000 members, published *The Way of the Bootstrapper: Nine Action Steps for Achieving Your Dreams*. I trusted the advice of this young up-and-coming leader in the religious denomination that my family had embraced for five generations. According to Flake,

> Bootstrapping is a way of taking responsibility for and building your own life while bringing reality to your dreams. You can be kept down only if you don't see those metaphorical boots that offer you a way out of your current predicament. Bootstrappers do not see themselves as victims but have confidence in their ability to rise beyond the limited expectations that others may have imposed on them. They develop inner strength from their experience and sufferings, which allows them to persevere even in the face of challenging odds. (Flake, 1999)

I believed every word of Floyd Flake's advice (1999) for us to "pull ourselves up by the bootstraps, turn obstacles into springboards, build stronger families and communities, and make our dreams come true" (p.3). But as I looked more closely at his personal story, I began to question whether or not he was aware of his own privilege. In 1986, Reverend Flake became a member of Congress and began to use community development block grants and other resources to revive then failing Queens, New York, neighborhood around the modest Allen A.M.E. church he had pastored since 1976. By the end of his term in Congress, he had built the Greater Allen Cathedral, an institution with more than 25,000 members, of which he remains CEO. Flake left Congress in 1997, when construction on the 23-million-dollar 93,000-square-foot, 2,500-seat Greater Allen Cathedral was completed. By then, hundreds of millions of federal dollars and other resources had been invested to revive this community in which the cathedral is located.

Though these were all great things for the community, for the Flakes, and for the church, I would argue that privilege was at play, as well as a bit of "corporate welfare." Traditional conservatism frowns on handouts and welfare for struggling individuals and poor families, but has no hesitation when it comes to corporate tax breaks and loopholes, pet projects funded by elected officials in their local communities, and the favorable treatment by the government or certain corporations. It became apparent that this pastor had a pretty reliable pair of boots and straps, and that he was also counting on the boots and straps of others to achieve his dream.

All this to say that, regardless of my faith, my trust in my own abilities, and my belief in personal empowerment and responsibility, the bootstrapper mentality fell flat for me when I encountered the many structural barriers that supersede self-determination. My real education began in 1997 when, despite being raised in a family that believed in my personal potential, I found myself bootless, strapless, and imprisoned the year that the Greater Allen Cathedral opened. As I was processed through the U.S. criminal justice system on multiple occasions, a few things became obvious to me through my own observations and interactions:

1. Money—for expert witnesses, private attorneys, and psychiatric reports (i.e., economic privilege)—made a huge difference in court outcomes.
2. The majority of defendants who have access to the aforementioned privilege are white.
3. White defendants are not seen as privileged, but as superior, invoking the vestiges of chattel slavery that permitted the enslavement of an entire group based on the supposition that they were inferior beings.

At that time, I was forced to critically examine the criminal justice system and the policies that drive it. Besides the blatant disparities that work against African Americans in the court system, largely resulting from the stark economic inequality caused by 400 years of chattel slavery, in prison I became aware of the educational disparities among the women incarcerated with me. Though I had had the advantage of having lived in an affluent area with an excellent public school system, most of the women in prison with me had only had access to poor quality education. They had not failed to pull themselves up by their bootstraps; they had been left barefoot by lack of access to quality educational resources.

Learning to Lead

I took on the role of peer tutor in adult basic education and high school equivalency classes. I began seeing with fresh eyes the criminal justice system, the public education system, and the racial stratifications that were not previously apparent. All of the women I was tutoring in basic education classes were women of color, mostly from poor backgrounds. Hearing them talk about the scarcity of resources in their local schools; their inability to navigate bureaucratic systems on behalf their children; and the realities of community trauma caused by overpolicing, addiction, unemployment, and discrimination made me consider the relationship between access to education and mass incarceration.

I saw that these women were not incapable of learning. On the contrary, many of them had never been properly challenged. Some had obvious learning difficulties that were never addressed, and many had never been encouraged to perform well in the classroom. Some had even been told more about their limitations than about their potential.

Having flunked out of college during my rebellious years, I never thought myself qualified to teach. In prison, however, I learned just how privileged I was. I grew up in an area with much greater resources than those of my students. Imparting that knowledge to others made me feel both valued and ashamed; valued because I was using my knowledge to help others, and ashamed because I had, in my mind, wasted the wonderful opportunity afforded me.

I heard many harrowing stories. I learned of a girl, 18 years of age, who lived on the street after dropping out of school and aging out of foster care. I met a young mother accused of murdering her child simply because she was never taught how to care for an infant. Almost all of my students were victims of the drug trade plaguing their communities. The more I listened, the more I was confronted with my privilege. I knew I had an obligation to help break the cycle of poverty and incarceration.

Wacquant's Peculiar Institutions

When I left prison, I joined an organization called College & Community Fellowship (CCF) and earned my degree with their support. In addition to providing a community in which to study, CCF offered seminars in which I learned to analyze the link between educational access and mass incarceration. At CCF, I learned about the work of Loïc Wacquant, and his notion of "peculiar institutions." Wacquant cites four peculiar institutions in the United States. These institutions are peculiar because of their connection to race-based chattel slavery and its byproduct, the creation of a "racial caste line," which structurally divides whites and blacks (Wacquant, 2002). Racial division was a consequence, not a precondition, of slavery in the United States. Wacquant's first peculiar institution is chattel slavery, which existed from the Colonial era to the Civil War and was the pillar of the U.S. economy. Jim Crow, the second institution, was a system of legally enforced discrimination that anchored the South from the end of reconstruction to the civil rights movement. The third is the ghetto, corresponding with the conjoint urbanization and proletarianization of African Americans from the great migration of 1914 until the 1960s, and climaxing with the explosive urban riots addressed by the report of the Kerner Commission, which was established by President Lyndon B. Johnson to investigate the causes of the 1967 race riots in the United States.

The fourth peculiar institution, currently thriving, is that of mass incarceration. At CCF, my fellow students and I began to see that reentry mirrored some of Wacquant's peculiar institutions. Racial structures clearly inform mass incarceration but remain marginally unnamed and untouched by virtually the entire gamut of reforms, models, and proposals. The quality of the solutions depends on the ethnicity of those affected by the problem.

REENTRY: A POSSIBLE FIFTH PECULIAR INSTITUTION

More than 700,000 men and women—and children aged as young as 16 years—exit state and federal correction facilities and return to their communities each year to face daunting uncertainty. This process, called *reentry*, has been a principal site for policy-makers and stakeholders who claim to embrace the moral principle that "America is a land of second chances." There is bipartisan agreement that the nation must address the escalating economic and societal costs associated with incarcerating more than 2 million people each year.

As I began to form my own thinking around these issues, I saw similarities to Wacquant's peculiar institutions emerging in the newly formed "prisoner reentry indus-try." Prisoner reentry, as an institution, could easily become the fifth peculiar institution. Reentry provides cheap labor, as those leaving prison are willing to take jobs at almost any wage; reentry models often offer harsh treatment of individuals, funneling them toward transitional housing, short-term employment, and manual labor. Historically, reentry strategies exclude access to postsecondary education,[1] which is proven to increase wages and decrease recidivism. Too often, reentry success is defined as subsistence: basic shelter, food, and low-wage employment. Many funding streams and best-practice models lend themselves to work-focused, cookie-cutter programs. These do not place emphasis on individual talents, and do not help foster the ambitions, educational or otherwise, of their workers. Ultimately, they provide little hope of long-term economic stability. There continue to be few expectations from reentering individuals beyond criminal desistance.

---

[1] The formation of the Second Chance Act in 2004 excluded any reference to education. George W. Bush cited work and crime reduction as major goals, implying that the purpose of the Act was to keep ex-cons from committing crimes rather than to offer opportunity for the good life.

When I was released from prison in 2001, reentry was already an industry, largely run by educated whites. Though the industry continues to make a concerted effort to hire people who have been directly affected by the criminal justice system, these positions rarely rise above low-level supervisory roles.

Many reformers believe that the costs of prison and policing have forced an about-face in criminal-justice policy. If efforts are focused solely on reentry, or "fixing" individuals and populations, possibilities of reform are limited. Despite claims that current reform efforts are fueled by a desire to offer second chances to those who have been found by the courts to have broken the social contract, Americans continue to rank public safety, security, and social control above other political, social, and economic aims. This reality is reflected in foreign policy, in immigration policy, and in escalating surveillance practices and police brutality around the country. Unless criminal justice reforms adopt new practical and theoretical understandings of racial justice, they will only be minimal and, in the long run, susceptible to quick reversal.

When reentry reform advocates began articulating the root issues underlying persistent challenges to the criminal-justice-involved population, there existed no adequate research to support the realities that these advocates knew to be true. Among the research that did exist, the lived experience of those in communities most affected was not accounted for. Much of this literature objectified its subjects, rather than including them. Marc Mauer's *Race to Incarcerate*, Christian Parenti's *Lockdown America*, and Jeremy Travis's *But They All Come Back*, all representative early works, were largely grounded in numbers, not participatory analysis including formerly incarcerated individuals and their families. These works, it is true, moved the needle of public conversation, but the solutions they suggested would only extend the power of the justice system through drug courts, reentry courts, and increased community supervision.

Reentry Extends Penal Forms Beyond the Prison Walls

In some ways, the focus on reentry for the past 12 years has led to the extension of the criminal justice system into new and old social institutions. Drug courts, reentry courts, community supervision (e.g., parole), and use of technology to increase surveillance in the community all point to the expansion of the system of punishment into our backyards, while at the same time purporting to be part of a trend toward rehabilitation and "second chances." Rather than providing exits to the criminal justice system, these entities often become feeders to the system itself. For example, a significant amount of the increased use of incapacitation since 1980 can be credited to the large numbers of men and women returning to incarceration via parole violations (Petersilia, 2000). In fact, Travis and Lawrence (2002) stated that, in 1999, more adults returned to incarceration on parole violations than were initially incarcerated—for any reason—in 1980 (Travis & Lawrence, 2002). Thus, the lengthening of the current reentry process extends involvement with the criminal justice system rather than shortens it. We must rethink this "peculiar institution" to create reforms that meet the needs of all who are affected and succeed where other reforms have fallen short.

LIMITATIONS OF CURRENT REENTRY REFORM EFFORTS

Many strategies for reform focus on personal responsibility and transformation (i.e., the bootstrapper mentality), as well as the deceptive separation of "deserving" and "undeserving" beneficiaries of reform efforts. First-time nonviolent offenders are often seen as deserving of redemption, whereas all other offenders are subject to increased scrutiny and continued demonization. For example, the Department of Justice released 6,000 federal prisoners in late 2015, but 2,000 of these were immediately deported. Such strategies indicate incremental progress, but much work remains to be done.

It will take many policy interventions and partnerships to move toward a steady process of decarceration. National systems and policies affect everybody. The problem is that systems and policies often do not inspire the civic engagement required to change bad policies until a particular policy touches a particular population at its core. However, many of the people who experience disadvantage at the hands of problematic systems and policies are those who would fall into the falsely dichotomous category of the "undeserving." When a fundamentally unjust or oppressive policy affects a specific community, and basic human rights are denied due to this policy's implementation, then the affected community will oppose this policy with the level of investment and energy that is required to sustain a movement. For example, people who are not farmers may not care about farm subsidies until they understand how it affects them. Similarly, people born into wealth, without the benefit of social consciousness, may not understand how milk prices rising above five dollars a gallon creates hardship for millions of families. Politicians and moguls who are unaware of the privileges, networks, and opportunities that allowed them to succeed may actually believe that the solution to unemployment is for young people to borrow money from their parents to start a business. Thus, it is a critical first step toward reform for those most affected by mass criminalization and incarceration to play key leadership roles in the decarceration movement.

REFORM HINGES ON NEW UNDERSTANDINGS OF RACIAL JUSTICE

A racialized form of social control, this process of reentry undermines formerly incarcerated individuals' capacity for development. Reentry, as practiced, is a form of oppression, and a peculiar institution indeed—it generates a population compelled to work for subsistence-level wages, with little hope of upward mobility. This process racializes through the distribution of life-and-death chances in practices that are aimed not only at bodies but at the very capacities for development, creativity, and leadership of the formerly incarcerated (Nixon et al., 2008).

The racism that has been central to mass criminalization has been transformed into a crude evolutionary or "biopolitical" racism. This new form of racism measures the potential, or perceived lack thereof, of whole populations. It makes *the measure of a population's life capacity, or seeming lack thereof,* represent that population's risks to the vitality, security, and future of society as a whole (Nixon et al., 2008). This racism widens the net of marginalization through contact with the criminal justice system. It therefore creates raced-based barriers that limit this population's capacity to successfully lead a decarceration movement that reflects the best possible outcomes for them, their families, and their communities.

Mass incarceration has rendered many communities devastated and these effects are inextricably linked to race. Therefore, current discourse on reform will be wrought with shortcomings if not viewed in this context. Unless criminal justice reforms adopt new practical and theoretical understandings of racial justice, they will only be minimal and, in the long run, susceptible to quick reversal. Having those most affected by the issue— a population that is disproportionately African American—in leadership will help to counteract the racism and structural oppression embedded in the current criminal justice system by illuminating these issues in the context of criminal justice reform.

PEOPLE IN REENTRY HAVE THE CAPACITY TO LEAD

Beginning in the early 2000s, Eddie Ellis, one of the founders of the Greenhaven Prison think tank, began to hold regular meetings of formerly incarcerated individuals around the country. For those of us currently on the front lines, this was the beginning of the contemporary movement to more fully include the formerly incarcerated in conversations about the criminal justice system. My personal focus was on postsecondary education.

The Need for Higher Education

The concept of increasing access to higher education for people involved with the criminal justice system was seen as impossible. Even those who cared deeply about the issue were focused on subsistence and did not believe that formerly incarcerated individuals were capable of more. One step toward moving decarceration efforts forward is to increase the leadership capacity of those most affected by this issue through access to higher education and adequate support to see these educational opportunities through to completion. Obtainment of education beyond high school diplomacy provides access to higher wage job opportunities and increases skills that may be applied to leadership in the decarceration movement. This, invariably, will open the door for an increased number of those most affected by the criminal justice system to ascend to higher level positions within the system itself, where they were previously relegated to lower level supervisory roles, at best, or, at worst, absent from decision-making positions. As well, access to higher wage jobs creates economic stability, not only for individuals but also for the communities in which they live—communities that often have disproportionately suffered economic depletion from mass incarceration.

True Reform Requires Leadership from Directly Affected Individuals in Research, Practice, and Policy

Another arena in which those most affected by the issues of mass incarceration and its extension through reentry can lead is research. Though scholarly conversations, research, and data about this issue are undoubtedly necessary, and powerful allies with resources and connections to stakeholders and decision makers are essential, American society needs to embrace the experiences, intelligence, capacity, and vigilance of communities directly affected by these issues.

Those directly affected by reentry policies realize that such efforts, though noble, are insufficient. Programs such as My Brother's Keeper (a national initiative formed by the Obama administration to promote the success of young black men) employ strategies that go much further than reentry programming by investing heavily in certain populations. But even these programs are problematic. Those they aim to help—young black males, in the case of My Brother's Keeper—are cast in the role of a problem to be fixed. When a targeted population feels that they are valuable only as a test of proposed reforms, they may feel objectified. Thus, young black males have become the nonparticipatory targets of reform, making it less possible to address the racism that led to mass criminalization and the surrogate racism that has been the effect of these policies (Nixon et al., 2008).

Organizing a Movement Led by Those Most Affected

It is essential that there be autonomous organizing among women and men in and beyond prison, in collaboration with various other leaders. "Prisoners in reentry" must reclaim that categorization to become a "population for ourselves." This does not mean separating from the larger society. Instead, it means creating opportunity to align with others who might share interests in social, political, and economic change.

Reform efforts are limited by an absence of leadership by those whom these efforts are meant to address. There must be a restructuring of the power dynamic in decarceration efforts, as well as in the communities that have most been oppressed by excessive social control and criminalization. If not engaged as thought and movement leaders toward a more just society, people with criminal records remain a subjugated population—one to be researched, judged, evaluated, and programmed.

Directly affected leaders, organizers, and advocates are banding together to make a case for their participation in the national conversation about decarceration. Unless their voices are heard, they are at risk to suffer statistical death with enormous implications for those populations who have been most affected by mass criminalization.

CONCLUSION

The pendulum of reform is swinging. Where it will rest remains to be seen. The 2010s have seen the emergence of bipartisan coalitions.[2] These coalitions, formed in the name of public safety, do not typically include the input of those of us whose experience has exposed the fallacies of the bootstrapper mentality. In pursuing this course, the U.S. criminal justice system runs the risk of perpetually pitting the perceived "deserving" against the "undeserving," even in the search for a fairer, smaller system.

In July 2016, a *Politico* headline read, "Criminal Justice Reform Gains Bipartisan Momentum" (Bade, 2015), indicating a growing belief that there is a bipartisan shift away from mass criminalization. If so, what is the vision for communities decimated by years of tough-on-crime policies? What does the nation see for them in the long term? The causal relationship between disinvestment in certain communities and the ballooning system of criminalization and imprisonment has become so unwieldy that influencers in multiple sectors and across the political spectrum agree that a major overhaul—if not a full dismantling—is inevitable.

Why, then, has the United States not yet seen a clear and swift move toward mass decarceration? What kind of leadership will it take to create and sustain a social and political movement that invests in the long-term social and economic success of communities most marginalized by neglect, underresourced social institutions, and overpolicing? Answering these questions requires a critical examination of the systemic and structural issues that inform mass criminalization. These issues remain largely unnamed and untouched by the majority of reentry models, and are excluded from many front-end proposals.

The support and development of leaders with criminal convictions will come about not as a result of a better program for "taking responsibility," or as a result of a more effective "personal transformation" than others. It certainly will not come about because directly affected individuals' histories are devoid of incidents that can be categorized as "violent crime" and render them "underserving" of the benefits to be ushered in by proposed reform. The success of these leaders is a result of a more radical approach: postsecondary education in and beyond prison. When arguing for higher education as a strategy for social, political, and economic change is considered radical for any population, it calls to question the values and motives that are used to decide who gets and does not get access to freedom from ignorance. With meaningful participation of directly affected individuals at the highest level of reform efforts, the United States can change course, avoiding a future mired in the fundamentally unjust criminal justice system.

---

[2] See http://rightoncrime.com and http://www.coalitionforpublicsafety.org/.

REFERENCES

Bade, R. (2015, July 15). Criminal justice reform gains bipartisan momentum. *Politico.* Retrieved from http://www.politico.com/story/2015/07/criminal-justice-reform-gains-bipartisan-momentum-120125

Flake, F. H. (1999). *The way of the bootstrapper: Nine action steps for achieving your dreams.* New York, NY: Amistad.

Nixon, V., Clough, P. T., Staples, D., Peterkin, Y. J., Zimmerman, P., Voight, C., & Pica, S. (2008). Life capacity beyond reentry: A critical examination of racism and prisoner reentry reform in the U.S. *Race/Ethnicity: Multidisciplinary Global Contexts, 2*(1), 21–43.

Petersilia, J. (2000). When prisoners return to communities: Political, economic, and social consequences. *Federal Probation, 65*(1), 3–8.

Rodriguez, M. N., & Emsellem, M. (2011). 65 million "need not apply." The National Employment Law Project. Retrieved from http://www.nelp.org/content/uploads/2015/03/65_Million_Need_Not_Apply.pdf

Shodell, E. (1984). *It looks like yesterday to me.* Port Washington, NY: Port Washington Public Library.

Travis, J., & Lawrence, S. (2002). Beyond the prison gates: The state of parole in America. The Urban Institute. Retrieved from http://www.urban.org/research/publication/beyond-prison-gates

Wacquant, L. (2002). From slavery to mass incarceration. *New Left Review, 13,* 41–60.

7

Prisoner Reentry in an Era of Smart Decarceration

Reuben Jonathan Miller

BACKGROUND

On March 26, 2015, Van Jones and Newt Gingrich, two unlikely political allies, led a bipartisan summit on criminal justice reform (Hortwitz, 2015). That same evening, the White House released a video of President Barack Obama interviewing David Simon, the famed director of *The Wire*, on the consequences of the drug war in poor and working class communities. On July 16, 2015, President Obama toured El Reno Federal Penitentiary, holding a 45-minute conversation with six men convicted of nonviolent drug offenses (White House, 2016). In November 2015, on the heels of historic drug policy reform, 6,000 people were discharged from federal prisons and halfway houses, representing the largest one-time release of prisoners from federal custody (Schmidt, 2015).

By January 2016, a coalition of 70 police chiefs and prosecutors published an open letter calling for the passage of the Sentencing Reform and Corrections Act of 2015. In March of that same year, the Act was endorsed by the National District Attorney's Association, the International Association of Chiefs of Police, and the Major County Sheriff's Association, three highly influential law enforcement organizations. Expanding provisions under the Second Chance Act of 2007, the Sentencing Reform and Corrections Act of 2015 calls for an end to life sentences and a modest reduction in mandatory minimum sentences for some nonviolent offenses. It expands the ability of formerly incarcerated people to seal and expunge juvenile records, also for nonviolent offenses, and eliminates most cases of juvenile solitary confinement. Finally, the act enhances support for drug treatment, mental health services, job training, and vocational counseling.

Though this moment of bipartisan support for criminal justice reform seems sudden, the efforts of these political actors follow the work of countless, previously unknown, formerly incarcerated people, their loved ones, and prisoner rights activists who have worked on these issues for the greater part of three decades (Davis, 1998; Critical Resistance, 2016; Sentencing Project, 2016). The success of these campaigns has set the stage for the current debate on the use of incarceration and the state of policing in the United States. It has provided insight on the effects of mass incarceration on the life chances of the poor, and especially poor people of color. It has fueled criminal justice reform at the local level, bringing about modest declines in the U.S. prison population, and a fairly dramatic decrease of the prison census in states like New York and Michigan (Martin & Price, 2016). A combination of political pressure, fiscal constraint, and a series of well-timed lawsuits has led to a number of historic prison closings and ultimately the largest, successful decarceration effort in U.S. history, the California prison realignment.

Given the success of these campaigns, and the promise of more to come, this chapter asks, "What does it mean for so many people to return home after prison?" And, in the spirit of this volume, "What should prisoner reentry look like in an era of smart decarceration?" *Reentry* is the process of leaving jails or prison and returning to the community (Travis, Solomon, & Waul, 2001). Joan Petersilia (2009) adds to this definition the role of social service organizations and the outcomes of formerly incarcerated people, calling reentry a "complex and multifaceted social problem." Most scholarship on prisoner reentry documents the barriers formerly incarcerated people face or raises technical questions about the efficacy of reentry programs. Though such questions are important, they fail to capture the broader implications of prisoner reentry, or the deep levels of vulnerability brought about in its wake.

In this chapter, I assess the problems and possibilities of prisoner reentry in supporting and maintaining decarceration. Examining the legal exclusion of formerly incarcerated people, the targeting of poor communities for police intervention, and the vulnerable social position of the formerly incarcerated upon release, I suggest the problem of prisoner reentry is ultimately a problem of citizenship. That is, formerly incarcerated individuals are loosely tethered to the political economy and culture of the city because they have an alternate set of rights, restrictions, and responsibilities that justify and reproduce social inequities. I critically evaluate the work of the prisoner reentry program, the rehabilitative strategy of choice in the current age (Petersilia, 2009; Travis, 2009) and ask whether the current efforts to rehabilitate the formerly incarcerated through prisoner reentry interventions are appropriate given the scale of the problem. I argue that reentry programs alone are an inadequate response to mass incarceration, and its community analogue, *mass supervision*—the formal and informal sanctions that govern how formerly incarcerated people can live, work, and travel (McNeill & Beyens, 2013; Miller & Alexander, 2016).

This suggests that social service solutions cannot alone adequately address social problems. With the challenge of reentry reimagined to suit the era of decarceration,

I offer suggestions that leverage the strengths of prisoner reentry programs, taking advantage of their position within the communities they serve to broker relationships between the formerly incarcerated and the resource rich social institutions best suited to help them. Doing so addresses the material, psychosocial, and emotional needs of formerly incarcerated people, which I suggest prisoner reentry programs are well positioned to do, while providing mezzo (i.e., organizational and institutional) level intervention strategies to help establish long-term access to economic, social, and civic life. Community partners are essential to accomplishing this goal, which is key to smart and sustainable decarceration.

FROM PRISON TO COMMUNITY AND BACK AGAIN

The number of formerly incarcerated people living in disadvantaged urban and rural neighborhoods has increased precipitously, from just over 1 million people in 1977 to nearly 5 million in 2014, with 600,000 returning home annually (Kaeble, Maruschak, & Bonczar, 2015). Apart from its size, mass incarceration's primary feature is "the concentration of incarcerations' effects" (Garland, 2001, p. 1), which has diminished the life chances of the poor, and especially poor people of color in the United States (Alexander, 2010; Western, 2006; Wakefield & Uggen 2010). Incarcerated and formerly incarcerated individuals are overwhelmingly poor, disproportionately comprising racial and ethnic minorities, and would be considered an "at-risk group" by any measure of population health (Dumont, Brockmann, Dickman, Alexander, & Rich, 2012). They face complex social problems, ranging from poverty, unemployment, and social isolation to health problems, addictions, and premature death (Dumont et al., 2012). The concentration of these trends in poor urban and rural neighborhoods sheds light on their disparate impact.

RACE AND THE PROBLEM OF PUNISHMENT

Racial disparities in the criminal justice system remain quite jarring. Even after recent declines in the incarceration rate of African Americans, they are twice as likely to be arrested, six times as likely to be incarcerated, and serve longer prison terms compared with their white counterparts (Starr & Rehavi, 2013). In addition, African Americans and Latinos are stopped and searched by police at much higher rates than whites, despite being less likely to have broken a law (New York Times Editorial Board, 2013). These disparities persist even when controlling for the evidence available to the arresting officer, the kinds of crimes committed in the area, or the reported race of the suspect (Gelman et al., 2012; Goel, Rao, & Shroff, 2015). Likewise, experimental data on police shooting simulations show that both police officers and civilians were more likely to shoot unarmed African American men than they were to shoot white men (Correll et al., 2007). In fact, there is evidence of a racial hierarchy when it comes to police shootings: Unarmed African

American men were most likely to be shot in police simulations, followed, in order, by Latinos, whites, and Asians (Correll et al., 2007).

The data are clear: African Americans are consistently viewed as more criminal, more dangerous, and less deserving of care than whites (Gilens, 1999). Given these attitudes, it is clear why African Americans make up over 65% of the nations' incarcerated population despite being only 13% of the total U.S. population (Carson & Sobel, 2014). It also becomes apparent why African American men even without criminal records have worse labor market outcomes than white men who do (Pager, 2008). Such attitudes also explain the staggering reality that poor whites are less likely to be incarcerated than even wealthy blacks (Zaw, Hamilton, & Darity, 2016).

Examining survey and administrative data on men born between 1965 and 1969, Pettit and Western (2004) showed that 60% of African American men who drop out of high school and 30% of those who graduate will be incarcerated by their early 30s, leading them to theorize incarceration as a life course event. But if incarceration is a normal life course trajectory, so too are repeated rounds of recidivism and reentry. Tracking recidivism rates for 400,000 people released from prisons in 30 states, Durose, Cooper, and Snyder (2014) found a 77% recidivism rate after 5 years. A third were rearrested within the first 6 months and half within a year; even more striking, the sample averaged 10 arrests (Durose, Cooper, & Snyder, 2014). From these findings, one may conclude that not only do *they all come back*, to borrow the title from Jeremy Travis's (2005) book on prisoner reentry, but many are rearrested frequently and within a short period of time.

The larger point is that formerly incarcerated people, who are overwhelmingly comprise composed of poor African American and Latino men, face challenges that extend beyond their conviction. Even without a record, they would be targeted for criminal justice intervention and face barriers to their full participation in the labor and housing market. They are enmeshed within systems that presume their deviance, dependence, and criminality. The criminal record itself, however, adds additional barriers that must be addressed to promote sustainable decarceration.

RECORDS, RISK, AND RESPONSIBILITY

Formerly incarcerated individuals face a number of barriers upon reentering society. The conditions of their release and the legal and regulatory exclusion they face due to the mark of a criminal record make it all the more difficult to keep and maintain employment, stay housed, and avoid contact with the criminal justice system (Miller & Alexander, 2016; Pager, 2008). These collateral consequences of criminal convictions coupled with shifts in social welfare policy draw formerly incarcerated individuals' families, employers, landlords, and social service providers into the penal dragnet, making them responsible for their management (Comfort, 2007; deVuono-Powell, Schweidler, Walters, & Zohrabi, 2015). Social service providers contract with the state to address the needs of formerly incarcerated individuals, but there are simply too few human service agencies to effectively do so (Taxman, Perdoni, & Harrison, 2007). Just 25% of individuals incarcerated in state and federal prisons and less than 10% of those in community corrections who have addiction treatment needs have access to daily treatment (Taxman et al., 2007). Even the celebrated Second Chance Act provided social service providers with just $30 per month per formerly incarcerated individual—enough, according to Wacquant (2010), to purchase a sandwich each week.

Therefore, various caregivers—family, friends, strangers—act as an informal social safety net for formerly incarcerated individuals encumbered with criminal records (deVuono-Powell et al., 2015). This social situation renders the formerly incarcerated subject to trends in an already hostile labor market. This deep, largely unaccounted for vulnerability places the formerly incarcerated in great need, while making them among the most undesirable candidates for help. A loved one may be evicted if they house an "ex-offender," whereas employers and landlords could be subject to lawsuits if an "ex-offender" under their jurisdiction breaks a law or causes harm to others (May, 1995). A social service agency can be sued for the actions of their clients (Dolnick, 2012). Helping simply puts caregivers at risk, changing the very nature of their relationships with formerly incarcerated individuals.

The burden of soliciting care from well-meaning strangers falls on the shoulders of formerly incarcerated people and their families (Miller, 2014; Miller & Alexander, 2016). To secure support, each interaction with almost any member of the general public must occur in such a way that puts them at ease. That is, the formerly incarcerated individual must convince the other—on whom they have come to depend for food, clothing, shelter, employment, or housing—that they have "changed their life" (Miller, 2014). To do so, they must demonstrate that they have taken responsibility for their criminal actions and their precarious social situations, and commit to good decision-making in the future (Miller, 2014).

This plays out in informal interactions between recently released individuals and members of their family and friendship networks; in formal interactions with the police, courts, and human service agencies; and in the activism and advocacy in which formerly incarcerated people engage (Miller & Alexander, 2016; Miller, Williams Miller, Zeleskov Djoric, & Patton, 2015). The responsibility to convince others that they are "good people" to receive formal and informal support is unique to those with the mark of a criminal record. So too is the set of laws that manage them and the organizations and institutions that support, monitor, and sanction their behavior.

CITIZENSHIP IN THE CARCERAL AGE

Nearly 48,000 laws, regulations, and administrative sanctions exclude formerly incarcerated people from full participation in social, political, and economic life (Heck, 2014). Though these restrictions vary greatly from state to state, they include more than 25,000 laws barring access to employment, 16,000 limiting entrepreneurship by constraining access to occupational licenses and certifications, 1,970 regulations listed under family/domestic rights, and 1,373 entries that limit their access to housing (Heck, 2014). This does not include the conditions of the formerly incarcerated individuals' release, which determine with whom they can associate, how often they have to check in with a parole officer, where they can go or live, and what they can do during their transition from prison to home. Violation of any of these conditions may result in arrest or reincarceration (Grattet, Petersilia, Lin, & Beckman, 2009; Latessa & Smith, 2007).

Life under such conditions is referred to as living in an age of mass supervision (McNeill & Beyens, 2013). Given the formal and informal mechanisms that constrain and control this group, and their unique legal position, Miller and Alexander (2016) argue that mass supervision has produced a novel form of citizenship they call *carceral citizenship*, which is based on the presumption that one has committed a crime. Carceral citizens have unique rights, restrictions, and responsibilities. For example, they must complete programs when required by the state and refrain from otherwise legal activity (e.g., drinking alcohol, crossing state lines). Therefore, they experience social life in ways that are unique to members of their class, and are not typically shared by even the most marginalized people who have traditionally been marked by their race, religion, ethnicity, or gender. Carceral citizens face constitutionally justified forms of exclusion based solely on the presumption of legal guilt, rather than exclusion based on a protected status (Miller & Alexander, 2016). If the degree of disadvantage associated with carceral expansion is even in part a result of carceral citizenship, any decarceration treatment must account for these largely structural barriers to succeed.

PRISONER REENTRY IN AN ERA OF MASS SUPERVISION

In an examination of mass incarceration's impact on poor black Chicagoans, neighborhoods with high concentrations of arrests were nearly identical to those where prisoners were annually returned (Street, 2002). The robust literature on neighborhood effects has drawn similar conclusions (Sampson & Loeffler, 2010; Travis; Western, & Radburn, 2014). Though these findings are in some ways intuitive, people recently released from prison or jail are highly transient. They struggle to make ends meet, moving residences multiple times each year (Harding, Wyse, Dobson, & Morenoff, 2014). Therefore, prisoners are not necessarily returned to their home communities upon release, but to neighborhoods *like* their home. Social service providers describe these spaces as *receiving communities*, noting that they are among the few areas willing to take in large numbers of returning prisoners (Peck & Theodore, 2008). Thus, in some inner-city neighborhoods, as many as 70% of the men have a felony conviction (Street, 2002).

The police, court system, and even human service agencies tasked with addressing the needs of formerly incarcerated people, known colloquially as prisoner reentry organizations, are overwhelmingly concentrated within these same racially segregated and disadvantaged urban areas (Miller, 2014). As a result, prisoners are arrested from, returned to, and offered rehabilitative services within neighborhoods *like* the ones they call home (Miller, 2014).

Given the costs of carceral expansion (fiscal and otherwise), policymakers have turned their attention to prisoner reentry. The research on prisoner reentry reveals the impact of incarceration on the life chances of the criminalized poor and the many barriers they face on release, shaping the design of prisoner reentry programming (Miller, 2014; Western, 2008). Unfortunately, the hardships faced by formerly incarcerated people and their subsequent negative social outcomes are most often interpreted as human capital deficiencies—deficiencies in their skill sets—rather than social problems, leading to micro-level, rather than structural, interventions (Hackett, 2013). A cognitive-behavioral therapy-inspired "evidence base" has emerged on the effective treatment of formerly incarcerated people that uses employment and recidivism as gold standards in program evaluation and seeks to address the decision-making processes of program participants (Gottschalk, 2015).

Prisoner reentry programs attempt to help formerly incarcerated people avoid crime and secure and maintain employment through social skills training, workforce development programs, substance abuse treatment, group and individual therapy, and a series of psychoeducational treatment groups (Miller, 2014). These services have been shown to reduce recidivism and increase employment outcomes for program participants (Petersilia, 2004; Seiter & Kadela, 2003; Visher & Travis, 2003). Most rigorous studies, however, find these interventions have modest to short-lived effects (e.g., Bloom, 2006; Cook, Kang, Braga, Ludwig, & O'Brien, 2015), with some negative effects on recidivism and employment, attributing participant outcomes to the increased surveillance. This suggests that human capital investment cannot overcome the mark of a criminal record. One may invest in the skill sets of program participants, but without removing barriers to employment, the chances of increasing their labor market participation are greatly diminished. The same holds true for housing. A program participant who completes a "life skills" course may have acquired the kind of habits one needs to pay the rent on time, but if they are discriminated against in the housing market, they will not be able to use them.

Proponents of reentry services put great stock in cognitive interventions that address "criminogenic risks" and bolster human capital. Such interventions are greatly needed, given the target populations' degree of disadvantage and vulnerability. The most successful programs, however, offer cognitive-behavioral therapy inspired programs and human capital interventions along with education and employment placement programs, housing assistance, and long-term support through comprehensive case management (Duwe, 2013). In other words, the most effective programs address the psychological, social, and *material needs* of program participants, and support them in the long term. Human capital investment, by itself, cannot overcome the constraints of a hostile labor or housing market. Participants, staff, administrators, and program planners from the most effective reentry programs understand this inherent limitation. They instead implement interventions designed to foster the development of social capital—connections to resource-rich social groups—in addition to their human capital interventions, providing their client base with both new or enhanced sets of skills to help them navigate the social world and simultaneously places where they can put those skills into practice.

<h3 style="text-align:center">THE EMMAUS ROAD WAY</h3>

The problem of prisoner reentry is ultimately a problem of citizenship, rather than one of choice, decision-making, skills deficits, or criminality. Admittedly, prisoner reentry programs, as social service organizations, cannot fully address structural barriers. Mass incarceration has produced a series of government-sized problems that cannot be solved by even the most robust and well-funded human service agency. Furthermore, the needs of formerly incarcerated people require engagement with a number of varied but interdependent systems, such as labor, healthcare, education, and housing. Yet in the face of their limitations, prisoner reentry organizations are well positioned to make a difference in their communities and support decarceration efforts already underway.

Moving beyond the limitations of human capital investment, reentry staff and administrators at the most successful reentry programs implemented interventions designed to foster the development of social capital, defined here as one's connections to resource rich social groups (see McNeill, Farrall, Lightowler, & Maruna, 2012; Miller, Patton, & Delva, in press). For example, an organization I have previously called Emmaus Road (Miller, 2014), a residential prisoner reentry program in a large Midwestern city, employs a brokerage model, connecting local businesses, church organizations, social service providers, and universities with the people they serve. Emmaus Road leveraged the needs of local universities to provide university students with training opportunities with their need for skilled and consistent therapeutic services. In doing so, the organization connected with a number of social work and psychology programs throughout the city, contracting them to provide weekly one-on-one psychotherapy sessions and supervised weekly treatment groups for each of their clients. Because doctoral psychology students conducted the weekly therapy sessions to complete the internship requirements for their PhD, Emmaus Road residents had access to a skilled, trained, and relatively experienced psychotherapist for the duration of their time in the program. In addition, graduate students conducted treatment groups, such as weekly psychotherapy and anger management classes, under the guidance of a practicing clinical supervisor to complete their fieldwork requirement. Not only does this university partnership provide access to quality services for participants, but also the school provides ongoing professional development and training for the organization's staff—increasing the connections between the reentry organization and a resource-rich institution.

In addition to these weekly sessions, Emmaus Road connected with local businesses and faith-based organizations to form affinity groups with their clients. These groups included chess clubs, foreign language courses, poetry and writing groups, running clubs, and cooking classes. They provided community members who had ethical commitments to serve the less fortunate with opportunities for extended interactions with formerly incarcerated men. Though initially a vehicle for service, Emmaus Road often engendered friendships, opening up new resource channels and professional networks for the clients. Aside from the opportunity to interact with professionals in lines of work many of the clients found interesting, community partners would often refer them for employment, housing opportunities, or professional development, and serve as references.

To help their clients find work and housing after they completed programming, Emmaus Road hired job developers, job retention counselors, and full-time housing specialists to forge relationships with local landlords and employers. Upon completion of Emmaus Road's job-training program, which provided the clients with the soft skills necessary in the labor market, Emmaus Road staff would refer clients to employers and landlords, vouching for their character and work ethic. Emmaus Road also partnered with the Chicago public school system, a local university, and a number of PhD students and professors to provide the clients with an opportunity to earn high school diplomas and college credit, should they want to, at a local workforce development program. Finally, Emmaus Road partnered with local unions and culinary arts programs to offer certification in food services, warehouse management, and green technology.

The results of these combined efforts were striking. An evaluation of Emmaus Road conducted by an independent research firm shows that over a 6-month treatment period, there was a 62% reduction in recidivism among residents and formerly incarcerated clients who applied but were waitlisted. In addition to significantly lower recidivism, graduates were four times as likely to acquire full-time employment. When they did recidivate, they stayed out of prison for longer periods of time. In addition to these more formal benchmarks, the clients I encountered during my time conducting research at Emmaus Road repeatedly expressed satisfaction with the services they received. They often discussed their belief that they should "give back" to other formerly incarcerated individuals by engaging in mentorship relationships, and reported aspirations of opening a reentry program in their home communities. Though these findings raise important questions about the employment trajectories of formerly incarcerated people, Emmaus Road remains among the most well respected programs in its host city among city officials, other reentry service providers, foundation officers, and formerly incarcerated people themselves.

By brokering relationships with community entities such as local businesses and universities, Emmaus Road addresses reentry challenges at the organizational level and effectively works to influence the ways in which systems interact with individuals returning to the community. This differs from other reentry models that use a "people-changing" approach—using individual-level interventions to transform individuals into "employable" citizens. The brokerage model centers on access to employment and housing rather than an exclusive focus on individual employability and tenant readiness. In effect, the brokerage model improves social capital in addition to human capital. Through the development of interpersonal relationships, both those fostered by the organization's staff and the participants themselves through the affinity groups, participants in the Emmaus Road model secured long-term employment and housing, a stark contrast to transitional job typical of reentry programs, which last an average of 90 to 180 days, and temporary housing (Miller, 2014). The implementation of complementary social and human capital interventions allows Emmaus Road to address both structural constraints and individual needs to promote successful reentry. Investing in multilayered services that address both individual and structural reentry facilitators, as exemplified in the Emmaus Road model, could prove an effective strategy in the context of mass reentry and smart decarceration.

A WAY FORWARD

To summarize, carceral citizenship has transformed the urban landscape and pulled formerly incarcerated individuals' families and community members into the penal dragnet through four key processes:

1. More than 48,000 laws, regulations, and administrative sanctions restrict former prisoners from full participation in social, civic, and political life (Heck, 2014).
2. Limited service availability results in formerly incarcerated individuals' reliance on already vulnerable networks of care (Taxman et al., 2007).
3. The concentration of criminal justice interventions in poor African American and Latino communities leads to disproportionate minority contact at every point in the criminal justice process (Miller, 2014; Miller & Alexander, 2016).
4. The return of thousands of prisoners to the "inner city" reconcentrates social disadvantage and diminishes the life chances of formerly incarcerated people, their partners, families, and friends.

There are many lessons one might draw from the collaborative model offered at Emmaus Road to address these processes. Whereas most other reentry programs are limited by their emphasis on cognitive interventions and human capital investment, the Emmaus Road model leverages community partnerships to address the needs of its target population. More specifically, it attempts to meet the mutual needs of its service population and its community partners. Emmaus Road provides opportunities for extended engagement between community members and residents at its facilities, allowing for the formation of alliances between them. The model takes an interdisciplinary approach, offering vocational, educational, psychological, and social services through their partnerships with universities, faith-based actors, local businesses, and landlords. Equally important, it meets the material needs of its clients, providing them with food, clothes, and shelter as they move through programming, and vouches for residents, sending out job developers and housing specialists into the labor and housing market on behalf of their clients.

Such a holistic approach to reentry planning is key to the promotion of smart decarceration. With literally millions of displaced formerly incarcerated people, and real resource limitations, finding ways to engage in partnerships that are mutually beneficial may make the difference between the smooth run of a well-supported program and the failure of an ineffective one.

If the problem of reentry is ultimately a problem of citizenship, and criminal records constrain the participation of formerly incarcerated people in the political economy and culture, no manner of human capital investment or cognitive intervention will result in successful community reintegration. However, transdisciplinary partnerships that leverage the strengths of existing organizations and communities, broker relationships, and increase access to social capital are in the best position to begin the work needed to move from an era of mass incarceration—and mass supervision—to one of smart decarceration. To adequately address these issues, one must think beyond the psychologies, rationalities, and traumatic experiences of formerly incarcerated individuals and help bridge the gap between their resource poor social situations and resource rich social institutions.

REFERENCES

Alexander, M. (2010). *The new Jim Crow: Mass incarceration in an age of color blindness.* New York, NY: the New Press.

Bloom, D. (2006). *Employment-focused programs for ex-prisoners: What have we learned, what are we learning, and where should we go from here?* MDRC. Retrieved from http://www.mdrc.org/publication/employment-focused-programs-ex-prisoners

Carson, E. A., & Sobel, W. J. (2014). *Prisoners in 2014.* Washington, DC: Bureau of justice statistics.

Comfort, M. (2007). Punishment beyond the legal offender. *Review of Law and Social Science, 3,* 271–296.

Cook, P. J., Kang, S., Braga, A. A., Ludwig, J., & O'Brien, M. E. (2015). An experimental evaluation of a comprehensive employment-oriented prisoner re-entry program. *Journal of Quantitative Criminology, 31*(3), 355–382.

Correll, J., Park, B., Judd, C. M., Wittenbrink, B., Sadler, M. S., & Keesee, T. (2007). Across the thin blue line: Police officers and racial bias in the decision to shoot. *Journal of Personality and Social Psychology, 92*(6), 1006.

Critical Resistance. (2016). *History.* Retrieved from http://criticalresistance.org/about/history/

Davis, A. (1998). Masked racism: Reflections on the prison industrial complex. *Color Lines, 1*(2), 11–13.

deVuono-Powell, S., Schweidler, C., Walters A., & Zohrabi, A. (2015). *Who pays? The true cost of incarceration on families.* Ella Baker Center. Retrieved from http://whopaysreport.org/

Dolnick, S. (2012, July 16). Finances plague company running halfway houses. *New York Times.* Retrieved from http://www.nytimes.com/2012/07/17/nyregion/nj-halfway-house-operator-plagued-by-financial-woes.html?_r=0

Dumont, D. M., Brockmann, B., Dickman, S., Alexander, N., & Rich, J. D. (2012). Public health and the epidemic of incarceration. *Annual Review of Public Health, 33,* 325.

Durose, M. R., Cooper, A. D., & Snyder, H. N. (2014). *Recidivism of prisoners released in 30 states in 2005: Patterns from 2005 to 2010.* US Department of Justice. Retrieved from http://www.bjs.gov/content/pub/pdf/rprts05p0510.pdf

Duwe, G. (2013). *What works with Minnesota prisoners: A summary of the effects of correctional programming on recidivism, employment, and cost avoidance.* St. Paul, Minnesota: Minnesota Department of Corrections. Retrieved from http://www.doc.state.mn.us/pages/files/6213/9206/2384/What_Works_with_MN_Prisoners_July_2013.pdf

Goel, S., Rao, J. M., & Shroff, R. (2015). *Precinct or prejudice: Understanding racial disparities in New York City's stop-and-frisk policy.* Retrieved from https://5harad.com/papers/frisky.pdf

Gelman, A., Fagan, J., & Kiss, A. (2012). An analysis of the New York City police department's "stop-and-frisk" policy in the context of claims of racial bias. *Journal of the American Statistical Association.* Retrieved from http://www.stat.columbia.edu/~gelman/research/published/frisk9.pdf

Grattet, R., Petersilia J., Lin, J., & Beckman, M. (2009). Parole violations and revocations in California: Analysis and suggestions for action. *Federal Probation, 73*(1), 2–11.

Heck, M. (2014). *The testimony of Mathias H. Heck Jr. on behalf of the American Bar Foundation for the hearing on collateral consequences of criminal convictions and the problem of over-criminalization of federal law.* Washington DC: Committee on the Judiciary Task Force on Over-Criminalization of the United States House of Representatives.

Hortwitz, S. (2015, August 15). Unlikely allies. *The Washington Post.* Retrieved from http://www.washingtonpost.com/sf/national/2015/08/15/clemency-the-issue-that-obama-and-the-koch-brothers-actually-agree-on/

Garland, D. (2001). *Mass imprisonment: Social causes and consequences.* London, UK: Sage.

Gilens, M. (1999). *Why Americans hate welfare: Race, media, and the politics of anti-poverty policy.* Chicago, IL: University of Chicago Press.

Gottschalk, M. (2015). *Caught: The prison state in lockdown America.* Princeton: Princeton University Press.

Hackett, C. (2013). Transformative visions: Governing through alternative practices and therapeutic interventions at a women's reentry center. *Feminist Criminology, 8*(3), 221–242.

Harding, D. J., Wyse, J., Dobson, C., & Morenoff, J. (2014). Making ends meet after prison. *Policy Analysis and Management, 33*(2), 440–470.

Kaeble, D., Maruschak, L. M., & Bonczar, T. P. (2015). *Probation and parole in the United States, 2014.* Bureau of Justice Statistics, US Dept of Justice, and Office of Justice Programs. Retrieved from http://www.bjs.gov/index.cfm?ty=pbdetail&iid=5415

Latessa, E. J., & Smith, P. (2007). *Corrections in the community.* New York, NY: Routledge.

Martin, W., & Price, J. (2016). *Decarceration and justice disinvestment.* Lanham, MD: Rowman and Littlefield.

May, B. E. (1995). Character component of occupational licensing laws: A continuing barrier to the ex-felon's employment opportunities. *North Dakota Law Review, 71,* 187. Retrieved from http://heinonline.org/HOL/LandingPage?handle=hein.journals/nordak71&div=19&id=&page=

McNeill, F., & Beyens, K. (2013). *Offender supervision in Europe.* New York, NY: Springer.

McNeill, F., Farrall, S., Lightowler, C., & Maruna, S. (2012). *How and why people stop offending: Discovering desistance.* Retrieved from http://www.iriss.org.uk/sites/default/files/iriss-insight-15.pdf

Miller, R. (2014). Devolving the carceral state: Race, prisoner reentry and the micro-politics of urban poverty management. *Punishment and Society, 16*, 305–335.

Miller, R., & Alexander, A. (2016). The price of (carceral) citizenship: Punishment, surveillance and social welfare policy in an age of carceral expansion. *Michigan Journal of Race and Law, 21*(2), 290–314.

Miller, R., Patton, D., & Delva, J. (in press). Group work in the shadow of criminal justice expansion. In C. Gavin, L. Gutierrez, & M. Galinski (Eds.), *Handbook of social work with groups.* New York, NY: Guilford Press.

Miller, R., Williams Miller, J., Zeleskov Djoric, J., & Patton, D. (2015). Baldwin's Mill: Race, carceral expansion and the pedagogy of repression, 1965–2015. *Humanity and Society, 39*(4), 456–475.

New York Times Editorial Board. (2013, August 13). Racial discrimination in stop-and-frisk. *New York Times.* Retrieved from http://www.nytimes.com/ 2013/ 08/ 13/ opinion/ racial-discrimination-in-stop-and-frisk.html?r=0

Pager, D. (2008). *Marked: Race, crime, and finding work in an era of mass incarceration.* Chicago, IL: University of Chicago

Peck, J., & Theodore, N. (2008). Carceral Chicago: Making the ex-offender employability crisis. *Urban and Regional Research, 32*(2), 251–281.

Petersilia, J. (2009). *When prisoners come home: Parole and prisoner reentry.* New York, NY: Oxford University Press.

Petersilia, J. (2004). What works in prisoner reentry: Reviewing and questioning the evidence. *Federal Probation, 68,* 4.

Sampson R. J., & Loeffler, C. (2010). Punishment's place: The local concentration of mass incarceration. *Daedalus, 139*(3), 20–31.

Schmidt, M. S. (2015, October 6). U.S. to release 6,000 inmates from prisons. *New York Times.* Retrieved from http://www.nytimes.com/2015/10/07/us/us-to-release-6000-inmates-under-new-sentencing-guidelines.html?_r=0

Sentencing Project. (2016). *About the Sentencing Project.* Retrieved from http://www.sentencing-project.org/about-us/

Taxman, F. S., Perdoni, M. L., & Harrison, L. D. (2007). Drug treatment services for adult offenders: The state of the state. *Substance Abuse Treatment 32*(3), 239–254. doi: 10.1016/ j.jsat.2006.12.019

Seiter, R. P., & Kadela, K. R. (2003). Prisoner reentry: What works, what does not, and what is promising. *Crime and Delinquency, 49*(3), 360–388.

Starr, S. B., & Rehavi, M. M. (2013). Mandatory sentencing and racial disparity: Assessing the role of prosecutors and the effects of Booker. *Yale Law Journal, 123,* 2.

Street, P. (2002). Race, prison, and poverty: The race to incarcerate in an age of correctional Keynesianism. *History Is a Weapon.* Retrieved from http://www.historyisaweapon.com/defcon1/streeracpripov.html

Travis, J. (2005). *But they all come back: Facing the challenges of prisoner reentry.* Washington, DC: Urban Institute Press.

Travis, J. (2009). *What works for successful prisoner Reentry?* US House of Representatives Committee on Appropriations: Subcommittee on Commerce, Justice, Science, and Related Agencies. Retrieved from http://www.jjay.cuny.edu/Travis_Congressional_Testimony.pdf

Travis, J., Solomon, A. L., & Waul, M. (2001). *From prison to home: The dimensions and consequences of prisoner reentry.* Washington, DC: The Urban Institute. Retrieved from http:// www. urban.org/UploadedPDF/from_prison_to_home.pdf

Travis, J., Western, B., & Radburn, S. (2014). *The growth of incarceration: Exploring causes and consequences.* Washington, DC: National Academy's Press.

Visher, C. A., & Travis, J. (2003). Transitions from prison to community: Understanding individual pathways. *Annual Review of Sociology, 29,* 89–113.

Wacquant, L. (2010). Class, race, and hyperincarceration in revanchist America. *Socialism and Democracy, 28*(3), 35–56.

Wakefield, S., & Uggen, C. (2010). Incarceration and stratification. *Annual Review of Sociology, 36,* 387–406.

Western, B. (2008). Reentry: Reversing mass imprisonment. *Boston Review.* Retrieved from http://bostonreview.net/bruce-western-reentry-reversing-mass-imprisonment

Western, B. (2006). *Punishment and inequality in America.* New York, NY: Russell Sage Foundation.

White House. (2016). *Fact Sheet: President Obama announces new actions to reduce recidivism and promote reintegration of formerly incarcerated individuals.* Office of the Press Secretary. Retrieved from https://www.whitehouse.gov/the-press-office/2016/06/24/fact-sheet-president-obama-announces-new-actions-reduce-recidivism-and

Zaw, K., Hamilton, D., & Darity, W., Jr. (2016). Race, wealth and incarceration: Results from the National Longitudinal Survey of Youth. *Race and Social Problems, 8*(1), 103–115.

8

Community and Decarceration

DEVELOPING LOCALIZED SOLUTIONS

Kathryn Bocanegra

BACKGROUND

A community-centered approach is relevant to current scholarship on reducing prison populations. Scholars of mass incarceration emphasize two critical policy changes to reduce prison populations: (1) admissions and (2) length of stay (Clear & Austin, 2009). To reduce the consequences of 4 decades of correctional expansion, the scale of punishment of incarcerated[1] individuals must also be reduced. Past policy changes—determinate sentencing policies and sentencing guidelines—have actually increased the prison population by keeping more people incarcerated for longer periods of time. Sentencing policy that affects admissions includes incarcerating individuals who could be better served in noncarceral settings (e.g., community treatment centers) and policies regarding technical parole and probation violators. There is sufficient evidence that changing these policies will reduce the national prison population (Berman, 2008; Clear & Austin, 2009).

However, exclusively focusing on reducing prison populations without considering the sustainability of such an effort is potentially dangerous. Rapid deinstitutionalization not preceded by thoughtful consideration of where these individuals will go could cause the same whiplash as the 1963 deinstitutionalization of state mental health institutions

---

[1] The term "incarceration" in this chapter refers to confinement in both jails and state prison facilities. The contours of federal incarceration or detainment facilities (such as juvenile detention centers or immigration detention centers) are not included in this analysis.

and asylums. An exclusive focus on number of jail and prison admissions and length of stay is insufficient for smart decarceration, because it considers only where people end up (incarcerated) and not where they come from and return to.

In this chapter, I first establish the "case for place" by describing the concentration of crime, mass incarceration, and mass reentry in discrete geographic areas. Building from this foundation, I explore community-centered smart decarceration by reviewing existing evidence and past attempts. Lessons learned from empirical research subsequently provide insight into new pathways for achieving safe and sustainable reductions in jail and prison populations while redressing the harm caused to communities of color. I conclude by highlighting the remaining questions and challenges to community-centered approaches in decarceration—a call to action for scholars and practitioners alike.

THE CASE FOR PLACE

There is clear evidence of a social concentration of incarceration among four axes: socioeconomic status, gender, age, and race/ethnicity (Clear, 2009). Incarceration is not an "equal opportunity" punishment, and it disproportionately affects particular segments of the general population (Frost & Gross, 2012). Those involved with the criminal justice system are overwhelmingly male, African American young adults with less than a high school education. Effectively, the American penal institution has entrenched the social contours of inequality along these axes and sustained it across the life course, thus normalizing the experience of incarceration among certain populations. Western and Pettit (2010) argue that the social and economic disadvantage resulting from such a dynamic is largely underestimated because it is invisible, it is cumulative, and it is intergenerational. However these sociodemographic contours of incarceration fail to account for the places incarcerated individuals come from and return to.

Emerging scholarship highlights evidence for a fifth axis of concentration: place. Multiple empirical studies have determined that the majority of state correctional populations come from a small number of highly disadvantaged communities[2] (Clear & Austin, 2009; Sampson & Loeffler, 2010; Urban Institute, n.d.).

An Urban Institute study in Maryland revealed that 60% of released prisoners return back to six specific communities of Baltimore's total of 55 community areas (Visher, Kachnowski, La Vigne, & Travis, 2004). These six communities have the city's highest

---

[2] The terms "community" and "neighborhood" are used interchangeably and clarified where necessary. *Community* often refers to a connection based on a shared quality (e.g., shared religious belief, place of residence, racial identity) and can transcend geographic boundaries. *Neighborhood* is a distinctly spatial construct and refers to a specific territory that often bears a particular identity. When used in this chapter, both "community" and "neighborhood" are referencing primarily geographic territory. Provided the spatial and social concentration of incarceration within a particular group of individuals, the term "community" references the shared beliefs and disposition of such individuals on the criminal justice system.

rates of extraction (i.e., incarceration rates), highest proportions of female-headed households, and some of the most violent neighborhoods (Visher et al., 2004). Similarly, in Cleveland the majority of released prisoners return back to five of 36 community areas (Visher & Courtney, 2007), and in Chicago there is a concentration in five of 77 community areas (Visher & Farrell, 2005). These studies substantiate that reentry is taking place on a large scale in a handful of localities.

Community as the Epicenter of Crime and Victimization

The "case for place" provides an alternative lens for decarceration efforts to understand prison and jail cycling and prevention strategies. The prevailing approach to criminal justice reform has been to institute changes in the response to individual crimes, prosecution of individual cases, and management of individual offenders (Clear, 1998). This alternative lens challenges the individual case orientation strategy.

Place matters. "High stakes," "high incarceration," "high impact areas," and "hot spots" are rotating terms that reference localities where criminal justice responses to crime are concentrated at extreme levels. In high stakes communities there is evidence of spatial clustering of crime, incarceration, and supervision (Weisburd & Eck, 2004). For example, just 3% of all street segments and intersections generated more than half of all gun violence in Boston (Braga, Papachristos, & Hureau, 2010). Left in the wake in such places are the victims of the crimes, their families, and all of the individuals exposed to crime. Exposure to regular incidents of violence normalizes victimization and creates ecological backdrops for child development in such places. Young men and women are socialized to navigate their community and schools with the fear of encountering violence. Furthermore, incarceration casts a shadow on the proximal processes of child development as it ensnares parents, siblings, and people in the immediate social network of youth (Murray, Farrington, & Sekol, 2012; Santiago & Galster, 2014). There is a strong link between exposure to violence, victimization, and subsequent offending (Ousey, Wilcox, & Fisher, 2011). Furthermore, juveniles have higher rates of offending and demonstrate the most robust association between victimization and perpetration (Jennings, Higgins, Tewksbury, Gover, & Piquero, 2010). Therefore, the young people left in the wake of crime are at high risk of perpetuating the cycle of concentrated violence in that particular place.

Community as the Epicenter of Punishment

Incarceration trends are not equitably distributed across urban landscapes. In some cities, areas of concentration could be neighborhoods, whereas in other cities they could be zip codes, districts, or even further geographically defined areas. These areas of concentrated mass incarceration have been called "million dollar blocks," given that the criminal justice system spends millions of dollars removing individuals from them (Cadora, 2014).

Rather than being invested in the community infrastructure, these resources are being used to incarcerate neighborhood residents, which contributes to these neighborhoods' loss of human capital.

In an analysis of the spatial concentration of incarceration in Chicago, Sampson and Loeffler revealed, "there is a dense and spatially contiguous cluster of areas in near-west and south-central Chicago that have rates of incarceration some eight times higher (or more)" (2010, p. 3), whereas other spatial contiguities in the cities are virtually untouched by the incarceration boom. Similar to crime, "there is a great deal of stability in the spatial logic of incarceration" over time (2010, p. 3). Though crime rates are made public through media distribution, the concentration of incarceration and its disproportionate impact within discrete geographic confines are not discussed as a public matter. For this reason, mass incarceration is a normalized reality for some urban residents and a distant social "issue" for others.

Community as the Epicenter of Surveillance

Not only are crime and mass incarceration concentrated within particular spatial contiguities but also mass reentry is geographically confined. First, it is important to acknowledge the scale at which reentry from prison and jails is occurring. Miller (2015) argues that the United States status quo is one of "mass supervision," with approximately 78 million Americans living with criminal records and 20 million with felony convictions (in comparison to approximately 750,000 inmates in jails and approximately 1.6 million inmates in state and federal prisons on any given day). Second, these masses are most often returning to the same places from which they come. Since the mid-1980s the majority of prison releases on a national level were to major metropolitan areas, a trend that has provocatively been described as "a recursive and deeply regressive relationship . . . between the prison system on one hand and African-American ghetto neighborhoods on the other" (Peck & Theodore, 2008, p. 254). The spatial clustering of individuals under correctional surveillance has implications for local public safety and reentry outcomes. Through evaluating postrelease outcomes of more than 31,000 parolees in three major Ohio cities, Chamberlain and Wallace (2015) uncovered that the concentration of parolees in a particular neighborhood exerts an independent effect on individual recidivism. The study demonstrates that returning citizens who reintegrated into neighborhoods with high concentrations of formerly incarcerated individuals had higher recidivism rates than those returning to neighborhoods with lesser concentration of former inmates, perhaps due to the limitations in developing prosocial networks or the exhaustion of local reentry resources.

The confluence of such factors raises the question of whether neighborhood incarceration is part of neighborhood disadvantage, rather than a restorative response to neighborhood problems. It should come as no surprise that the same communities bearing the heaviest imprint of the criminal justice system are also those with the highest rates of poverty, minority concentration, poor health outcomes, and fewest resources. The focus on communities has been one of surveillance, enforcement, and extraction without a concomitant process of investment, engagement, and solutions. Therefore, while the federal government and state institutions take measures to dismantle the criminal justice system's overly punitive approach, immediate solutions can be implemented at the community level to alleviate the consequences of historical racism, discrimination, and postindustrial divestment of labor market resources. Such solutions are wider in scope than individualistic responses to crime and provide a rich experimental context for evaluating solutions that could be replicated at scale throughout state governments.

Ecological Consequences

There are clear ecological consequences of the disproportionate burden of crime, incarceration, reentry, and supervision that particular neighborhoods bear. One could even call this penal regime the "war on neighborhoods" (Chicago's Million Dollar Blocks, n.d.). The practice of incarceration "does not end at the boundaries of the prison" (Brown, 2014, p. 377) and extends into locations to which formerly incarcerated individuals return. Contrary to the often-used "warehouse" descriptor for prisons and jails, the walls of such institutions are highly permeable. The average "inflow" and "outflow" from institutions can be roughly equivalent. When this trend is considered in conjunction with the high rates of recidivism, it becomes clear that the same individuals are cycling in between the criminal justice system and their communities (Peck & Theodore, 2008). This dynamic, also known as *prison cycling* or *prison migration*, has negative public safety implications, an area of particular concern for achieving meaningful decarceration.

Crime and Incarceration: A Bidirectional Relationship

It is often purported that incarceration enhances public safety and reduces community violence. Contrary to this assumption, two studies illustrate the bidirectional relationship (i.e., forced removal and eventual return) between crime and incarceration.

Coercive mobility is the forced removal of individuals through incarceration. The coercive mobility thesis elaborates on prison cycling (Clear, Rose, Waring, & Scully, 2003) by considering the bidirectional quality of prison cycling often within the same place. Clear and colleagues (2003) compared the effects of coercive mobility to high residential mobility. High residential mobility has a deleterious effect on community life: It engenders isolation and a low degree of social integration, decreases the likelihood of collective action, and reduces social cohesion and commitment to a particular locality (Sampson & Loeffler, 2010). According to the thesis, forced removal of large numbers of individuals disrupts social ties, weakens social networks, and damages informal social control mechanisms—all of which adversely affects public safety.

The coercive mobility thesis challenges the widely held assumption about crime and incarceration by suggesting that concentrated mass incarceration can produce the very issue it is trying to resolve: crime. Clear tested the thesis in Tallahassee, Florida, resulting in evidence that incarceration decreases crime rates *up to a certain point*; however, once a particular threshold is reached (i.e., the "tipping point"), increased incarceration results in increased crime rates (Clear et al., 2003). He examined prison admissions from Leon County (where Tallahassee is situated) and prison releases to Leon County as well as crime data from the Tallahassee police department. Analysis indicated that increasing prison admissions had a negligible effect on crime the following year and revealed a strong positive effect of releasing offenders into a community and crime rates one year later.

Several other empirical studies confirmed the "tipping point" concept in the coercive mobility thesis in communities in Baltimore and Portland, Oregon (Lynch & Sabol, 2004; Renauer et al., 2006). The consensus of these studies indicates that the incapacitative benefits of incarceration are limited due to the destabilizing effects of the forced removal of a significant number of individuals and the depletion of familial, economic, and political social supports (Renauer, Cunningham, Feyerherm, O'Connor, & Bellatty, 2006). The threshold is different for each community; there is no universal local incarceration threshold past which crime rates start to increase. Nonetheless, such research further elucidates the differential impact incarceration has based on spatial and social location. The evidence also confirms the strategic outline developed within the Smart Decarceration Initiative to consider both public safety and well-being and reductions in prison populations together, not as separate or distinct operations (see Chapter 1).

Fagan, West, and Hollan (2002) demonstrate how incarceration becomes an embedded force that affects community ecology through the churning effect on social networks, destabilization of informal social control mechanisms, and generation of more punitive police enforcement. By describing incarceration as an "ecological force," the authors contend that incarceration becomes a local factor that shapes the dynamic interrelations between people, their peer networks, community, and societal structures (Fagan et al., 2002). For example, in response to changes in drug law and policy, the New York Police Department implemented aggressive policing initiatives targeting drug sellers. Two examples include "Operation Pressure Point," targeting outdoor retail drug markets, and the expansion of Tactical Narcotics Teams into minority neighborhoods where crack is sold. As a result of these tactics, the number of felony drug arrests skyrocketed as did the proportion of felony drug offenders in local jails and prisons. Such initiatives also raised complaints from minority citizens about the disproportionate minority impact of such measures and criminal justice measures imposed considering that most offenders were nonviolent and presented no public safety threat. Their statistical analysis of crime trends and incarceration data reveal "there are social, economic, legal, and political mechanisms through which incarceration is transformed from an acute external shock to an enduring internal feature of the neighborhood fabric" (Fagan et al., 2002, p. 1554).

To prove their point, jail admission rates grew despite declining drug arrests and serious crime rates. The study concludes with the disturbing, yet proven, revelation that in high stakes communities, incarceration becomes endogenous, or "grown from within" (Fagan et al., 2002, p. 1589). In other words, the assumed primary "generator" of incarceration is no longer crime.

The evidence reviewed thus far describes how the social structure of neighborhoods and social control measures become integrated. When the penal system was expanded to its current reach, it created a self-generating system within particular communities; incarceration begets more incarceration. Such communities have been stripped of their infrastructure, the majority of men have criminal backgrounds, and there is little viable local employment or resources available to support families. The main government institution, then, to intervene in such circumstances regardless of the crime level would be the prison system.

COMMUNITY-CENTERED SMART DECARCERATION

In the era following mass incarceration, high stakes communities are sites where optimal impact in achieving safe and sustainable decarceration can be realized. Institutions across the criminal justice spectrum (from police to parole) operate with a jurisdictional focus that ranges widely in geographic scope, most typically, though, at a municipal level. Given the breadth of such municipalities, most agencies operate as centralized bureaucracies with standardized operations to facilitate some level of efficiency. Strategies that embrace the notion of *community justice* function with a smaller operational focus of justice, where different localities formulate different solutions to address the public safety concerns and needs of their respective justice-involved populations. The definition of community justice is rooted in "the actions of citizens, community organizations, and the criminal justice system . . . shifting the focus from individual conscience to social mores, and from individual goods to the common good" (Karp & Clear, 2000, p. 323). A community-centered approach responds to crime with consideration of its implications for the quality of life of the victim(s) and the affected locality. Such an approach is distinct from adversarial processes or "negative social control" measures typically exercised by the criminal justice system, which extract individuals from their community and invest public dollars in their confinement. From a community justice perspective, policing and incarceration neither address the root cause of crime nor repair the harm it causes. Thus, community justice attempts to strengthen community bonds between offenders and their victims to repair harm inflicted, and also to recognize that offenders are integral parts of local social networks and could be conceptualized as a resource to their communities.

In this section, I critically analyze responses that embrace a community focus of justice. It is important to keep in mind that community-centered solutions can achieve smart decarceration when community stakeholders formulate and continually evaluate them through an iterative process. In the absence of these key elements, community-centered solutions can aggravate the existing disparities within the criminal justice system and contribute to incarceration rates. Therefore, community-centered solutions should not be considered the "silver bullet" of decarceration. Rather, they are a strategy that could achieve considerable progress in decarceration strategies with significant impact within populations most affected by mass incarceration.

Community and Policing

The criminal justice system can be compared to a hydraulic system, with the flow and pressure determined by one of the primary gatekeepers of the system: the police. Two of the police's primary functions are to protect citizens and prevent future crime. As such, crime prevention strategies since the 1990s have focused on using "intelligence" (i.e., data) to identify and target (1) high crime places, or (2) high crime networks (e.g., gangs). Both strategies arguably adhere to more localized/focused deterrence strategies within a more collaborative framework (as promoted within a community justice framework). Most famous among these strategies is "broken window policing," where community neglect or apathy (e.g., broken windows, abandoned property) is seen as a breakdown of social infrastructure and indicative of a larger social issue. Law enforcement strategies along this line of logic that address minor offenses have the potential to ward off more serious criminal activity. Individuals caught engaging in crimes that disturb the quality of life (e.g., vandalism, prostitution) would be severely punished. In addition, police target areas of urban decay in partnership with residents to transform blighted areas into viable public spaces.

Policing strategies targeting high crime networks often use social network analysis as a prevention strategy. *Social network analysis* allows police to map out crime networks and generate patterns of interactions and social behaviors of social actors within the network. Two different forms of policing using social network analysis to drive crime prevention strategies include the Boston Ceasefire model and Violence Reduction Strategies. Both strategies embody "pulling levers" tactics for law enforcement, in which police target specific individuals presenting specific criminal behaviors (e.g., carrying and using firearms) to use specific sanctions and punishment as a deterrence mechanism (Braga, Papachristos, & Hureau, 2010). Community members are often engaged in assisting police with the delivery of deterrence messages. For example, the mother of a homicide victim could be called on to speak to a group of gang-involved individuals about the consequences of their activities on the street.

On the surface, such policing strategies are ostensibly consistent with the goals of smart decarceration. Data should inform policing strategies and, as public servants, police officers should collaborate with community. However, evaluation of such policing efforts has yielded mixed results. For example, a recent evaluation of Violence Reduction Strategies revealed a 32% reduction in gunshot victimization 1 year following the intervention within the targeted gang factions (Papachristos & Kirk, 2015). However, the acclaimed success has been viewed with suspicion, considering the quasiexperimental design claiming to compare treatment and nontreatment groups without any way to verify noninterference between the "treated" gang factions and the "control" gang factions (Gravel & Tita, 2015). At best there are marginal gains in public safety.

At worst, aggressive data-driven policing leads to the overpolicing of black communities. "Being overpoliced for the small stuff, and underpoliced for the important stuff, alienates the community, undercuts cooperation and fuels private violence: which itself often then drives even more intrusive policing, more alienation, lower clearance rates, and still more violence" (Kennedy, 2015). Sustained over time, such practices have developmental implications for young men and women of color. Elijah Anderson explains, "The intensified police presence in poor black communities fosters a negative association in residents from a young age," one that leads them to believe that the police exist not to "protect and serve" but to criminalize and humiliate them (2014). Stop-and-frisk practices in communities of color serve as examples of such humiliation. Police contact, especially involuntary contact, is a moment of "legal socialization" for young men of color (Tyler, Fagan, & Geller, 2014). A statistically significant association has been confirmed between the number of police stops one witnesses or personally experiences and a diminished sense of police legitimacy (Tyler et al., 2014). A lowered perception of police legitimacy in turn influences one's conformity to the law and willingness to cooperate with the law. The police scholar Anthony Braga concedes,

> an inappropriate police focus on particular people and places—one where the police, in isolation from the community, identify the areas of focus, and where entire neighborhoods are defined as trouble zones—can contribute to racial disparity and mass incarceration problems that harm disadvantaged neighborhoods. (2015, p. 233)

Such tactics, in the end, work against one of the goals of smart decarceration by aggravating existing social disparities within the criminal justice system. Though policing is clearly necessary in poor and minority communities, its current delivery is flawed. This is exemplified by the police-related deaths of Michael Brown (Ferguson), Oscar Grant (Oakland), Cary Ball (St. Louis), LacQuan McDonald (Chicago), and Freddy Gray (Baltimore) among many, many others. In the summer of 2016, national attention was brought to incidents of civilian-inflicted deaths of police officers as well in Dallas, Texas, and Baton Rouge, Louisiana. Police legitimacy, implicit bias, and procedural justice have been topics of conversation in light of such tragedies.

Though a community-centered approach to policing is largely agreed on as an effective way to improve public safety, there is less agreement on how to do it without intentionally or unintentionally harming the perception of reciprocal cooperation between police and communities of color. The International Union of Police Associations indicated they "welcome changes to operations" (Majumdar, 2016). The Black Lives Matter movement, the American Civil Liberties Union, and the National Urban League have all published specific recommendations for police reform and accountability. Their recommendations largely agree on reform in the following areas: end "broken windows policing," use body cameras and dashboard cameras, and institute independent civilian oversight committees to create transparency and accountability to communities.

Community and the Court

Most criminal courts in large urban settings operate in a centralized bureaucratic manner. Individuals arrested for a particular crime filter through a single court site and location. Such courthouses review a range of cases from misdemeanor complaints to violent felony convictions. Following the drug court model, *community courts* are "neighborhood focused courts that attempt to harness the power of the justice system to address local problems" (Center for Court Innovation, 2016). Their genesis is tied to the implementation of "broken windows policing" strategies in New York City under the governance of Mayor Rudy Giuliani. When the mayor declared a war on low-level offenses with zero-tolerance policies enforced by the police, massive numbers of individuals flooded an anemic court system for misdemeanor crimes. Subsequently, New York City started the first community courts (e.g., Midtown Community Court, Red Hook Center, the Brooklyn Defenders) to manage arraignments for the large number of misdemeanor crimes (Thompson, 2002).

Community courts typically focus on just one neighborhood and handle criminal cases focusing on quality-of-life crimes. All use a problem-solving approach to administering justice (versus an adversarial approach) and center solutions on strengthening community. For example, judges in community courts participate in community forums and help connect clients to different local service providers. As a result, judges have increased discretion in how cases are processed and sentenced. Furthermore, community courts enable collaboration between judges, prosecutors, defense attorneys, law enforcement, and community practitioners in ways that are not typical in centralized court systems.

Community courts exemplify the ideals of community justice. Evaluations of Midtown Community Court and Red Hook Center demonstrate that clients of community courts have lower recidivism rates, are more compliant with parole conditions, and have better treatment outcomes (Lee et al., 2013; Sviridoff et al., 2005). A form of alternative sanctioning often used in community courts is to replace short-term jail sentences with community service and social service interventions. Clients processed through community courts report that they feel as though they received better treatment in community court versus criminal court, thus enhancing the legitimacy of the criminal justice system (Lee et al., 2013). One of the reasons why community courts report better outcomes for their clients is more efficient case processing. In addition clients receive better sanctions that are more localized and tailored to their needs. As a result of a more fair and just experience in the court, the clients' attitudes and behaviors toward the system could positively change; "a public that feels respected will be more respectful towards the court" (Sviridoff et al., 2005, pp. 6–9).

Though their individually tailored sanctions and integrated supports result in fewer individuals sent to prison, it is unclear whether community courts substantially reduce prison populations. When an individual sanctioned within a criminal court is non-compliant with alternative arrangements (e.g., social services), they tend to go to prison for longer periods of time (Sevigny, Fuleihan, & Ferdik, 2013). This is consistent with a meta-analysis conducted on drug courts that finds that any benefits from sending fewer people to prison is counterbalanced by longer sentences imposed on individuals who do not comply with treatment (Shaffer, 2011). In other words, community courts can reduce the experience of incarceration for many individuals, "but do not appear to reduce the aggregate, near-term burden placed upon correctional resources" (Sevigny et al., 2013, p. 425).

Furthermore, community courts usually do not deal with felony crimes or serious offenses that can drive prison populations. Based on some arguments that they grew out of problematic "broken windows policing," community courts primarily deal with the consequences of oversurveillance and overpolicing of communities of color. As a result, "community courts ratify arrests that should never have been made, and legitimate cases that should never have been brought" (Steinberg & Albertson, 2016, p. 997). Steinberg and Albertson further argue that community courts' extension of "broken windows policing," with an overly punitive focus on low-level crimes, has exacerbated the disproportionate minority representation within the criminal justice system. One way to interpret such a concern is that system reform within the courts is already too far downstream to effectively reduce prison populations and reduce racial disparities. The more urgent need is to examine where these individuals are coming from (community areas), assess what supports are necessary and available to prevent crime in these places, and address police practices that are ushering people into contact with the system in the first place.

This point raises the question of whether community courts necessarily operate in the interest of communities of color. The "community" aspect of the court should pervade every dimension of functioning within the setting—from the way judges exercise judicial discretion to the engagement of local service providers in crafting alternative sanctions. There is no systematized definition of the community component of such courts; therefore, community participation can be limited to roles such as occasional advisory board meetings. For example, within just a few years of the beginning of the Midtown Court in New York City, there was broad agreement that the priorities of the court had shifted away from the local residents and more toward law enforcement and the business community (Sviridoff et al., 2005). Lee and colleagues (2013) find that successful community courts engender meaningful community participation in the courts by ensuring the following components:

- *Select a proper community court judge* who is willing to engage in community spaces (e.g., town hall meetings) and is comfortable in dealing directly with clients generate to open, collaborative environments within the courtroom.
- *Promote a community identity.* Community courts with a marked community identity inspire local ownership and engagement and can dispel the perception that the institution is a governmental outpost.
- *Seek local knowledge.* All court actors should actively seek out local knowledge to assist in accurate decision-making and sanctioning. Such principles can ensure that a community justice ideal is realized within the courthouse, even if significant reductions in prison populations are not attained.

Community and Supervision

Community corrections—primarily probation and parole—are considered meaningful alternatives to incarceration. Community corrections provide more cost-effective solutions to managing offenders who present low risk to public safety while at the same time keeping families and social networks intact. *Adult probation* is usually an alternative to incarceration that permits an individual convicted of an offense to live and work in the community while complying with several court-ordered mandates, which may include participation in social service interventions, payment of fines or restitutions, or community service. *Adult parole* typically follows a period of incarceration and is considered part of the sentence served. An individual is usually put on parole after an evaluation from a prisoner review board and when he or she is deemed no longer a threat to public safety.

Both probation and parole have multiple competing goals: accountability, recidivism reduction, offender rehabilitation, and alternative to incarceration. The function of community supervision has changed significantly with the rise of mass incarceration. When comparing 2010 levels to 1980 levels of the American population under the control of the U.S. correctional system, there were 3.8 times more people on parole (840,676 versus 220,438) and 3.6 times more people on probation (4.06 million versus 1.12 million) (Glaze & Parks, 2011).

This tremendous growth has not been accompanied with an increase in resources allocated to support adequate service provision. Traditional supervision methods that focus primarily on offender management and compliance with court mandates are not effective in recidivism reduction or in offender rehabilitation (Latessa, 2013). In fact, inadequate community supervision can actually increase prison populations. Overworked probation and parole officers with large caseloads in underresourced communities struggle finding adequate time and social services for clients under supervision to assist in compliance with their court mandates. Such factors can increase the vulnerability of clients going back to prison for a technical violation of their supervision requirements. In the state of Illinois the number of individuals returned to the Department of Corrections for technical violations has ranged from 6,000 to 10,000 annually since 2010. Such high numbers of technical violators raises the question why community supervision so often fails and what evidence-based practices exist to support successful reintegration. This analysis is urgent, as a decarceration strategy advocated by some state governments has to allow for more offenses to be "probationable" to reduce prison populations. Such an effort could lead to "back-end net-widening" of the prisons (Tonry & Lynch, 1996).

The Maryland Division of Parole and Probation integrated research findings to implement a strategy called Proactive Community Supervision (PCS). One of the components of this model is to use a place-based strategy in which individuals are supervised within their own communities. Such a practice stands in contrast to other standard probation/parole practices of mandating individuals to meet with their supervisor in a centralized office (often far from their community of residence). Through an evaluation that uses a random selection-individual match design, the PCS intervention produced statistically significant differences in rearrests and warrants for technical violation rates (Taxman et al., 2006). The place-based focus of PCS is attributed to the successful outcomes reported. Probation and parole officers implementing PCS conduct home visits and meet with clients in local facilities close to their home, such as a social service agency or a faith-based institution. Officers are also active in the community and participate in local public safety meetings and events.

Similarly, the Maricopa County Adult Probation department in Arizona adopted a community-oriented supervision structure in 1996. Coronado is a neighborhood in Maricopa County to which a large number of formerly incarcerated individuals returned. A satellite probation office was set up in Coronado for individuals on supervision to receive support within their home community, a model that was then expanded to five additional neighborhoods. The probation officers chose to set up their office inside of a local church that provided space to other community service providers, such as legal services, adult education resources, and ESL classes. Next, probation officers conducted a series of small house meetings and discussions with local leaders to understand their concerns about situating a probation office within their community. Within this context, they also established their department as a support in addressing local needs. For example, a block club president asked the assistance of probation officers and their clients with a particular neighborhood project. This community-centered approach resulted in increased compliance with mandates when compared with a control group of probationers who reported to a central office outside the neighborhood (Clear, 2002).

In both Maryland and Maricopa County, data analysis helped identify areas of concentrated mass reentry. These localities served as intervention sites where community supervision services were structured to meet the needs of parolees and improve public safety. The model is upheld as exemplary in the partnership network developed with community organizations and neighborhood leaders: "Partnerships reduce the chances that cases fall through the cracks" (Clear & Karp, 2002, p. 39).

However, similar to community policing and community courts, community-centered supervision can increase the consumption of correctional resources. The actual practice of probation or parole supervision matters greatly in determining outcomes. To reverse the trend of reflexivity in the system (i.e., increasing rates of prison admissions for technical violations of supervision), a rehabilitative focus must be prioritized (Phelps, 2013). When a therapeutic approach or treatment component is integrated into community supervision, the outcomes—particularly recidivism reduction—change significantly. One example of the integration of a therapeutic approach into community supervision is the training of officers in a set of core correctional practices that include skills such as anticriminal modeling, effective reinforcement, structured learning, problem solving, and cognitive restructuring (Latessa, 2013). Such changes could reduce the number of individuals receiving technical violations or committing new crimes, and thus effectively reduce prison populations and advancing the smart decarceration goal of enhancing public safety.

Drawing from these examples, a robust community-based supervision model would incorporate the following components. First, it would move beyond the modus operandi of "offender management." Second, probation and parole departments would incentivize officers to develop local systems of care and support for clients in high stakes communities. A natural consequence of such efforts would be a broadening of the officers' concept of "who is my client" beyond the individual and reaching into their immediate family, peer, and community contexts. Finally, community-based supervision would consider the civic participation of their clients as a vital reintegration component, an effort to rehabilitate their status as citizens.

BEYOND THE SYSTEM: RETHINKING JUSTICE REINVESTMENT

Smart decarceration will not take place through additional investments in the criminal justice system. Given that community clearly lies both upstream of mass incarceration and downstream of its impact, a wiser strategy would be to build more resilient, protective communities. One option is to invest more resources, and not just more surveillance, into high stakes communities, areas that have typically experienced a half-century of divestment due to political and economic shifts in urban environments.

Embracing this notion, *justice reinvestment* broadly refers to strategies that reduce prison populations while steering reinvestment back into the hardest hit communities (Austin et al., 2013). The goals of the justice reinvestment were to make state governments accountable to high stakes communities through data analysis of correctional populations, identifying investment/reinvestment opportunities, and organizing the demand of high incarceration localities. Several states enacted justice reinvestment legislation with mixed results, including Connecticut (2004), Kansas (2007), Texas

(2007), Rhode Island (2008), and Arizona (2008) (Austin et al., 2013). In all states that enacted justice reinvestment reform, none reinvested correctional savings back into the targeted "million dollar blocks." All savings went to support some aspect of the criminal justice system, such as law enforcement or probation. California is the only state that has effectively diverted correctional savings back into the hardest hit communities through Proposition 47, which was not connected to the official justice reinvestment effort. A 2013 analysis by the American Civil Liberties Union has attributed the failure of justice reinvestment to the following five causes: (1) the failure to affect sentencing legislation on admissions and length of stay, (2) failure to involve local stakeholders, (3) failure to focus on the long-term sustainability of the efforts, (4) abandonment of reinvestment in high incarceration communities, and (5) absence of structural incentives to pursue noncarceral public safety strategies.

A better strategy for building stronger, more resilient communities could be justice "preinvestment." In other words, the capacity of high stakes communities sending and receiving large numbers of individuals to the criminal justice system must be built up before, not after, population reductions and prison savings are realized. Otherwise, reductions in prison populations run the risk of repeating the history of decommissioning state mental health institutions in the 1960s. Although the state hospital population went down by over 60% between 1965 and 1975, the majority of the individuals did not receive community-based care and ended up homeless, in jails, or in prisons (Gralnick, 1985).

A separate government approach to decarceration is to defund state prisons by dismantling state financial apparatuses that pay for corrections. Ball argues that the "correctional free lunch" problem is at the heart of the overuse of prisons (2013). Though local agencies (e.g., police and court systems) drive criminal justice responses, in most cases the state pays for imprisonment costs. An alternative funding apparatus would be to proportion block grants to local governments (such as a county) to cover all of their criminal justice needs ranging from police to incarceration. This would enhance the autonomy of local governments in designing public safety strategies as well as forcing them to internalize the costs of their decisions. Such a strategy may or may not reduce incarceration levels. Some localities may decide to incarcerate at the same rate and have the will to pay for it. Such a decision, however, would reflect local values of that particular geography rather than the easiest/most low-cost option available.

If government-led justice reinvestment has a dubious future in reducing incarceration, what potential strategies exist to redress the "enmeshment" of the prison and the ghetto (Wacquant, 2001)? Two possibilities exist: community organizing led by the formerly incarcerated and community development. Inclusive community development initiatives have the potential to reverse the decades of divestment that have taken place in high stakes community areas. Evidence suggests that residential involvement in local initiatives can improve sense of control, empowerment, individual coping, and health behaviors (Wallerstein & Duran, 2006). Such organizing strategies—when inclusive of individuals with felony convictions—hold potential for community building and systems change. Community building strategies that hold potential for decarceration include expansion of prevention and early intervention programs as well as specific supports needed for the justice-involved populations. California, for example, reinvested the majority of prison savings realized through Proposition 47 into underperforming schools across the state. Such a strategy clearly addresses the problematic "school-to-prison-pipeline" often cited as a stimulant of mass incarceration (Meiners & Winn, 2010). The inclusion of the formerly incarcerated in development efforts is essential, as they are best able to articulate the needs of individuals who are in contact with the criminal justice system.

Organizing led by formerly incarcerated individuals also holds great potential for enhancing the collective citizenship of historically disenfranchised communities. Some scholars have even gone so far as to argue "some of the most interesting political work around the country is happening among organizations trying to mobilize those segments of society too often deemed deviant . . . people incarcerated and reentering their communities" (Cohen, 2004, p. 41). The work of coalitions and organizations focused on individuals with felony convictions not only facilitates the restoration of citizenship to the formerly incarcerated but also rehabilitates citizenship in their neighborhoods (Owens, 2014). Combined, inclusive development and organizing efforts could effectively extract "high incarceration neighborhoods from the shackles of criminal justice governance" (Cadora, 2014, p. 280).

CONCLUSION

In an era of smart decarceration, measures must be taken to shift spatial patterns and reverse trends of surveillance and extraction from marginalized communities. Community-centered solutions move beyond trying to fix a broken system through reforms recommended by system stakeholders. The approach outlined in this chapter identifies the residents of high incarceration communities as the primary stakeholders in decarceration efforts. Such a perspective can inspire justice innovation through leveraging the collective history of communities that have become penal outposts in the past half-century. Community residents, activists, leaders, and service providers must be prepared to offer their own decarceration plans constructed in partnership with the formerly incarcerated in this new era. You cannot bang down the door of reform and present yourself empty-handed. The evidence reviewed indicates a change in tide in criminal justice reform—those who have thus far not been recognized as sources of wisdom and innovation must now prepare *their* case for *their* place.

REFERENCES

Anderson, E. (2014, August 13). What caused the Ferguson riot exists in so many other cities, too. *Washington Post*. Retrieved from https://www.washingtonpost.com/posteverything/wp/2014/08/13/what-caused-the-ferguson-riot-exists-in-so-many-other-cities-too/

Austin, J., Cadora, E., Clear, T. R., Dansky, K., Greene, J., Gupta, V., . . . Young, M. C. (2013). *Ending mass incarceration: Charting a new justice reinvestment.* Washington, DC: The Sentencing Project.

Ball, W. D. (2013). *Defunding state prisons.* Santa Clara University. Retrieved from http://digitalcommons.law.scu.edu/cgi/viewcontent.cgi?article=1606&context=facpubs

Berman, D. A. (2008). Reorienting progressive perspectives for twenty-first century punishment realities. *Harvard Law and Policy Review Online, 3,* 1–20.

Braga, A. A. (2015). Better policing can improve legitimacy and reduce mass incarceration. *Harvard Law Review, 129,* 233.

Braga, A. A., Papachristos, A. V., & Hureau, D. M. (2010). The concentration and stability of gun violence at micro places in Boston, 1980–2008. *Journal of Quantitative Criminology, 26*(1), 33–53.

Brown, E. (2014). Expanding carceral geographies: Challenging mass incarceration and creating a "community orientation" towards juvenile delinquency. *Geographica Helvetica, 69,* 377.

Cadora, E. (2014). Civics lessons: How certain schemes to end mass incarceration can fail. *The ANNALS of the American Academy of Political and Social Science, 651,* 277–285.

Center for Court Innovation. (2016). *Overview of community courts.* Retrieved from http://www.courtinnovation.org/topic/community-court

Chamberlain, A. W., & Wallace, D. (2015). Mass reentry, neighborhood context and recidivism: Examining how the distribution of parolees within and across neighborhoods impacts recidivism. *Justice Quarterly,* 1–30.

Chicago's Million Dollar Blocks. (n.d.). Website. Retrieved from http://chicagosmilliondollarblocks.com/

Clear, T. R. (1998). *Community justice as public safety* (pp. 11–14). Paper delivered to the Conference of the American Society of Criminology, Washington, DC.

Clear, T. R. (2002). The problem with "addition by subtraction": The prison-crime relationship in low-income communities. In M. Chesney-Lind & M. Mauer (Eds.), *Invisible punishment: The collateral consequences of mass imprisonment,* 181–194. New York, NY: The New Press.

Clear, T. R. (2009). *Imprisoning communities: How mass incarceration makes disadvantaged neighborhoods worse.* New York, NY: Oxford University Press.

Clear, T. R., & Austin, J. (2009). Reducing mass incarceration: Implications of the iron law of prison populations. *Harvard Law and Policy Review, 3,* 307.

Clear, T. R., & Karp, D. R. (2002). *What is community justice? Case studies of restorative justice and community supervision.* Thousand Oaks, CA: Sage.

Clear, T. R., Rose, D. R., Waring, E., & Scully, K. (2003). Coercive mobility and crime: A preliminary examination of concentrated incarceration and social disorganization. *Justice Quarterly, 20*(1), 33–64.

Cohen, C. J. (2004). Deviance as resistance: A new research agenda for the study of black politics. *Du Bois Review, 1*(1), 27–45.

Fagan, J., West, V., & Hollan, J. (2002). Reciprocal effects of crime and incarceration in New York City neighborhoods. *Fordham Urban Law Journal, 30,* 1551.

Frost, N. A., & Gross, L. A. (2012). Coercive mobility and the impact of prison-cycling on communities. *Crime, Law and Social Change, 57*(5), 459–474.

Glaze, L. E., & Parks, E. (2011). Correctional populations in the United States, 2011. *Population, 6*(7), 8.

Gralnick, A. (1985). Build a better state hospital: Deinstitutionalization has failed. *Psychiatric Services, 36*(7), 738–741.

Gravel, J., & Tita, G. E. (2015). With great methods come great responsibilities. *Criminology and Public Policy*. Retrieved from http://onlinelibrary.wiley.com/doi/10.1111/1745-9133.12147/abstract

Jennings, W. G., Higgins, G. E., Tewksbury, R., Gover, A. R., & Piquero, A. R. (2010). A longitudinal assessment of the victim–offender overlap. *Journal of Interpersonal Violence, 25*(12), 2147–2174.

Karp, D. R., & Clear, T. R. (2000). Community justice: A conceptual framework. *Boundaries Changes in Criminal Justice Organizations, 2,* 323–368.

Kennedy, D. (2015, April 10). Black communities: Overpoliced for petty crimes, ignored for major ones. *Los Angeles Times*. Retrieved from http://www.latimes.com/opinion/bookclub/la-reading-los-angeles-kennedy-ghettoside-20150404-story.html

Latessa, E. J. (2013). *Evaluation of the effective practices in community supervision model (EPICS) in Ohio*. Doctoral dissertation, University of Cincinnati.

Lee, C. G., Cheesman, F., Rottman, D., Swaner, R., Lambson, S., Rempel, M., & Curtis, R. (2013). *A community court grows in Brooklyn: A comprehensive evaluation of the Red Hook*. Community Justice Center Final Report. Williamsburg, VA: National Center for State Courts.

Lynch, J. P., & Sabol, W. J. (2004). Assessing the effects of mass incarceration on informal social control in communities. *Criminology and Public Policy, 3*(2), 267–294.

Majumdar, B. (February 3, 2016). *Law enforcement agencies welcome changes to operations*. Retrieved from http://multibriefs.com/briefs/IUPA/IUPA020916.php

Meiners, E. R., & Winn, M. T. (2010). Resisting the school to prison pipeline: The practice to build abolition democracies. *Race Ethnicity and Education, 13*(3), 271–276.

Miller, R. J. (2015, September). *Rethinking reentry: Reimagining community corrections in an age of mass supervision*. Presented at Inaugural Smart Decarceration Initiative Symposium in St. Louis, MO.

Murray, J., Farrington, D. P., & Sekol, I. (2012). Children's antisocial behavior, mental health, drug use, and educational performance after parental incarceration: A systematic review and meta-analysis. *Psychological Bulletin, 138*(2), 175.

Ousey, G. C., Wilcox, P., & Fisher, B. S. (2011). Something old, something new: Revisiting competing hypotheses of the victimization-offending relationship among adolescents. *Journal of Quantitative Criminology, 27*(1), 53–84.

Owens, M. L. (2014). Ex-felons' organization-based political work for carceral reforms. *Annals of the American Academy of Political and Social Science, 651*(1), 256–265.

Papachristos, A. V., & Kirk, D. S. (2015). Changing the street dynamic. *Criminology and Public Policy, 14*(3), 525–558.

Peck, J., & Theodore, N. (2008). Carceral Chicago: Making the ex-offender employability crisis. *International Journal of Urban and Regional Research, 32*(2), 251–281.

Phelps, M. S. (2013). The paradox of probation: Community supervision in the age of mass incarceration. *Law and Policy, 35*(1–2), 51–80.

Renauer, B. C., Cunningham, W. S., Feyerherm, B., O'Connor, T., & Bellatty, P. (2006). Tipping the scales of justice the effect of overincarceration on neighborhood violence. *Criminal Justice Policy Review, 17*(3), 362–379.

Sampson, R. J., & Loeffler, C. (2010). Punishment's place: The local concentration of mass incarceration. *Daedalus, 139*(3), 20–31.

Santiago, A. M., & Galster, G. C. (2014). The effects of childhood exposure to neighborhood and community violence: Impacts on the safety and well-being of low-income, minority children. *Journal of Community Practice, 22*(1–2), 29–46.

Sevigny, E. L., Fuleihan, B. K., & Ferdik, F. V. (2013). Do drug courts reduce the use of incarceration? A meta-analysis. *Journal of Criminal Justice, 41*(6), 416–425.

Shaffer, D. K. (2011). Looking inside the black box of drug courts: A meta-analytic review. *Justice Quarterly, 28*(3), 493–521.

Steinberg, R., & Albertson, S. (2016). The underbelly of the beast: Misdemeanor practice on the era of broken windows policing: Broken windows policing and community courts: An unholy alliance. *Cardozo Law Review, 37*, 995–1127.

Sviridoff, M., Rottman, D. B., Weidner, R., Cheesman, F., Curtis, R., Hansen, R., & Ostrom, B. (2005). *Dispensing justice locally: The impacts, costs and benefits of the Midtown Community Court.* New York, NY: Center for Court Innovation.

Taxman, F. S., Yancey, C., & Bilanin, J. E. (2006). *Proactive community supervision in Maryland: Changing offender outcomes.* Maryland Division of Parole and Probation. Retrieved from https://www.dpscs.state.md.us/publicinfo/publications/pdfs/PCS_Evaluation_Feb06.pdf

Thompson, A. C. (2002). Courting disorder: Some thoughts on community courts. *Washington University Journal of Law and Policy, 10*, 63.

Tonry, M., & Lynch, M. (1996). Intermediate sanctions. *Crime and Justice, 20*, 99–144.

Tyler, T. R., Fagan, J., & Geller, A. (2014). Street stops and police legitimacy: Teachable moments in young urban men's legal socialization. *Journal of Empirical Legal Studies, 11*(4), 751–785.

Urban Institute. (n.d.). *Returning home study: Understanding the challenges of prisoner reentry.* Retrieved from http://www.urban.org/policy-centers/justice-policy-center/projects/returning- home-study-understanding-challenges-prisoner-reentry

Visher, C. A., & Courtney, S. M. (2007). *One year out: Experiences of prisoners returning to Cleveland.* Urban Institute. Retrieved from http://www.urban.org/research/publication/one-year-out-experiences-prisoners-returning-cleveland

Visher, C., & Farrell, J. (2005). *Chicago communities and prisoner reentry.* Urban Institute. Retrieved from http://www.urban.org/research/publication/chicago-communities-and-prisoner-reentry

Visher, C. A., Kachnowski, V., La Vigne, N. G., & Travis, J. (2004). *Baltimore prisoners' experiences returning home.* Washington, DC: Urban Institute.

Wacquant, L. (2001). Deadly symbiosis when ghetto and prison meet and mesh. *Punishment and Society, 3*(1), 95–133.

Wallerstein, N. B., & Duran, B. (2006). Using community-based participatory research to address health disparities. *Health Promotion Practice, 7*(3), 312–323.

Western, B., & Pettit, B. (2010). Incarceration and social inequality. *Daedalus.* Retrieved from https://www.amacad.org/content/publications/pubContent.aspx?d=808

Weisburd, D. L., & Eck, J. E. (2004). What can police do to reduce crime, disorder, and fear? *Annals of the American Academy of Political and Social Science, 593*, 42–65.

PART III

Rethinking Policy and Practice

9

Minimizing the Maximum

THE CASE FOR SHORTENING ALL PRISON SENTENCES

Nazgol Ghandnoosh

APPETITE FOR DECARCERATION

Crime rates have been plummeting for over 2 decades in the United States. The murder rate and reported rates of violent and property crimes fell by half between 1991 and 2014 (Federal Bureau of Investigation [FBI], 2016). Yet the incarceration rate continued to soar during much of this period. In recent years, the criminal justice landscape has begun to shift. The public has grown less punitive, and policymakers and practitioners have also changed course. Though these developments are promising, I demonstrate in this chapter that they have yet to reach the scale needed to produce meaningful decarceration.

Waning Punitive Sentiment

A 2014 poll by the Pew Research Center revealed that a growing majority of Americans (63%) supported moving away from mandatory prison terms for nonviolent drug crimes (compared to 47% in 2001). Public opinion has grown less punitive for more serious crimes as well. Mark Ramirez (2013) has charted historical changes in punitive sentiment, which he defines as public support for the death penalty, harsher judicial sentencing, increased law enforcement authority, and increased spending for tougher police enforcement (Figure 9.1).

He found that "public support for all four policies increased during the 1970s, plateaued in 1994, and declined afterward" (Ramirez, 2013, p. 338). By 2013, only a slim majority of Americans supported these punitive policies.

FIGURE 9.1 Punitive sentiment in the United States, 1950–2013.
Source: Data from Mark D. Ramirez.

Bipartisan Political Support for Decarceration

Political leaders are also increasingly eschewing the tough-on-crime rhetoric and policies of the past, particularly for nonviolent crimes. In a 2015 speech about the criminal justice system, President Barack Obama said, "For nonviolent drug crimes, we need to lower long mandatory minimum sentences—or get rid of them entirely." Until that point, then Attorney General Eric Holder had been the administration's champion for criminal justice reform, advocating for policies and practices that were "smart on crime," rather than—or rather than just—"tough on crime" (U.S. Department of Justice, 2013). Many of the 2016 presidential candidates also echoed this sentiment early in the election cycle (Chettiar & Waldman, 2015). And advocacy groups from across the political spectrum, including the American Civil Liberties Union (ACLU) and the Center for American Progress on one end, and Koch Industries and Americans for Tax Reform on the other, have supported the growing political consensus that the United States should scale back punishments for nonviolent crimes.

Reforms Have Initiated Decarceration

This changing climate has paved the way for reforms. Four states have led the nation by decarcerating by over 20% since reaching their peak prison populations between 1999 and 2014: New Jersey, New York, Rhode Island, and California (The Sentencing Project, 2016). They achieved this through a mix of measures such as drug sentencing reforms, reduced prison admissions for technical parole violations, and diversion for persons convicted of lower-level crimes (Mauer & Ghandnoosh, 2014). Through reforms like these,

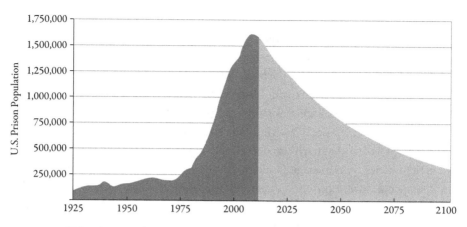

FIGURE 9.2   U.S. prison population: Historical and projected based on 2012 rate of decarceration. *Source*: Mauer and Ghandnoosh (2013).

39 states have at least modestly downsized their prison populations (The Sentencing Project, 2016). The federal prison population has also contracted, by 3% from 2011 to 2014 (The Sentencing Project, 2016; Haile, 2015).

"Can we wait 88 years to end mass incarceration?"

Despite these developments, the overall scale of decarceration has been very modest.[1] The U.S. prison population grew for 37 consecutive years beginning in 1973, increasing by almost 700% (Mauer & Ghandnoosh, 2013). This trend began to reverse in 2010, but the pace of contraction has been slow: a total decline of 3% by 2014. Mauer and Ghandnoosh (2013) estimated that at 2012's annual rate of decarceration—1.8%, the greatest yet—it would take until 2101 for the prison population to return to its 1980 level (Figure 9.2).

This modest and slow pace of decarceration falls short of the goal articulated by several scholars, advocates, and political analysts: a 50% reduction sometime within the next 15 years (Tonry, 2014; Eckholm, 2014; JustLeadershipUSA, 2016; Gingrich & Jones, 2014). Though even halving the U.S. incarceration rate would leave us at twice the level in England and Wales and over four times that of Germany (International Centre for Prison Studies, 2016), we appear to be far from reaching even this target anytime soon.

MEANINGFUL DECARCERATION REQUIRES REDUCING ALL SENTENCES

Existing reform efforts and proposals have not made a significant dent in mass incarceration because they have been limited to a small group of incarcerated individuals. One

---

[1] In contrast, the juvenile justice system has decarcerated more substantially and quickly, halving the number of youth in placement since 2000 (Nellis, 2015; Rovner, 2015).

constraint has been geographic: Decarceration has not occurred evenly across states. California's 34,000-prisoner reduction between 2009 and 2014 accounted for three-quarters of the nationwide decline in incarceration levels during this period (Carson, 2015; Carson & Sabol, 2012). But the bigger obstacle has been the narrowing of reforms to nonviolent crimes, and often to only drug crimes (see Subramanian & Moreno, 2014).[2]

"Even if every person in state prison for a drug offense were released today, mass incarceration would persist," write Ryan King and colleagues (2015). People with drug convictions made up half of the nearly 193,000 people in *federal* prisons in 2014, while those with violent convictions made up a slim minority (7%) (Carson, 2015). But among the 1.3 million people in *state* prisons, this pattern is reversed: 16% had drug convictions while 53% were convicted of violent crimes (Carson, 2015). Thus if the United States released all imprisoned individuals whose most serious offense was a drug crime, its total prison population would decline by 20%. The resulting imprisonment rate, 382 per 100,000, would be two and a half times higher than before the era of mass incarceration (Travis, Western, & Redburn, 2014).

Ending the War on Drugs would have a profound impact on our criminal justice system: In addition to reducing prison admissions for drug convictions, it would also affect people whose nondrug convictions and parole or probation revocations are related to substance abuse. But ending the drug war would leave the other major drivers of mass incarceration largely intact, as described next.

Increased Punitiveness Toward Violent Crimes

Alfred Blumstein showed that in addition to escalated drug law enforcement, the main causes of state prison population growth between 1980 and 2010 were the increased likelihood that arrests would result in prison sentences, and that people would serve longer sentences (Travis et al., 2014; see also Raphael & Stoll, 2013). Recent research reveals the persistence of these trends for violent crimes (Beckett, Knaphus, & Reosti, 2015). In fact, efforts to scale back sentences for lower level offenses are often coupled with measures to expand sentences for serious and violent crimes (Gottschalk, 2015; Seeds, 2015).

The trend toward increasing punitiveness with regard to serious and violent crimes is most pronounced at the extremes. Ashley Nellis (2013) estimated that between 2008 and 2012, the United States continued its "historic rise in life sentences." By 2012, 159,520 individuals (one of every nine imprisoned individuals) were serving life sentences, a 12% rise since 2008.[3] The subset of individuals sentenced to life *without* the possibility of parole

---

[2] Some exceptions to this trend are in the areas of the death penalty (Death Penalty Information Center, 2013) and juvenile life without parole (Rovner, 2016).

[3] The majority of these prisoners are African American or Latino (47% and 16%, respectively; see Nellis, 2013). On how this racial/ethnic composition creates an obstacle for reform, see Ghandnoosh (2014), showing that white Americans' association of crime with African Americans and Latinos is related to their greater support for punitive policies.

grew even more dramatically, by 22% since 2008. By contrast, the total U.S. prison population *declined* by 2% during this period (Carson, 2014; West & Sabol, 2010). And while a majority of these lifers (64%) had homicide convictions (Nellis, 2013), their numbers increased during a period in which the murder rate fell by 13% (FBI, 2016).

As Nellis (2013) explains, the growth in the "lifer" population is due to the greater rate at which people are given these sentences, and to the greater amount of time they serve before being released. California, a state with one-quarter of the country's lifer population, illustrates both of these trends.

The Expansion of Life Sentences and the Erosion of Parole in California

After California passed its "three strikes and you're out" law in 1994, people whose third felony conviction (of any type, until 2012's Proposition 36) was preceded by two serious or violent felonies were mandated to serve a 25-years-to-life sentence. The state has rigorously enforced this law, and in recent years, nearly 8,000 Californians were serving such indeterminate life sentences (California Department of Corrections and Rehabilitation, 2013).[4] Their release from prison depends on discretionary parole approval. These "three strikers" have not yet come up for parole review (Weisberg, Mukamal, & Segall, 2011), but the experience of the state's 26,000 other parole-eligible lifers demonstrates the hurdles they may face.

Through low rates of parole grants by the parole board, gubernatorial overrides of the parole board's decisions, and long waits between parole reviews, California has significantly prolonged the parole approval process. The parole board granted parole in 5% of scheduled hearings between 1991 and 2013, and governor reversals—an additional level of oversight made possible after a 1988 referendum—cut this rate to 3.1% (Ghandnoosh, 2017; see Ghandnoosh, 2016). In 2008, voter-approved Marsy's Law (Proposition 9) increased wait times between hearings, from 1–5 years to 3–15 years. As a result of these polices and practices, the average time served for lifers with murder convictions *released* between 1990 and 2010 has reached 20 years (Weisberg et al., 2011). But according to a spokesperson from California's department of corrections, " 'the average sentence for a prisoner serving a life sentence with the possibly of parole in California is death,' " with more lifers with murder convictions dying in prison than being released between 2000 and 2011 (Mullane, 2012, p. 147). Other states have used these and other strategies to prolong lengths of stay for these incarcerated individuals, or abolished their parole eligibility altogether (Ghandnoosh, 2017; Schwartzapfel, 2015).

The United States cannot end mass incarceration as long as the punitive approach dominates for individuals convicted of serious and violent offenses (Mauer & Cole, 2015; Pfaff, 2015; The Economist, 2015). The remainder of this chapter demonstrates that it is possible to scale back these excessive sentences while protecting public safety.

---

[4] In addition, California's three-strikes law has enhanced sentences for nearly 35,000 people for their second felony.

MASS INCARCERATION'S LIMITED CONTRIBUTION
TO THE CRIME DROP

Understanding mass incarceration's limited contribution to the crime drop of the last 2 decades strengthens the case for dramatic decarceration. Rates of crime reported to the police in the United States grew dramatically beginning in the 1960s, until finally climbing back down in the early 1990s.[5] The murder rate, in particular, began to climb in the 1960s, 1970s, and much of the 1980s, until beginning its deep descent in 1992 (FBI, 2016). During this period, the U.S. prison population exploded: quadrupling between 1972 and 1991, the period of the crime wave, and then doubling again between 1991 and 2014, during the dramatic crime drop (Figure 9.3).

By 2014, the U.S. murder rate was at its lowest point since 1960, while the imprisonment rate was three times higher than in 1960. To what extent has the increased confinement of people in prisons, from about 200,000 in 1973 to 1.5 million in 2014, accounted for this dramatic crime reduction?

Reviewing the research on this question, the authors of a National Research Council report (Travis et al., 2014, p. 4) concluded that "the increase in incarceration may have caused a decrease in crime, but the magnitude of the reduction is highly uncertain and the results of most studies suggest it was unlikely to have been large." Specifically, mass incarceration accounted for as much as 35% or as little as 6% of the crime drop in the 1990s, depending on the type of crime under investigation as well as the methodology and assumptions used by analysts, and it has made almost no contribution to the crime drop since the turn of the century (Baumer, 2008; Roeder, Eisen, & Bowling, 2015; Western, 2006). To further appreciate the weak relationship between incarceration and crime, consider the following examples of jurisdictions that experienced a crime drop without expanding incarceration and that decarcerated without experiencing a crime wave.

A Global Crime Drop Without Mass Incarceration

A global perspective—revealing crime reductions in countries that did not become more punitive—helps to understand why mass incarceration takes only partial credit for the crime drop in the United States. Canada offers the clearest contrast. Though Canada has had a much lower homicide rate and incarceration rate than the United States, changes in the two countries' homicide rates have "tracked each other very closely" since the 1960s (Thompson & Gartner, 2014, p. 92). Yet unlike the United States, the drop in Canada's

---

[5] In contrast to rates of crime reported to the police during the 1970s and 1980s, rates of crime reported on victimization surveys fluctuated for violent crimes and decreased for property crimes during this period (Beckett & Sasson, 2004; Lauritsen, Rezey, & Heimer, 2015).

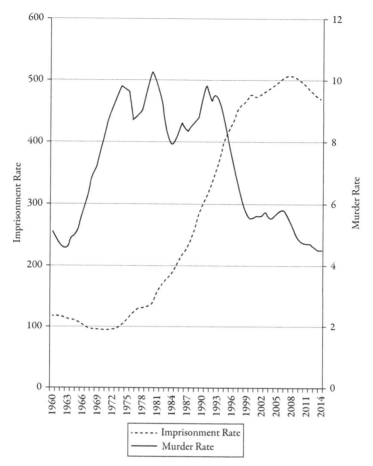

FIGURE 9.3 Murder and imprisonment rates per 100,000 residents in the United States, 1960–2014.
Source: FBI's Crime in the United States series; Sourcebook of Criminal Justice Statistics online; Carson (2015).
Note: Imprisonment rate excludes population in jails. Murder rate includes nonnegligent manslaughter.

homicide rate has occurred alongside very modest growth in its incarceration rate (Figure 9.4) (Doob & Webster, 2006; Zimring, 2007).

Like the United States, Canada's 2013 homicide rate had returned to its 1960s levels. But unlike the United States, Canada's imprisonment rate increased by just 14% between it 1960s average and 2013.

Many other countries also experienced crime drops without expanding incarceration. Tseloni and colleagues (2010) found that between 1988 and 2004, the United States was among 26 countries that experienced comparable reductions in crimes such as assault and personal theft. But countries that implemented more punitive carceral or policing policies, such as the United States and the United Kingdom, did not experience sharper crime reductions than those that did not (see also Tonry & Farrington, 2005).

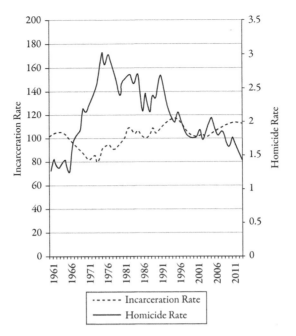

FIGURE 9.4 Homicide and incarceration rates per 100,000 residents in Canada, 1961–2013.
Source: Data from Anthony N. Doob and Cheryl Marie Webster (Doob & Webster, 2006; Zimring, 2007).
Note: Incarceration rate consists of federal and provincial incarcerated individuals, including remand populations.
Homicide rate includes murder, manslaughter, and infanticide.

Fewer Prisoners, Less Crime in New Jersey, New York, and California

Within the United States, states that led in decarceration continued to share the benefits of the nationwide crime drop. Mauer and Ghandnoosh (2014) have shown that during the periods when New York, New Jersey, and California reduced their prison populations by over 20%, they also saw their crime rates decline at a similar and sometimes faster pace than the national average (Table 9.1 presents updated figures).

"During the period that the prison population was declining in these states," they add, "crime rates were declining not only in these states but in virtually all states" (Mauer & Ghandnoosh, 2014, p. 8). And yet most states continued to increase their prison populations amid the crime drop. In fact, an analysis by The Pew Charitable Trusts (2015) revealed that the 10 states with the largest *declines* in imprisonment rates between 2009 and 2014 experienced a 16% decline in crime rates, while the 10 states that had the greatest *increases* in imprisonment rates experienced a comparable, 13%, decline in crime rates. In addition to demonstrating that decarceration is not at odds with public safety, these analyses reinforce that a decrease in crime rates is not enough to bring about decarceration: States must change policies and practices to downsize prisons.

TABLE 9.1

State and National Imprisonment and Crime Trends

State	Peak Imprisonment Year	Prison Population Change, Peak Year to 2014		Violent Crime Rate Change, Peak Year to 2014		Property Crime Rate Change, Peak Year to 2014	
		State	National	State	National	State	National
New Jersey	1999	−31%	+16%	−37%	−30%	−42%	−31%
New York	1999	−28%	+16%	−35%	−30%	−36%	−31%
California	2006	−22%	0%	−26%	−24%	−23%	−22%

Source: *FBI's Crime in the United States series; Bureau of Justice Statistics' Prisoners Series.*

WHY REDUCING ALL SENTENCES WOULD NOT HARM PUBLIC SAFETY

Mass incarceration has had a limited impact on U.S. crime rates because of the diminishing returns of incarceration. When incarceration reaches high levels, imprisoning more people makes a weaker contribution to public safety because "the offender on the margin between incarceration and an alternative sanction tends to be less serious" (Raphael & Stoll, 2014, p. 10). Such diminishing returns come from casting too wide a net—sending too many people to prison—and from keeping people in prison for too long. Below, I focus on long sentences and elaborate on two reasons that they lose their efficacy: Incapacitation is unnecessary when people age out of crime and increased sentence severity has limited deterrent value.

People Age Out of Crime

One of the key functions of prisons is to incapacitate people who are likely to cause harm to others. There are limits and costs to this effect: When drug sellers are removed from communities they are often readily replaced, criminally active groups of young people persevere after the loss of some members, and incarceration can exacerbate postrelease offending (Travis et al., 2014). But society is safer when certain individuals are incarcerated. A key question is: for how long? The answer depends on the direct value of imprisoning harmful individuals through incapacitation and on the indirect value of deterring crime through the threat of long sentences.

Maturity and Social Controls

The "age-crime curve," a long-standing and well-tested concept in criminology, charts the proportion of individuals in each age group that is committing crime (Loeber & Farrington, 2014). The bell-shaped graph (Figure 9.5) depicts the increased prevalence

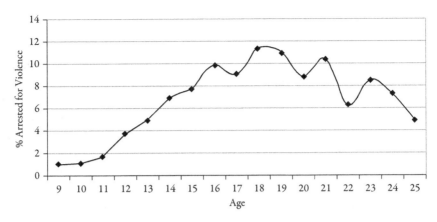

FIGURE 9.5 Age-crime curve.
Source: Loeber and Farrington (2014), based on the Pittsburgh Youth Study

of offending in late childhood, its peak in the teenage years, and its gradual decline in the early 20s.

Though there is considerable variation in the shape of the curve depending on factors such as type of crime committed and socioeconomic status, "crime declines with age *even for active offenders*" (Sampson & Laub, 2003, p. 330, emphasis in original).

Why do individuals age into and out of criminal careers? A key factor in the onset of criminal activity is the transition, between adolescence and adulthood, away from the external controls of guardians to the internal controls of youth themselves. As children grow, the combination of greater individual freedom and incomplete psychological maturation elevates risk of offending (Piquero, Hawkins, & Kazemian, 2012; Sampson & Laub, 1993). During adolescence and into early adulthood, young people gain cognitive capability before they learn to self-regulate by controlling their impulses, considering the impact of their actions on others, delaying gratification, and resisting the influence of peers (Steinberg, Cauffman, & Monahan, 2015).

Drawing on research on adolescent development, the Supreme Court banned capital punishment and limited life-without-parole sentences for crimes committed under age 18 (Steinberg, 2013). Yet "psychosocial development is far from over at age 18," write Laurence Steinberg and colleagues (2015, p. 8), noting that maturation slows at around age 22, and continues in the mid-twenties. Criminal careers finally fade during adult years not only because of greater maturity but also because individuals acquire other forms of social control that promote desistance from crime, such as family and work responsibilities (Piquero et al., 2012; Sampson & Laub, 1993).

These findings help to determine for how long harmful individuals should be incapacitated. Because the propensity to commit crime declines with age, there is little public safety benefit in incapacitating someone who has aged out of crime. Alex Piquero and colleagues (2012, p. 40) observe that existing studies show that "criminal careers are of a short duration (typically under 10 years), which calls into question many of the long-term sentences that have characterized American penal policy."

The Lower Recidivism Rates of Older Adults

Recidivism patterns also reveal that the United States incapacitates people for too long. Older individuals and those who have served time for the most serious offenses are among the least likely to be arrested after release from prison (Durose, Cooper, & Snyder, 2014; Langan & Levin, 2002). In fact, studies consistently show that people who have completed sentences of life with the possibility of parole have some of the lowest recidivism rates (Gottschalk, 2012). But given the human and fiscal costs of prolonged incarceration, the pursuit of near-zero rates of recidivism for lifers is misguided. A closer look at California, whose stringent parole process was described earlier, illustrates this point.

Former California lifers with murder convictions have a "minuscule" recidivism rate for new crimes: among a group of 860 individuals convicted of murder who were paroled since 1995 in California, less than 1% were sentenced to jail or prison for new felonies, and none recidivated for life-term crimes (Weisberg et al., 2011). This compares to the approximately one-in-three rate of reincarceration for new crimes for all formerly imprisoned individuals in California within 3 years of their release (Fischer, 2005).[6] Few policymakers or practitioners advocate for lowering the state's overall recidivism rate by prolonging sentences, but this is the approach used for those with life sentences. The gravity of these individuals' crimes should not cloud the assessment of how to use limited resources to promote public safety. As the authors of the National Research Council report (Travis et al., 2014, p. 337) state, "Because recidivism rates decline markedly with age, lengthy prison sentences, unless they specifically target very high-rate or extremely dangerous offenders, are an inefficient approach to preventing crime by incapacitation."

The Limited Deterrent Value of Longer Sentences

Long prison sentences can promote public safety not only by incapacitating people who pose a significant criminal threat but also by deterring others from criminal offending. So how effective are long prison sentences in deterring crime? Surveying research on this question, Durlauf and Nagin (2011, p. 38) write, "for the general incarceration of aged criminals to be socially efficient, it must have a deterrent effect on younger criminals . . . . Simply no reliable evidence is available that such an effect is sufficiently large to justify the costs of long prison sentences." They recommend that statutes such as California's

---

[6] An additional one-third of released prisoners were reincarcerated for technical parole violations, which Petersilia (2008) notes is often associated with criminal activity proven by the lower evidentiary standard of civil law.

three-strikes law be repealed or greatly narrowed. In the next section, I examine this law's limited impact and discuss the reasons for its limitations.

The Limited Payoff of California's Costly Three-Strikes Law

As described earlier, California's three-strikes law "strikes out" people convicted of a third felony offense by imposing a mandatory 25-years-to-life sentence. When Helland and Tabarrok (2007) compared crime rates among individuals previously convicted of two strike-eligible offenses with a comparable group previously convicted of just one strike-eligible offense, they found that the first group had an approximately 20% lower arrest rate.[7] But they also determined that the imprisonment cost of the three-strikes law, $4.6 billion, far exceeded its public safety contribution—a 2% reduction in the felony crime rate (Zimring, Hawkins, & Kamin, 2001). They concluded that a comparable investment in other measures, of which I present several examples below, would have made a greater dent in crime.

Why Long Sentences Have a Limited Impact on Crime Decisions

The threat of prolonged prison sentences has a limited impact on people's decision-making for several reasons. First, people who break the law may correctly predict that they will not be caught (Mauer, 2006). As Nagin (2013, p. 202, emphasis in original) elaborates, the "*certainty of apprehension* and not the severity of the legal consequence ensuing from apprehension is the more effective deterrent." Second, most people who commit crime are not aware of the legal penalties that they will face (Robinson & Darley, 2004). Finally, substance use and mental health issues may distort the decision-making of even those who are familiar with criminal sentencing (Robinson & Darley, 2004). Factors like these help to explain why studies find that ratcheting up penalties is a high-cost policy with limited public safety payoff.

HOW TO BETTER ALLOCATE PUBLIC RESOURCES TO PROMOTE PUBLIC SAFETY

The pursuit of punitive but ineffective policies has come at the expense of investments in effective crime prevention, drug treatment, and rehabilitative programs. In 2012, the United States spent over $80 billion on federal, state, and local corrections—compared to about $13 billion (adjusted for inflation) in 1971 (Kyckelhahn, 2015; U.S. Department of Justice, 1990). But there has not been a concomitant investment in crime prevention and drug treatment programs, despite public support for these policies—especially from people of color who are most likely to be crime victims (Ghandnoosh, 2014).

---

[7] The familiarity of "two strikers" with this sentencing policy likely increased its deterrent effect.

The High Cost of Incarcerating the Elderly

The soaring cost of corrections is driven not just by the large number of people in prison but also by the higher cost of its fast-growing segment: older incarcerated individuals (Horwitz, 2015). Since 2000, people aged 45 years or older have been the fastest growing age group in state and federal prisons, while the number of individuals aged 25 to 44 years has remained stable and the population aged younger than 25 years has contracted (Beck & Harrison, 2001; Carson, 2015) (Figure 9.6).

Even more specifically, the number of incarcerated individuals aged 55 years or older has more than tripled between 2000 and 2014, reaching over 150,000. This population has grown largely because of longer sentences and a recent uptick in the age of admission (Luallen & Kling, 2014; Porter, Bushway, Hui-Shien, & Smith, 2016).

Imprisoning older individuals is extremely expensive due to the cost of providing medical care in high security environments. A National Institute of Corrections (2004) study estimates that taxpayers pay over twice as much annually to imprison an elderly individual compared to a younger one. The provision of medical care is especially costly for elderly incarcerated individuals because prisons generally lack systems to "monitor chronic problems or to implement preventative measures," and must often transport individuals off-site, with security, for medical care (American Civil Liberties Union, 2012, p. 29; Human Rights Watch, 2012). These expenses come at the cost of investing in effective crime prevention and drug treatment policies.

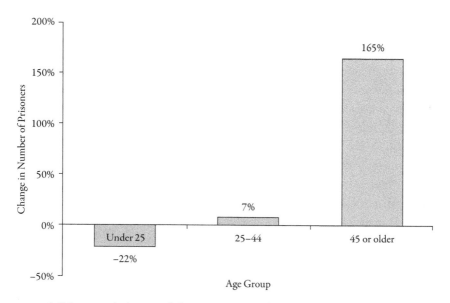

FIGURE 9.6 Prison population growth from 2000 to 2014 by age group.
Source: Beck and Harrison (2001); Carson (2015).

Reallocate Investments Toward Crime Prevention

Increasing access to high-quality early education and reducing residential segregation are two types of investments that would tackle crime at its roots. Preschool education for 3- and 4-year-olds improves later educational outcomes and has been shown to reduce contact with the criminal justice system (Heckman, Malofeeva, Pinto, & Savelyev, 2010; The Sentencing Project, 2013). Yet as the Department of Education (2015) acknowledges, "Children in countries as diverse as Mexico, France, and Singapore have a better chance of receiving preschool education than do children in the United States." Early family/parent training, such as Nurse-Family Partnership programs, also reduces behavior problems among young children (Piquero, Farrington, Welsh, Tremblay, & Jennings, 2009) and should therefore be expanded.

Urban areas with concentrated residential poverty, which are disproportionately inhabited by people of color, have higher crime rates (Peterson & Krivo, 2012; Sampson, Morenoff, & Raudenbush, 2005). Since 2000, "high-poverty neighborhoods and the population living in them has risen at an alarming pace" (Jargowsky, 2015). By promoting housing mobility, programs such as Moving to Opportunity improve young people's educational and employment prospects (Chetty, Hendren, & Katz, 2015) while decreasing criminal justice contact related to violent crime (Kling, Ludwig, & Katz, 2005; Sciandra et al., 2013).[8] We should therefore expand these programs and build on recently renewed efforts to end housing discrimination based on race (see Badger, 2015; Liptak, 2015).

Expand Drug Treatment Programs

In a 2004 survey, 17% of individuals in state prisons said that they committed their crimes to obtain money for drugs, and one-third said that they were under the influence of drugs at the time of their offense (Mumola & Karberg, 2006). Yet in that year, only 40% of individuals in state prisons who met the criteria for drug dependence or abuse had received professional drug treatment or participated in a drug abuse programs since their admission (Karberg & James, 2005; Mumola & Karberg, 2006).[9] The rate was even lower among individuals in jails (18%).

People with limited economic resources also struggle to get timely treatment for substance abuse in their communities. In the 1990s, substance abuse treatment programs that served indigent patients became less likely to provide "treatment on demand" (entry within 48 hours of request) whereas private for-profit programs serving affluent individuals grew more accessible (Friedmann, Lemon, Stein, & D'Aunno, 2003). The gap

---

[8] I thank Reed Jordan for his guidance on this topic.

[9] Other effective rehabilitation policies, such as access to higher education, have been eclipsed in the era of mass incarceration (Davis, Bozick, Steele, Saunders, & Miles, 2013).

between capacity and the need for treatment persists today—though it may be narrowed by the Affordable Care Act—and it is especially pronounced for people under community supervision (Jones, Campopiano, Baldwin, & McCance-Katz, 2015; Gorman, 2014). In 2006, "the prevalence rate of unmet treatment needs for substance alcohol or illicit drug use among parolees was about three times higher (24.2%) than the rate for the rest of the population in the community (8.5%)" (Sung, Mahoney, & Mellow, 2011, p. 46). Reducing spending on incarceration can free up resources to meet these needs.

HOW TO SHORTEN ALL PRISON SENTENCES

Prisons promote public safety by incapacitating and rehabilitating harmful individuals and by deterring others from breaking the law. But because prisons inflict suffering, they should not be overused. Moreover, prisons produce diminishing returns at high levels of incarceration. Yet mandatory sentencing laws, life without parole sentences, and politicized parole policies have created penal excess. Marc Mauer (2015) observes,

> the notion that punishment should be no greater than necessary to achieve a legitimate public purpose has been one of the central conceptions of justice shared by Western nations since the Enlightenment. But in recent decades, the concept of parsimony in punishment has been lost.

To expand existing reform efforts, some observers propose reclassifying certain violent crimes as nonviolent (Neyfakh, 2015; Roth, 2015). But as I have shown in this chapter, achieving meaningful decarceration requires reducing excessive punishment for crimes that most would consider serious or violent. In what follows, I outline three policy reforms to shorten sentences for all incarcerated individuals.

Establish an Upper Limit on Prison Sentences

During his historic address before a joint session of Congress in 2015, Pope Francis called for an abolition of the death penalty, stating, "A just and necessary punishment must never exclude the dimension of hope and the goal of rehabilitation." The death penalty is not the only form of punishment with these characteristics: sentences of life without parole also foreclose hope and make rehabilitation irrelevant. As I have shown, endless as well as excessive incarceration incapacitate many people when they do not pose an unreasonable risk to public safety and displace effective crime-prevention policies. The United States should join other democratic nations, including Germany, France, and Italy (Appleton & Grøver, 2007; van Zyl Smit, 2006), and abolish sentences that amount to death in prison (see also Tonry, 2014; Henry, 2012).

In addition, the federal government and states should, as Mauer (2015; Goldstein, 2015) has suggested, establish an upper sentencing limit of 20 years. This maximum should be used sparingly and can be extended in exceptional circumstances for individual who pose persistent risk to public safety. Curbing the maximum penalty *at the time of sentencing* would respect the human dignity of the convicted and recognize their possibility for rehabilitation and redemption.

Because sentencing structures are generally proportional, a reduced maximum sentence would exert downward pressure on penalties for less serious crimes (Mauer, 2015). In carrying this out, judges should be guided in their sentencing decisions not by legislators setting mandatory minimum sentences, but by sentencing commissions setting sentencing guidelines. As specialized administrative agencies, sentencing commissions are more insulated from political pressures, and their expertise makes them "much better suited than legislatures to develop, monitor, and over time revise sentencing standards" (Tonry, 2014, p. 20). To be just, sentencing reforms should apply retroactively to individuals sentenced under earlier schemes (Haile, 2016), and to be equitable, they should incorporate the goal of reducing racial disparities (Ghandnoosh, 2015).

Depoliticize and Professionalize the Parole Process for Life Sentences

Policymakers and practitioners have increased lengths of stay in prison not only by imposing long sentences, but also by delaying the decision to release individuals on parole (Ghandnoosh, 2017). Parole decision-making has grown more politicized and less professionalized as governors, who often wield significant influence in this process, have practiced extreme caution and sometimes brandished their punitiveness as campaign tools. Indeterminate sentencing—which requires discretionary parole approval—is therefore in need of major reform.

Parole decisions should not be driven by politics but by professional assessments of public safety risk. The few states that allow governors to reverse the parole board's decisions should repeal this authority, as Maryland has recently attempted (see Rabner, 2015). Parole boards should be composed of professional staff making meaningful assessments of rehabilitation and acting in the interest of public safety. Michael Tonry (2014) has recommended narrowing and standardizing this decision-making process through presumptive sentencing guidelines established by a sentencing commission, and parole guidelines established by the parole board. States should also reduce the protracted wait times for initial parole hearings and in between hearings (Ghandnoosh, 2017).

Develop a Meaningful Process of Geriatric Release

Finally, states and the federal government should develop and implement meaningful geriatric and medical release programs for the elderly and infirm. The Vera Institute of Justice recommends that jurisdictions answer questions such as "Are eligibility requirements and exclusions too narrow, resulting in too small a pool of inmates who qualify? Are application procedures confusing or burdensome? Are cases reviewed in a timely fashion? Are releases frequently denied at the final stage of the process?" (Chiu, 2010, p. 11). Given that incarceration exacerbates the already poor health of many incarcerated individuals, Vera also recommends lowering the age at which these individuals are considered elderly.

CONCLUSION

A growing chorus of judges now decries the harsh sentences imposed on defendants because of mandatory minimum sentencing laws or politically charged parole policies (Gertner, 2007; Kozinski, 2015; Rakoff, 2014; see also Clifford, 2015 and Van Meter, 2016). After imposing a mandatory sentence of 10 years on Mark Weller for selling methamphetamine, U.S. District Judge Mark Bennett remarked, "I would have given him a year in rehab if I could" (Bennett, 2012; Saslow, 2015). Judges who impose indeterminate sentences for violent crimes are also troubled when they realize how long parole boards keep people imprisoned (Ghandnoosh, 2017). When now-retired California Superior Court Judge Robert W. Armstrong sentenced Flozelle Woodmore to 15 years to life for second-degree murder in 1986, he "had expected that she would serve 'much less' than 15 years, as was customary for second-degree murders in that era" (*San Francisco Chronicle*, 2007). Yet Woodmore, now deceased, was not released until having served 21 years because of five gubernatorial overrides of the parole board's decision to grant parole—including after her victim's relatives requested her release (Karmali, 2007).

The exasperation of these judges is a clear signal that the American criminal justice system is out of balance. Criminological research has established that growing sentence lengths are a major cause of mass incarceration and an ineffective tool for promoting public safety. Long sentences have little deterrent effect and they keep many people imprisoned after they pose little risk to public safety. They not only waste the lives and damage the spirits of the people serving these sentences, they also impede public investments in effective crime prevention, drug treatment, and other rehabilitative programs that promote healthier and safer communities. Establishing an upper limit on sentence lengths, creating professional and depoliticized parole procedures, and meaningfully carrying out geriatric and medical release programs would move the United States closer to achieving meaningful decarceration.

REFERENCES

Appleton, C., & Grøver, B. (2007). The pros and cons of life without parole. *British Journal of Criminology, 47*(4), 597–615.

American Civil Liberties Union. (2012). *At America's expense: The mass incarceration of the elderly.* New York, NY: Author.

Badger, E. (2015, July 8). Obama administration to unveil major new rules targeting segregation across U.S. *Washington Post*. Retrieved from http://www.washingtonpost.com

Baumer, E. (2008). An empirical assessment of the contemporary crime trends puzzle: A modest step toward a more comprehensive research agenda. In A. Goldberger & R. Rosenfeld (Eds.), *Understanding crime trends: Workshop report* (pp. 127–176). Washington, DC: National Academies Press.

Beck, A., & Harrison, P. (2001). *Prisoners in 2000.* Washington, DC: Bureau of Justice Statistics.

Beckett, K., Knaphus, E., & Reosti, A. (2015). *The end of mass incarceration? The contradictions of criminal justice policy and practice.* Manuscript submitted for publication.

Beckett, K., & Sasson, T. (2004). *The politics of injustice: Crime and punishment in America.* Thousand Oaks, CA: Sage Publications.

Bennett, M. W. (2012, October 24). How mandatory minimums forced me to send more than 1,000 nonviolent drug offenders to federal prison. *The Nation.* Retrieved from https://www.thenation.com/article/how-mandatory-minimums-forced-me-send-more-1000-nonviolent-drug-offenders-federal-pri/

California Department of Corrections and Rehabilitation. (2013). *Prison census data as of June 30, 2013.* Sacramento, CA: California Department of Corrections and Rehabilitation.

Carson, E. A. (2014). *Prisoners in 2013.* Washington, DC: Bureau of Justice Statistics.

Carson, E. A. (2015). *Prisoners in 2014.* Washington, DC: Bureau of Justice Statistics.

Carson, E. A., & Sabol, W. (2012). *Prisoners in 2011.* Washington, DC: Bureau of Justice Statistics.

Chettiar, I., & Waldman, M. (Eds.). (2015). *Solutions: American leaders speak out on criminal justice.* New York, NY: Brennan Center for Justice at New York University School of Law.

Chetty, R., Hendren, N., & Katz, L. F. (2015, May). *The effects of exposure to better neighborhoods on children: New evidence from the moving to opportunity experiment.* Working Paper No. 21156. Cambridge, MA: National Bureau of Economic Research.

Chiu, T. (2010) *It's about time: Aging prisoners, increasing costs, and geriatric release.* New York, NY: Vera Institute of Justice.

Clifford, S. (2015, August 26). From the bench, a new look at punishment. *New York Times.* Retrieved from http://www.nytimes.com/2015/08/27/nyregion/from-the-bench-a-new-look-at-punishment.html?_r=0

Davis, L. M., Bozick, R., Steele, J., Saunders, J., & Miles, J. (2013). *Evaluating the effectiveness of correctional education: A meta-analysis of programs that provide education to incarcerated adults.* Washington, DC: Rand Corporation.

Death Penalty Information Center. (2013). *The death penalty in 2013: Year end report.* Washington, DC.

Doob, A., & Webster, C. (2006). Countering punitiveness: Understanding stability in Canada's imprisonment. *Law and Society Review, 40*(2), 325–367.

Durlauf, S., & Nagin, D. (2011). Imprisonment and crime: Can both be reduced? *Criminology and Public Policy, 10*(1), 13–54.

Durose, M., Cooper, A., & Snyder, H. (2014). *Recidivism of prisoners released in 30 States in 2005: Patterns from 2005 to 2010.* Washington, DC: Bureau of Justice Statistics.

Eckholm, E. (2014, November 6). A.C.L.U. in $50 million push to reduce jail sentences. *New York Times.* http://www.nytimes.com/2014/11/07/us/aclu-in-dollar50-million-push-to-reduce-jail-sentences.html

The Economist. (2015, July 20). *The moral failures of America's prison-industrial complex.* Retrieved from http://www.economist.com/blogs/democracyinamerica/2015/07/criminal-justice-and-mass-incarceration

Federal Bureau of Investigation (FBI). (2016). *Uniform crime reports as prepared by the National Archive of Criminal Justice Data*. Retrieved from http://www.ucrdatatool.gov.

Fischer, R. (2005). *Are California's recidivism rates really the highest in the nation? It depends on what measure of recidivism you use*. Irvine, CA: University of California Irvine Center for Evidence-Based Corrections.

Friedmann, P., Lemon, S., Stein, M., & D'Aunno, T. (2003). Accessibility of addiction treatment: Results from a national survey of outpatient substance abuse treatment organizations. *Health Services Research, 38*(3), 887–903.

Gertner, N. (2007). From omnipotence to impotence: American judges and sentencing. *Ohio State Journal of Criminal Law, 4*(523), 523–539.

Ghandnoosh, N. (2014). *Race and punishment: Racial perceptions of crime and support for punitive policies*. Washington, DC: The Sentencing Project.

Ghandnoosh, N. (2015). *Black lives matter: Eliminating racial inequity in the criminal justice system*. Washington, DC: The Sentencing Project.

Ghandnoosh, N. (2016). *Rehabilitation amidst retribution: How intimate ties help and harm California prisoners' parole prospects*. Manuscript submitted for publication.

Ghandnoosh, N. (2017). Delaying a second chance: The declining prospects for parole on life sentences. Washington, DC: The Sentencing Project.

Gingrich, N. & Jones, V. (2014, May 22). Prison system is failing America. *CNN*. Retrieved from http://www.cnn.com

Goldstein, D. (2015, March 20). Too old to commit crime? *New York Times*. Retrieved from http://www.nytimes.com

Gorman, A. (2014, April 5). Despite Obamacare, a gaping hole in addiction treatment. *USA Today*. Retrieved from http://www.usatoday.com

Gottschalk, M. (2012). No way out? Life sentences and the politics of penal reform. In C. J. Ogletree & A. Sarat (Eds.), *Life without parole: America's new death penalty?* New York: New York University Press.

Gottschalk, M. (2015). *Caught: The prison state and the lockdown of American politics*. Princeton, NJ: Princeton University Press.

Haile, J. (2015, October 5). Federal prisoners decline, but it's not a trend yet. *Open Society Voices*. New York, NY: Open Society Foundations. Retrieved from https://www.opensocietyfoundations.org

Haile, J. (2016). Farewell, fair cruelty: An argument for retroactive relief in federal sentencing. Manuscript submitted for publication.

Heckman, J., Malofeeva, L., Pinto, R., & Savelyev, P. (2010). *Understanding the mechanisms through which an influential early childhood program boosted adult outcomes*. Chicago, IL: University of Chicago Press.

Helland, E., & Tabarrok, A. (2007). Does three strikes deter? A nonparametric estimation. *Journal of Human Resources, 42*, 309–330.

Henry, J. (2012). Death in prison sentences: Overutilized and underscrutinized. In C. J. Ogletree & A. Sarat (Eds.), *Life without parole: America's new death penalty?* New York: New York University Press.

Horwitz, S. (2015, May 2). The painful price of aging in prison. *Washington Post*. Retrieved from http://www.washingtonpost.com

Human Rights Watch. (2012). *Old behind bars: The aging prison population in the United States*. New York, NY.

International Centre for Prison Studies. (2016). *Highest to lowest: Prison population rate.* Retrieved from http://www.prisonstudies.org/highest-to-lowest/prison_population_rate?field_region_taxonomy_tid=All

Jargowsky, P. A. (2015). *Architecture of segregation: Civil unrest, the concentration of poverty, and public policy.* New York, NY: The Century Foundation.

Jones, C., Campopiano, M., Baldwin, G., & McCance-Katz, E. (2015). National and state treatment need and capacity for opioid agonist medication-assisted treatment. *American Journal of Public Health, 105*(8), e55–63.

JustLeadershipUSA. (2016). https://www.justleadershipusa.org/about-us/

Karberg, J. C., & James, D. J. (2005). *Substance dependence, abuse, and treatment of jail inmates, 2002.* Washington, DC: Bureau of Justice Statistics.

Karmali, A. (2007, September). Flozelle Woodmore finally freed. *National Lawyers Guild San Francisco News.* San Francisco, CA. Retrieved from http://www.nlgsf.org/sites/default/files/news/Sept07_Newsletter.pdf

King, R., Peterson, B., Elderbroom, B., & Pelletier, E. (2015). *Reducing mass incarceration requires far-reaching reforms.* Washington, DC: Urban Institute. Retrieved from http://webapp.urban.org/reducing-mass-incarceration/

Kling, J., Ludwig, J., & Katz, L. (2005). Neighborhood effects on crime for female and male youth: Evidence from a randomized housing voucher experiment. *Quarterly Journal of Economics, 120*(1), 87–130.

Kozinski, A. (2015). Criminal law 2.0. *Georgetown Law Journal, 103*(5), iii–xliv.

Kyckelhahn, T. (2015). *Justice expenditure and employment extracts, 2012.* Washington, DC: Bureau of Justice Statistics.

Langan, P., & Levin, D. (2002). *Recidivism of prisoners released in 1994.* Washington, DC: Bureau of Justice Statistics.

Lauritsen, J. L., Rezey M. L., & Heimer, K. (2015). When choice of data matters: Analyses of U.S. crime trends, 1973–2012. *Journal of Quantitative Criminology, 32*(3), 1–21.

Loeber, R., & Farrington, D. (2014). Age-crime curve. In G. Bruinsma & D. Weisburd (Eds.), *Encyclopedia of criminology and criminal justice* (pp. 12–18). New York, NY: Springer.

Luallen, J., & Kling, R. (2014). A method for analyzing changing prison populations: Explaining the growth of the elderly in prison. *Evaluation Review, 38*(6), 459–486.

Mauer, M. (2006). *Race to incarcerate.* New York, NY: The New Press.

Mauer, M. (2015, March 11). *Testimony to Charles Colson Task Force on Federal Corrections: A proposal to reduce time served in federal prison.* Retrieved from http://sentencingproject.org/doc/publications/sen_Colson_Task_Force_Testimony.pdf

Mauer, M., & Cole, D. (2015, May 23). How to lock up fewer people. *New York Times.* Retrieved from http://www.nytimes.com

Mauer, M., & Ghandnoosh, N. (2013, December 20). Can we wait 88 years to end mass incarceration? *Huffington Post.*

Mauer, M., & Ghandnoosh, N. (2014). *Fewer prisoners, less crime: A tale of three states.* Washington, DC: The Sentencing Project.

Mullane, N. (2012) *Life after murder: Five men in search of redemption.* New York, NY: Public Affairs.

Mumola, C., & Karberg, J. C. (2006). *Drug use and dependence, state and federal prisoners, 2004.* Washington, DC: Bureau of Justice Statistics.

Nagin, D. S. (2013). Deterrence in the twenty-first century: A review of the evidence. In M. Tonry (Ed.), *Crime and Justice: A Review of Research, 42,* 199–263.

National Institute of Corrections. (2004). *Correctional health care: Addressing the needs of elderly, chronically ill, and terminally ill inmates.* Washington, DC: U.S. Department of Justice.

Nellis, A. (2013). *Life goes on: The historic rise in life sentences in America.* Washington, DC: The Sentencing Project.

Nellis, A. (2015). *A return to justice: Rethinking our approach to juveniles in the system.* Washington, DC: Rowman & Littlefield.

Neyfakh, L. (2015, March 4). OK, so who gets to go free? *Slate.* Retrieved from http://www.slate.com

Obama, B. (2015). *Remarks by the President at the NAACP conference.* Retrieved from https://www.whitehouse.gov/the-press-office/2015/07/14/remarks-president-naacp-conference

Petersilia, J. (2008). California's correctional paradox of excess and deprivation. *Crime and Justice: A Review of Research, 37,* 207–278.

Peterson, R., & Krivo, L. (2012). *Divergent social world: Neighborhood crime and the racial-spatial divide.* New York, NY: Russell Sage Foundation.

Pew Charitable Trusts. (2015). *Imprisonment, crime rates fell in 30 states over five years.* Retrieved from http://www.pewtrusts.org/en/multimedia/data-visualizations/2015/imprisonment-crime-rates-fell-in-30-states-over-five-years

Pew Research Center. (2014). *America's new drug policy landscape.* Washington, DC. Retrieved from http://www.people-press.org/2014/04/02/section-1-perceptions-of-drug-abuse-views-of-drug-policies/

Pfaff, J. (2015, July 26). For true penal reform, focus on the violent offenders. *Washington Post.* Retrieved from https://www.washingtonpost.com

Piquero, A., Farrington, D., Welsh, B., Tremblay, R., & Jennings, W. (2009). Effects of early family/parent training programs on antisocial behavior and delinquency. *Journal of Experimental Criminology, 5,* 83–120.

Piquero, A., Hawkins, J., & Kazemian, L. (2012). Criminal career patterns. In R. Loeber & D. P. Farrington (Eds.), *From juvenile delinquency to adult crime: Criminal careers, justice policy, and prevention* (pp. 14–46). New York, NY: Oxford University Press.

Porter, L. C., Bushway, S. D., Hui-Shien, T., & Smith, H. L. (2016). How the U.S. prison boom has changed the age distribution of the prison population. *Criminology, 54*(1), 30–55.

Rabner, N. (2015, February 20). Bill would remove governor from decision-making on parole for lifers. *Capital News Service.* Retrieved from http://cnsmaryland.org

Rakoff, J. S. (2014, November 20). Why innocent people plead guilty. *New York Review of Books.* Retrieved from http://www.nybooks.com

Ramirez, M. D. (2013). Punitive sentiment. *Criminology, 51*(2), 329–364.

Raphael, S., & Stoll, M. (2013). *Why are so many Americans in prison?* New York, NY: Russell Sage Foundation.

Raphael, S., & Stoll, M. (2014). *A new approach to reducing incarceration while maintaining low rates of crime.* Washington, DC: The Hamilton Project, The Brookings Institution.

Robinson, P., & Darley, J. (2004). Does criminal law deter? A behavioural science investigation. *Oxford Journal of Legal Studies, 24*(2), 173–205.

Roeder, O., Eisen, L., & Bowling, J. (2015). *What caused the crime decline?* New York, NY: Brennan Center for Justice at New York University School of Law.

Roth, A. (2015, July 24). Let's consider leniency for many "violent" offenders too. *Los Angeles Times.* Available at http://www.latimes.com

Rovner, J. (2015). *Declines in youth commitments and facilities in the 21st century.* Washington, DC: The Sentencing Project.

Rovner, J. (2016). *Juvenile life without parole: An overview.* Washington, DC: The Sentencing Project.

Sampson, R., & Laub, J. (1993). *Crime in the making: Pathways and turning points through life.* Cambridge, MA: Harvard University Press.

Sampson, R., & Laub, J. (2003). Life-course desisters? Trajectories of crime among delinquent boys followed to age 70. *Criminology, 41*(3), 301–340.

Sampson, R. J., Morenoff, J. D., & Raudenbush, S. W. (2005). Social anatomy of racial and ethnic disparities in violence. *American Journal of Public Health, 95*(2), 224–232.

San Francisco Chronicle. (2007, April 8). *A prisoner of politics.* Editorial. Retrieved from http://www.sfgate.com

Saslow, E. (2015, June 16). Against his better judgment. *Washington Post.* Retrieved from http://www.washingtonpost.com

Schwartzapfel, B. (2015, July 11). How parole boards keep prisoners in the dark and behind bars. *Washington Post.* Retrieved from http://www.washingtonpost.com

Sciandra, M., Sanbonmatsu, L., Duncan, G., Gennetian, L., Katz, L., Kessler, R., . . . Ludwig, J. (2013). Long-term effects of the moving to opportunity residential mobility experiment on crime and delinquency. *Journal of Experimental Criminology, 9*(4), 451–489.

Seeds, C. (2015). *Bifurcation nation: Strategy in contemporary American punishment.* Manuscript in preparation.

The Sentencing Project. (2016). *U.S. prison population trends 1999–2014: Broad variation among states in recent years.* Washington, DC: The Sentencing Project.

The Sentencing Project. (2013). *Ending mass incarceration: Social interventions that work.* Washington, DC: The Sentencing Project.

Steinberg, L. (2013, July). The influence of neuroscience on US Supreme Court decisions about adolescents' criminal culpability. *Nature Reviews Neuroscience, 14,* 513–518.

Steinberg, L., Cauffman, E., & Monahan, K. (2015). *Psychosocial maturity and desistance from crime in a sample of serious juvenile offenders.* Washington, DC: Office of Juvenile Justice and Delinquency Prevention.

Subramanian, R., & Moreno, R. (2014). *Drug war détente? A review of state-level drug law reform, 2009–2013.* New York, NY: Vera Institute of Justice.

Sung, H.-E., Mahoney, A. M., & Mellow, J. (2011). Substance abuse treatment gap among adult parolees: Prevalence, correlates, and barriers. *Criminal Justice Review, 36*(1), 40–57.

Thompson, S., & Gartner, R. (2014). The spatial distribution and social context of homicide in Toronto's neighborhoods. *Journal of Research in Crime and Delinquency 2014, 51*(1), 88–118.

Tonry, M. (2014). Remodeling American sentencing: A ten-step blueprint for moving past mass incarceration. *Criminology and Public Policy, 13*(4), 503–533.

Tonry, M., & Farrington, D. P. (2005). Punishment and crime across space and time. *Crime and Justice, 33,* 1–39.

Travis, J., Western, B., & Redburn, S. (Eds.). (2014). *The growth of incarceration in the United States: Exploring causes and consequences.* National Research Council. Washington, DC: National Academies Press.

Tseloni, A., Mailley, J., & Garrell, G. (2010). Exploring the international decline in crime rates. *European Journal of Criminology, 7*(5), 375–394.

U.S. Department of Justice. (1990). Bureau of Justice Statistics report, 1989. Bureau of Justice Statistics. Retrieved from https://www.bjs.gov/index.cfm?ty=pbdetail&iid=3254

U.S. Department of Justice. (2013). *Smart on crime: Reforming the criminal justice system for the 21st century*. Washington, DC: U.S. Department of Justice.

Van Meter, M. (2016, February 25). One judge makes the case for judgment. *The Atlantic*. Retrieved from http://www.theatlantic.com

van Zyl Smit, D. (2006). Life imprisonment: Recent issues in national and international law. *International Journal of Law and Psychiatry, 29*, 405–421.

Weisberg, R., Mukamal, D., & Segall, J. (2011). *Life in limbo: An examination of parole release for prisoners serving life sentences with the possibility of parole in California*. Stanford, CA: Stanford Criminal Justice Center, Stanford Law School.

West, H. C., & Sabol, W. J. (2010). *Prisoners in 2009*. Washington, DC: Bureau of Justice Statistics.

Western, B. (2006). *Punishment and inequality in America*. New York, NY: Russell Sage Foundation.

Zimring, F. E. (2007). *The great American crime decline*. Oxford, UK: Oxford University Press.

Zimring, F. E., Hawkins, G., & Kamin, S. (2001). *Punishment and democracy: Three strikes and you're out in California*. New York, NY: Oxford University Press.

10

Reforming Civil Disability Policy to Facilitate Effective and Sustainable Decarceration

Carrie Pettus-Davis, Matthew W. Epperson, and Annie Grier

BACKGROUND

A largely punishment- and retribution-oriented approach to crime and criminal behavior ushered in an era of mass incarceration in the United States. During this era, *civil disabilities*—legal rights or privileges that are revoked or restricted because of a criminal conviction—proliferated. An estimated 40,000 laws produce civil disabilities nationwide, which has created a patchwork of policies that severely limits the rights and daily behaviors of people with criminal convictions (Laird, 2013). The expansion of civil disabilities penalizes offenders beyond the limits of their criminal sentence, hence the alternative term for civil disabilities: *collateral consequences*.

An era of decarceration will require movement away from punishment-oriented policies and practices toward a rehabilitation approach—one grounded in a treatment-focused orientation that provides evidence-driven services and supports to reduce risks of reoffending. Civil disabilities, as currently enacted, will encumber any large-scale effort toward decarceration, particularly those efforts that are rooted in rehabilitation. The commitment to a justice system with a rehabilitation focus is undermined by practices and policies that inhibit reentry and the very factors that are correlated with successful reintegration and reduced reoffending.

The misalignment between rehabilitative goals and civil disabilities creates a crack in the justice system through which thousands of men and women fall each year—to the detriment of the nation's public safety and well-being. Immediately redressing this misalignment is critical to turning the tide on mass incarceration. Despite ample discourse on civil disabilities and the likelihood that these public policies counterbalance rehabilitative goals, there has been little empirical investigation into the conflict between civil disabilities and rehabilitation practices, and limited study of the impact of civil disability statutes on recidivism for people with felony convictions.

The purpose of this chapter is to call attention to the misalignment between rehabilitative goals and civil disabilities and propose ways to address civil disabilities through means that promote, rather than inhibit, decarceration. We provide an overview of civil disabilities in the United States, their history, and current trends. We then examine the role of civil disabilities in decarceration efforts. We argue that civil disabilities, as they currently stand, work against the rehabilitative aims of evidence-driven corrections and efforts to reverse mass incarceration. Finally, we recommend steps to align policies around civil disabilities with rehabilitative practices to promote public safety and public well-being in the era of decarceration.

DEFINITION, HISTORY, AND TRENDS

Civil disabilities in the United States are anachronistic punishments carried over from the European practice of "civil death," in which a person was permanently excluded from civic participation as a result of certain criminal convictions (Chin, 2012). Civil disabilities are legal penalties or sanctions that limit convicted individuals' access to social, economic, and political participation (Pinard, 2006) without constitutional protections related to criminal law such as effective assistance of counsel, proportionality of punishment, and adequacy of notice (Chin & Holmes, 2001). Examples of civil disabilities include ineligibility for housing, student loans, professional licensure, certain forms of employment, and denial of voting and parental rights.

Scholars describe the modern landscape of civil disabilities as a national quilt of policies inconsistently enacted and lacking justification or a cogent rationale (Ewald, 2005). To be sure, in some cases the rationale is clear. For example, restrictions on where a sex offender can live in proximity to parks or schools is clearly prompted by fear and concerns for public safety. Denial of food stamps to persons with certain felony convictions could be argued from a limited public resources perspective where only law-abiding citizens are deemed worthy of public assistance. However, much of the rationale for civil disabilities becomes murky when considering the practical implications of many of these policies. For example, restricting food stamps from a convicted felon may also affect that individual's innocent children. Other justifications for civil disabilities seem invalid at face value. What is the basis for uniformly denying people with a felony conviction, despite offense type, from becoming a barber or working in waste management?[1]

---

[1] See http://abacollateralconsequences.org.

By the mid-20th century, many attorneys and criminal justice professionals argued that civil disabilities threatened reintegration of prisoners to communities and therefore should be reconsidered and, in many cases, eliminated (Love, 2011). In 1955, the National Council on Crime and Delinquency called for the restoration of all civil rights of former prisoners upon completion of their sentence to strengthen the former prisoner's ties to the community (Chesney-Lind & Mauer, 2002; Demleitner, 1999). In 1956, the National Conference on Parole called for the elimination of civil disability laws that infringed on the rights of personals with a criminal conviction, citing such laws as "archaic." Some state legislatures made efforts to disassemble civil disability laws and, instead, worked to enact nondiscrimination laws that applied to the employment and licensing of persons with a criminal conviction within certain fields (Demleitner, 1999). By 1983, the American Bar Association predicted that civil disabilities would become extinct, pointing to many state level reforms as indicators of a national consensus that arbitrary social exclusions work against the goals of reintegration and that criminals could and should be rehabilitated (Love, 2011).

These predictions proved false. The mid-1980s served as a major tipping point, as the United States fully engaged in a war on drugs and a tough-on-crime philosophy. For example, New York increased from having 125 civil disabilities in 1976 to more than 1,000 active civil disability statutes in 2011 (Radice, 2012). The exponential growth in civil disability policy adoption at the state level was led by passage of the Comprehensive Crime Control Act of 1984, which enacted guidelines for judicial sentencing, eliminated indeterminate sentencing, phased out parole, reinstituted the federal death penalty, and increased penalties for marijuana-related offenses and gun-related offenses (U.S. Congress, 1984). The Crime Control Act of 1984 was followed by the Anti-Drug Abuse Act of 1986 and the Anti-Drug Abuse Amendment Act of 1988, which created mandatory minimum sentences for federal drug offenses and increased penalties for drug offenses. Combined, these three acts prompted an era of longer and more severe sentences and reduced discretion in sentencing that could take into account individual circumstances.

The proliferation of civil disabilities was consistent with attitudes driving the dominant response of the criminal justice system—the idea that people needed to be severely punished for their crimes, and that punishment should continue for a long time. The reach of federal civil disability legislation expanded dramatically at the latter end of the 1990s, with laws that limited whether people could obtain education and where they could live (e.g., Higher Education Act of 1998 and Quality Housing and Work Responsibility Act of 1998). The Crime Act of 1994 required each state to implement a public sex offender registration law or lose 10% of federal funding for criminal justice programs (Travis, 2005). Given the emphasis on drug offenders for most federal civil disability policies, it is clear that the War on Drugs was an underlying driver on much of states' civil disability policy adoption. Outside of federal incentives, it is less clear what drove states to become so aggressive in their enactment of civil disabilities. In 1996, the Personal Responsibility and Work Opportunity Reconciliation Act denied federal cash assistance and food stamps to those convicted of state or federal drug offenses. The lifetime disqualification applied to otherwise eligible individuals in all states unless the state chose to opt out (Mauer & McCalmont, 2013). In 2016, 18 states have opted out completely, while 26 states have only a partial ban on receiving Supplemental Nutrition Assistance Program benefits. Additionally, 14 states have lifted the ban on Temporary Assistance to Needy Families and 23 states uphold only a partial ban on benefits (Hager, 2016).

Some estimates speculate that individuals with a criminal conviction potentially face up to 50,000 legally mandated civil disabilities including restrictions on housing, employment, educational opportunities, receiving public benefits, termination of parental rights, and civic engagement—including voting, serving on a jury, and holding public office (LaFollette, 2005; Laird, 2013).

THEORY AND EMPIRICAL SUPPORT FOR EXAMINATION

In light of the dearth of empirical data, theory helps to explain why and how civil disabilities and rehabilitation practices are misaligned and how this misalignment may be problematic. Both age-graded theory and life-course theory offer an explanation as to how civil disability policies create civic and social isolation for individuals with criminal histories that can be prohibitive to successful rehabilitation. Additionally, civil disability policies disrupt civic and civil participation beyond incarceration in ways that affect not only the individual, but also social structures such as families, workplace, and communities.

Age-Graded Theory

Sampson and Laub's (2003) age-graded theory of crime demonstrates how civil disabilities may interfere with rehabilitative goals that largely focus on integration versus exclusion. According to the age-graded theory of crime, an individual desists from crime as a result of a positive interlocking experience between individuals and social conditions that occurs within a structural context shaped by historical factors. Structural events such as employment or marriage function as turning points for individuals to change from engagement in crime to law-abiding living (Laub & Sampson, 1993). These positive structural events act as vehicles for positive social support and attachments to others unlikely to engage in crime. For example, returning to school changes daily routine activities in ways that are more structured and removed from locations or activities that foster criminality. Sampson and Laub's (1994) empirical research supports the theoretical propositions that positive social bonds in the context of work, school, and family in adulthood promote desistance from crime. Yet people reentering society from prison or jails are barred from many of these structural opportunities through civil disabilities.

Life-Course Theory

Prominent contemporary criminological perspectives fall under life-course theory. Life-course theory proposes that individuals isolated from prosocial social contexts and positive social support from social networks, and individuals who feel unable to excel given their criminal background are at a substantially increased risk to continue engaging in crime. Life-course theorists note that social ties are important at all ages but that the salience of different types of bonds to society change during adulthood (Sampson & Laub, 1990, 1994). For example, in childhood, bonds to parents are more salient than employment, which takes a more prominent role in adulthood. Civil disabilities by definition isolate individuals from some major aspects of civic and social participation, particularly those associated with criminogenic needs and social bonds such as poor histories in work, school, family, and peers. Empirical data on the connection between criminogenic needs and civil disabilities support life-course theoretical propositions (Martinez & Christian, 2009; Miller & Ngugi, 2009; Davis, 2013; Visher, Bakken, & Gunter, 2013).

Empirical Support for Disruption

Some researchers have examined how civil disabilities affect positive structural events and positive social networks that can prevent reengagement in crime. For example, several studies looked at the impact of residency restriction and public notification laws specific to sex offenders. These studies report profound negative effects across several life domains such as routine housing disruption, loss of employment, threats to self and family, being harassed and having personal property damaged, undoing of positive social support, homelessness, and financial hardship (Levenson & Prescott, 2008; Levenson, D'Amora, & Hern, 2007; Mercado, Alvarez, & Levenson, 2008; Tewksbury & Mustaine, 2009). The impact of civil disabilities is also undiscerning; sex offenders at low risk of reoffending are equally affected by civil disability policies as those at high risk of reoffending (Levenson & Prescott, 2008).

Pogorzelski, Wolff, Pan, and Blitz (2005) investigated the effects of civil disabilities on access to resources for 3,073 reentering individuals with mental illnesses. They found that nonviolent offenders were permanently denied access to public housing and welfare benefits (drug offense specific) and faced conditional restrictions on education, driving, custody of children, expungement of criminal records, and voting. Violent offenders experienced lifetime consequences for their felony offenses in the domains of employment, public housing, education, voting, jury participation, adoption and foster care, and expunging criminal records. Other research on the impact of civil disabilities has shown that consequences of civil disabilities extend beyond access to resources and include stress, depression, shame, and hopelessness (Levenson et al., 2007; Mercado et al., 2008; Tewksbury & Mustaine, 2009). Thus, civil disabilities perhaps started in some logical ways but have ended up invading people's lives in ways that may not have been anticipated. Such empirical associations with civil disabilities are expected given the extent to which these policies can prohibit persons with criminal histories from accessing formal and informal supports to leave a life of crime. In this way, civil disabilities may lead to more crime.

SHIFTS IN STATE-LEVEL POLICY IN THE ERA OF MASS INCARCERATION

In 2004, the Legal Action Center (LAC) produced the first comprehensive report of civil disabilities (LAC, 2004). The report concluded that people with criminal records "face a daunting array of counterproductive, debilitating, and unreasonable roadblocks in almost every important aspect of life" (LAC, 2004, p. 7). The LAC updated this report in 2009 and, in doing so, inventoried and ranked the severity of civil disabilities by state. Emblematic of the inconsistency of civil disability policy, there was no consistent geographic or demographic pattern for those states with the least or most severe civil disabilities. According to the LAC report, Illinois has the least number of civil disabilities followed by New York, California, Hawaii, and New Hampshire. The states with modest ranking scores included Kansas, Arizona, Florida, Rhode Island, and North Dakota. Those states ranked as having the most severe civil disabilities were Alaska, Virginia, South Carolina, Georgia, and Pennsylvania. Whether increased attention will result in less severe or fewer civil disabilities is yet to be seen. In the LAC's 2009 update on state level civil disabilities, they found that 28 states removed or reduced the severity of some civil disabilities between 2004 and 2009, but that the other 22 states created new civil disabilities. No single state or set of states appears to lead in removing or lessening civil disabilities.

Ewald (2012) found that civil disabilities are more restrictive in states where African Americans are underrepresented in their state legislature; however, in three states where African Americans were "overrepresented" in the legislature compared to the proportion of African Americans in the state, the states are among the least restrictive fifth of the distribution. To identify the factors that may predict the severity or restrictiveness of civil disabilities, Ewald (2012) created state-level composite scores of civil disability policies (e.g., voting, public office, jury service, driver's license, cash assistance and food stamps for families in poverty, public records, employment, firearms). Ewald found that the top fifth of states score almost twice as high in restrictiveness as the bottom fifth of states. This finding indicates that a person living in one state may have a very different experience with reintegration than if that person lived in another state. Across all states, the factors that positively predicted restrictiveness of civil disabilities included being a southern state, state incarceration rates, and size of the African American population. The factors associated with less restrictive civil disabilities included the proportion of citizens reporting a liberal ideology and states with a greater proportion of African American legislators.

The Vera Institute examined shifts in state level civil disability policies from 2009 to 2014 (Subramanian, Moreno, & Gebreselassie, 2014). The report found that 41 states have enacted laws that increase relief from civil disabilities, reduce civil disabilities, give people more information on civil disabilities, or formed tasks forces to examine civil disabilities. However, the report also noted that the reforms have not gone far enough because they are largely limited to a narrow set of offenses and that relief mechanisms are inaccessible to most. These legislative reforms have also given little attention to the crime-related risks that civil disability driven exclusions from civic participation may impose.

One concern about the vast nature of civil disabilities is that there are so many that defendants, defense attorneys, prosecutors, and judges are often not aware of or cannot stay current on active collateral consequences of conviction. In 2010, a U.S. Supreme Court decision pointed to a shift in thinking about civil disabilities. The U.S. Supreme Court decision in *Padillia v Kentucky* requires criminal defense attorneys to advise noncitizen clients about the risks of deportation associated with a guilty plea. This is the first court decision that has required any acknowledgment of civil disability policies during the criminal process.

Pointing to the "collective weight" of civil disabilities on individuals with criminal histories, and by association their families, in 2001 the American Bar Association established a Task Force on Collateral Sanctions to assess the growing policy barriers to civic participation of people with felony convictions. In 2003, the Criminal Justice Section of the American Bar Association strongly recommended that states limit and codify civil disabilities. In 2009, the U.S. Department of Justice awarded the American Bar Association financial support to develop a national inventory of civil disabilities made available to the public and searchable by state. The inventory, referred to as the National Inventory of the Collateral Consequences of Conviction is up to date as of April 2014 (American Bar Association, 2013). The development of the National Inventory of the Collateral Consequences of Conviction provides one resource for identifying civil disabilities.

COMMITMENT TO REHABILITATION: EVIDENCE-BASED CORRECTIONS

As a renewed focus on the negative consequences of civil disabilities emerged in the 21st century, so too did attention to corrections-based rehabilitative practices. The turn of the century marked the beginning of what Petersilia and Cullen (2014) refer to as evidence-based corrections. During this time, researchers, practitioners, and intervention developers gradually but widely embraced criminogenic (i.e., crime-producing) needs as targets for rehabilitative interventions. In response to the complex and multiple needs that incarcerated individuals face when they are released, a class of multimodal interventions referred to as reentry interventions emerged at the beginning of the 21st century. These programs addressed other basic needs of releasing prisoners such as obtaining driver's licenses, public assistance eligibility, child support payment, and reconnecting with family in addition to criminogenic needs related issues of employment, education, housing, and cognitions. These comprehensive reentry programs are seen as necessary because of the multiple policy-imposed obstacles that formerly incarcerated individuals encounter that prohibit their full participation in society such as employment. For example, not having a valid driver's license limits employment opportunities and contributes to people not being able to maintain a job once they find one.

An evidence-based corrections approach asserts that it is the responsibility of criminal justice interventions to actively address criminogenic needs to achieve reductions in recidivism and public safety improvements (Petersilia & Cullen, 2014). Criminogenic needs are risk factors amenable to change that influence a person's criminal behavior. Over 2 decades of empirical research have yielded a set of central criminogenic needs that are consistently predictive of reengagement in crime among formerly incarcerated persons (Andrews & Bonta, 2010). These criminogenic needs include (1) poor school or work history; (2) associations with others who engage in criminal behaviors while also being isolated from law-abiding individuals; (3) impulsive, aggressive, pleasure-seeking personality pattern in opposition of conventional norms (i.e., antisocial personality pattern); (4) attitudes or thinking that rationalizes engaging in criminal behaviors; (5) abuse of alcohol or illicit substances; (6) problematic relationships with loved ones or family; and (7) low level or no involvement in positive leisure or recreational activities such as hobbies or volunteering (Andrews & Bonta, 2010). Because of the empirical association of criminogenic needs with reincarceration and crime, evidence-based corrections interventions aim to address these criminogenic needs. Some interventions hone in on one criminogenic need (e.g., employment programs) whereas other interventions attempt to address multiple criminogenic needs (e.g., transitional housing programs, which often address issues such as substance use or employment while also addressing housing).

In many ways, addressing criminogenic needs entails increasing access to many life domains, including education, employment, housing, and social life; however, civil disability policies actually exclude access to many of these same domains. Given the tensions between civil disabilities and evidence-based corrections, it is important to examine the ways in which rehabilitative programs seek to include formerly incarcerated individuals in full social participation. When thinking about ways to maximize the effectiveness of interventions, researchers, policymakers, and stakeholders should examine how the misalignment of civil disability policies and rehabilitative practices presents barriers to achieving rehabilitation goals. In the sections that follow, we discuss areas of focus in rehabilitative practices and the impact of civil disabilities on these domains.

Employment

Employment and education programs are popular rehabilitation interventions. Research shows that employment status and level of education are strong predictors of recidivism among released prisoners (Berg & Huebner, 2011; Nally, Lockwood, Ho, & Knutson,

2014; Visher, Debus, & Yahner, 2008). Employment programs prepare and assist formerly incarcerated individuals to overcome barriers to obtaining and retaining employment. The range of types of employment programs include job readiness classes that focus on attitudinal, behavioral, and technical skills needed to obtain work; job training programs that focus on specific trades or vocations; transitional employment programs that usually involve small crews under close supervision performing manual labor; and job placement and development programs that help to connect formerly incarcerated persons with both temporary and permanent employment.

There is a high need for employment and education programs because many incarcerated people have poor education and sporadic work histories. For example, although 41% of individuals incarcerated in jails and around 83% of those in state prisons nationally report being employed in the month before incarceration, up to two-thirds report an income at or below poverty level, earning less than $1,000 per month during that time (Harlow, 2003; James, 2004). Obtaining and maintaining employment after incarceration is difficult. In a study of 740 released state prisoners, 43% of respondents had been employed at one point after incarceration, but only 31% remained employed 2 months after incarceration (Visher et al., 2008). Interviews with these same respondents 8 months after incarceration indicated continued job instability: 65% of respondents reported they had been employed at some time after incarceration, but only 47% were employed at the time of the interview. Earning prospects after incarceration are also dire; a history of incarceration reduces annual income for men by 40% (Western & Pettit, 2010). Moreover, a study of 6,529 released individuals incarcerated in state prisons found unemployment rates of 65.6% between the recessionary period of 2008–2009 compared to 9.9% for the general population (Nally, Lockwood, & Ho, 2011).

Unemployment and low wages post incarceration are problematic because they are predictive of recidivism. For example, in a study of 740 released individuals, those who were unemployed 2 months after release from prison had a 23% probability of reincarceration compared to 16% of those employed, but they were earning $7 or less an hour. As wages increased, the likelihood of reincarceration decreased to 8% probability at $10 per hour (Visher et al., 2008). In a study of reincarceration among 6,561 state prisoners, those who were employed after release were nearly 63% less likely to be reincarcerated than their unemployed counterparts (Nally et al., 2014).

Civil disabilities impede pathways to suitable employment for adults with criminal histories. Passing a criminal background check is the most prevalent prerequisite for obtaining occupational licensure or securing many employment opportunities (Rodriguez & Avery, 2016). However, this one informal policy can lead to a multitude of veiled reasons for denial of employment. Various policies affect employment availability and narrow qualifications that exclude persons with criminal histories. For example, there could be as many as 800 entire occupations nationwide that impose lifetime disqualifications for persons with a felony conviction (Bushway & Sweeten, 2007). Furthermore, civil disabilities pose temporary or permanent bans from employment based on offense type and impose mandatory or discretionary bans for certain professions based on offense type. Lastly, certain professional licensures are restricted by type of offense. The American Bar Association (2016) found that there are more than 12,000 occupational licensing restrictions for individuals with any type of felony and more than 6,000 similar restrictions based on misdemeanors. Many of these restrictions are mandatory, and even more impose a permanent or lifetime disqualification once enforced (Rodriguez & Avery, 2016). Combined, these civil disabilities provide barriers to one of the most empirically supported pathways out of the cycle of reincarceration—employment.

Education

Directly tied to employment, education programs aim to equip formerly incarcerated participants with needed literacy and numeracy proficiency required for employment. Educational programs include adult basic education for formerly incarcerated individuals performing below a ninth-grade level, high school level education equivalency, postsecondary education, and vocational education, which includes certification in various trades.

Over two-thirds of individuals incarcerated in state prisons and 44% of those in jails report less than a high school education at incarceration compared to 18% of the general population (Harlow, 2003). A study of 6,561 individuals in state prisons found that reincarceration rates were nearly 9 percentage points higher among released prisoners without high school credentials than those with a high school degree and 23 percentage points higher compared to those released prisoners with a college degree (Nally et al., 2014). Those who participate in high school or GED programs have 30% lower odds of recidivating than those who needed the programs but did not participate (Davis, 2013).

As with employment, civil disabilities prevent persons with criminal histories from accessing important avenues to education, such as denial of admission to some schools and disqualification for some loans and scholarships. A survey of 273 colleges showed that more than half not only inquire about an applicant's criminal history on the initial application but also use this information in the admissions process (Weissman, Rosenthal, Warth, Wolf, & Messina-Yauchzy, 2010). Even if given consideration, many applicants with a criminal conviction are tasked with additional requirements that may be challenging to meet, such as obtaining official court documents related to the charges, getting references from corrections officials, or securing official records from a correctional institutions regarding education services while incarcerated (Blakinger, 2015).

Housing

Housing stability promotes mental, physical, and economic well-being of individuals, despite incarceration history, particularly during times of adversity (Geller & Curtis,

2011). Although some housing-specific programs exist specifically for formerly incarcerated individuals, housing has primarily been addressed by corrections case managers and parole officers. Generally, housing programs and services aim to mitigate personal (e.g., strained relationships, affordability) and public policy (e.g., public housing restrictions, private landlord exclusions) barriers to housing. Some examples of housing programs for releasing prisoners include halfway houses or transitional facilities; housing specialists to assist correctional case managers in locating appropriate housing; temporary and long-term rent subsidies; master leasing with subleasing to formerly incarcerated individuals; and supportive housing programs for formerly incarcerated individuals with other needs, such as mental illnesses (Roman & Travis, 2006).

Housing programs respond to the fact that many formerly incarcerated individuals have unstable housing experiences before and after incarceration. Homelessness is four to six times greater among those incarcerated in state prisons than in the general population (Greenberg & Rosenheck, 2008) and 14% of those in jails reported being homeless in the year prior to their admission into jail (James, 2004). A study of more than 48,000 formerly incarcerated individuals in state prisons released to New York City between 1995 and 1998 found that 5,510 (11.4%) of those released resided in a homeless shelter at some point during a 2-year period after incarceration (Metraux & Culhane, 2006). Another study of 3,000 New York City men found that those with recent incarceration histories face 69% greater odds of housing insecurity than men without incarceration histories within a 12-month period. Unstable housing can be problematic for anyone, but it poses additional risks for formerly incarcerated individuals because unstable housing can increase the likelihood of reincarceration. Metraux and Culhane (2006) found that the odds of being reincarcerated are 1.17 times greater for formerly incarcerated individuals that experience a shelter stay than for those who did not experience a shelter stay in the two years after prison. Lutze, Rosky, and Hamilton (2014) found that those with periods of homelessness in the year following prison experienced two times greater risks for new convictions and prison readmissions. In a study of more than 2,000 individuals formerly incarcerated in state prisons, Makarios, Steiner, and Travis (2010) found that each time an individual moved, the odds of recidivism increased by 196%. Despite the difficulties with housing stability faced by formerly incarcerated individuals, few successful interventions exist that reduce risks for both unstable housing and reincarceration. Simply providing housing does not reduce risks for continued crime for formerly incarcerated individuals (Miller & Ngugi, 2009). In fact, when compared to being released to a private residence, being released to transitional housing increased the odds of rearrest (Clark, 2014). When housing is combined with other services and provided to formerly incarcerated individuals at high risk of reoffending, recidivism can be reduced by 12%, and the successful approach of combined services was supported in findings from a reentry housing program in Washington (Lutze et al., 2014; Miller & Ngugi, 2009).

Housing is effective in reducing reincarceration; however, civil disabilities play a critical role in stymying housing and its needed accompanying services to formerly incarcerated individuals. Policies affect the affordability and location of housing for adults with criminal histories. Offense type can affect stays in homeless shelters, evictions of self and family, and denial of public housing or a lease by a landlord. For example, public housing authorities are permitted to deny admission to any household in which a family member has been previously evicted for a drug-related crime. Also, they may deny acceptance to any public, federally assisted Section 8 housing if any adult applicant has been convicted of a drug-related crime, violent offense, or other crime that may be perceived by public housing authority employees as a threat to the health, safety, or enjoyment of other residents. Likewise, in the private housing market, landlords are able to deny housing based on the wide availability of criminal background checks. Finally, municipal ordinances restrict where persons with certain offenses may reside. These myriad challenges to securing safe and affordable housing leave many individuals reentering the community after incarceration in a tenable situation that puts their successful reentry at risk.

Family

Perhaps the most profound impact of the surge in federal civil disability laws was on the composition of the family unit. Nearly 90% of formerly incarcerated individuals rely heavily on family for support after incarceration, and over half of all prisoners have children aged younger than 18 years (Mumola, 2000). Yet strained and tumultuous relationships with family are predictive of reincarceration. Individuals incarcerated in prisons who have more contact with their families and who report positive relationships overall are less likely to be reincarcerated (Martinez & Christian, 2009). For men, over 80% receive some form of assistance from family while reentering from incarceration, and most name family support as the most important factor in helping them to stay out of prison. Almost half of men cited spending time with their children as a motivator for remaining out of prison (Visher & Courtney, 2007). Fathers who spend time with their children are also more likely to have a successful reentry (Bahr, Armstrong, Gibbs, Harris, & Fisher, 2005; Visher et al., 2013). Additionally, families of reentering adults may provide a durable emotional barrier that shields them from the disorienting experiences common to reentry (Maruna, 2001; Sampson & Laub, 2003). Thus, interventionists recognize that it is important to provide formerly incarcerated individuals and families the resources and skills to reconnect in positive ways.

However, civil disabilities disrupt family composition and impede successful familial reintegration. For example, because formerly incarcerated individuals are restricted, sometimes permanently, in the types of employment they can obtain and where they can live, the possibility of reducing strain on families and facilitating positive reconnections is substantially limited. The Adoption and Safe Families Act of 1997 made any family member with a criminal record ineligible to care for a child of an incarcerated parent (LAC, 2009). As a result, children could be taken from parents or grandparents if they had prior criminal justice involvement regardless of when or how substantial. Provisions of the law also mandated that states bar individuals with certain types of criminal convictions from becoming foster parents or adoptive parents, so that people with criminal histories would be denied the opportunity to adopt. Finally, this act specified that parental rights could be permanently terminated if a child had been in foster care for 15 months of the most recent 22 months; therefore, mothers or fathers who were incarcerated for more than 15 months and had a child in foster care could have their parental rights permanently severed and lose their children to adoption without even being consulted.

Civil Disabilities: A Tale of Two States

Given the varied and wide reach of civil disabilities, it is useful to explore a "typical" scenario of a recently released prisoner. "Trey" will experience scenarios in two different states, Virginia and Illinois. In this scenario, Trey was convicted of an aggravated robbery and a drug offense, served time in prison, and was released back to his community. The examples of civil disabilities here (Table 10.1) are limited to those that are mandatorily, and often permanently, imposed by state laws in both states. These examples do not include the volumes of discretionary state laws also widely enacted. Virginia and Illinois are chosen as case examples because the Legal Action Center, in its 2009 report, ranked Virginia a state with one of the most extensive networks of civil disabilities and Illinois as the state with the least extensive set of civil disabilities.

It should be noted that the decreased civil disabilities imposed on Trey in Illinois, though much improved from those in Virginia, are not ideal. Trey remains limited in his pursuit of full rehabilitation and societal reintegration, even in states with the most liberal of policies. Improvements in civil disability policy are needed, across the entire country, if we are to make a permanent shift from a system with a focus on punishment to one of rehabilitative aims.

IMPLICATIONS FOR RESEARCH AND REFORM

State and federal governments are experimenting with decarceration-oriented reforms such as justice reinvestment initiatives, changing criminal codes, reconsidering sentencing laws, and using less restrictive correctional practices. But the experiments are proceeding without a true understanding of how civil disability policies might influence the potential feasibility and success of criminal justice reforms. Because governments are increasingly less willing and less fiscally able to support incarceration as the default response to crime, the number of people being released from jails and prisons is unprecedentedly high. There is an urgent need to investigate how to align public policy and rehabilitative practices to support reforms and ensure that people release from incarceration with the greatest possible chance of success to ultimately reduce crime.

TABLE 10.1

Civil Disabilities: A Tale of Two States

Virginia	Illinois

Employment

- Permanently banned from numerous career paths, including healthcare, respite services, assisted living, nursing facility care, behavioral health or developmental services, private security services, waste management, law enforcement, child care, private school employment, social services boards, child welfare, bail enforcement, tow truck driver, and having a commercial driver's license.
- Employers are allowed to deny Trey employment based on having a criminal record. Virginia allows for widespread public access to criminal records. Trey's offense record is readily available to any potential employers.
- May need alternative transportation to and from work because his driver's license may be revoked up to 1 year due to drug offense.

- Cannot work in child or elderly care services or any Medicaid managed healthcare facility or child facility funded by Department of Human Services; cannot be an officer, consultant, or adviser for a labor organization, employed as a mentor for children of prisoners, or work in AmeriCorps; in airports, cannot work in security or as a bag handler, and cannot go unescorted through security areas; cannot operate a commercial vehicle or drive for care-based organizations, religious organizations, or private carrier companies providing public transportation; cannot be employed by or volunteer with Illinois HOPE program, law enforcement, or park districts.
- Potential employers have readily available access to his criminal history and can choose not to hire him based on criminal background.
- Able to retain a driver's license.

Housing

- Barred from certain housing options.
- Not allowed to obtain a public housing lease.
- Restricted from living with family members (including an intimate partner) that have foster or adoptive children.
- Cannot reside at a home-based child, adult, or family day center.

- After assessment, may be eligible for public housing.

Positive Social Networks and Civic Engagement

- Permanent ban from being an adoptive or foster parent.
- Cannot marry an immigrant.
- Ineligible for some retirement benefits, food stamps, and unemployment benefits.
- Voter registration will be canceled.
- Right to vote is permanently revoked.

- After several years, able to become an adoptive or foster parent after passing an individualized assessment.
- Not eligible for TANF or food stamps.
- Voter registration suspended during incarceration.
- Eligible to vote upon release.

In 2009, the Uniform Law Commission developed the Collateral Consequences of Conviction Act that is a standardized procedural approach to limiting and codifying civil disabilities that can be adopted by states (Uniform Law Commission, 2009). The act also creates two forms of relief from civil disabilities aimed at facilitating full integration of those who have completed sentences for felony convictions.[2] The first is an Order of Limited Relief, which permits a court or agency to lift the automatic bar of a collateral sanction. For example, an occupational licensing agency or public housing authority may relieve a restriction that would otherwise disqualify an individual from certain occupational fields or housing units. The second form of relief is a Certificate of Restoration of Rights. This certificate is awarded based on concrete and objective information that demonstrates a reentrant's progress toward rehabilitation. This certificate may be presented to potential landlords, employers, or licensing agencies where there is discretionary enforcement of civil disabilities. Widespread adoption of these two forms of relief can alleviate the impacts of both mandatory and discretionary civil disabilities. As of 2014, one state has adopted the act and four states have introduced legislation for consideration.

Other potential opportunities to alleviate the burden of civil disabilities is to notify defendants about potential civil disabilities affected by their particular charge, especially at or before formal notification of charges (which may impact pleas and plea bargains). Another opportunity to mitigate civil disabilities is to require that they be authorized by statute rather than ordinance or informal policy. This could lead to equitable enforcement and allow both legal and non-legal entities to have a firm understanding of what civil disabilities are in place in any given state. Finally, if a conviction has been overturned or pardoned, including convictions from other jurisdictions, or an offense expunged, civil disabilities should be automatically and immediately lifted and civil rights restored.

Further research is needed to inform both state and federal civil disability policies in ways that align with rehabilitative practice to better understand what leads to the adoption of civil disability policies. This research could answer questions such as, "What are the intended effects of any given category of civil disability policy?" For example, if limited resources are driving the adoption of policies such as limiting public assistance to people with felony histories, there should be research into whether civil disabilities leads to more criminal offending—as criminal offending is highly costly given the costs associated with law enforcement, courts, corrections, and victimization. Research is also needed that examines what different types of civil disabilities actually accomplish. Do civil disabilities promote public safety in some cases? Do they make crime more likely in other cases? Do civil disabilities contribute to racial and economic stratification? Do they contribute to disproportionate criminal justice contact for some groups? For example, the Sentencing Project argues a racial impact study of civil disabilities is needed (Schrantz & McElroy, 2008).

---

[2] See www.uniformlaws.org.

Finally, how will researchers and policymakers know that reducing, aligning, or integrating civil disability policies with rehabilitative practices is successful in terms of individual and societal well-being? The answers to these types of questions can inform courts as well as policymakers who are operating on intuition and perceptions of public opinion rather than theory and data. Although civil disabilities are not formally a part of what courts refer to as the criminal process, research is needed to articulate how they interact with the criminal process including how civil disabilities relate to recidivism. More theoretical, conceptual, and empirical work is needed to outline what is risked and gained by reversing a given set of civil disability policies.

With rare exception (e.g., Reentry Net), contemporary rehabilitation programs work around civil disabilities. Advocates of civil disability reforms have proposed several options for states and the federal government to adopt that would help move beyond the broad reach of civil disabilities. For example, individualized disabilities at sentencing, consideration of disabilities that will be faced as a part of sentencing, and predetermined shelf lives of civil disabilities. One proposal that most closely approximates integrating rehabilitation practices and civil disabilities is certificates of rehabilitation in which individuals are no longer subject to certain civil disabilities after they have completed rehabilitation programming. Despite a lack of research into the effectiveness of certificates of rehabilitation, a growing number of states are adopting this model.

The current quilt of civil disability policies restrict, if not eliminate, participation for those with criminal convictions in social structures such as family, housing/neighborhoods, the workplace, and civic engagement. This social and civic isolation robs both individuals and communities of human capital and works counter to our aims of establishing and maintaining public safety and well-being. Major shifts in policy are required to support of evidence-driven rehabilitation and decarceration. Only then can we end the informal extension of criminal justice sanctions through civil disability policy. We must align our nation's civil disability policies with rehabilitative practice to facilitate effective and sustainable decarceration.

REFERENCES

American Bar Association. (2013). National Inventory of the Collateral Consequences of Conviction.

Andrews, D. A., & Bonta, J. (2010). Rehabilitating criminal justice policy and practice. *Psychology, Public Policy, and Law, 16*(1), 39.

Bahr, S. J., Armstrong, A. H., Gibbs, B. G., Harris, P. E., & Fisher, J. K. (2005). The reentry process: How parolees adjust to release from prison. *Fathering, 3*(3), 243.

Berg, M. T., & Huebner, B. M. (2011). Reentry and the ties that bind: An examination of social ties, employment, and recidivism. *Justice Quarterly, 28*(2), 382–410.

Blakinger, K. (2015). Why colleges should admit more ex-felons. *The Washington Post*. Washington, DC. Retrieved from https://www.washingtonpost.com/posteverything/wp/2015/06/21/why-colleges should-admit-more-ex-felons/

Bushway, S. D., & Sweeten, G. (2007). Abolish lifetime bans for ex-felons. *Criminology and Public Policy, 6*(4), 697–706.

Chesney-Lind, M., & Mauer, M. (Eds.). (2002). *Invisible punishment: The collateral consequences of mass imprisonment.* New York, NY: The New Press.

Chin, G. J. (2012). The new civil death: Rethinking punishment in the era of mass conviction. *University of Pennsylvania Law Review, 160,* 1789.

Chin, G. J., & Holmes, R. W., Jr., (2001). Effective assistance of counsel and the consequences of guilty pleas. *Cornell Law Review, 87,* 697.

Clark, V. A. (2014). Predicting two types of recidivism among newly released prisoners first addresses as "launch pads" for recidivism or reentry success. *Crime and Delinquency, 62*(10), 1364–1400.

Davis, L. M. (2013). *Evaluating the effectiveness of correctional education: A meta-analysis of programs that provide education to incarcerated adults.* Santa Monica, CA: Rand Corporation.

Demleitner, N. V. (1999). Reforming juvenile sentencing. *Federal Sentencing Report, 11,* 243.

Ewald, A. (2005). *A crazy-quilt of tiny pieces: State and local administration of American criminal disenfranchisement law* (Vol. 16). Sentencing Project.

Ewald, A. C. (2012). Collateral consequences in the American states. *Social Science Quarterly, 93*(1), 211–247.

Ewald, A. C., & Smith, M. (2008). Collateral consequences of criminal convictions in American courts: The view from the state bench. *Justice System Journal, 29*(2), 145–165.

Geller, A., & Curtis, M. A. (2011). A sort of homecoming: Incarceration and the housing security of urban men. *Social Science Research, 40*(4), 1196–1213.

Greenberg, G. A., & Rosenheck, R. A. (2008). Homelessness in the state and federal prison population. *Criminal Behaviour and Mental Health, 18*(2), 88–103.

Hager, E. (2016). *Six states where felons can't get food stamps.* The Marshall Project.

Harlow, C. W. (2003). *Education and correctional populations.* Bureau of Justice Statistics Special Report. Retrieved from https://www.bjs.gov/content/pub/pdf/ecp.pdf

James, D. (2004). *Profile of Jail Inmates, 2002.* Bureau of Justice Statistics Special Report.

LaFollette, H. (2005). Consequences of punishment: Civil penalties accompanying formal punishment. *Journal of Applied Philosophy,* 241–261.

Laird, L. (2013). Doing time extended: Ex-offenders face tens of thousands of legal restrictions, bias and limits on their rights. *ABA Journal, 99*(6), 50–55.

Laub, J. H., & Sampson, R. J. (1993). Turning points in the life course: Why change matters to the study of crime. *Criminology, 31*(3), 301–325.

Legal Action Center. (2004). *After prison: Roadblocks to reentry; A report on state legal barriers facing people with criminal records.* Retrieved from https://lac.org/roadblocks-to-reentry/

Legal Action Center. (2009). *After prison: Roadblocks to reentry.* Retieved from https://lac.org/roadblocks-to-reentry/

Levenson, J. S., D'Amora, D. A., & Hern, A. L. (2007). Megan's law and its impact on community re-entry for sex offenders. *Behavioral Sciences and the Law, 25,* 587–602.

Levenson, J. S., & Prescott, D. S. (2008). Treatment experiences of civilly committed sex offenders: A consumer satisfaction survey. *Sexual Abuse: A Journal of Research and Treatment 21*(1). doi:10.1177/1079063208325205

Love, M. C. (2011). Paying their debt to society: Forgiveness, redemption, and the uniform collateral consequences of conviction act. *Howard Law Journal, 54*(3).

Lutze, F. E., Rosky, J. W., & Hamilton, Z. K. (2014). Homelessness and reentry a multisite outcome evaluation of Washington state's reentry housing program for high risk offenders. *Criminal Justice and Behavior, 41*(4), 471–491.

Makarios, M., Steiner, B., & Travis, L. F. (2010). Examining the predictors of recidivism among men and women released from prison in Ohio. *Criminal Justice and Behavior,* 0093854810382876.

Martinez, D. J., & Christian, J. (2009). The familial relationships of former prisoners: Examining the link between residence and informal support mechanisms. *Journal of Contemporary Ethnography, 38*(2), 201–224.

Maruna, S. (2001). *Making good: How ex-convicts reform and rebuild their lives.* Washington, DC: American Psychological Association.

Mauer, M., & McCalmont, V. (2013, November). *A lifetime of punishment: The impact of the felony drug ban on welfare benefits.* The Sentencing Project.

Mercado, C. C., Alvarez, S., & Levenson, J. (2008). The impact of specialized sex offender legislation on community reentry. *Sexual Abuse: A Journal of Research and Treatment, 20*(2), 188–205.

Metraux, S., & Culhane, D. P. (2006). Recent incarceration history among a sheltered homeless population. *Crime and Delinquency, 52*(3), 504–517.

Miller, M., & Ngugi, I. (2009). *Impacts of housing supports: Persons with mental illness and ex offenders.* Olympia, WA: Washington State Institute for Public Policy.

Mumola, C. J. (2000). *Incarcerated parents and their children.* Bureau of Justice Statistics Special Report.

Nally, J. M., Lockwood, S. R., & Ho, T. (2011). Employment of ex-offenders during the recession. *Journal of Correctional Education, 62*(2), 117–131.

Nally, J. M., Lockwood, S., Ho, T., & Knutson, K. (2014). Post-release recidivism and employment among different types of released offenders: A 5-year follow-up study in the United States. *International Journal of Criminal Justice Sciences, 9*(1), 16.

Petersilia, J., & Cullen, F. T. (2014, June). Liberal but not stupid: Meeting the promise of downsizing prisons. Liberal but not stupid: Meeting the promise of downsizing prisons. *Stanford Journal of Criminal Law and Policy, 2.*

Pinard, M. (2006). Integrated perspective on the collateral consequence of criminal convictions and reentry issues faced by formerly incarcerated individuals. *Boston University Law Review, 86,* 623.

Pogorzelski, W., Wolff, N., Pan, K. Y., & Blitz, C. L. (2005). Behavioral health problems, ex offender reentry policies, and the "Second Chance Act." *American Journal of Public Health, 95*(10), 1718–1724.

Radice, J. (2012). Administering justice: Removing statutory barriers to reentry. *University of Colorado Law Review, 83,* 715.

Rodriguez, M. N., & Avery, B. (2016). Unlicensed and untapped: Removing barriers to state occupational license for people with records. National Employment Law Project. Retrieved from http://www.nelp.org/publication/unlicensed-untapped-removing-barriers-state-occupational-licenses/

Roman, C. G., & Travis, J. (2006). Where will I sleep tomorrow? Housing, homelessness, and the returning prisoner. *Housing Policy Debate, 17*(2), 389–418.

Sampson, R. J., & Laub, J. H. (1990). Crime and deviance over the life course: The salience of adult social bonds. *American Sociological Review, 55*(5), 609–627.

Sampson, R. J., & Laub, J. H. (1994). Urban poverty and the family context of delinquency: A new look at structure and process in a classic study. *Child Development, 65,* 523–540.

Sampson, R. J., & Laub, J. H. (2003). Life-course desisters? Trajectories of crime among delinquent boys followed to age 70. *Criminology, 41,* 555–592.

Schrantz, D., & McElroy, J. (2008). *Reducing racial disparity in the criminal justice system: A manual for practitioners and policy makers.* Sentencing Project.

Subramanian, R., Moreno, R., & Gebreselassie, S. (2014). *Relief in sight?* Vera Institute of Justice. Retrieved from https://storage.googleapis.com/vera-web-assets/downloads/Publications/relief-in-sight-states-rethink-the-collateral-consequences-of-criminal-conviction-2009-2014/legacy_downloads/states-rethink-collateral-consequences-report-v4.pdf

Tewksbury, R., & Mustaine, E. (2009). Stress and collateral consequences for registered sex offenders. *Journal of Public Management and Social Policy, 15*(2), 215–239.

Travis, J. (2005). *But they all come back: Facing the challenges of prisoner reentry.* Washington, DC: The Urban Institute.

Uniform Law Commission. (2009). *Collateral Consequences of Conviction Act.*

US Congress, House of Representatives. (1984). *Comprehensive Crime Control Act of 1984.*

Visher, C. A., Bakken, N. W., & Gunter, W. D. (2013). Fatherhood, community reintegration, and successful outcomes. *Journal of Offender Rehabilitation, 52*(7), 451–469.

Visher, C. A., & Courtney, S. M. (2007). *One year out: Experiences of prisoners returning to Cleveland.*

Visher, C. A., Debus, S., & Yahner, J. (2008). *Employment after prison: A longitudinal study of releases in three states.* Urban Institute, Justice Policy Center.

Weissman, M., Rosenthal, A., Warth, P., Wolf, E., & Messina-Yauchzy, M. (2010). *The use of criminal history records in college admissions reconsidered.* The Center for Community Alternatives. Retrieved from http://www.communityalternatives.org/pdf/Reconsidered-criminal-hist-recs-in-college-admissions.pdf

Western, B., & Pettit, B. (2010). Incarceration and social inequality. *Daedalus, 139*(3), 8–19.

11

A Public Health Approach to Decarceration

STRATEGIES TO REDUCE THE PRISON AND JAIL POPULATION AND SUPPORT REENTRY

Ernest Drucker

BACKGROUND: FROM PUNISHMENT TO PUBLIC HEALTH

The United States incarcerates more people than any other nation in the world. In 2015, it had more than two million people behind bars and another five million on parole and probation (U.S. Bureau of Justice Statistics, 2010). As one measure of this system's punitive policies, the United States also holds more of its citizens in isolation and solitary confinement than all the other prisons of the world combined.

Another 10 to 14 million are arrested every year, and more than 10 million have histories of felony convictions and time served in prisons (Suede, 2014). Astonishingly, between 70 million and 100 million—or as many as one in three Americans—have some type of criminal record (The Sentencing Project, n.d.). Not included in these numbers is the massive impact of incarceration on the families of the incarcerated—on people who have committed no crime at all yet suffer from devastating effects of their family member's imprisonment.

With more than two million still behind bars daily, the first priority for decarceration must be to release those who represent little or no significant threat to public safety. But releasing people from jails and prisons will not be enough—the stigma of incarceration has a long-lasting debilitating effect on the millions who have returned from prison to their communities, dooming more than half to failure and reincarceration within 3 years of leaving prison. There are high rates of recidivism among released prisoners;

for example, in a study of 404,638 prisoners in 30 states after their release from prison, Durose, Cooper, and Snyder (2014) found the following:

- Within 3 years of release, about two-thirds (67.8%) of released individuals were rearrested.
- Within 5 years of release, about three-quarters (76.6%) of released individuals were rearrested.
- Of those rearrested, more than half (56.7%) were arrested by the end of the first year.

Researchers and policymakers must confront the impact of this stigmatic identity and the many restrictions it imposes on formerly incarcerated individuals. To be successful, a paradigm shift is necessary that replaces these impediments to successful reentry with positive places and opportunities for this population in the outside world.

The good news is that the United States is in the midst of a sea change in attitudes and policies about its 40-year epidemic of mass incarceration. As incarceration is recognized as a major determinant of the nation's health and well-being, many from across the political spectrum are calling for major changes to bring down the drivers of mass incarceration, such as drug laws and their mandatory sentencing policies (Drucker, 2013). With this growing awareness of the need to decarcerate the nation, new questions are being raised about the attitudes and beliefs about the use of imprisonment and the role of reentry policies and practices in perpetuating the impacts of punishment and increasing its high social costs after release from prisons.

Mass incarceration directly contributes to many current problems in the communities and populations that it affects the most: low-income individuals and racial minorities. Incarceration's role in perpetuating America's long legacy of racial and class disparities beginning with slavery are clear indicators of America's social and political dysfunction (Alexander, 2010). This is most clearly visible in the great divide now visible between police and communities of color as seen in the Black Lives Matter movement, and the growing focus on worsening patterns of social and economic disparities in America (Miller, 2016). The current practices that sustain mass incarceration are linked to the issues that form its political and practical foundations: sentencing policies, prison and jail conditions, and alternatives to incarceration (e.g., the use of probation, parole, special courts).

This view of the broad impact of mass incarceration lends itself to a public health analysis I first developed in *A Plague of Prisons*, which made the case that mass incarceration is a deadly epidemic that spreads its effects across generations of individuals, families, and communities. In this chapter, I extend this public health analysis and its argument to the issues and challenges of decarceration and argue for the usefulness of the public health model to aid in the vital task of ending the American epidemic of incarceration and, of equal importance, healing those who have survived its blows. I explore how the public health model can inform the decarceration movement's approach to each stage of the process leading to incarceration: arrests and the decision to incarcerate individuals, the negative effects of the conditions of incarceration, and the reform of the process of reentry (Drucker, 2013). Through primary, secondary, and tertiary prevention strategies, decarceration can (1) identify vulnerable populations, (2) transform jails and prisons from institutions of punishment to agents of rehabilitation and public health, and (3) restore formerly incarcerated individuals' civil rights.

DECARCERATION AND PUBLIC HEALTH

Decarceration involves more than getting individuals out of jails and prison; it means getting the traumatic effects of jails and prisons out of them. It represents a new application of the public health model: to inform a national movement in developing new ideas and policies to end the overuse of incarceration and restore a sense of citizenship. Based on the contemporary understanding of the harms imprisonment inflicts on individuals, it is possible to develop new social and political interventions at the community level that can help to reintegrate millions of formerly incarcerated individuals into society. These public health principles of *prevention* serve as the basis to distinguish the emerging concept of decarceration from the simple notion of reentry. Applied to large numbers of formerly incarcerated individuals reentering communities, "smart decarceration" can help end the epidemic of mass incarceration by interrupting the recurrent cycle of recidivism.

A New Kind of Epidemic

A collective social, financial, and public health burden on society, mass incarceration can be considered a *new kind of epidemic* (Drucker, 2013). This epidemic results in chronic disabilities that affect a very large portion of the U.S. population, especially among low-income minority populations, where the immediate public health effects of mass incarceration now include reduced life expectancy, higher infant mortality, and elevated rates of acute and chronic illness on those who have been in prison and for their families (Massoglia, 2008).

Health Risks and Limitations of Social Reintegration at Reentry

When released from jail or prison, individuals face increased health risks (e.g., relapse to drug use, problems getting access to healthcare) and greatly reduced prospects of establishing stable lives in the community. This failure to readapt to "life on the outside" (Gonnerman, 2004) is due in part to the incapacitating restrictions of having been incarcerated (e.g., difficulty finding employment and housing), which compromises their ability to deal with all too common postrelease social and mental health problems. Such restrictions limit formerly incarcerated individuals' ability to reestablish ties to family and community and often lead to a high probability of recidivism.

Formerly incarcerated individuals also face a dramatically increased risk of death within the 2 to 4 weeks after being released from prison—a 10- to 12-fold increase in mortality rates from drug overdose, suicide, homicide, and heart disease (Binswanger et al., 2007) relative to other periods in their lives. This phenomenon has also been observed in released individuals in other nations (e.g., the United Kingdom, Australia), thought to be a measure of the stresses associated with release when their failures become publicly visible to their families (Andrews & Kinner, 2012). These issues point to the public health realities related to mass incarceration and the utility of applying a public health lens to decarceration.

The Public Health Framework: Three Stages of Prevention

In contrast to clinical medicine, which is inherently an individual matter, public health deals with entire populations. Like clinical medicine, public health is action oriented. It has an analytic stage employing diagnostic models, and is explicitly aimed at identifying and applying interventions designed to reduce death and disease in both individuals and populations. In adopting a public health approach, decarceration efforts are less likely to blame and stigmatize individuals; instead, decarceration can focus on the adverse policies and pathogenic environments imposed on entire populations (Drucker, 2013). Applied to the U.S. prison population, this model offers a new framework for creating alternative structures and interventions for formerly incarcerated individuals, designed to foster successful reentry.

Decarceration priorities must address all of the major elements of the criminal justice system that determine the size of the prison and jail population and the rates of incarceration and likelihood of success after release. By focusing on alleviating the burdens of the "chronic disease" effects of incarceration on populations and the generally poorly resourced communities in which they live (Clear, 2009) the public health prevention model can focus on the concrete steps of primary, secondary, and tertiary prevention and their impact on the size and characteristics of the U.S. prison population.

PRIMARY PREVENTION

The first aim of the public health approach to epidemic disease is prevention of incidence (i.e., to stop its spread by reducing the number of new cases), termed *primary prevention*. Applied to mass incarceration, primary prevention's first objective is to have fewer people entering jails and prisons. Often called the "the front door" approach, primary prevention is seeing a growing national campaign, with many states already beginning to reduce the size of their prison populations by reducing new admissions and reforming arrest and sentencing practices (Eckholm, 2015; Parsons, Drucker, & Clear, 2015; The Sentencing Project, 2015).

By minimizing admissions to jails and prisons, a primary prevention approach aims to divert individuals from not only the experience of incarceration but also the cascade of consequences that follows. First, it is important to understand major differences in jail and prison admission patterns. Whereas prison admissions to state or federal institutions typically involve sentences of a year or more of incarceration, 85% of all jail admissions are for brief periods of detention, typically a week or less (Spaulding et al., 2010). Longer jail stays are often for those who cannot make bail while awaiting trial or bargaining for release and are not yet convicted or sentenced. Though short lengths of jail stays may be less traumatic than longer prison sentences, they reach a broader population, with 11 million individuals per year spending time in jail (Subramanian, Delaney, Roberts, Fishman, & McGarry, 2015). Given frequent arrests or summonses, many more have lives disrupted by even a short time behind bars. Though 40% of those with a first *prison* admission do not return to prison, 65% of those released from prison will be back again within 5 years (Durose et al., 2014)—and back again and again thereafter. The fact that admission to jail or prison greatly predicts subsequent episodes of incarceration demonstrates the importance of primary prevention strategies.

Primary prevention looks to early intervention for diversion of individuals from all stages of punishment, with the goals of minimizing the harms associated with the adverse impacts of arrest and even short-term detention (most often due to the inability to make bail), which can immediately lead to loss of employment, child custody, and housing, all basic issues essential to successful reentry. Each depends on establishing a base in local communities, often the home communities from which prisoners come. Therefore, an initial primary prevention step would be to develop an inventory to assess the available assets in the community in which the bulk of prison and jail admissions originates. The idea is to place each such community (focusing on those that have large numbers of reentering prisoners) and equip them to support individuals who are being diverted from first time incarceration. These practices could also be applied to individuals reentering from jail or prison, the outcome of which would be public safety improvements. This becomes both an investment in support for preventing incarceration and a basis of identifying and maintaining existing positive social and community ties and establishing new services and supports based on restorative justice practices.

As the goal becomes keeping more people out of jails and prisons, important tools for primary prevention of incarceration now include the reform of drug laws and other sentencing practices, and policy changes and legal challenges to bail that disproportionally targets the poor for pretrial detention (Schlanger, 2003).

Drug Law Reform

Reform of drug laws and sentencing practices is a promising step to reducing new commitments to prisons. Federal sentencing changes (especially ending long mandatory sentences for drug offenses) have reduced prison populations by over 20% in several states (Carson, 2015). There are calls to release as many as 40,000 more prisoners now in federal prisons serving out their long sentences for nonviolent drug offenses with plans for new more moderate sentencing policies, but with little chance of their being applied retroactively (Mauer, 2011). In addition, state-by-state changes in drug laws and sentences have produced significant changes in the number of drug cases arrested and sentenced to prisons (Parsons et al., 2015). As more and more states soften or eliminate punitive drug laws, there will be considerable reductions in the numbers of people entering prisons.

Bail Reform

Bail reform is another important primary prevention step to reducing excessive jail stays as well as the number of new prison entrants. Recent studies show that extended pretrial detention, which can be more dangerous than prison, can lead to increased likelihood of recidivism—especially for younger prisoners (Lowenkamp, VanNostrand, & Holsinger, 2013). New approaches to bail must be based on offenders' risk to public safety (i.e., the severity of their crimes) rather than on their ability to raise a few hundred dollars in cash. According to New York state's Chief Judge, Jonathan Lippman, New York's "intolerable" bail system has created a "two-tiered system of justice, one for those with money and one for those without" (Glazer, 2015).

> Those arrested on misdemeanors or nonviolent felonies and can make bail, return to home work while they wait for their day in court . . . [but] the poor don't enjoy *such luxuries.* They are incarcerated . . . by the thousands, they sit in dangerous prisons like the Rikers Island complex for months, sometimes years, because they cannot afford bail as low as $1,000. After months of delay, many simply give up, plead guilty and accept what is often a rotten deal that sends them back into society with a criminal record . . . pretrial detention can tear apart the very fabric of people's lives, [where] they lose their jobs, their housing. They can lose their place in school or their health in these rough and unsafe prisons. (Pinto, 2015)

To prevent this sort of damaging progression of events, there are now calls for a complete overhaul of the bail system based on the federal system, "where a judge has broad discretion to decide whether a suspect is a flight risk or a danger to society" (New York Times Editorial Board, 2015). One possible solution would be to appoint a senior judge in each New York City borough to review every misdemeanor case in which a defendant fails to pay bail. The review would take place within 10 days of arraignment to determine whether bail should be reduced. The judge would order periodic reviews for people in custody awaiting trial on felony charges to either expedite the trial or reduce the bail. A pilot program in Manhattan Criminal Court would allow judges to release some defendants charged with misdemeanors to be monitored electronically with a bracelet.

The borough judges would ask state and city judges to offer defendants less onerous alternatives to putting up cash or using bail bonds with high fees.

Key Task in Primary Prevention: Identify Vulnerable Populations
and Divert Them from Incarceration

For primary prevention efforts to succeed in reducing jail and prison admissions, researchers and practitioners must identify appropriate target populations to divert from incarceration. Decades of criminological research have articulated multiple predictive risk factors for criminal activity (i.e., school and job functioning, substance abuse, antisocial thoughts and attitudes), but these matters are often not addressed prior to incarceration. The primary prevention lens challenges decarceration efforts to target subpopulations for early intervention at the time of arrest to avoid unnecessary incarceration—often involving police in Law Enforcement Assisted Diversion.[1] Another target population of focus is people in poverty, as there is also a growing awareness of and motivation (part of it financial) to reduce the high rates of incarceration associated with poor people's failure to make bail. This is increasingly being seen in the context of "debtor prisons" and other throwbacks to medieval criminal justice practices that the United States formally disavows but still practices (Stillman, 2014).

Another subpopulation to focus on is youth who commit violent crimes. *Restorative justice* models, such as the Common Justice program at the Vera Institute of Justice in New York City, employ innovative alternative-to-incarceration services. Working with one of the most important and difficult populations—young people aged 16 to 24 years who commit violent felonies—Common Justice aims to reduce violence, facilitate the well-being of those harmed, and transform the criminal justice system's response to serious crime. Common Justice provides participants with "a respectful and effective means of accountability, an equitable and dignified avenue to healing, and the tools to break cycles of violence" (Vera Institute of Justice, n.d.).

Common Justice uses the terms "harmed party" and "responsible party" to describe the person who survives harm and the person who causes harm, respectively. These terms recognize someone's role in a given event and acknowledges that that it does not constitute the person's entire identity. A harmed party is owed certain things by the responsible party as a result of the harm he or she endured. If and only if the harmed party welcomes the process, the responsible and harmed parties are diverted into a victim–offender mediation program with intensive preparatory and follow-up components. This approach seeks to develop and employ a humane, event-centered language for talking about people involved in crime and violence.[2]

---

[1] See http://leadkingcounty.org.
[2] See http://www.vera.org/project/common-justice.

In the public health approach to decarceration, *secondary prevention* acknowledges the fact that it is impossible to prevent all new cases of arrest and incarceration, no matter how unjust and socially destructive they may be. Through secondary prevention, decarceration can further reduce the size of the prison population by releasing more prisoners who pose no harm to public safety, such as older adults and those determined to be low risk (Law, 2016). This approach addresses both individuals and populations affected by mass incarceration. In addition, it offers specific plans and programs to heal the many wounds of the affected populations, both the victims of crime and the victims of mass incarceration.

Decarceration efforts must use secondary prevention to minimize the negative impacts of incarceration as the response to all social tensions and individual criminal actions. The evidence (Mauer & Ghandnoosh, 2014) proves that recidivism can be decreased while incarcerated individuals are released more quickly without compromising public safety. However, much remains to be done to address the circumstances of those already arrested, going through the criminal courts, and entering jails and prisons. To this end, secondary prevention can be achieved by sentencing reform, which shortens prison stays and promotes restorative justice programs that offer alternatives to extended punishment.

Key Tasks in Secondary Prevention

All too often, U.S. prisons and jails are overly punitive places where violence and victimization at the hands of staff or other prisoners is a regular occurrence. These facilities often lack the capacity to provide supportive services needed to address recidivism risks. Secondary prevention leads to the rethinking of the function of prisons and jails for those who must be confined for reasons of public safety, given the risk they may pose to others. This can be accomplished through incarceration-based programs with rehabilitative objectives and outcomes—especially drug treatment, mental and behavioral health services, and access to higher education—whereby rehabilitative outcomes can become achievable goals (Kenner, 2015). For example, college-in-prison programs across the country have converted the prison experience for a small number of prisoners from one of primarily punishment to one of personal growth and advancement through higher education (Halkovic et al., 2013).

Although there are nearly 1.5 million people in jail or prison in the United States today that meet criteria for substance use disorders, only about 11% receive substance abuse treatment while incarcerated (Taxman & Kitsantas, 2009). For those with substance abuse disorders for whom incarceration cannot be avoided, there must be greater access to substance abuse treatment services behind bars. The United States can learn much from prison programs in other nations that have successfully maintained incarceration rates from 80% to 90% lower than those of the United States (Drucker, 2013). Effective models of restorative justice and reconciliation programs within prisons are now being developed in some countries with very long histories of violent prisons, such as Rwanda and South Africa (Dreisinger, 2015).

TERTIARY PREVENTION

In clinical medicine, *tertiary prevention* is the term used for chronic "incurable" conditions where interventions are aimed not at cure but instead seek to minimize suffering and the extent of physical and mental disability among those with longer term cases of any disease. It focuses on both the individual and the collective effects of long-term health problems and often employs community interventions to address entire populations, reduction of risky human behavior, and the social structures and resources that support risk reduction in both physical and social environments.

Applied to mass incarceration and decarceration, tertiary prevention seeks to minimize the chronic effects imposed by incarceration and its adverse impact on formerly incarcerated individuals upon reentry. Tertiary prevention can lead to environmental changes that can improve formerly incarcerated individuals' life prospects and experience upon release (e.g., employment training, access to healthcare, higher education). The sustained adverse impact of imprisonment on social and economic life outside of prison must now be approached via collective solutions for restoring the very communities most affected by high rates of imprisonment and lowering the likelihood of recidivism—a form of relapse (Clear, 1996). This step involves building new community-based models and structures for the education, employment, housing, and healthcare for the formerly incarcerated population (Gates, Artiga, & Rudowitz, 2014).

There are new models of community leadership by formerly incarcerated individuals. For example, Glenn Martin, a formerly incarcerated individual himself, started a community leadership training program for other formerly incarcerated individuals called Just Leadership USA.[3] Such programs are growing into a network of restorative justice programs and represent an emerging crucial asset of reentry communities. They recognize the social capital of reentering individuals and their roles in immunizing new generations of minority youth at risk of future incarceration (Coates, 2015).

Key Tasks for Tertiary Prevention

To promote sustainable decarceration, the criminal justice system must provide meaningful support—not just supervision—for people after release. Carrying a criminal record

---

[3] See https://www.justleadershipusa.org/about-us/.

severely restricts formerly incarcerated individuals' access to education, employment, housing, and full participation in society and the economy—a long line of restrictions and disenfranchisements that systematically obstruct their efforts at social and family reintegration. To deal with the reentry surge of decarceration, new services are necessary to accommodate housing and employment needs.

Because many newly released individuals have difficulty reintegrating into society, programs, such as the day labor work crews (Finn, 1998), that help them prepare for, find, and keep jobs are necessary. In addition to enabling the participants to earn a daily income, day labor work crews help them structure their lives and develop good work habits. These are steps along the way to placing ex-offenders in permanent, unsubsidized, full-time jobs that provide benefits and compensation above minimum wage. Such programs typically offer ongoing services to all placed participants for at least 6 months after placement. Three-fourths of participants placed remain employed at the same job after 1 month, and about half still work at that job after 6 months (Finn, 1998).

Health and mental healthcare needs also must be addressed, which is now more possible due to provisions of the Affordable Care Act. Such provisions extend the 8th Amendment right of prisoners to healthcare while incarcerated, making care available after release in the states that have agreed to extend their Medicaid services. Rather than simply addressing individual cases under the restrictions of parole supervision, which tends to focus on individual failures, tertiary prevention focuses on readapting individuals to living in communities as full citizens following periods of incarceration by recognizing their special needs (especially around drugs and mental health). Restoration of felons' voting rights is now the subject of aggressive steps to reverse a century of civic death through voting disenfranchisement—currently affecting millions of American's right to vote (Chung, 2016).

The work of the criminologist Shadd Maruna (2001) created a conceptual framework for addressing a fundamental issue of reentry. It analyzes the lives of repeat offenders who, by all statistical measures, should have continued on the criminal path but instead created lives of productivity and purpose and asks the fundamental question beyond the details of reentry and rehabilitative services: Can "hardened criminals" really reform (Maruna, 2001)? By providing a narrative analysis of the lives of repeat offenders who created lives of productivity and purpose, Maruna answers that question as "yes," and shows how criminals who desist from crime often construct powerful narratives that aid them in making sense of their pasts, finding fulfillment in productive behaviors, and feeling in control of their future (Maruna, 2001).

The additional work of tertiary prevention, then, must focus on providing the kinds of concrete individual and structural supports necessary to facilitate such optimism. Also necessary are opportunities for individuals—especially those who cannot avoid reincarceration—to develop desistance narratives.

DISCUSSION

Maruna's approach links to the work of Deborah Small—a legal scholar, community organizer, and founder of Break the Chains—a program designed to enable communities of color to address the consequences and frame new alternatives to the War on Drugs. Small speaks of "decarceration as healing," and argues that the growth of the decarceration "movement" has potential to play a central role for healing some of the issues currently plaguing our society, specifically institutional racism, income inequality, overcriminalization, and educational failure (Small, 2015). She argues that decarceration can address "the lingering impact of centuries of racist ideology on the American psyche and associated white privilege" while working for "a sustainable model of full employment for all those people currently caught up in the criminal justice system who have been essentially excluded from the mainstream economy," providing for "a new basis for satisfaction, self-esteem, and meaning to many whose lives have been devoid of such opportunities" (Small, 2015).

As described in this chapter, the public health approach can help achieve this goal by considering the wide spectrum of population health and social data (not just crime rates) as a means of identifying and measuring the driving forces of the mass incarceration epidemic. An effective or "smart" decarceration strategy should address the underlying social significance of excess punitiveness and work to reverse its many adverse effects.

Incorporating a public health model for decarceration can help to transform the criminal justice system and society in ways that work together to prevent incarceration by addressing its root causes and alleviating its damaging effects. By identifying and intervening early with populations vulnerable to incarceration, primary prevention strategies have the potential to significantly alter trajectories that would likely otherwise result in the revolving door experience of incarceration and recidivism. Secondary prevention approaches acknowledge the notion that incarceration for punishment only does little to benefit society, and that every effort should be made to provide meaningful rehabilitative services for those behind bars. Tertiary prevention aims to recognize and repair the myriad burdens and obstacles that individuals experience upon release and reentry, so that formerly incarcerated individuals have the greatest chance for not returning to jail or prison. Applying prevention lenses to the monumental task of decarceration provides a proactive framework for addressing the multilayered and complex causes and effects of incarceration on society's health and well-being.

The relevance of a public health approach to decarceration is underscored by healthcare reform advances through the Affordable Care Act. For those states that have enacted Medicaid expansion, many criminal-justice-involved populations that were previously uninsured are now eligible for health insurance. This provides unique and unprecedented opportunities to access evidence-based behavioral health and primary health services for populations vulnerable to incarceration, which can reduce the likelihood of first time or repeat imprisonment via all three prevention strategies (Heller, 2016). Leveraging the Affordable Care Act can help to make life on the outside possible for former prisoners and reduce the likelihood of reimprisonment, making this a powerful mechanism for decarceration.

CONCLUSION

The United States is at a seminal moment in the struggle to reverse mass incarceration. A major shift in thinking about drug policies, drug laws, and their mandatory long prison sentences marks a nascent recognition of their role in creating mass incarceration and making it one of the most pressing problems in America. Many Americans acknowledge that the overuse of imprisonment (not drugs or crime per se) sustains the institutions of mass incarceration. The new goal is to end it. This involves getting millions out of prison and jail and keeping them out, and replacing the current system of punishment to one premised on individual rehabilitation and public health.

The current political climate about the use of mass incarceration makes this new approach very timely. There is now a broad and growing base of support for ending mass incarceration in America (Chettiar, 2015). The great value of decarceration as an alternative to the cyclical recurrence of arrest and recidivism is that it offers a new paradigm—a shift to a strategy that directly addresses the underlying social pathogenicity of the criminal justice system's excessive punitiveness. This attitude is a key to reversing the course of the catastrophic epidemic of mass incarceration in America. Incorporating a public health approach to the tasks of decarceration will help to realize this paradigm shift and, as this book proposes, pursue policies and programs that are necessary to advance both public safety *and* public health for the nation.

REFERENCES

Alexander, M. (2010). *The new Jim Crow*. New York, NY: The New Press.

Andrews, J. Y., & Kinner, S. A. (2012). Understanding drug-related mortality in released prisoners: A review of national coronial records. *BMC Public Health, 12*(270). doi:10.1186/1471-2458-12-270

Binswanger I. A., Stern, M. F., Deyo, R. A., Heagerty, P. J., Cheadle, A., Elmore, J. G., & Koepsell, T. D. (2007). Release from prison—A high risk of death for former inmates. *New England Journal of Medicine, 356,* 157–165. doi:10.1056/NEJMsa064115

Carson, E. A. (2015). *Prisoners in 2014*. U.S. Department of Justice: Office of Justice Programs, Bureau of Justice Statistics, NCJ 248955. Retrieved from http://www.bjs.gov/content/pub/pdf/p14.pdf

Chettiar, I. M. (2015, April 27). A national agenda to reduce mass incarceration. *NYU Brennan Center for Law And Justice*. Retrieved from https://www.brennancenter.org/analysis/national-agenda-reduce-mass-incarceration

Chung, J. (2016). *Felony disenfranchisement: A primer*. The Sentencing Project. Retrieved from http://www.sentencingproject.org/publications/felony-disenfranchisement-a-primer/

Clear, T. R. (2009). *Imprisoning communities: How mass incarceration makes disadvantaged neighborhoods worse*. New York, NY: Oxford University Press.

Clear T. R. (1996). Backfire: When incarceration increases crime. *Journal of the Oklahoma Criminal Justice Research Consortium, 3*, 7–18.

Coates, T. (2015, October). The black family in the age of mass incarceration. *The Atlantic*. Retrieved from http://www.theatlantic.com/magazine/archive/2015/10/the-black-family-in-the-age-of-mass-incarceration/403246/

Dreisinger, B. (2015). *Incarcerated nations*. New York, NY: The Other Press.

Drucker, E. (2013). A plague of prisons: The epidemiology of mass incarceration in America. New York, NY: The New Press.

Durose, M. R., Cooper A. D., & Snyder, H. N. (2014). Recidivism of prisoners released in 30 states in 2005: Patterns from 2005 to 2010. Bureau of Justice Statistics Special Report, NCJ 244205.

Eckholm, E. (2015, February 26). Out of prison, and staying out, after 3rd strike in California. *New York Times*. Retrieved from http://www.nytimes.com/2015/02/27/us/california-convicts-are-out-of-prison-after-third-strike-and-staying-out.html?_r=0

Finn, P. (1998). Successful job placement for ex-offenders. The Center of Employment Opportunities. Retrieved from https://www.ncjrs.gov/txtfiles/168102.txt

Gates, A., Artiga, S., & Rudowitz, R. (2014, September 5). *Health coverage and care for the adult criminal justice-involved population*. The Kaiser Family Foundation. Retrieved from http://kff.org/uninsured/issue-brief/health-coverage-and-care-for-the-adult-criminal-justice-involved-population/

Glazer, E. (2015, October 15). *New York City's big idea on bail*. The Marshall Fund. Retrieved from https://www.themarshallproject.org/2015/10/15/new-york-city-s-big-idea-on-bail#.tEwLDCeVV

Gonnerman, J. (2004). *Life on the outside: The prison odyssey of Elaine Bartlett*. New York, NY: Picador.

Halkovic, A., Fine, M., Bae, J., Campbell, L., Evans, D., Gary, C., . . . Tejawi, A. (2013). *Higher education and reentry: The gifts they bring*. John Jay College of Criminal Justice: Prisoner Reentry Institute. Retrieved from http://johnjayresearch.org/pri/files/2013/11/Higher-Education-in-Reentry.pdf

Heller, D. (2016). *The Affordable Care Act (ACA) and healthcare reform is a vehicle for decarceration*. Retrieved from http://decarceration.org/2016/01/10/healthcare-reform-is-a-vehicle-for-decarceration

Kenner, M. (2015). *The Bard prison initiative*. Retrieved from http://bpi.bard.edu/what-we-do. 2015

Law, V. (2016, June 18). Aging, sick and incarcerated: The need for compassionate release. *Truthout*. Retrieved from http://www.truth-out.org/news/item/36464-aging-sick-and-incarcerated-the-need-for-compassionate-release

Suede, M. (2014, June 5). What percentage of the U.S. adult population has a felony conviction? *Libertarian News*. Retrieved from https://www.libertariannews.org/2014/06/05/what-percentage-of-us-adult-population-that-has-a-felony-conviction/

Lowenkamp, C. T., VanNostrand, M., & Holsinger, A. (2013). *The hidden costs of pretrial detention*. The Arnold Foundation. Retrieved from http://www.pretrial.org/download/research/TheHiddenCostsofPretrialDetention-LJAF2013.pdf

Maruna, S. (2001). *Making good: How ex-convicts reform and rebuild their lives*. Washington DC: American Psychological Association.

Mauer, M. (2011). *Sentencing reform amid mass incarcerations—Guarded optimism*. The Sentencing Project. Retrieved from http://sentencingproject.org/wp-content/uploads/2016/01/ABA-Sentencing-Reform-Amid-Mass-Incarcerations-Guarded-Optimism.pdf

Mauer, M., & Ghandnoosh, N. (2014). *Fewer prisoners, less crime: A tale of three states*. The Sentencing Project. Retrieved from http://www.sentencingproject.org/publications/fewer-prisoners-less-crime-a-tale-of-three-states/

Massoglia, M. (2008). Incarceration as exposure: The prison, infectious disease, and other stress-related illnesses. *Journal of Health and Social Behavior, 49,* 56–71.

Miller, R. W. (2016, July 12). Black Lives Matter: A primer on what it is and what it stands for. *USA Today*. Retrieved from http://www.usatoday.com/story/news/nation/2016/07/11/black-lives-matter-what-what-stands/86963292/

New York Times Editorial Board. (2015, October 2) Bail reform for indigent suspects. *New York Times*. Retrieved from http://www.nytimes.com/2015/10/03/opinion/bail-reform-for-indigent-suspects.html

Parsons, J., Drucker, E., & Clear, T. (2015). *A natural experiment in reform: Analyzing drug policy change in New York City*. National Institute of Justice. Retrieved from https://www.ncjrs.gov/pdffiles1/nij/grants/248524.pdf

Pinto, N. (2015, August 13). The bail trap. *The New York Times*. Retrieved from http://www.nytimes.com/2015/08/16/magazine/the-bail-trap.html

Schlanger, M. (2003). *Differences between jails and prisons*. Prisons Seminar, Harvard Law School, Spring 2003. Retrieved from https://www.law.umich.edu/facultyhome/margoschlanger/Documents/Resources/The_Difference_Between_Jails_and_Prisons%20.pdf

The Sentencing Project. (2015). *Trends in U.S. correction*. The Sentencing Project. Retrieved from http://sentencingproject.org/wp-content/uploads/2016/01/Trends-in-US-Corrections.pdf

The Sentencing Project. (n.d.). *Criminal justice facts*. The Sentencing Project. Retrieved from http://www.sentencingproject.org/criminal-justice-facts/

Small, D. (2015). *Decarceration as healing*. Decarceration.org. Retrieved from http://decarceration.org/2015/11/22/decarceration-as-healing/

Spaulding, A. C., Perez, S. D., Seals, R. M., Hallman, M. A., Kavasery, R., & Weiss, P. S. (2010). Diversity of release patterns for jail detainees: Implications for public health interventions. *American Journal of Public Health, 101*(51), S347–S352.

Stillman, S. (2014, June 23). Get out of Jail, Inc. *The New Yorker*. Retrieved from http://www.newyorker.com/magazine/2014/06/23/get-out-of-jail-inc

Subramanian, R., Delaney, R., Roberts, S., Fishman, N., & McGarry, P. (2015). *Incarceration's front door*. Vera Institute of Justice. Retrieved from http://archive.vera.org/sites/default/files/resources/downloads/incarcerations-front-door-report.pdf

Taxman, F. S., & Kitsantas, P. (2009). Availability and capacity of substance abuse programs in correctional settings: A classification and regression tree analysis. *Drug and Alcohol Dependence*, 103(1), S43–S53.

U.S. Bureau of Justice Statistics. (2010). *Prison inmate characteristics*. Retrieved from http://www.bjs.gov/index.cfm?ty=tp&tid=132

12

Community Interventions for Justice-Involved Individuals

ASSESSING GAPS IN PROGRAMMING TO PROMOTE
DECARCERATION

Faye S. Taxman and Amy Murphy

BACKGROUND

Decarceration, as a social movement, has accelerated policy reform of the justice system. Much of the discussion focuses on reforming (1) sentencing; (2) pretrial release and supervision; (3) use of risk–need assessment information at all decision points; (4) early release through earned discharge efforts; and (5) justice reinvestment. These welcome policy shifts were designed to reduce and ease the penal severity of mass incarceration practices. These are critical reforms that can undoubtedly change the shape of the justice system. Though well intentioned, such reforms overlook the individual-level factors that lead to offending behavior and the research on evidence-based practices to tackle criminal behavior. Attention to individual-level issues is critical given the end goal of decarceration is not simply to reduce incarceration but also to reduce offending and recidivism. Decarceration is built on a framework of addressing mass incarceration by addressing human conduct and behavior that drives criminal behaviors.

By a conservative estimate, *evidence-based programs*—interventions found to be effective based on rigorous research—reduce recidivism by 20% to 30% through addressing the human conditions that affect involvement in criminal behavior (Caudy, Tang, Ainsworth, Lerch, & Taxman, 2013; Nagin, Cullen, & Jonson, 2009). Such gains could be even greater with significant expansions to programs for the *justice-involved population* (JIP)—those who are or were previously incarcerated in prison or jail. Taxman and

colleagues (2008; 2013) estimate that about 10% of the JIP can have access to any services (e.g., therapeutic, educational, vocational) on any given day, meaning that the lack
of quality programs constrains the system's ability to reduce individual-level recidivism
rates. Expanding service capacity with quality programs appropriate for the JIP can have
a dramatic impact on recidivism and build the social capital of communities. The logic
is simple—treatment has a greater impact on reducing recidivism than punishment does.
For example, using the number needed to treat (NNT) concept (see Cook & Sackett,
1995), treatment provided to eight members of the JIP prevented one recidivism event,
whereas punishment provided to 33 members of the JIP prevented just one (Caudy et al.,
2013). Expanding the capacity of the system to offer services to 50% of the JIP would
greatly decrease recidivism rates. Given the social justice and citizenship issues that confront the JIP, quality programming can facilitate rehabilitation and promote secondary
and tertiary prevention, especially in underserved communities.

In this chapter, we present an overview of the risk–need–responsivity (RNR) framework.[1] The chapter then showcases findings from case studies from two jurisdictions
that used the methodological framework to survey the quality of their existing programs,
determine the needs of their probationers, and identify gaps in services. To yield the
greatest reductions in recidivism, the case studies illustrate how a strong methodological
approach can facilitate a better understanding of the capacities of the systems, treatment
needs of the populations, and emphases on evidence-based programming.

BEHAVIORAL HEALTH NEEDS OF THE JUSTICE-INVOLVED POPULATION: RISK–NEED FACTORS

Regardless of the justice setting—pretrial, prison, jail, probation, parole—members of
the JIP have a variety of social and behavioral issues linked to criminal behavior. In the
criminal justice context, such issues are expressed in terms of risk and needs (Andrews &
Bonta, 2010) as well as lifestyle-type stabilizers and destabilizers that affect how a person
functions (Taxman et al., 2014).

Risk is an actuarial measure of the likelihood that an individual will become involved
in the justice system. The predictors of risk include the age of first arrest, number of
arrests/convictions, number of prior probation violations, and number of escapes from
prison/jail. In addition to these basic factors, risk assessment instruments may use a
number of other measures present in a particular population. Risk is usually classified as
low, medium, or high, depending on the instrument and jurisdiction. Instruments generally predict risk of any arrest (for any offense), although some instruments differentiate

---

[1] The Center for Advancing Correctional Excellence at George Mason University developed this methodological tool with support from the Bureau of Justice Assistance and the Substance Abuse and Mental Health
Services Administration and the Public Welfare Foundation.

among recidivism for felony offenders, misdemeanors, and those who haven't been convicted (Barnes & Hyatt, 2012).

Needs refers to changeable factors correlated with recidivism, including antisocial personality, antisocial peers, antisocial values, antisocial attitudes, substance abuse, low employment, educational deficits, and poor leisure time activities. Among the JIP, the prevalence of substance use disorders is four times higher than in the general population (Center for Behavioral Health Statistics and Quality, 2015; Taxman, Perdoni, & Harrison, 2008; Wooditch, Tang, & Taxman, 2014).

Certain factors—*(de)stabilizers*—affect the stability of the JIP in the community and their ability to function. For example, mental illness is twice as prevalent among the JIP as in the general population (Thomas, Spittal, Kinner, & Taxman, 2015). Other destabilizers include homelessness, food insecurity, residence in a high-concentration area of crime, poor employment background, and low educational attainment. These factors also affect the JIP's success under correctional control. Given the complex configurations of risk–need–(de)stabilizers the JIP presents, it is challenging to identify the combination of programming and social controls to improve individual outcomes.

AN APPROACH TO UNDERSTANDING PROGRAM-RELATED ISSUES

Smart and sustainable decarceration involves allowing more individuals to remain in the community. To achieve this, it is crucial to first identify the community resources that are available, needed, and of high quality enough to improve outcomes. After a community becomes aware of the available programs, then the question is whether there are sufficient interventions to prevent incarceration or other involvement in the justice system. This is the goal of the RNR methodology.[2]

The RNR methodology enables communities to better understand issues at three levels: (1) individual, (2) program, and (3) jurisdictional/system. The individual-level decision-support process uses algorithms to match clients to programs and services, regardless of place in the justice system (e.g., pretrial, jail, community supervision). The program-level analysis methodology categorizes programs and assesses the quality of programming and the implementation of evidence-based practices (e.g., corrections, education, employment, restorative justice in behavioral health programming). The jurisdiction-level approach compares program capacity to client needs using client characteristics data in the system and the available programming (see Taxman & Pattavina, 2013; Taxman et al., 2014).

The RNR methodology uses three supportive databases (one each for prison, jail, and community corrections) of more than 20,000 risk–need profiles, with separate

---

[2] This chapter discusses of the concepts of RNR, but the actual RNR Simulation Tool is available at http://gmuace.org/tools.

datasets for individuals on pretrial supervision, incarcerated in jail, incarcerated in prison, and on probation and parole supervision. For data-rich jurisdictions (i.e., those with assessment information on criminal justice risk, offenses, behavioral and psychosocial health needs, and outcomes/recidivism), the database can be augmented to include local data for the simulations. For jurisdictions that lack these data, the supporting database can be reweighted to reflect the characteristics of the population based on available data, which may include rates of recidivism, age distribution, criminal justice risk levels, offense categories, gender distributions, and other key characteristics. Details of the tool's development and the sources of the databases can be found in Taxman and Pattavina (2013).

The Individual-Level Approach: Matching Individuals to Appropriate Programs

The individual-level methodology uses risk–need information from clients to identify the appropriate type of programming and dosage amount. Criminal justice risk (e.g., criminal history, prior criminal justice experience), needs (e.g., substance abuse, criminal cognitions, antisocial peers, antisocial values, dysfunctional family, employment/leisure time activities), and (de)stabilizers (e.g., mental health condition, housing, food security, family support) pose a challenge to justice actors (e.g., probation officers, case managers, pretrial workers, counselors) who make assessment and referral decisions. The individual-level algorithms assist in prioritizing such needs by assigning clients to the appropriate services based on the risk–need–(de)stabilizer formulas. The algorithms prioritize substance abuse and criminal lifestyle, given their direct relationship to recidivism reductions. See Taxman et al. (2014) for a description of the algorithms.

The Program-Level Approach: Implementing Quality Programming

The program quality methodology allows jurisdictions to evaluate their programs in terms of the target behaviors being addressed (classification), the quality of the programming (Crites & Taxman, 2013), and areas to improve programming. It estimates how well programs adhere to evidence-based practices and treatment knowledge base as defined by the behavioral health and correctional research literature and calculates scores in six categories—risks, needs, responsivity, implementation, dosage, and restrictiveness. Each of the domains is scored ranging from 0% to 100%.

First, the program quality methodology uses an online survey to acquaint program administrators with the programs available in their jurisdiction and gleans the quality measures from the core correctional practices literature, behavioral health programming, and evaluation studies on quality aspects of programs. The results from the online survey are used to classify programs into six categories based on their primary targets, including

diagnosable behavioral health disorders (e.g., substance abuse, antisocial behaviors, rehabilitation needs) addressable through the Affordable Care Act. Another result from the
program survey is a report on the adherence to evidence-based practices, treatments, and
implementation and identifies areas where programs could benefit from further development (Box 12.1).

   Within each of the six reporting domains, the reports detail how programs can make
quality, implementable, and evidence-based improvements to advance client-level outcomes. These implementation strategies pertain to systems issues (e.g., sharing information, clearer eligibility criteria) and program-specific issues (e.g., staffing, program
components, use of certain tools). Programs should develop improvement plans around
these diagnostic reports that can track their progress. Often these efforts are done as part
of quality improvement collaborative learning teams that assist individual programs in
making substantive changes.

The Jurisdiction-Level Approach: Planning for Service Needs

Operable at program, agency, system, and jurisdiction/state levels, the jurisdiction-level
methodology uses risk–need individual-level data to analyze the service capacity needs,
examine the distribution of available services, and identify gaps in services. The system
can make these calculations for the overall population or subpopulations as desired.
Within the methodology, a simulation tool consisting of a national database of risk–need
profiles enables jurisdictions to apply them to their own jurisdiction-specific data. Once
the data are available, the underlying models convert risk–need profiles into targets for
programming. The underlying models also indicate the dosage (i.e., treatment hours/
intensity) level and service augmentation necessary to meet social and behavioral health
needs of the population.

BOX 12.1

SAMPLE SYSTEMIC ISSUES IDENTIFIED THROUGH THE ONLINE SURVEY
OF PROGRAMS

- The lack of information sharing between justice agencies and treatment providers
- Referrals to programs that do not meet the need of individuals
- Unclear referral criteria
- The need for training in cognitive behavioral approaches and engagement
  strategies
- The dearth of treatment programs

CASE STUDY OF SAN FRANCISCO, CALIFORNIA

The San Francisco Adult Probation Department (APD) supervises more than 6,000 probationers in San Francisco, California. From 2013 to 2015, the jurisdiction used the RNR Simulation Tool and the methodology to understand the programming needs of their population, understand the quality of services, and identify gaps in service needs. Special attention was given to differentiating the needs of the population by females, AB-109 clients (Public Safety Realignment Assembly Bill [AB] 109 ordered that individuals serving prison sentences for nonviolent, nonserious, nonsex offenses be moved to community corrections supervision [California Department of Corrections and Rehabilitation, 2013]), domestic violence offenders, clients with mental health diagnoses, clients experiencing housing instability, and clients aged 25 years and younger.

Characteristics of the San Francisco Probationers

The San Francisco APD used data from various sources to identify the characteristics of their probation population. The sources include the Correctional Offender Management Profiling for Alternative Sanctions (COMPAS) risk and needs assessment instrument, the APD case management system, the San Francisco Court Management System, and arrest data. The San Francisco APD provided data on all probationers (both standard and AB-109) whom APD supervised. The simulation model used these data sources to examine population needs and create an analytical file.

Figure 12.1 illustrates the risk levels of the various types of populations the APD supervised. The AB-109 clients tend to be older and at higher risk for future recidivism. The highest risk populations are individuals who have a mental health disorder, are aged 18 to 25 years (i.e., young adults), released under AB-109, and the general probation population. The lower risk population included those with a domestic violence conviction and females. The variation of risk level among different subpopulations illustrates some of

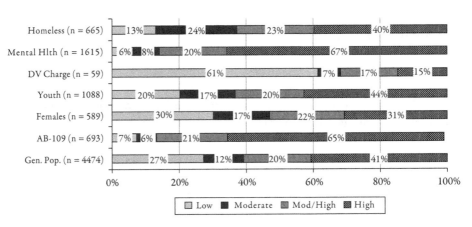

FIGURE 12.1 Risk level distribution of the probation population.

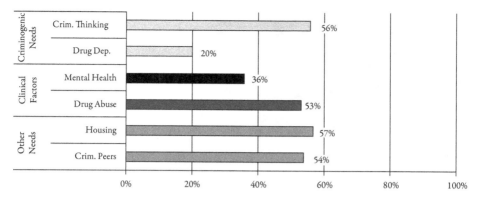

FIGURE 12.2 General probation population needs per COMPAS ($N = 4,474$).

the challenges that justice agencies confront regarding the various needs of the clientele. The challenges include balancing criminal justice risk with needs to access appropriate programs and services.

Figure 12.2 illustrates the needs of the APD clientele: housing, criminal peers, criminal cognitions, and drug abuse. The analysis uses criteria from the *Diagnostic and Statistical Manual of Mental Disorders*, fifth edition (DSM-5), to identify the degree to which individuals had mild, moderate, or severe substance use disorders. Those with severe substance use disorders tended to use opioids, cocaine, and methamphetamines, whereas those with mild or moderate substance use disorders tended to use marijuana less frequently. Figure 12.2 illustrates how some (de)stabilizers such as mental health and unstable housing were prevalent in this population. Though these (de)stabilizers were not directly related to recidivism, they had an indirect effect that required consideration in programming.

Figure 12.3 shows the different needs of subpopulations. Probationers aged 18 to 25 years had lower rates of substance use disorder, but higher rates of criminal thinking than other age groups. Programs achieve better outcomes by tailoring their services to individual needs. To achieve this responsivity principle, programs must address issues such as gender responsiveness, mental health, and literacy rates.

Overall, 20% of APD clients were substance-dependent, and, of those, 37% had a co-occurring mental health diagnosis. More than half (56%) of APD's clients had criminal thinking/antisocial cognitions; half (53%) of those with criminal thinking abused substances, and 36% had a mental health diagnosis. Such comorbid conditions must be addressed in programs to ensure positive outcomes.

Programming in San Francisco

Eighteen programs in San Francisco used the online survey of programs to identify the available programs, which included programs for substance dependence, criminal

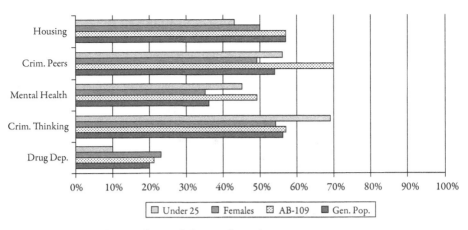

FIGURE 12.3 Major factors affecting different subpopulations.

thinking, self-improvement, interpersonal skills, and life skills. The programs had a mean score of 41 (out of 100), with slightly better scores in addressing risks of the clients, addressing responsivity, and having high-quality implementation. The lowest scoring domain was dosage (i.e., appropriate clinical hours). The programs that had highest quality services were the two criminal thinking programs and the four self-improvement programs. The life skills programs tended to embrace fewer evidence-based practices. The programs devoted to domestic violence probationers tended to have higher quality programming, given that they tend to serve a more homogeneous population.

The San Francisco APD used the online survey to examine the common programmatic quality issues that affect the 18 programs. Improvements in the use of evidence-based practices included (1) prioritizing high-risk clients for greater intensity of treatment, especially with front-loading services during the first 60 days after release; (2) integrating criminal thinking into a greater range of services; (3) developing integrated care models in which probation officers and treatment providers understand common goals; (4) expanding substance abuse programming for women and including trauma-informed care; and (5) training probation officers and treatment providers to use positive incentives (rewards) to enhance participation in treatment.

Gaps in Services

By combining data on the risk–need profiles of the probationers with the characteristics of the available programs, it was possible to assess a jurisdiction's capacity to address needs of those under correctional control. Figure 12.4 illustrates the results of the gap analyses in the APD. The greatest capacity in available programming was for substance dependence disorders (APD programs have the capacity to provide services for 18% of probationers), followed by substance abuse treatment (10% of probationers), criminal thinking (9% of probationers), and life skills (7% of probationers).

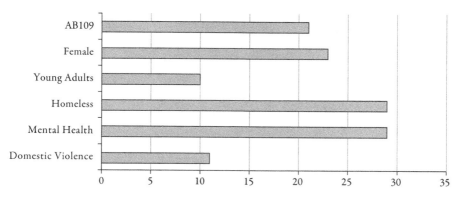

FIGURE 12.4 Gaps in substance dependence programming among subpopulations.

Figure 12.5 illustrates that the largest gap in treatment capacity was for programs target-ing criminal thinking/criminal cognitions (Group B). The system had sufficient capacity for substance abuse treatment. In most other areas, though, there was a need for greater capacity in the available programming.

Significant gaps exist in cognitive restructuring programming for AB-109 clients, individuals with mental health needs, and young adults (Figure 12.6). This is an area where the jurisdiction needs more extensive programming. Clients in this system would benefit from more strength-based cognitive restructuring programming that focuses on improvements in quality of life and desistance. A strength-based approach would work to help individuals see their value and build resilience to the factors that affect involve-ment in crime.

The analysis also found that some subpopulations have a greater need for programs that focus on self-improvement, problem-solving skills, impulsivity control, and man-aging risky situations. These types of programs can include less intensive substance abuse treatment, domestic violence treatment, and other programs that aim to increase

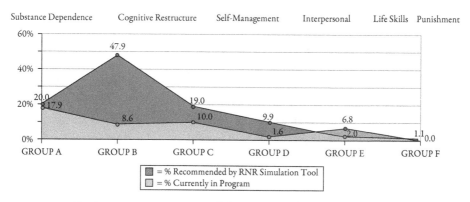

FIGURE 12.5 Gap between programming needed and programming available in the San Francisco APD.

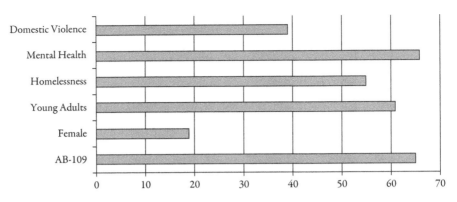

FIGURE 12.6 Gaps in cognitive restructuring programming among subpopulations.

participants' self-control. These skills can help individuals learn to manage their own behaviors and to resist social pressures that may lead to continued offending behavior (Botvin & Wills, 1984; Botvin, Griffin, & Nichols, 2006). Many of the existing programs in this category only target substance abuse (not serious dependence) and management of risky situations. The greatest gap is for individuals who are supervised in the Domestic Violence Unit.

The gaps in services are even more pronounced among the subpopulations of AB-109 clients and youthful clients. These graphs demonstrate why it is critical to look not only at the needs of the general population at the aggregate but to also examine needs of subpopulations, especially those that are particularly vulnerable (e.g., homeless people, women, those suffering from mental health disorders).

Lessons from San Francisco

The RNR methodology assisted the APD examine their system in a holistic fashion that strengthened its existing core services and realigned its service capacity to meet the needs of the population. The tool's gap analysis provided APD the information necessary to guide and further develop the programming in their jurisdiction. There is a clear need for more and better programming that addresses criminal thinking/cognitive restructuring, particularly for the young adult population and the AB-109 population, which, interestingly, tends to be older. Stable and affordable housing is a major issue throughout the San Francisco area, and this need is especially pronounced among APD clients. More than half of APD clients report unstable housing, and this group has higher than average rates of rearrest and reconviction (62% and 21%, respectively). These figures only account for those individuals who report homelessness or reliance on public housing, not those who may be "couch surfing" or living in other unstable situations, such as in a criminogenic environment or with antisocial peers.

In San Francisco, the RNR methodology spurred an interest in revising and updating data sharing systems, especially in increasing the adoption of evidence-based research into programming. The APD faced challenges with tracking probationers as they progressed through treatment. Through use of these methods, the APD learned how updating data systems to allow limited access to treatment providers would lead to shorter lags in receiving information about clients. Doing so would also ease the flow of communication between APD and providers, which would help hold programs, officers, and clients accountable. An updated system would also allow the department to improve its system for referrals and facilitate appropriate sequencing of programming for clients with multiple needs.

The process also facilitated increased use of existing resources, including ones to avoid incarceration. By strengthening the community programing, use of the RNR methodology created more opportunities to use community programming instead of incarceration. In addition, the efforts led to stronger efforts to address noncompliance on supervision, which is often a driver of new intakes to incarceration.

CASE STUDY OF SANTA CRUZ, CALIFORNIA

The AB-109 policy shift in California resulted in an increase in the number of individuals under parole and probation supervision in Santa Cruz, California. The Santa Cruz Probation Department used the RNR methodology to examine their probationer population need and determine the types of programs that would meet their needs. Figure 12.7 displays the *primary* needs of the population based on the risk–need profile of probationers, the available programming as reported by the programs that completed the jurisdictional capacity for delivering services, and the gap between what is needed and what is offered.

As the gap analysis indicates, the Santa Cruz Probation Department was well equipped to address substance use disorders, but it had a significant gap in programming that addresses criminal thinking/antisocial cognitions. This is an issue found in numerous jurisdictions—criminal thinking is a nascent concept, and programming and assessments that address it are scarce. The Santa Cruz Probation Department identified addressing

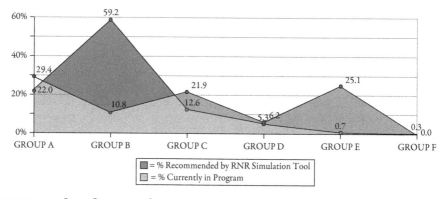

FIGURE 12.7 Santa Cruz gap analysis.

this gap as a goal and sought out additional providers who could deliver programming in this area.

In 2013 and again in 2015, the Santa Cruz Probation Department requested that organizations that provide treatment and programming for clients complete the AJC portal of the RNR Simulation Tool. In the initial 2013 cohort, 36 programs completed the portal, and 25 completed it in 2015 (Figure 12.8). Given the shift in services the Santa Cruz Probation Department made, the change in the number and types of programs reflected the needs of the probationers. These changes included a greater requirement for programs addressing serious and criminogenic needs and fewer programs addressing life skills.

Figure 12.8 shows the distribution of programs in 2013 and 2015. Though the mean total score, representing how adherent the program is to evidence-based practices, was 55% in 2015 and 51% in 2013, 12 of the 15 programs that completed a reassessment saw improvements in their scores, increasing in critical area. From 2013 to 2015, the average program score increased in all six domains (Figure 12.9). The areas in which the programs showed greatest strengths were responsivity and restrictiveness. Responsivity refers to how well a program can adapt to clients' characteristics and learning style, and restrictiveness reflects a program's ability to employ controls to help constrain individual behavior while the client is stabilized in the program. The area where programs had the lowest scores was dosage; programs in all jurisdictions tend to struggle with providing a dosage amount that meets the recommended thresholds, and the best way to address this is to have clients complete a sequence of programs so the cumulative dosage will come closer to the recommended number of treatment hours.

In addition to shifting services to address the gaps, the Santa Cruz Probation Department made strategic improvements in the service delivery system. It improved the referral process by directing probationers to services based on primary need and sharing

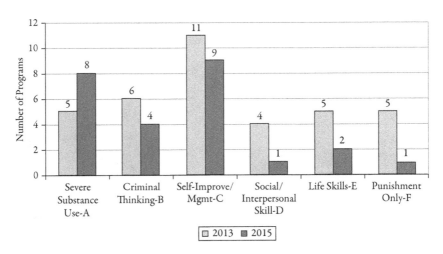

FIGURE 12.8 Distribution of AB-109 programs.

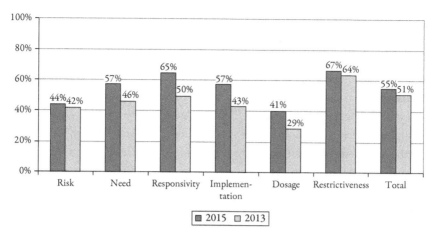

FIGURE 12.9 Average domain scores in Santa Cruz.

the risk–need information (COMPAS results) with the service providers. It contracted with new providers for services to fill in the identified gaps. It added new performance criteria for treatment providers to ensure that providers make improvements on their online survey domain scores. The department adjusted annual training to focus on enhancing cognitive behavioral skills of treatment providers, which was observed in San Francisco as well.

As noted in both of these case studies, there is a need for more programing efforts to address cognitive restructuring and criminal lifestyles. In both communities, individuals with these needs are typically handled in substance abuse programming, which is not the main driver of their criminal behavior. More attention to the appropriate type of programming should lead to greater results for the individuals, including reductions in recidivism and less reliance on incarceration. The expansion of services in the community then can reduce the demand for jail space.

CONCLUSION

In the early 2000s, there was a movement away from therapeutic, clinical programs in prison to reentry or life skill programming (Phelps, 2012). This movement was spurred by the realization that there was a need for discharge planning as part of the transition from incarceration to the reentering the community. The research community emphasized the importance of more clinical training while the corrections field reduced the availability of such programs. The research literature continues to build evidence about strong clinically based programs, particularly those that employ a cognitive behavioral framework and emphasize skill development among the clientele. The list of effective clinically based programs includes therapeutic community, cognitive behavioral therapies for substance use disorders and antisocial cognitions, drug treatment courts, family interventions (i.e., multisystemic therapies), and medication-assisted treatments for opioid and alcohol dependencies (Johnston & Cullen, 2016). Applying the RNR principles in probation and parole supervision settings focuses on validated risk and need assessment tools, linking individuals to services based on their target needs, providing cognitive behavioral programming, and using rewards to reinforce positive behavior (Drake, 2012). Other promising strategies include motivational interviewing, advocacy case management, contingency management, emotional skills, and secondary education/GED. Ineffective sanctions that do not reduce recidivism include intensive supervision, boot camps, psychosocial education groups, nondirective counseling, case management, and incarceration. The knowledge base regarding "what works" is growing stronger, but the field lags behind in providing the most effective services.

As the two case studies on programs for the JIP illustrate, few jurisdictions have the array of interventions that embrace evidence-based practices and treatments, and jurisdictions often do not have good quality programming. Both case studies and other work (see Taxman & Pattavina, 2013) using the online survey of programs (i.e., RNR Program Tool) illustrate how the current availability of programs is limited—it does not address the full breadth of program components and suffers from implementation issues. The interventions lack fidelity, which hinders their ability to have an impact on reducing recidivism.

Though improving the quality of and number of evidence-based programs for the JIP is a major challenge, it has enormous potential for reducing recidivism and promoting smart decarceration. The expansion of programs, with more individuals able to participate in programming, would facilitate a change in the corrections environment and culture—involvement in programming will be a routine activity instead of an activity in which select individuals participate (Caudy et al., 2013). By making programming a more prominent piece of justice system processes, jurisdictions can place greater emphasis on intermediate or proximal outcomes related to improvements in functioning and reducing mental health symptoms and drug using behaviors. This means that policies to reduce incarceration should involve expanding programs and services that are designed to meet the needs of individuals in the justice system.

Both case studies demonstrate how assisting individuals and their communities with the factors that lead to incarceration requires a long-term commitment to implement programs and services that fit within the evidence-based practices and treatment knowledge base. For too long, funded programs have received insufficient resources to address the needs of the clients. Almost universally, the programs do not have sufficient duration, given the severity of needs of the clients—most programs are 3 to 4 months, yet the research literature recommends 200 to 300 hours of clinical programming for most of the JIP (Bourgon & Armstrong, 2005). There is also a need for more evidence-based programming to address criminal lifestyles and cognitions. Right now there is a shortage of programs, and the existing programs have not been adequately evaluated (Taxman & Caudy, 2015). Finally, more attention should be given to the clinical skills of the staffing for the programs. Many programs can only afford to staff programs with those who have lived experience, volunteers, and paraprofessionals, yet the research literature emphasizes the importance of having masters-level clinical staffing (Knudsen, Ducharme, & Roman, 2007). Information from the program tool can also add to the need of areas to develop evidence about interventions. More importantly, the efforts taken to address areas of deficiency can also be studied to learn more about making sustainable improvements to interventions.

Smart decarceration policies and practices focus on building strengths and capacity that can prevent the use of incarceration as the major tool of crime control and prevention efforts. Incarceration grew as a result of concerns about the efficacy of correctional programs or the "nothing works" rhetoric (see Martinson, 1974). Unraveling mass incarceration then requires attention to building infrastructure and capacity to assist individuals and communities with the ingredients of crime and disorder in their community including substance abuse, mental illness, criminal lifestyle, and antisocial behavior. The best place to address these issues is in the communities where they occur. But that means it is important to understand the needs of the individuals in different communities, and then build the infrastructure of programs, interventions, and other capacities to address crime-producing issues. Decarceration requires attention to these infrastructure issues that have long been neglected.

Strengthening community supports, as part of decarceration, has the benefits of building resiliency in our communities and the individuals that reside in these communities. The RNR methodology has usually referred to what corrections could do. But the methodologies that are demonstrated in this chapter illustrate a need to attend to the fidelity of programs and interventions as well as the depth of the programs. Fidelity is an investment in the people that work in the programs and services to ensure that they have the skills and resources to prevent and control criminal behavior. Decarceration is an effort to invest in people as part of the strategy to reduce and control crime, and this often includes those that are the facilitators or levers of support. Smart decarceration then can embrace the RNR methodology as a strategy to identify how to strengthen efforts at the individual, program, and community levels, with sufficient resources to meet the needs of the U.S. population.

REFERENCES

Andrews, D. A., & Bonta, J. (2010). *The psychology of criminal conduct*. Cincinnati, OH: Anderson.

Barnes, G. C., & Hyatt, J. M. (2012). *Classifying adult probationers by forecasting future offending.* National Criminal Justice Reference Service. Retrieved from https://www.ncjrs.gov/pdffiles1/nij/grants/238082.pdf

Botvin, G. J., Griffin, K. W., & Nichols, T. D. (2006). Preventing youth violence and delinquency through universal school-based prevention approach. *Prevention Science, 7,* 403–408.

Botvin, G. J., & Wills, T. A. (1984). Personal and social skills training: Cognitive-behavioral approaches to substance abuse prevention. In C. S. Bell & R. Battjes (Eds.), *Prevention research: Deterring drug abuse among children and adolescents* (pp. 8–49). NIDA Research Monograph. Rockville, MD: Department of Health and Human Services.

Bourgon, G., & Armstrong, B. (2005). Transferring the principles of effective treatment into a "real world" prison setting. *Criminal Justice and Behavior, 32*(1), 3–25.

California Department of Corrections and Rehabilitation. (2013, December 1). *Realignment report*. Retrieved February 25, 2015, from http://www.cdcr.ca.gov/realignment/index.html

Caudy, M., Tang, L., Ainsworth, S. A., Lerch, J., & Taxman, F. S. (2013). Reducing recidivism through correctional programming: Using meta-analyses to inform the RNR Simulation Tool. In F. S. Taxman & A. Pattavina (Eds.), *Simulation strategies to reduce recidivism: Risk need responsivity (RNR) modeling in the criminal justice system.* New York, NY: Springer.

Center for Behavioral Health Statistics and Quality. (2015). *Behavioral health trends in the United States: Results from the 2014 National Survey on Drug Use and Health* (HHS Publication No. SMA 15-4927, NSDUH Series H-50). Retrieved from http://www.samhsa.gov/data/

Cook, R. J., & Sackett, D. L. (1995). The number needed to treat: A clinically useful measure of treatment effect. *British Medical Journal, 310,* 452–454.

Crites, E., & Taxman, F. S. (2013). The responsivity principle—Determining the appropriate program and dosage to match risk and needs. In F. S. Taxman & A. Pattavina (Eds.), *Simulation strategies to reduce recidivism: Risk need responsivity (RNR) modeling in the criminal justice system.* New York, NY: Springer.

Knudsen, H. K., Ducharme, L. J., & Roman, P M. (2007). The adoption of medications in substance abuse treatment: Associations with organizational characteristics and technology clusters. *Drug and Alcohol Dependence, 87,* 164–174.

Martinson, R. (1974). What works?—Questions and answers about prison reform. *The Public Interest,* 22–54. Retrieved from http://www.pbpp.pa.gov/research_statistics/Documents/Martinson-What%20Works%201974.pdf

Nagin, D. S., Cullen, F. T., & Jonson, C. L. (2009). Imprisonment and reoffending. In Michael Tonry (Ed.), *Crime and justice: A review of research* (pp. 115–200). Chicago, IL: University of Chicago Press.

Phelps, M. S. (2012). The place of punishment: Variation in the provision of inmate services staff across the punitive turn. *Journal of Criminal Justice, 40*(5), 348–357.

Taxman, F. S., & Caudy, M. (2015). Risk tells us who, but not what or how: Empirical assessment of the complexity of criminogenic needs to inform correctional programming. *Criminology and Public Policy, 14*(1), 71–103.

Taxman, F. S., & Pattavina, A. (2013). *Simulation strategies to reduce recidivism: Risk need responsivity (RNR) modeling in the criminal justice system.* New York, NY: Springer.

Taxman, F. S., Pattavina, A., & Caudy, M. (2014). Justice reinvestment in the US: The case for more programs. *Victims and Offenders, 9*(1), 50–75.

Taxman, F. S., Perdoni, M., & Caudy, M. (2013). The plight of providing appropriate substance abuse treatment services to offenders: Modeling the gaps in service delivery. *Victims and Offenders, 8*(1), 70–93.

Taxman, F. S., Perdoni, M. L., & Harrison, L. D. (2008). Drug treatment for adult offenders: The state of the state. *Substance Abuse Treatment, 32*(3), 239–254.

Thomas, E. G., Spittal, M. J, Kinner, S. A., & Taxman, F. S. (2015). Health-related factors predict return to custody in a large cohort of ex-prisoners: New approaches to predicting reincarceration. *Health and Justice*. doi:10.1186/s40352-015-0022-6

Wooditch, A., Tang, L., & Taxman, F. S. (2014). Which criminogenic need changes are most important in promoting desistance from crime and substance use? *Criminal Justice and Behavior, 41*(3), 276–299.

13

Empirical Means to Decarcerative Ends?

ADVANCING THE SCIENCE AND PRACTICE

OF RISK ASSESSMENT

Julian Adler, Sarah Picard-Fritsche, Michael Rempel, and Jennifer A. Tallon

---

BACKGROUND

With more than four million people imprisoned or under correctional control in the United States (Bureau of Justice Statistics, 2014), there is unprecedented consensus regarding the need to stem the tide of mass incarceration. In 2015, the American popular press dedicated dozens of articles to the problem of mass incarceration, and spokespeople on both sides of the political aisle have championed the cause of decarceration. Meanwhile, leading scholars and policy reformers are determined to see major change efforts proceed in line with recent advances in criminal justice science, including the lessons learned from previous reform initiatives.

Accordingly, increasing numbers of jurisdictions are turning to the field of evidence-based practice, but in particular to actuarial risk assessment, in an attempt to systematically revise pretrial release and sentencing practices. Simply put, though efforts to assess individual criminal risk are as old as the justice system itself, the actuarial approach to risk assessment can be distinguished from traditional approaches by its grounding in the statistical analysis of the patterns of large groups of offenders over time. The prevailing assumption about the *actuarial risk assessment* approach is that it allows for more accurate classification of individuals into subgroups with similar levels of risk—either the risk of failing to appear for court, general reoffending, or violent reoffending. For many reformers, data-driven decision making is a welcome antidote to long-standing and largely unquestioned discretionary habits that have contributed to the problems driving mass incarceration (e.g., money-based pretrial release decisions [wherein those who can afford bail are released while others are detained], overreliance on oftentimes flawed professional judgment to determine risk to the community, the default use of short-term jail sentences).

Risk Assessment: From Traditional to Actuarial (and Its Challenges)

The move toward *actuarial assessment* and away from professional judgment at the pretrial and sentencing stages can be aptly termed a "sea change" in criminal justice reform. By a conservative estimate, the use of actuarial methods has increased more than fivefold over the since the 1990s (Harcourt, 2007; Starr, 2015a). Moreover, there are now at least five competing, proprietary risk assessment "systems" actively marketed to jurisdictions across the country. For example, in 2015, the Laura and John Arnold Foundation announced the rollout of its pretrial risk assessment tool (the Public Safety Assessment) in 29 jurisdictions, "including three entire states—Arizona, Kentucky, and New Jersey— as well as three of the largest cities in the country—Charlotte, Chicago, and Phoenix" (Laura and John Arnold Foundation, 2015).

At its core, risk prediction involves the retrospective use of statistics to create evidence-based classifications (e.g., low-, moderate-, and high-risk) of an individual's risk of a future offense or risk of failing to appear for scheduled court appearances. Although the specific algorithms can vary significantly across risk assessment instruments, and indeed instruments created based on data from differing jurisdictions will inevitably vary to a degree, they all draw their measures from the same broad categories that 30 years of research has consistently linked to risk.

ACTUARIAL RISK ASSESSMENT TOOLS

Popular risk assessment systems currently on the market range from short, public domain tools that rely on static (i.e., untreatable) risk factors to complex, proprietary decision triage and case management systems.[1] All, however, include some range of variables concerning a defendant's criminal history. Specifically, nearly all tools include one or more measures of prior arrests or convictions, either over an individual's lifetime or a recent period (i.e., 3 to 5 years) before the current case. Other common criminal history measures linked with risk include prior arrests or convictions for specific crimes or charge severities; separate measures of juvenile priors; age at first arrest or conviction, prior incarceration, probation or parole history, failure to appear in court on prior cases, and the existence of cases that are currently open at the time that a new arrest occurs. In short,

---

[1] Major risk assessment systems currently on the marked include the Public Safety Assessment (PSA), the Ohio Risk Assessment System (ORAS), the Level of Services Inventory (LSI, LSI-R, LSI-CMI), the Risk an Needs Triage System (RANT) and the COMPAS.

combinations of criminal history variables are consistently highly predictive and accessible through administrative records and so play a significant part in all risk assessment tools.

THE RISK-NEED-RESPONSIVITY MODEL

Many instruments also integrate dynamic or "needs-based" factors (see Chapter 12), reflecting simultaneous advances in theories of crime prevention, and in particular, the risk-need-responsivity (RNR) model of offender rehabilitation (Latessa, Smith, Lemke, Makarios, & Lowenkamp, 2009; Taxman, Henderson, Young, & Farrell, 2012). Supported by over 3 decades of meta-analytic research (e.g., Andrews, Bonta, & Hoge, 1990; Lipsey, 2009), RNR is largely responsible for reviving rehabilitative correctional practice from the blow wrought by the "nothing works" sentiments of the 1970s (e.g., Martinson, 1974). Among other implications, the RNR model concurs that criminal history is key predictor of risk but also draws attention to seven additional treatable risk factors: antisocial attitudes, criminal social networks, antisocial personality or temperament (e.g., impulsive decision-making), school or work deficits, family dysfunction, lack of prosocial leisure activities, and substance abuse.

Two of RNR's key principles, the *risk principle* and the *need principle*, may prove pivotal to successful pretrial and sentencing reform efforts. The risk principle posits that intensive intervention (including therapeutic treatment or supervision) is most effective with higher-risk individuals but can have counterproductive effects with lower-risk individuals (Andrews & Dowden, 2006; Lowenkamp, Latessa, & Smith, 2006). This principle directly implicates the need for valid methods for discerning risk level and is extensively supported in the empirical literature (Bonta & Andrews, 2007; Latessa & Lowenkemp, 2006). Less often noted is the need principle, which suggests that correctional intervention should focus on the specific criminogenic needs of the individual. This principle supports a preference for decarcerative responses to crime, especially when viewed in concert with a growing body of literature on the criminogenic nature of jails and prisons, discussed in detail later. Importantly, when understood in tandem, the risk and need principles logically imply that low-risk individuals should be off-ramped as soon as possible to avoid unnecessary incarceration, whereas only individuals at *higher* risk levels (i.e., moderate or higher) should be targeted for treatment. In other words, public safety is best protected by allowing low-risk individuals do what their risk level indicates they were prone to do in the first place—namely, show up for their court dates and not reoffend.

Higher-risk individuals have the most to gain from evidence-based treatment interventions designed to reduce risk. This concept contradicts historic practice in many jurisdictions, where treatment is often reserved for low-risk individuals who do not need it and may be harmed by it (e.g., if the treatment interferes with school or employment obligations or creates psychological stigma). In such jurisdictions, moderate- and high-risk individuals face high rates of incarceration, though treatment may well have yielded greater public safety benefits. Indeed, research shows that incarceration at best does not deter reoffending and has often been linked to *increased* reoffending after release (Cullen, Jonson, & Nagin, 2011). Conversely, by following the need principle and the responsivity principle, the latter of which encourages the use of cognitive behavioral approaches adapted to the particular needs of the individual, it is actually possible to *reduce* risk below the level where it was assessed at baseline.

CRITICISMS OF ACTUARIAL RISK ASSESSMENT

Although actuarial risk assessment is intended as a means to shift individuals away from jails and prisons and thereby reduce the negative collateral consequences of incarceration, the practice is not without criticism.

Some contend that empirical assessment methods lend new and seemingly objective credence to long-entrenched racial and socioeconomic biases in the criminal justice system (e.g., Harcourt, 2015; Starr 2015b). As the critique proposes, if criminal history is built into assessment tools, racially disproportionate arrest practices can lead members of minority groups to accumulate longer rap sheets—and then have their criminal history counted against them in risk assessment algorithms. Furthermore, in tools that explicitly consider employment status or other socioeconomic measures as a risk factor, those who are economically disadvantaged can be punished in the risk calculus (i.e., the risk assessment will add risk points for those who have not completed a high school education, for example).

Others have suggested that proponents and practitioners confuse the underlying science of actuarial assessment for something more akin to prophecy (e.g., Hannah-Moffat, 2010). A corollary to this critique is the idea that actuarial risk assessment "carries echoes of *Minority Report*: locking people up for crimes they might commit in the future" (Barry-Jester, Casselman, & Goldstein, 2015). And still others raise pragmatic concerns about the vagaries of implementation; as criminologist William R. Kelly observes, "evidence-based programs and practices are not self-implementing or self-executing" (2015, p. 93).

Given the near ubiquity of risk assessment in current criminal justice reform efforts, we understand the criticisms in the debate about actuarial methods; however, we are equally concerned that the question of *whether* to use actuarial tools for the purposes of justice reform has eclipsed the more imminent question of *how* to do so most effectively and responsibly. Thus, we focus on the latter question. Actuarial risk assessment practice is neither monolithic nor zero-sum, and much can be done to improve its design and implementation—even as the field continues to wrestle with its long-term viability and appropriateness.

To this end, we offer three general principles to advance the practice of actuarial risk assessment as the trend and the debate continue. The first principle, *maximized accuracy and transparency*, concerns assessment tool creation and validation. We advise jurisdictions to maximize the accuracy of instruments they employ while making every practicable effort to eschew secret recipes and black boxes. We suggest that risk assessment items, weighting, and scoring algorithms—and past performance in objective validation studies—be openly disclosed and thoroughly explained to users, including the identification and analysis of any potential "proxy" variables (i.e., variables thought to "stand in" for socioeconomic status). The second principle, *judicious implementation*, cautions jurisdictions to pay equally careful attention to how risk assessment instruments are implemented, taking into account the need for structured decision-making and the challenges posed by probabilistic models. Finally, the third principle, *decarcerative purpose*, holds that risk assessment instruments should be affirmatively used to both increase and *broaden* the identification of candidates for alternatives to pretrial detention and incarceration. In light of the known criminogenic effects of incarceration and the demonstrated efficacy of rehabilitative intervention, we advise jurisdictions to maximize the safe and appropriate use of community-based alternatives. Put simply, risk assessment should not become an instrument of fear to attempt to lock up more individuals who pose anything more than a low risk, in lieu of using sound assessment, supervision, and treatment practices capable of ensuring public safety by reducing risk.

Prelude: The Slog from "Is" to "Ought"

Before turning to these three principles, we draw attention to one of the most striking yet undernoted features of evidence-based justice reform efforts: Empirical data is inherently nonprescriptive. Though policy decisions can and should be carefully informed by rigorous empirical analysis, the data point itself is always—often agonizingly—silent on its possible applications in criminal justice settings. In other words, there is an unavoidable logical break between the scientific evidence and the resulting evidence-based practice or policy. For example, as discussed earlier, it is largely assumed by their advocates that risk assessment tools will have decarcerative effects. Yet, no matter how empirically valid is a risk prediction algorithm, or what advocates may *believe* are the logical uses of the information, the information itself and its real-world application are intrinsically separate matters.

In her 2013 examination of the tensions between the natural sciences and social policy, the rhetorician Lynda Walsh traces this cardinal insight to the year 1740 and philosopher David Hume's *Treatise on Human Nature*: As Walsh recounts, "policy could not be logically derived from science. Scientific statements were statements about what the current state of the world 'is'; policy amounted to statements about what we 'ought' to do about the state of the world" (p. 86). Walsh goes on to describe Hume's prescient realization about how scientific evidence ultimately gets transformed into evidence-based practice and policy: The "logical gap between 'is' and 'ought' could not be bridged without the application of something extra: a priori values" (p. 86). In a similar vein, the noted criminologist Michael Tonry (2011) has observed that "normative arguments based on ideas about justice and moral rights and wrongs often trump instrumental ones" (p. 638) in policy debates about penal reform.

Turning specifically to the subject of actuarial risk assessment, it is, for example, empirically known that men are at higher risk to recidivate than women, and that crime risk peaks around the late teens (Farrington, 1986; Gendreau, Little, & Goggin, 1996; Hirschi & Gottfredson, 1983). Accordingly, some jurisdictions choose to include sex and age in their actuarial risk assessment tools, but others affirmatively omit these variables. Epistemologically, these decisions to include or exclude particular criminogenic factors reflect—largely unnoticed—value differences, *not* empirical discrepancies. Parenthetically, in these very examples, omitting sex and age may seem like a neutral ethical decision to all demographic groups, but in fact the very omission of such factors is detrimental to the risk score of those who might have been scored lower (women and older offenders) had sex and age been considered. We therefore encourage the reader to bear the "is/ought" distinction in mind (as well as the empirical ramifications of alternative value choices) as we consider the various decisions jurisdictions have to make in developing and implementing risk assessment instruments.

Principle #1: Maximized Accuracy and Transparency

Some policymakers may be receptive to the implementation of risk assessment tools because they are informed by empirical data. However, the bulk of the science of risk assessment concerns probabilistic predictions about the future behavior of defendants, the accuracy of which may vary substantially from one tool to the next. For this reason, we advise jurisdictions to double-down on predictive accuracy when developing or selecting a preexisting instrument. Additionally, we advise policymakers to bear in mind that the creation of risk assessment instruments is often rife with myth and opacity. (For example, an actuarial assessment instrument reduces uncertainty about behavior and treatment, but it does not produce certainty, just as a weather report does not guarantee rain.) For policymakers who are inherently less sympathetic than others to the assessment enterprise, this uncertainty often results in reactive devaluation and the unfounded mistrust of scientific findings. To avoid the premature rejection of actuarial risk assessment, to promote greater decisional fairness and accountability in the courtroom, and to advance the science of risk prediction, we also strongly suggest that instrument developers follow a principle of full disclosure regarding the science behind risk assessment. This includes the selection of assessment items, the weighting of items and domains, and the scoring algorithms and performance of the resulting tools.

Accuracy

At its core, the empirical science that underlies risk assessment is one of probability (risk assessment tools will never be accurate in every individual case); for this reason, predictive power is crucial to actuarial risk assessment. *Probability* can be defined as the number of specific outcomes over all possible outcomes. For example, the probability of flipping a coin and having it land on tails is one out of two, or 50%. When dealing with the complexities of human behavior, actuarial risk assessments indicate the likelihood of future criminal behavior given the presence and combination of specific risk factors that have shown to be predictive of either failing to appear for court, reoffending, or reoffending violently. As the scholars Eric Silver and Lisa Miller summarized, "by stating that this person has a 30% risk of violence, the model is in effect [simply] stating that 30 out of 100 persons with these characteristics will act out violently" (Silver & Miller, 2002, p. 143). The more accurate and transparent the classification, the more useful it is to decision makers.

In general, the most important statistic for evaluating a tool's predictive accuracy is the area under the curve (AUC) statistic. In intuitive terms, the AUC reflects the extent to which a tool outperforms chance (.500) in accurately predicting who will and will not reoffend. The AUC ranges from 0.500 to 1.000; generally, an AUC of 0.500–0.600 is considered poor, 0.600–0.700 is acceptable, 0.700–0.800 is good/very good, and 0.800 plus is excellent (but rare). The greater an instrument's predictive accuracy, the less likely it is that the tool will produce false positives (e.g., a lower-risk defendant scores as higher risk) or false negatives (e.g., a higher-risk defendant scores as low risk). Of course, what even a highly calibrated instrument can tell us about any individual defendant is open to interpretation. A defendant may be in a high-risk classification because of his or her age and criminal history, but as indicated above, that does not mean that everyone in that category is predestined to reoffend. That said, the AUC offers a measure of assurance to decision makers that the risk classification resulting from the risk assessment accurately reflects the chance that a given defendant will either fail to appear for court, reoffend, or reoffend violently.

It is important to note that maximizing predictive accuracy often comes at the expense of being able to "shop off the rack" for an assessment tool that is ready to "plug and play." The industry standard for maximizing predictive accuracy is local validation (Austin, 2006). An instrument that accurately predicts reoffending among felony-level defendants in a largely rural jurisdiction in the Midwest may not perform as well in a largely urban jurisdiction in California. Even in the case of brief assessment tools that only consider criminal history variables without interviewing the defendant, there is considerable variation and nuance across jurisdictions with respect to which specific criminal history variables are most predictive. Accordingly, we advise jurisdictions to either develop their own instruments using local data or revalidate—and potentially modify—any off-the-rack instrument using local data.

We encourage jurisdictions to also consider whether temporary "eccentricities" (e.g., policing innovations or drug use epidemics) may be influencing the development or validation of the tool. The best tool will be the one that can provide a reliable and valid basis for intervention or risk reduction in the local jurisdiction over time. "Overfitting" tools to a particular set of data in a highly local setting can be problematic; for example, if an instrument were created for a local jurisdiction based on a particular year of data, the arrest patterns or other dynamics in that one year may have created an unrepresentative defendant population when compared with subsequent years. In short, the goal is maximizing predictive accuracy for one's jurisdiction in the long run.

Finally, although it is possible to create fairly accurate risk profiles based on criminal background alone, gathering dynamic risk data (e.g., information on current substance use or antisocial thinking patterns) both improves accuracy and allows for the possibility of risk reduction through targeted alternatives to incarceration. Given the importance of such factors that reflect an individual's current clinical needs or socioeconomic context (Austin, 2006; Monahan & Skeem, 2014), good risk assessment may require defendant interviews to maximize predictive accuracy. Forthcoming research from the Center for Court Innovation drawn from in-depth interviews with a large sample of defendants in New York City suggests that risk of reoffending is optimally predicted based on a combination of static criminal history variables gleaned from administrative databases (e.g., prior convictions, prior warrants for failure to appear in court, currently open cases) and dynamic needs (e.g., substance use, residential stability, employment stability) gleaned from interviews.

Transparency

Regardless of whether a jurisdiction decides to develop an assessment instrument from scratch or to import a tool from another jurisdiction, it is prudent to avoid the "black box" phenomenon that haunts so many reform efforts (i.e., we observe a particular treatment "working" and quickly replicate it prior to understanding *how*, *why*, or for *whom* it works). Although there is near consensus at this point regarding the drivers of risk, the relative strength and interactive nature of these factors in any given assessment tool often remains a closely guarded scientific secret. There are lots of tools on the market, and the makers of these tools tend to have a proprietary (and often financial) interest in advancing their product and protecting their intellectual property. Thus, the "black box" is already an unwelcome guest at the development table, particularly given the significant collateral consequences that a misunderstood cumulative risk score may produce—detention versus freedom.

We implore instrument developers to reverse this trend, beginning with disclosing the assessment items, weighting, and scoring algorithms for public and user examination and to include the identification and analysis of the potential impact of any "proxy" variables during technical assistance efforts. For example, if unemployment both predicts risk *and* is highly correlated with race, age, or neighborhood, transparency about this should be promoted to allow jurisdictions to make ethical decisions about how to respond to this "reality." A cumulative risk score *only* undermines such efforts. Developers can further promote transparency and better decision-making through publishing the results of an instrument's performance (including AUC statistics) in validation studies—and publication of results must include *all* results, not just ones that are favorable to an instrument. Given the nascence of the science and the high-stakes implications for pretrial release and sentencing decisions, it is detrimental to allow proprietary interests to trump the broader, public interest in accurate risk prediction methods. When a developer has a stake in the use of an instrument—particularly when the developer markets or promotes that instrument—the onus is on the developer to back up claims by making the science available and accessible to interested parties.

Moreover, failure to promote transparency raises concerns about the fairness of legal proceedings that take actuarial risk information into account without judges, defenders, and other stakeholders having a full understanding of how a risk score or category was produced. As Starr (2015b) opines, "if judges or policymakers would be embarrassed to embrace ideas like 'we should increase people's sentences for being poor' openly, then they should not do so covertly by relying on a risk score that is substantially driven by such factors" (p. 122). The only way for proponents of the practice to effectively defend both the integrity and science of actuarial risk prediction is to make it explicitly clear how an instrument's scoring system works.

Principle #2: Judicious Implementation

A risk assessment instrument is not a magic bullet; the significant time and resources that are invested in developing and validating these instruments will not affect decision-making without concerted efforts toward proper implementation. For example, the comprehensive evaluation of the implementation of the Virginia Pretrial Risk Assessment Instrument (VPRAI) could inform the release of low-risk, nonviolent felony offenders to probation in lieu of incarceration (Ostrom, Kleiman, Cheesman, Hansen, & Kauder, 2002). Under Virginia's policy, over a period of 5 years, more than 500 prison-bound offenders were recommended for release to diversion based on the results of a short risk assessment tool. Evaluators found that those diverted according to the assessment guidelines were less likely to recidivate than those the tool recommended for detention, in support of the tool's validity. At the same time, judges made decisions contradicting the risk assessment guidelines in a quarter of the more than 2,000 cases examined in the research. Of greater concern, in the majority of these override cases, judges provided no rationale for not adhering to the risk assessment results. Similarly, Arizona judges using the Coconino County Risk Assessment Tool were able to follow recommendation guidelines for low- and high-risk defendants, but did not consistently follow recommendations for moderate risk level defendents (Levin, 2010). While the existence of a risk assessment tool does not obviate the need for judicial discretion, ideally, its exercise should be as transparent and justifiable as risk-based decision-making. For example, a judge may choose to deviate from a risk tool based on sensitivity to a victim or a particularly persuasive argument by either the prosecutor or the defender; but unless that judges makes a clear record of the rationale, there is no reliable method for distinguishing that exercise of discretion from one born of bias or caprice.

Overcoming Institutional Inertia

At first, the solution to these types of implementation problems seems simple: Develop and implement structured decision-making matrices that distill probability information into practice recommendations (Baglivio, Greenwald, & Russell, 2015). In other words, proponents should look to develop a new set of default system responses based on a defendant's risk level and possibly other salient factors (e.g., whether the current charge is classified as violent or nonviolent, whether the defendant has an immediately treatable clinical need). Though a separate body of literature expands on the potential of structured decision-making, it is important to emphasize the likelihood that most jurisdictions will struggle to make continued use of new decision-making models. Proponents can also reasonably expect—but are encouraged to persevere through—some regression to preexisting practice. Indeed, there may be some merits to local resistance to the imposition of externally developed decision-making grids based on the idea that local practitioners know their jurisdictions—the judicious use and documentation of professional overrides (including the rationale for overrides) can actually improve the development of evidence-based decision-making models such as sentencing grids and provide practical guidance on overcoming practice inertia.

From Statistical Uncertainty to Misplaced Intuition

Despite the increasing efficacy of actuarially informed decision-making, implementation challenges may also turn on the inherently probabilistic nature of the instruments and how it conflicts with the way judges tend to understand and decide matters before them which is generally more individualistic and intuitive. Another reason risk assessments may not be conducive to immediate "plug and play" is that implicit bias across justice system decision points has been shown to be relatively widespread (Casey, Warren, Cheesman, & Elek, 2012; Guthrie, Rachlinski, & Wistrich, 2001, 2007; Rachlinski, Johnson, Wistrich, & Guthrie, 2009). Research indicates, for instance, that the chance of pretrial release is influenced by attitudes toward and stereotypes about certain types of offenders (e.g., offenders who show apparent symptoms of mental illness), which may be empirically inaccurate (Beattey, Matsuura, & Jeglic 2014). The literature on bail decisions has also demonstrated that judges may base their decisions on factors that may be only loosely or partly related to risk, including prosecutorial recommendations, the seriousness of the presenting charge, or an apparent lack of community ties (Phillips,

2012). Results of these and other studies have consistently displayed a judicial preference for expert opinion testimony as compared to actuarial information (Kwartner, Lyons, & Boccaccini, 2006; Poythress, 1983; Redding, Floyd, & Hawk, 2001)—even though actuarial information has proven to be more scientifically valid (American Psychological Association, 2011).

Judges' (and presumably other decision makers') ostensible difficulty with actuarial risk data may best be explained by the intuitive override model (Guthrie et al., 2007). The model draws from the social-cognitive literature on dual process models of information processing, but applies it to the specific context of judicial decision-making. Several varying "dual process" models have been articulated (see Chaiken, 1980; Epstein, 1994; Petty & Cacioppo, 1986), but these theories all propose that individuals process information along two independent pathways. One path emphasizes deliberate, rational processing based on careful consideration of information; the other is rooted in intuition. The intuitive path may sometimes lead to accurate decisions, but the intuitive mode is largely influenced by heuristics and preexisting attitudes that have the potential to lead to errors (Guthrie et al., 2007)—and the potential to unwittingly ignore relevant conflicting data.

For jurisdictions planning for or struggling with judicial fidelity to risk assessment information, the goal may essentially be to encourage judges to shift processing to the more deliberate, rational path. Somewhat ironically, the imposition of models that reflect the very probabilistic information that judges reject, such as structured decision-making grids, may promote shifting from intuitive to rational pathways. As Guthrie and colleagues (2007) note, a successful shift depends on the motivation of the individual and an environment that facilitates deliberate decision-making (e.g., providing judges with more time to render decisions, judicial education, creating tools to help guide decision-making).

Principle #3: Decarcerative Purpose

Risk assessment instruments—and, more generally, evidence-based practices—are only effective if used appropriately and for credible purposes. Given growing evidence of the detrimental effects of even short periods of incarceration, we advise jurisdictions to apply these instruments to increase and broaden the use of alternatives to pretrial detention and incarceration. Academic literature supports the preference for nonincarcerative responses to crime. Recent meta-analytic research suggests that the empirical status of deterrence theory, which underlies the majority of get-tough-on-crime measures, is weak at best (Pratt, Cullen, Blevins, Daigle, & Madensen, 2006). Indeed, incarceration has been shown to have little deterrent effect across the risk spectrum and instead may moderately increase the likelihood of reoffending (Cullen, Jonson, & Nagin, 2011; Langan & Levin, 2002). Criminological theorists typically attribute the criminogenic effects of incarceration to labeling (Spohn, 2007) or strain theories (Listwan, Sullivan, Agnew,

Cullen, & Colvin, 2013), and although the majority of such research has been conducted on longer-term prison populations, similar criminogenic effects have been documented in those studies of pretrial and jail populations that do exist (Dejong, 1997; Freudenberg, Daniels, Crum, Perkins, & Richie, 2008; Lim et al., 2012).

The Science and Practice of Risk Reduction

More recent work has directly applied actuarial risk information to elucidate the relationship between criminogenic risk, pretrial incarceration, and future offending. In their analysis of 153,407 defendants in Kentucky, Lowenkamp, VanNostrand, and Holsinger (2013) classified risk according to the Kentucky Pretrial Risk Assessment to determine the likelihood of pretrial failure. The criminogenic effects of pretrial incarceration were most pronounced for the low- and moderate-risk defendants, and the effects were lasting. Compared to those released within 24-hours, for example, low-risk defendants detained from 2 to 3 days were 40% more likely to fail pretrial. To place these findings in perspective, a leading scholar in the field of sentencing, Cassia Spohn, wrote, "incarceration may have transformed high-stakes offenders into low-stakes offenders with little to lose as a result of a new arrest" (Spohn, 2007, p. 47). With this perspective in mind, we argue that the use of risk assessment instruments for the promotion of therapeutic and community-based efforts that reduce the stigmatization and collateral consequences of incarceration is both ethically defensible and pragmatic for decarceration.

The emphasis on both *increasing* and *broadening* community-based and therapeutic alternatives to incarceration is purposeful. When we refer to *increasing* alternatives, this means using risk assessment instruments to increase identification of individuals who are appropriate for diversion. There is consensus regarding this pressing need to identify and off-ramp lower-risk defendants whom many jurisdictions would—in theory—be happy to release were they aware of their low-risk status. Currently, however, three out of five people in jail are awaiting trial and simply cannot afford to post bail, with 75% of these individuals being detained for nonviolent misdemeanor crimes (Subramanian, Delaney, Roberts, Fishman, & McGarry, 2015). The application of risk assessment instruments to increase release on recognizance decisions is an obvious antidote to the overuse of bail.

Rethinking High-Risk Incarceration

Broadening the use of assessment instruments to facilitate nonincarcerative treatment and recidivism reductions among moderate- to high-risk groups is a more complex matter, both conceptually and politically. Conventional criticism of risk assessment is that it will actually *increase* incarceration for moderate- and high-risk individuals; for example, judges will see a "high risk" actuarial classification and have a quite natural impulse to incarcerate. This is especially problematic if, as critics fear, individuals classified as high risk are more likely to be poor or from racial or ethnic minority groups.

It is one thing to point out that moderate- and high-risk individuals are precisely the group with whom intensive supervision and alternatives to incarceration have been proven most effective; it is another matter entirely to work with decision makers entrusted as guarantors of public safety to actually hold in abeyance the incarcerative impulse. Undoubtedly, such concerns fed Eric Holder's (2014) plea to minimize the use of risk assessment tools for the purpose of informing the decision to incarcerate and informing length of incarceration.

Moreover, the application of evidence-based practices toward "smart decarceration" will likely fail without reducing incarceration specifically among high-risk individuals for the following important reasons: (1) Mass incarceration is driven primarily by reoffense among high-risk populations (Glaze & James, 2006); (2) community-based supervision and therapeutic intervention are *most* effective with high-risk populations (Latessa & Lowenkamp, 2006); and (3) though incarceration has been shown to be *most* detrimental among lower-risk groups, even among the highest-risk populations there is no conclusive evidence that it has a risk-reduction effect, particularly given the absence of therapeutic services in many American jails today (Subramanian et al., 2015).

Drilling Down: Actuarial Assessment and Decarceration

We have several suggestions for the effective use of risk assessment instruments to broaden alternatives for high-risk populations. First, it is important to understand the subtleties of risk definitions and respond accordingly. For example, defendants who are assessed to be at high risk to reoffend (or to fail to return to court) may not be threats to public safety. Instead, they may be particularly appropriate candidates for alternatives to incarceration. Conversely, defendants who are assessed to be at higher risk of violence likely pose different—and often insurmountable— challenges in both pre- and postsentencing contexts, and stakeholders may need to consider whether they have the resources and wherewithal to manage the risk.

Second, jurisdictions should adopt risk assessment instruments that separately score and classify risk of general reoffense (i.e., for any crime) and risk of violent reoffense; then, in making the decision of whether to incarcerate, focus on risk of violent reoffense. Such an approach can aid in reducing incarceration for high-risk individuals whose risk is in fact both nonviolent and highly treatable.

Third, jurisdictions should economically collect and use information about dynamic needs in keeping with the need principle. This suggestion is rooted in the academic literature, which shows that properly targeted intervention among moderate- to high-risk groups with significant criminogenic needs is the most robust approach to recidivism reduction (Bonta & Andrews, 2007; Latessa & Lowenkamp, 2006). Though this strategy cannot be successful without some effort toward data collection on needs early in case processing, emerging findings from recent risk assessment development research suggests that these needs can be identified relatively efficiently (e.g., see forthcoming validation research from the Center for Court Innovation).

Finally, jurisdictions should make appreciable, real-time efforts to document the process and impact of the development or adoption of risk assessment instruments, to both avoid the inadvertent "net-widening" or racially disproportionate effects of new release sentencing policies, and also to contribute to the larger project of tempering and qualifying anxieties regarding the potentially negative consequences of decarceration.

CONCLUSION

It is premature to settle the debate about whether actuarial risk assessment helps or hinders the crisis of mass incarceration—or has a negative effect on public safety for that matter. The empirical question remains open. What is known is that a rapidly increasing number of jurisdictions are using risk assessment instruments to inform pretrial release and sentencing decisions and that much remains to be done to advance the science and practice of risk assessment. Returning to the distinction between "is" and "ought," we also recognize that empirical analysis will only get jurisdictions so far—at the end of the day, the questions of whether and how to effectuate decarceration reduce down to values.

On the subject of values, it is worth noting that risk assessment instruments received a major endorsement in a roundtable discussion by the Brennan Center for Justice, *Reducing Racial and Ethnic Disparities in Jails: Recommendations for Local Practice* (Eaglin & Solomon, 2015). One participant aptly made the case for why assessment instruments may be the more effective vehicles for advancing decarceration. Acknowledging that risk instruments that consider "things like prior arrests can create disparities when people of color tend to live in neighborhoods with more police patrolling them, which leads to more contact with police and more arrests for low-level offenses," the participant cautions that "the alternative to a risk assessment is a judge's gut feeling. That may be worse" (p. 28). A second participant in the roundtable framed the challenge as maximizing the benefits of actuarial risk assessment while safeguarding against and improving on the limitations of the current state of the science: "The key is to reduce or eliminate elements of the tools that produce disparities, and then put them to use" (p. 28). Ultimately, the report recommends the use of pretrial risk assessment tools as a strategy for decreasing racial disparities in jails, effectively preventing "decision makers from falling back on implicit biases that may cause them to assume that individuals of color are more dangerous and more in need of detention" (p. 28).

Of course, some critics maintain "it is also easy to imagine any number of incarceration reduction measures that do not incorporate actuarial risk assessment at all" (Starr, 2015b, p. 133). This may prove to be the case—eventually. But in light of the immediate mass incarceration crisis in the United States, we argue that all credible incarceration-reduction measures are worth considering at this juncture. At the end of the day, it is premature and even harmful to take zero-sum positions where the potential still lies for improving and refining practices with decarcerative potential.

REFERENCES

American Psychological Association. (2011). Amicus brief in *Coble v. State of Texas*. Retrieved from http://www.apa.org/about/offices/ogc/amicus/index-chron.aspx

Andrews, D. A., Bonta, J., & Hoge, R. D. (1990). Classification for effective rehabilitation: Rediscovering psychology. *Criminal Justice and Behavior, 17,* 19–52. doi:10.1177/0093854890017001004

Andrews, D. A., & Dowden, C. (2006). Risk principle of case classification in correctional treatment: A meta-analytic investigation. *International Journal of Offender Therapy and Comparative Criminology, 50,* 88–100. doi:10.1177/0306624X05282556

Austin, J. (2006). How much risk can we take? The misuse of risk assessment in corrections. *Federal Probation, 70,* 58–63.

Baglivio, M. T., Greenwald, M. A., & Russell, M. (2015). Assessing the implications of a structured decision-making tool for recidivism in a statewide analysis. *Criminology and Public Policy, 14,* 5–49. doi:10.1111/1745-9133.12108

Barry-Jester, A. M., Casselman, B., & Goldstein, D. (2015). *The new science of sentencing: Should prison sentences be based on crimes that haven't been committed yet?* The Marshall Project. Retrieved from https://www.themarshallproject.org/2015/08/04/the-new-science-of-sentencing

Beattey, R. A., Jr., Matsuura, T., & Jeglic, E. L. (2014). Judicial bond-setting behavior: The perceived nature of the crime may matter more than how serious it is. *Psychology, Public Policy, and Law, 20,* 411–420. doi:10.1037/law0000020

Bonta, J., & Andrews, D. A. (2007). Risk-Need-Responsivity Model for offender assessment and rehabilitation: 2007-06. Pennsyvania Board of Probation and Parole. Retrieved from http://www.pbpp.pa.gov/Information/Documents/Research/EBP7.pdf

Bureau of Justice Statistics. (2014). *Total adult correctional population, 1980–2014.* Retrieved from http://www.bjs.gov/index.cfm?ty=kfdetail&iid=487#figure

Casey, P. M., Warren, R. K., Cheesman, F. L., & Elek, J. K. (2012). *Helping courts address implicit bias: Resources for education.* National Center for State Courts. Retrieved from http://www.ncsc.org/~/media/Files/PDF/Topics/Gender%20and%20Racial%20Fairness/IB_report_033012.ashx

Chaiken, S. (1980). Heuristic versus systematic information processing and the use of source versus message cues in persuasion. *Journal of Personality and Social Psychology, 39,* 752–766. doi:10.1037/0022-3514.39.5.752

Cullen, F., Jonson, C., & Nagin, D. S. (2011). Prisons do not reduce recidivism: The high cost of ignoring science. *Prison Journal Supplement, 91,* 48S–65S. doi:10.1177/0032885511415224

Dejong, C. (1997). Survival analysis and specific deterrence: Integrating theoretical and empirical models of recidivism. *Criminology, 35,* 561–575. doi:10.1111/j.1745-9125.1997.tb01230.x

Eaglin, J., & Solomon, D. (2015). *Reducing racial and ethnic disparities in jails: Recommendations for local practice.* Brennan Center for Justice. Retrieved from https://www.brennancenter.org/sites/default/files/publications/Racial%20Disparities%20Report%20062515.pdf

Epstein, S. (1994). Integration of the cognitive and the psychodynamic unconscious. *American Psychologist, 49,* 709–724. doi:10.1037/0003-066X.49.8.709

Farrington, D. P. (1986). Stepping stones to adult criminal careers. In D. Olweus, J. Block, & Radke-Yarrow, M. (Eds.), *Development of antisocial and prosocial behavior.* New York, NY: Academy Press.

Freudenberg, N., Daniels, J., Crum, M., Perkins, T., & Richie, B. (2008). Coming home from jail: The social and health consequences of community reentry for women, male adolescents, and their families and communities. *American Journal of Public Health, 98,* S191–S202.

Gendreau, P., Little, T., & Goggin, C. (1996). A meta-analysis of the predictors of adult offender recidivism: What works! *Criminology, 34*(4), 575–608.

Glaze, L. E., & James, D. J. (2006). *Mental health problems of prison and jail inmates.* Washington, DC: Bureau of Justice Statistics. Retrieved from http://www.bjs.gov/content/pub/pdf/mhppji.pdf

Guthrie, C., Rachlinski, J. J., & Wistrich, A. J. (2001). Inside the judicial mind. *Cornell Law Review, 86,* 777–830.

Guthrie, C., Rachlinski, J. J., & Wistrich, A. J. (2007). Blinking on the bench: How judges decide cases. *Cornell Law Review, 93,* 1–43.

Hannah-Moffat, K. (2010). Actuarial sentencing: An "unsettled" proposition. *Justice Quarterly, 30,* 270–296. doi:10.1080/07418825.2012.682603

Harcourt, B. E. (2007). *Against prediction: Profiling, policing, and punishing in an actuarial age.* Chicago, IL: University of Chicago Press.

Harcourt, B. E. (2015). Risk as a proxy for race: The dangers of risk assessment. *Federal Sentencing Reporter, 27,* 237–243. doi:10.1525/fsr.2015.27.4.237

Hirschi, T., & Gottfredson, M. R. (1983). Age and the explanation of crime. *American Journal of Sociology, 89,* 552–584.

Holder, E. (2014). *Attorney General Eric Holder speaks at the National Association of Criminal Defense Lawyers 57th Annual Meeting and 13th State Criminal Justice Network Conference.* United States Department of Justice Office of Public Affairs. Retrieved from http://www.justice.gov/opa/speech/attorney-general-eric-holder-speaks-national-association-criminal-defense-lawyers-57th

Kelly, W. R. (2015). *Criminal justice at the crossroads: Transforming crime and punishment.* New York, NY: Columbia University Press.

Kwartner, P. P., Lyons, P. M., & Boccaccini, M. T. (2006). Judges' risk communication preferences in risk for future violence cases. *International Journal of Forensic Mental Health, 5,* 185–194. doi:10.1080/14999013.2006.10471242

Langan, P. A., & Levin, D. J. (2002). *Recidivism of prisoners released in 1994.* Washington, DC: Bureau of Justice Statistics, U.S. Department of Justice.

Latessa, E. J., & Lowenkamp, C. T. (2006). What works in reducing recidivism? *University of St. Thomas Law Journal, 3,* 521–535.

Latessa, E. J., Smith, P., Lemke, R., Makarios, M., & Lowenkamp, C. (2009). *Creation and validation of the Ohio Risk Assessment System: Final report.* Cincinnati, OH: University of Cincinnati Center for Criminal Justice Research.

Laura and John Arnold Foundation. (2015). *Public safety assessment.* Retrieved from http://www.arnoldfoundation.org/initiatives/case-studies/public-safety-assessment-2/

Levin, D. J. (2010). *Validation of the Coconino County pretrial risk assessment tool.* Washington, DC: Pretrial Justice Institute.

Lim, S., Seligson, A. L., Parvez, F. M., Luther, C. W., Mavinkurve, M. P., Binswanger, I. A., & Kerker, B. D. (2012). Risks of drug-related death, suicide, and homicide during the immediate post-release period among people released from New York City jails, 2001–2005. *American Journal of Epidemiology, 175,* 519–526. doi:10.1093/aje/kwr327

Lipsey, M. W. (2009). The primary factors that characterize effective interventions with juvenile offenders: A meta analytic overview. *Victims and Offenders, 4,* 124–147.

Listwan, S. J., Sullivan, C. J., Agnew, R., Cullen, F. T., & Colvin, M. (2013). The pains of imprisonment revisited: The impact of strain on inmate recidivism. *Justice Quarterly, 30,* 144–168. doi:10.1080/07418825.2011.597772

Lowenkamp, C. T., Latessa, E., & Smith, P. (2006). Does correctional program quality really matter? The impact of adhering to the principles of effective intervention. *Federal Probation, 5,* 201–220. doi:10.1111/j.1745-9133.2006.00388.x

Lowenkamp, C. T., VanNostrand, M., & Holsinger, A. (2013). *The hidden costs of pretrial detention.* The Arnold Foundation. Retrieved from http://www.arnoldfoundation.org/wp-content/uploads/2014/02/LJAF_Report_hidden-costs_FNL.pdf

Martinson, R. (1974). What works? Questions and answers about prison reform. *The Public Interest, 35,* 22–54.

Monahan, J., & Skeem, J. L. (2014). Risk redux: The resurgence of risk assessment in criminal sanctioning. *Federal Sentencing Reporter, 26,* 158–166. doi:10.1525/fsr.2014.26.3.158

Ostrom, B. J., Kleiman, M., Cheesman, F., Hansen, R. M., & Kauder, N. B. (2002). Offender risk assessment in Virginia. *Virginia Criminal Sentencing Commission.* Retrieved from http://www.vcsc.virginia.gov/risk_off_rpt.pdf

Petty, R. E., & Cacioppo, J. T. (1986). The elaboration likelihood model of persuasion. In L. Berkowitz (Ed.), *Advances in experimental social psychology* (pp. 123–203). New York, NY: Academic Press.

Phillips, M. T. (2012). *A decade of bail research in New York City.* New York: New York City Criminal Justice Agency.

Poythress, N. G. (1983). Psychological issues in criminal proceedings: Judicial preference regarding expert testimony. *Criminal Justice and Behavior, 10,* 175–194. doi:10.1177/0093854883010002003

Pratt, T. C., Cullen, F. T., Blevins, K. R., Daigle, L. E., & Madensen, T. D. (2006). The empirical status of deterrence theory: A meta-analysis. *Taking Stock: The Status of Criminological Theory, 15,* 367–396.

Rachlinski, J. J., Johnson, S., Wistrich, A. J., & Guthrie, C. (2009). Does unconscious racial bias affect trial judges? *Notre Dame Law Review, 84,* 1195–1246.

Redding, R. E., Floyd, M. Y., & Hawk, G. L. (2001). What judges and lawyers think about the testimony of mental health experts: A survey of the courts and bar. *Behavioral Sciences and the Law, 19,* 583–594. doi:10.1002/bsl.455

Silver, E., & Miller, L. L. (2002). A cautionary note on the use of actuarial risk assessment tools for social control. *Crime and Delinquency, 48,* 138–161. doi:10.1177/0011128702048001006

Spohn, C. (2007). The deterrent effect of imprisonment and offender's stakes in conformity. *Criminal Justice Policy Review, 18,* 31–50. doi:10.1177/0887403406294945

Starr, S. B. (2015a). The risk assessment era: An overdue debate. *Federal Sentencing Reporter, 27,* 205–206. doi:10.1525/fsr.2015.27.4.205

Starr, S. B. (2015b). Risk redux: The new profiling: Why punishing based on poverty and identity is unconstitutional. *Federal Sentencing Reporter, 27,* 229–236. doi:10.1525/fsr.2015.27.4.229

Subramanian, R., Delaney, R., Roberts, S., Fishman, N., & McGarry, P. (2015). *Incarceration's front door: The misuse of jails in America.* Retrieved from http://www.vera.org/sites/default/files/resources/downloads/incarcerations-front-door-report_02.pdf

Taxman, F. S., Henderson, C., Young, D. W., & Farrell, J. (2012). The impact of training interventions on organizational readiness to support innovations in juvenile justice offices. *Administration of Mental Health Policy and Mental Health Services Research.* doi:10.1007/s10488-012-0445-5

Tonry, M. (2011). Making peace, not a desert. *Criminology and Public Policy, 10*(3), 637–649.

Walsh, L. (2013). *Scientists as prophets: A rhetorical genealogy.* New York, NY: Oxford University Press.

PART IV

Moving from Concepts to Strategies

14

Imagining the Future of Justice

ADVANCING DECARCERATION THROUGH

MULTISECTOR SOCIAL INNOVATIONS

Margaret E. Severson

BACKGROUND

On a flight some years ago, I was seated next to a "futurist" employed by Intel who was returning from a meeting focused on imagining what comes next in computer technology. I asked him, What will come next? He told of a future in intuitive, smart computing; using hands-and-voice free technologies, a future where computers function and respond not to users' physical prompts but to their thoughts. Indeed, in the digital age, technologies once conceptualized as the lore of science fiction are being actively realized and produced.[1]

The impossible becoming possible inspires a similar suspension of disbelief for other seemingly intractable tasks, such those awaiting action in the U.S. criminal justice system. Certain key substantive objectives—realizing reductions in the numbers of people incarcerated in the nation's jails and prisons, reforms in policing and charging practices, and the adoption of fiscally and operationally viable diversion and reintegration strategies— seem ripe for the futurist's provocations. Thus, when imagining significant decarceration, the futurist might ask, What is the one change, one innovation to our current incarceration practice(s) that, if realized today, would result in a more perfect rendering of justice?

---

[1] Taking a cue from the ideas of the esteemed professor Todd Clear, readers are cautioned that nothing in this chapter should be interpreted as suggesting that incarceration is a profound or a singularly effective method of responding to criminal behavior.

There is plenty of room in this question for futurists of different motivations and interests to imagine the possibilities.

In this chapter, I explore the potential of futurist justice work, especially as related to decarceration efforts, within the framework of multisector social innovations, that is, through imagining the possibilities when individuals, organizations, institutions, and government come together to shape a new, more just use of incarceration. The hope moving forward is to free the imagination to generate ideas for a more perfect justice in incarceration practices, and to generate innovation(s) not yet imagined or realized that will significantly reduce the size of and growth in the incarcerated population.

The futurist (my attribution, not his) Josh Tetrick, CEO of the food company Hampton Creek, in ads in the *New York Times* (2015) inspired readers to imagine change, and the future, with this provocation, directed to our presidential candidates: "Ask yourself this question: What would it look like if we started over in food?" As if that were not enough to contemplate, Tetrick underscored his question with this statement: "Historic opportunities are missed because we fixate on what folks say they want. And what folks say they want in business (and politics) is limited by what they believe is possible."

Following his lead, it seems important to ask similar questions in the justice context. When thinking about potential innovations in justice, is what we say we want in a justice system limited by what we believe is possible? That question and those posed by other futurists are timely ones for the business of justice, particularly as the collective struggle for meaningful decarceration seems limited by our own inventions (e.g., arbitrary sentencing policies and practices, the transinstitutionalization of inmates from prisons to other places of confinement or forms of surveillance, non-evidence-supported crime-deterrence strategies, limited viable diversion options, reentry programs in need of reform), with little evidence to suggest that even a wide-scale deployment of these inventions, without something more—something perhaps not yet imagined—will have a major impact on criminal justice population reductions or on new incidents of criminal behavior (Austin et al., 2013; Fabelo & Thompson, 2015; Raphel & Stoll, 2013).

Throughout the American experience of criminal justice, the one sure lesson delivered is that there is no single fix, no silver bullet to prevent crime or to rehabilitate the crime doer. Though decarceration advocates present arguments for the more liberal use of diversion and sentencing alternatives and even for dramatic prisoner releases such as those imposed on the California prison system by the federal courts (*Brown v. Plata*, 2011) and through measures imposed by its legislature[2] and citizen referendum,[3] significant reductions in the rates and levels of imprisonment throughout in the United States are likely to take years, even decades, to realize.

---

[2] See California Assembly Bill (AB) 109, 2011, also known as Public Safety Realignment.
[3] See Proposition 47 (The Safe Neighborhoods and Schools Act) on November 4, 2014.

In the decarceration effort, what lies beyond the limits of what we believe is possible? What ideas, options, and strategies—perhaps inconceivable today but not tomorrow— might solve the challenges posed by a system that espouses justice, but often metes disadvantage? What kinds of policy structures and collaborations are necessary to consider and answer these questions? What would it look like if we could start over in justice, particularly in the use of incarceration and in efforts toward decarceration?

There are, of course, future-minded persons already working in criminal and social justice systems and on justice issues. For example, in *Places Not Cases*, Todd Clear (2005) advanced a radical idea for change in the business of probation. Rather than continuing to support a probation system that operates on an assigned case method, a method that "would lead someone uninformed about the topic to think that there must be some large and convincing literature showing the caseload system to be a profoundly powerful and effective method of doing the work" (2005, p. 173), Clear proposed moving the probation officer's focus to "place" instead, to the places and neighborhoods where probationers reside. Alas, change comes slowly, even for the futurist. Work with assigned and specialty caseloads continues to this day, as though the answers to recidivism lie somewhere in the realm of the supervising officers' offices. Even with more than 4.7 million adults subject to parole and probation supervision, the movement from case-based to place-based supervision remains "far from the norm" (Solomon et al., 2008).

Similarly, the notoriously overused prison and jail systems in the United States might also lead some to believe that there is ample evidence that locking people up is a "profoundly powerful and effective method" (Clear, 2005, p. 173) of preventing crime and changing behaviors. That the evaluation of one's movement toward or arrival at a state of rehabilitation is focused solely on change in the individual's thinking and behavior is difficult to comprehend. To suggest that the incarcerated person—who has likely faced the systemic oppression and social disenfranchisement of racism, classism, poverty, poor education and living conditions, un- or underemployment, hunger, and physical and mental health challenges—is solely responsible for his or her rehabilitation ignores the reality that there is a benefit to some for his failure to succeed.

Clearly incarceration is not the sole answer to many criminal behaviors, nor is it even the correct intervention for producing enduring positive behavior change. The futurist's question in this regard asks us to consider, What is possible even if not immediately palatable?

Embracing the long view for change is key to imagining and creating a new justice for incarceration and decarceration practices. Consider this: By the time Intel Corporation rolls out its hands-and-voice-free computer technology, more than 20 years will have passed since the idea was conceived (Eaton, 2009). Taking the long view encourages innovative thinking, optimism, and resolve: the formula needed to imagine a *just* decarceration.

Thus, this chapter is devoted to the future—examining what is and what might be, generating questions, asking "what ifs," setting out hypotheses and provocations—to inspire some preliminary shifts in thinking and action that will move the nation to a new way of realizing justice.

Justice, at least in the criminal context, has through history been frequently defined by how the victims and the offenders were treated and by the outcomes they met: vindication of or reparations for the victims; convictions and punishments for the offenders. Rather than the line of action between victims and offenders being so direct, recent innovations suggest that it is more complex; involve more stakeholders; include profiteers, philanthropists, and government and private actors; and insist that it must end in something more than win and lose.

The Historical Context

Ideas about the nature of and the challenges inherent in criminal justice are not new; centuries of thought about what justice is and how it should be delivered and experienced mark its imperfect evolution. Consequently, there are myriad notions of the appropriate punishment for crimes and for rehabilitation methods for incarcerated people reentering society. Eighteenth-century measures of deterrence accomplished through punitive actions such as severe isolation and physical brutality, gave way in the 19th century to a philosophy of social rehabilitation accomplished through structural mechanisms, such as physical labor and solitary or silent living conditions. In the 20th century, particularly in the 1970s, when the U.S. Supreme Court first issued seminal health- (*Estelle v. Gamble*, 1976) and conditions-related (*Bell v. Wolfish*, 1979) decisions, the federal courts engaged with jail and prison officials to identify and rectify unacceptable conditions of confinement and articulate the constitutional standards for the minimally adequate care and treatment of incarcerated persons. These legal actions contributed to the development of rehabilitative interventions focused on changing the incarcerated individual (Severson, 2009). In the 1990s and now well into the 21st century, social-structural-process interventions that correspond to individuals' risks, needs, and responsivity measures are being suggested as one component of an enthusiastic embrace of emerging evidence-based responses to criminal behaviors (Taxman, 2011).

The Criminal Justice System's Focus on Individual Change Through Incarceration

Common to all of these historical approaches is the focus on change in the individual; change in the individual's behavior, thinking, and ability to avoid detention. Indeed, at present, the central measurement of change or lack of change has only to do with the individual; the contributions to the change process or the absence thereof made by the external systems with which the individual interfaces are not measured in any meaningful way.

In reality, focusing on psychological and behavioral changes that occur in the individual perpetrator is not a good measure of whether justice has been served or of whether public safety has been advanced. The incessant focus on recidivism lessens the pressure for the necessary system changes and solutions, the kind of changes that might be furthered (if not accomplished) by multisector social innovations, ones that are measured by outcomes bigger than individual change.

Thus, thinking like a futurist might, one must wonder what justice would look like if the measurement of change changed. What if every time a formerly incarcerated individual returned to custody, the agencies, the businesses, and the forces involved in his or her recidivism were called to answer for their contributions to his or her failure? Might this demand for accountability, however ultimately expressed, be the future, or some part of it, of justice?

MULTISECTOR SOCIAL INNOVATIONS

Typing the words "multisector social innovation" into an academic database yields both topical (e.g., healthier communities [Horne, Bass, & Silva, 2013], learning networks and higher education institutions [Dlouha, Macháčková-Henderson, & Dlouhý, 2013], and health equity [Shrimali, Luginbuhl, Malin, Flournoy, & Siegel, 2014]) and goal-oriented (profitable change for private and public interests [Kanter, 1999], innovations for sustainable development [Petry et al., 2011], and financing social services through social impact bonds [Leventhal, 2013]) results. Key terms run through this body of literature, the descriptors for an array of conceptual ideas having to do with innovation, collaboration, sectoral contributions, the development and use of human and social capital, and social impacts. The term "multisector" denotes concerted action in decarceration work to achieve advances that could not otherwise be achieved through the actions of only one entity. For this paper, it refers to activities in the private, public, and academic sectors.

Until its dismantling under the Trump administration, President Obama's Office of Social Innovation and Civic Participation (OSICP) was often invoked in the literature as providing the structure for finding "novel answers to social problems" (The Economist, 2010). Distinguishing conventional innovation, which focuses "on the creation of better and more effective products, processes or services," from social innovation, which focuses "on finding ways to solve old problems and doing so in the public interest" (The White House, n.d.), the OSICP, which prioritized building a fairer and more equitable criminal and juvenile justice system, set out a series of principles that can still provide structure for thinking about, identifying, and securing multisector social innovations for decarceration. As a working framework for considering the process of achieving justice, the OSICP's principles underscored the following: (1) Doing "more with less" so that declining federal resources are expanded in quantity and reach through public and private partnerships; (2) building on the expertise of others who offer "unique capabilities and skills"; (3) leveraging "collective action" by bringing "together new coalitions of public and private actors . . . to solve problems" as only a collective can; (4) improving performance by increasing efficiencies and improving "the speed and agility of accomplishing a shared policy objective;" and (5) involving diverse partnerships of individuals and organizations in the problem-solving process.

The idea of relying on a decarceration-oriented partnership that includes private actors is at once frightening and intriguing. Much has been written on the consequences of the privatization of corrections (e.g., Carleton, 1984; Feeley, 2002; Kilgore, 2015), and new forms of social control are the consequences of entrepreneurs operating in the justice world. To be sure, a futurist might well imagine a justice system free of profit-making motivations. Disentangling the justice system from the grip of private, profit-driven entities will require the latter to be at the table of reform. If the futurist's questions about starting over in justice and incarceration are entertained and clear goals for mass reductions in the imprisoned and supervised populations are established; a broad representation of individuals, organizations, and government must be involved in the problem-solving process and action. Only then can both private and public actors be held accountable for actions that undermine progress.

A Focus on System Change Through Collaboration

The core focus of the OSICP principles is on system change through collaboration. A policy environment that supports partnerships fosters the collaboration needed to secure that change. This stands in contrast to the centuries of U.S. criminal justice theory and practice where rehabilitation has been defined and evaluated in terms of the individual offender's success; a success measured both substantively and temporally. *Substantive success* is defined, in part, as avoiding new arrests and returns to incarceration, securing a job, meeting the terms of one's postrelease supervision, and finding stable housing. Temporally, success is defined as the amount of time between release from incarceration and the experience of new criminal justice events such as law enforcement contacts, arrests, threats of parole revocation, and shock incarcerations. Thus, formerly incarcerated individuals are followed for 6, 12, 18, 24, 48, and 60 months after release, and their rehabilitation success (or failure) is attached to the time between events and also attached, by extension and assumption, to the belief that some change(s) has or has not occurred in the individual to hold (or not) trouble at bay. The underlying assumption that individual success is primarily a matter of time and individual will only serves to distract our attention from the other culprits of success and failure: the systems responsible for creating the opportunities for success, and for neglecting the conditions that contribute to failure. These systems include the private sector as well as the not-for-profits, policymaking and regulatory bodies, faith-based communities, and individual citizens.

Applying OSICP principles to justice systems, the measurement of justice realized moves away from the focus on the individual and toward a focus on the collective, shifting responsibility for success and for failure from the one to the many. Consequently, how the formerly incarcerated person fares in the community is evaluated in the context of the systems he or she encounters. How did local employers greet her? Was she offered a job, and if not, was feedback provided as to why? What services were received from housing, health, and family service agencies—how many services, for how long, and under what conditions? What did the faith community offer—childcare, housing support, or a place to find food and shelter? In essence, individual change no longer remains the primary marker of a just or unjust system; rather, how well the collaborators function and what their outputs are are recognized and embraced as being equally appropriate measures for evaluation and as the more salient markers of success.

In the end, concerted action to create viable alternatives to and meaningful changes in the use of incarceration is necessary to achieve advances that could not otherwise be achieved through the actions of only one individual.

The Justice Multisector

Keeping the language, spirit, and principles of social innovation in mind, the futurist might ask, What multisector innovation(s) not yet identified or deployed would inspire and support the success of the formerly incarcerated individual's reintegration? What multisector components are needed to achieve the objectives of a justice-centered decarceration movement, and how innovative do we dare be in the seeking of the fair and just outcomes of it?

The dangerous territory of the OSICP's emphasis on the inclusion of a "diverse" partnership raises the question of how private actors can be compelled to join in the decarceration effort. To start, public policy can mandate that corporate entities reaping financial benefit from incarceration contribute to justice reformation, and there are many such entities: private prison corporations (Corrections Corporation of America), health providers (Corizon), release monitors (BI Incorporated), builders (Turner Construction), food providers (Aramark), telephone service providers (Securus) and many other primary and secondary providers and recipients of the goods and services related to imprisonment. Another futurist question emerges: What can be expected of the private sector in the decarceration effort, and what mechanisms can be used to effect this effort?

Like most large-scale change, institutional reform and reductions in the imprisoned population will not happen all at once, but surely they are more likely to happen if guided by clear goals and a cohesive vision. To that end, some one entity must take the lead to create the structure within which certain objectives can be met. If, for example, the goal is to reduce the incarcerated population by one million people in the next two decades, many entities (e.g., families, lawmakers, supervising officers, people profiting from incarceration, nonprofit agencies expending resources on incarceration, researchers, philosophers, politicians) must come to the table determined to collaborate and innovate to keep people out of jail and prison. A justice agent—the district attorney, the chief judge, the sheriff—or agency, for example, might form and inform a jurisdiction's Criminal Justice Coordinating Council in part to identify the barriers that exist in the community and to open discussion for problem solving.

There are examples of public–private collaborations that can be used to inspire the justice work to be done. Affordable and supportive housing initiatives such as Housing First, though not perfectly executed, provides one such example of an evolving program to address homelessness. Housing First focuses in part on populations at risk for incarceration because of their homeless condition. Funding strategies are also developing, such as those where the grant of zoning and building permits is conditioned on the set-aside of a certain proportionate number of units for identified populations. In this funding scenario, an example of public–private collaborations, the builder has the opportunity to expand business and the otherwise not affordable housing stock becomes available to meet the needs of the entire community. Tax incentives and other tax policy initiatives can also be used to create affordable and supportive housing stock.

In a justice system with limited resources, saving its most extreme responses for its most extreme needs is necessary. Attitudinal and structural changes are needed for this new justice; the former must change the way we think and feel about incarceration, and the latter must change the way we think about policy and profitability. For example, the prison's contract with the telephone company[4] might contain incentives for its hire of formerly incarcerated persons or for its debt-forgiveness programs for families of prisoners. The nonprofit would be expected to train the incarcerated person for paid work and for volunteer work as well. The politician would commit to avoiding a tough-on-crime campaign in exchange for the public relations consultant's advice on talking points. The Chamber of Commerce would establish an informal system of communication and identify non-law-enforcement-related intervention strategies when shopkeepers become concerned about the accessibility of their businesses and the safety of their customers. The academic would offer the thinking context in which justice can be considered in a community, and her tenure process would honor the value of her service. Communities would be asked to help shape *just* responses for both the individual and the community, to behaviors that violate the law. And researchers would evaluate the collaborators' readiness to perform (risks), their ability to perform (needs), and their subsequent efforts and the system outcomes (responsivity) when evaluating the individual's outcomes. In essence, the challenge of rehabilitation would be shared with the incarcerated person and with the other collaborators and is one in which all who share in it are evaluated.

No doubt these ideas represent only the start of a new justice paradigm.

---

[4] For a look at the prison-telephone industry, visit http://www.prisonpolicy.org/phones/.

"Actuarializing" the Collaboration

At present, the burden of success in proving one's state of rehabilitation falls solely on the formerly incarcerated person. Current evaluative methods generally focus on identifying the reentering incarcerated person's criminogenic risks, needs, and the level of responsivity, using actuarial instruments like the Level of Service Inventory, Revised (LSI-R; Andrews & Bonta, 1995; Andrews, Bonta, & Hoge, 1990) to assess the static (inalterable) and dynamic (changeable) risk factors for recidivism. Actuarial instruments are favored over clinical judgments about the offender's risk for reoffending, as the former are touted as objective evidence-based assessment strategies.

These risk assessment actuarial strategies may work well as methods of building an understanding of who the individual incarcerated person is and where opportunities for his or her thinking and behavioral change might lie, but they do precious little to call into play the systems that must respond to the individual. Knowing more about the individual, indeed, assessing and reassessing him or her every 90, 180, or 360 days, only measures his or her change, not the changes that must happen *in the system* to bolster and support that change. Despite efforts to change the standards by which success and failure are judged, and in spite of the recognition that a change in focus from ultimate outcomes (recidivism and returns to incarceration) to intermediate outcomes (sobriety; securing employment and housing) is warranted, at present, all eyes remain on the individual (e.g., did he or she get a job, stay sober, return to jail, violate parole?). But it is precisely that focus that puts the individual at risk for reentry to the criminal justice system, if for no other reason than that he or she is being watched more closely than perhaps needed or desired. To all this the futurist might ask, What might it look like if we started over in evaluating risk for recidivism?

Building on the premise that the focus of rehabilitation should be on the systems involved as well as the individual's efforts, one answer: In the spirit of shared responsibility and shared liability, an assessment of the dynamic and static *system* risks, *system* needs, and *system* responsivity should be completed each time a success and a failure-to-(re) integrate occurs.

Consequently, an innovative collaboration between many of the stakeholders to an individual person's desistence or rehabilitation might be evaluated consistently with these inquiries:

- Was there an expectation that the formerly incarcerated person could and would be successful at release?
- Was there an assessment of the capacity of the external systems to meet that person's needs? Did the agency have the necessary resources and/or staff to do so? Did addressing the formerly incarcerated person's needs preempt services being delivered to another person? How did the system / agency respond and was that response adequate?

- Was a job placement agency involved that was equipped to find a job for a formerly incarcerated person? What efforts were made to do so—and what capabilities were put to the task?
- Was job training provided?
- Were jobs available that matched the capabilities of the released person? Was a decent, living wage offered?
- Was mentoring available?
- Did the employer receive an incentive consistent with the formerly incarcerated person's time in the community and his or her quality of freedom?
- What supports were in place to assist the formerly incarcerated person to assimilate into the job milieu?
- Was a support system in place to intervene when needed?
- Did everyone and every agency perform his or her duties?
- Were they capable of doing so?
- Were there gaps in responding to the formerly incarcerated person's questions or concerns and if so, who saw or should have seen and addressed these gaps? What did the system lack that directly or indirectly impacted the success of the formerly incarcerated person in his/her transition to the community?

The work of the multisector collaborations must be supported with clearly defined expectations, assessed for its capabilities to provide what is needed and promised, monitored for its process, and evaluated for its outcomes. This includes the collaborators' power to respond to misuses of power and privilege. If this occurs, the resulting innovations, efficiencies, and social impacts can be ensured beyond any identified persons or political agendas.

Multisector innovation, then, is the standard in a new revisioned justice system, judged on (1) its process—the building and sustaining of private and public collaborations and the realization of a shared vision among the strange bedfellows that make up various sectoral contributions; (2) its capabilities—what the collaborators and the individual formerly incarcerated person bring to the effort and the intersections of all efforts; (3) its outputs—contributions of human capital and beneficial social impacts; (4) its criminal justice outcomes—the fair administration of all justice systems toward a just end for the individual and the community and its community justice outcomes — the offering of a place to live and develop in the community, through relationships, social support, employment, housing, and minimal surveillance.

Moving Forward

Mass incarceration is, ultimately, a problem of troublesome entanglements. To war seriously against the disparity in unfreedom requires a war against a disparity in resources (Coates, 2015).

In generating decarceration strategies, it is important to be aware of and guard against being constrained by our own conventions and the rules we inherited about defining and achieving success. As implied in the idea of an actuarial assessment, the willingness to suspend the focus on the individual person's outcomes and on the belief that individualism and motivation are what it takes to achieve success is important in a country where much of how an individual fares in life is controlled by the opportunities available to him or her. More helpful would be a focus on the outcomes of the person–systems synergies that could tap opportunity, something encompassing, or perhaps a step beyond, what Taxman suggests when she argues for a "client-centered" and empowerment approach (Taxman, 2011). That focus must be inclusive and must account for the racial, ethnic, and class biases that pervade our system of justice and serve as barriers to the opportunities that further decarceration efforts. A focus on person–systems synergies must also take account of the barriers constructed as a result of the rise of the prison industrial complex, the third rail of justice that contaminates the relationship between doing crime and serving time. Until then, our fundamental social and political thinking reverts to the norm, to what is already known not to work: Expecting the individual to pull herself up by the bootstraps, when her boots were taken at the moment of arrest and justice entanglement and certainly at the moment of incarceration.

Person–System Synergies: The Power of the Collaboration

What are these person–system synergies, and how do we know them when they exist (i.e., what would be measured, and how)? The achievement of synergy implies that an outcome of the action of two or more joined forces is bigger, more robust, and more impactful that what would be realized by the action of any single force. Some might call this a "gestalt"; others might acknowledge, as did Aristotle, that the whole is greater than the sum of its parts. This phenomenon, this exponential power realized through concerted action, is exactly what is implied in multisector social innovations.

Expecting the power and effects of the combined energies of participants in reentry endeavors, for example, those of the case manager and the formerly incarcerated individual, or of the housing authority and the case manager, or of the mental health professional and the family of the formerly incarcerated person, to surpass the outcomes of any one of those entities acting solo, defines synergy. Thus, these synergies can be seen as the whole of the outcome, an outcome that cannot be attributed to a particular part of the response.

Consider this example: A formerly incarcerated individual returns to the community, has a job, feels good, and decides on payday to get high, which could result in a technical violation of her parole. Clearly, there is nothing synergistic about this event, nor is there anything that will likely be measured beyond her behavior. She used a substance forbidden by the terms of her release (terms that are rarely individualized); the parole officer, having the power to impose sanctions, takes action in response. That action may include a verbal admonition, the use of the popular "quick dip," or a return to incarceration. Seen in this light, the individual is cast as the problem.

Consider an alternative response, a synergistic one. A formerly incarcerated person is released, has a job, feels good, and decides on payday to get high. The supervising officer discovers this in a random urinalysis and immediately rules out detention as an option, because detention is reserved for those who pose an immediate risk to public safety. There are at least two other options. After an examination of the whole of the person's reintegration, one option is to do nothing. Perhaps forbidding the use of substances should not have been included in the supervision plan.

As an alternative, if the impact of substance use for this particular person (as opposed to all released persons) is assessed as being significant, option two might involve work to secure an evaluation for her for substance treatment services. The treatment services evaluator provides a bus pass for transportation to the evaluation and does so even though the formerly incarcerated person is working and might afford to purchase a pass. The pass is a gesture of good will. The employer recognizes that change and adaptation and assimilation is a process rather than a state-of-being, sees his/her support as a reinvestment in securing a stable workforce, and so makes adjustments to accommodate the evaluation. The supervising officer or a delegate calls the person to remind her of the appointment, and is encouraging about her progress in the community. Once evaluated and accepted into the program, even if a space is not immediately available for treatment, the other services continue. The parole officer makes regular, supportive contact; the evaluator gives the formerly incarcerated individual tips for staying clean; the agency calls daily to provide an update on the timing for admission. Perhaps the family is involved, queried about the pressures it feels in the reintegration process; asked what it can do, and what can be done on its behalf, to support the individual's success. In short, the formerly incarcerated individual, already recognized as being in need of a system of care, is viewed in the context of how that system responds rather than on the basis of a judgment about her individual success and failure; she is viewed as part of a responsive (or not) system that will ultimately form the basis for evaluation.

Finally, the assessment of accountability must also be part of an open, transparent process. Unlike the actuarial assessment of the individual's risks, needs, and responsivity, how well the system worked, the outcomes achieved and the weaknesses exposed, are evaluated in a forum where all the contributors—supporters and detractors included—are at the table. The formerly incarcerated person is asked about her decision to get high. The friends she was with are asked what they might have done differently to reinforce rather than undermine her progress. Her employer reports the pressures on the business to compensate for her absences and also on how the support for her impacted other employees. Perhaps a fiscal accounting is given. What did this transgression cost the person, her family, her employer, her friends and the various agencies involved? And then, the new plan for movement forward is devised.

Call this system accountability, the logical partner of synergy. The influence on each other, recognizing that one cannot be as powerful as the many, builds on the strengths of the individual and on the capacity of others to yield a stronger whole. Consequently, the actions of the system, like those of the individual, are part of the evaluation of success (or failure). In the end, not holding the system accountable simply encourages onlookers to believe that what matters is what is said about the system and not how the system actually works or does not work to further or inhibit decarceration and rehabilitation efforts and system change.

IMAGINING THE POSSIBILITIES FOR MULTISECTOR SOCIAL INNOVATION FOR INCARCERATION

Generating ideas in the futurist's style—some conservative in scope, others more radical, expansive, and controversial—provides a starting place for imagining multisector social innovations. Some additional ideas are set out here, and the reader is encouraged to engage in a generative process of addressing reductions in incarceration rates and amplified decarceration efforts. Once again, consider the question: What would it look like if we started over in the use of incarceration? We need not look far to find fairly dramatic examples of starting over. California's correctional realignment legislation (2011 Public Safety Realignment Act, AB-109) is an experiment in progress. Ordered to reduce its prison population by 30,000 people in a 2-year period, the state legislature enacted AB-109 to shift many of the imprisoned into parole and probation systems and into local county jail facilities (Quan, Abarbanel, & Mukamal, 2014). The outcomes of realignment in terms of recidivism, threats to public safety, and success at achieving permanent reductions in the state prison population are not yet known, but clearly the sheer boldness of the measure, undertaken after years of litigation about the conditions of confinement in California prisons, sends a message: There are strategies for decarceration. And so the futurist's question is formed: What if detention is not an option?

Thus, having arrived at the intersection of new ideas and possibilities for justice, what are the potentialities of multisector social innovations? Though a beginning rather than an exhaustive list, the futurist vision here is about many independent entities merging their interests to form an interdependent web of support for justice. These and other imaginings will raise significant questions and face formidable challengers, but the goal at this moment is not that *these* particular iterations of multisector social innovations be embraced, but that collectively the *need* for ideas such as these and other innovations be embraced. Here are a few ideas to get started:

As a component of the larger public health system, "interventions on the social context" (Draine & Hadley, 2011) must be primary considerations in criminal justice system change. Suggesting that incarceration is a public health issue is not a new idea, but applying it specifically to decarceration may well be. Public health does not start or stop in the jail or prison or probation/parole system; its cradle-to-grave reach means that the failures in public health systems, rooted in poverty and mental illness and their products (e.g., hunger; homelessness; racial, economic, and health disparities) are the precursors to and the consequences of incarceration (Draine, Salzer, Culhane, & Hadley, 2001). Viewed as a unifying approach to the health of all persons, including those involved in the justice system, a public health perspective should lead us to think first about where the breakdown is when we find a person entangled in the justice system. Is it lack of access to medication, the lack of shelter and food, poor job opportunities, chronic health conditions, and/or inadequate social supports? Once the contributors to justice interface are identified, the focus pivots to an inquiry about where and why the synergy broke down. Look to the partners: What system barriers made achieving success more difficult or even impossible? What must be done to pierce these barriers so that the further entrenchment in the system is mitigated? Operating the criminal justice system in ways consistent with supporting the public health has the promise to significantly impact crime, incarceration, and decarceration rates, but only if those responsible for the provision of resources are held accountable for the equitable distribution of them. Consequently, those with less get more. But those with more may also get more. The private food service corporation operating in the prison that, as part of its contract, employs formerly incarcerated persons in its community-based operations not only may enjoy the benefits of a reliable labor force but also may contribute to a safer community that is a consequence of its citizens earning a living wage.

Those who profit from mass incarceration must invest in rehabilitation efforts and in creating success stories. The massive increase in incarceration rates since 1970 and the costs associated with it are borne by all, but mostly by the perpetrators, their families, and their communities. Though simplistic, the reality of a retributive justice system demands payment from the perpetrators of crime—through the penalties of incarceration, fines, and restitution—for whatever injuries they caused. That this payment is seldom adequate or satisfying to the parties involved matters not. At the same time, third parties benefit from both the victim of a crime and the perpetrator: The former may seek retribution; the latter may pay it, but others profit from them both.

As part of the "justice reinvestment" movement, beyond asking states to reinvest its funds in ways that may reduce admissions into the prison and reduce lengths of stay as well, what is reasonable to ask of those who benefit from the *business* of incarceration? Where are profits made in the justice system—for example, by the construction company, the private prison corporation, the correctional health services company, the pretrial monitors, the telephone contractors, and others—and what portion of those profits can be leveraged in decarceration efforts? From the contractor, for example, demand the commitment of funds to secure affordable housing in the community where the construction is occurring. From the phone company, the provision of low- and no-cost phones and "minutes" for the formerly incarcerated person during a certain postrelease period. Encouraging profit-making from incarceration without insisting on corporate social responsibility to return some of the profits to the benefit of its payees threatens the desired outcomes of justice reform.

Every partner is evaluated for its contributions to successful reintegration. Having used this idea in the context of this chapter, little more need be said here. The measure of "successful" decarceration is no longer limited to a sole focus on the formerly incarcerated individual. Questions must be asked of the agencies and the individuals who are responsible for assisting in the person's reintegration to society, to identify the pathways to successes and to failures. It is important to understand the synergies that developed in the community to support the employment and housing of formerly incarcerated individuals and how these synergies endured, or not, and why. What if detention is not an option? Perhaps revisiting the principles of community and restorative justice will help direct us to better responses than that of banishment.

The most extreme sanctions—removal from the community, imprisonment without opportunity, and life and death in an institution—should be reserved for the persons whose level of risk to public safety is significant. Imagine there being no room in the local jail. Doing so necessarily forces us to identify our fears about personal safety and prioritize our objectives for public safety. This cannot be done without a value check as well. *Do I care more about physical safety than, for example, my possessions and if so, what are differential responses—beyond those defined by sentencing guidelines—to the crime?* In decarceration efforts, a person's level of risk to the community cannot be assessed in a vacuum. What systems can be called to the table to help mitigate that risk and to support the individual's success? Operating a justice system fed by the need for personal vindication and also by unexamined and unfounded prejudice, furthered by the use of traditional forms of punishment that banish the convicted from family and community, is no longer acceptable. Removal of a person from society should be reserved for those who pose the most danger to the public safety. Who are they? What entities must work together to more accurately assess the level of danger posed?

The language of justice must change; starting with the words "public safety," a concept too often conflated with promises of "personal safety." The important distinction between public and personal safety is easily lost in the emotional rhetoric of criminal justice. Public safety is the responsibility of government. It includes the government's obligation to provide law enforcement and detention services and to develop a system to ensure public safety through policy that emphasizes the protection of the public health. However, public safety mechanisms and initiatives such as forming a community policing division or developing a bike safety course are different from ensuring the impossible: personal safety. The latter necessarily implicates the rights of the individual to exercise free will. Government policy can optimize public safety but it cannot guarantee personal safety; such policy is not designed to prevent the individual person from being in the wrong place at the wrong time. When detention and imprisonment decisions are made, they must comport with public safety goals, not simply react to the tragic outcomes that can occur in the breach of personal safety.

Provide persons leaving jail and prison with enough money and resources to secure housing, employment, and childcare. Historically, jails have been seen as operating as an "extension[s] of the welfare system" (Welch, 1991) and accordingly, prisoners are expected to be poor (Sykes, 1958). To what end? To be poor in a society of riches is to underscore the insults already visited on the formerly incarcerated individual: dangerous living conditions, hunger, poverty, mental illness, and inadequate social and financial supports. To have taken a person's boots at admission and return them to the community with cheap slip-ons serves no valid purpose. And to those who might suggest that funding a person's reintegration will only reinforce their laziness and dependence: Produce the evidence.

That said, we must entertain seriously the idea that there will always be people that require support. So what if that is the case? When thinking about punishment and rehabilitation—locking people up, passing restrictive criminal laws and sentencing laws, and insisting on certain types of services to be provided to the incarcerated—these are after-the-fact responses; after the harm is done. Perhaps the need for indeterminate reentry programming assistance (e.g., acknowledgment of the need for one's Alcoholics Anonymous sponsor) stems from reentry programs being the only place the person can secure the needed supports to stay out of jail. This raises a value question: Do we believe that desistence is more important than dependence?

Think about and plan for prevention of (re)incarceration with the long view; the cradle-to-grave, whole-system view. Focus on place, not case; on where and how the formerly incarcerated individual lives; how he or she survives. Research suggests where one is born and raised has significant lifelong implications on socioeconomic class (Chetty, Hendren, Kline, & Saez, 2014). This information must be factored into decarceration efforts. In light of this body of research, we must entertain the idea that as a product of collaborative public and private efforts to devise multisectoral social innovations, the offering of material supports to a formerly incarcerated individual may have enduring personal and intergenerational benefits (Chetty, Hendren, & Katz, 2016; Chetty et al., 2014).

Devise strategies for the application of the principles of restorative justice, including the use of methods of community "justice" in ways that reemphasize the value of an inclusive process for rehabilitation, which might include victim–offender mediation, opportunities for shared decision-making (Coates, 2015), and community reconciliation processes. In the words of Dr. Faye Taxman, paying "greater attention to humanistic approaches that override the current 'catch 'em' reentry efforts" (Taxman, 2011, p. 933) may yield exponential benefits.

Normalize and support the formerly incarcerated person's agency; her freedom to make choices, a freedom enjoyed by the masses and one that should not be abridged simply because of the history of conviction and incarceration. The key word here is *normalize*. Not many reading this chapter are in danger of living under the constant surveillance of the police or the probation officer, watched for the slightest hint of an infraction or sign of derailment. And yet, most of those reading this chapter have derailed—operated a vehicle while intoxicated, taken someone else's prescription medications, cheated on taxes, took a sick day when not really sick. The normal life (i.e., yours, mine) is not the perfect life. Nor is it the life of the formerly incarcerated individual. In most cases, it was not perfect before his or her incarceration and it will not be perfect after his or her release. Some transgressions are in and of themselves learning experiences, and these experiences are a normal part of life—everyone's life.

CONCLUSION

Far from being a fantasy, assuming the futurist's position and imagining *what is necessary to realize significant decarceration* is a forward, fruitful, and hopeful exercise; one that underscores the power of the unafraid to imagine change and then work with others to make it happen. In the quintessential parallel process, we ask this very thing of the formerly incarcerated all the time: Imagine how your life could be and what you need to do or have to do to make it so. In the end, however, the formerly incarcerated individual is too often afraid, doubts her power to change, and lacks the partnerships needed to find and seize opportunities for success. Thus, the burden of achieving successful reintegration, and ultimately of meaningful decarceration, is on all justice-minded persons and organizations to work together and share the responsibility for successes and failures.

Taking the futurist's view should inspire us to ask of ourselves and others, What would it look like if we did this particular and major part of justice, the incessant and largely unproductive use of incarceration, over? The preceding pages provide a rationale for this approach and beginning ideas for realizing the possibilities for success at reintegration and the possibilities for success at decarceration.

The real imaginative work, that which will ultimately become incorporated in public policy and practice, remains to be done. As you consider all that is written here and elsewhere in this volume and reflect on your awareness of the need for change, be aware that at its heart the movement forward compels all of us to take that critical first step toward a new justice: *Just* imagine.

REFERENCES

Andrews, D. A., & Bonta, J. (1995). *LSI-R: The Level of Service Inventory-Revised.* Toronto, Ontario, Canada: Multi-Health Systems.

Andrews, D. A., Bonta, J., & Hoge, R. D. (1990). Classification for effective rehabilitation: Rediscovering psychology. *Criminal Justice and Behavior, 17,* 19–52.

Austin, J., Cadora, E., Clear, T., Dansky, K., Greene, J., Gupta, V., . . . Young, M. (2013). *Ending mass incarceration: Charting a new justice reinvestment.* The Sentencing Project. Retrieved from http://www.justicestrategies.org/publications/2013/ending-mass-incarceration-charting-new-justice-reinvestment

Bell v. Wolfish, 441 U.S. 520 (1979).

Brown v. Plata, 131 S. Ct. 1910, 1923 (2011).

Carleton, M. (1984). *Politics and punishment. The history of the Louisiana State Penal System*. New Orleans: Louisiana State University Press.

Coates, T. (2015). The black family in the age of mass incarceration. *The Atlantic Magazine*. Retrieved from http://www.theatlantic.com/magazine/archive/2015/10/the-black-family-in-the-age-of-mass-incarceration/403246/#Chapter%20VII

Chetty, R., Hendren, N., & Katz, L. F. (2016). The effects of exposure to better neighborhoods on children: New evidence from the Moving to Opportunity Experiment. *American Economic Review, 106*(4), 855–902. doi:10.1257/aer.20150572

Chetty, R., Hendren, N., Kline, P., & Saez, E. (2014). Where is the land of opportunity: The geography of intergenerational mobility in the United States. *Quarterly Journal of Economics, 129*(4), 1553–1623.

Clear, T. R. (2005). Places not cases? Re-thinking the probation focus. *The Howard Journal, 44* (2), 172–184.

Coleman v. Brown, 90-cv-00520 (E.D. Cal. June 6, 1994).

Dlouha, J., Macháčková-Henderson, L., & Dlouhý, J. (2013). Learning networks with involvement of higher education institutions. *Journal of Cleaner Production, 49*, 95–104. doi:10.1016/j.jclepro.2012.06.009

Draine, J., & Hadley, T. (2011). Public health and policy perspectives for psychiatry and law. *International Journal of Law and Psychiatry, 34*, 247–248.

Draine, J., Salzer, M. S., Culhane, D. P., & Hadley, T. R. (2001). Role of social disadvantage in crime, joblessness, and homelessness among persons with serious mental illness. *Psychiatric Services, 53*(5), 565–573.

Eaton, K. (2009). Intel's mind-reading chips: Replace your mouse with your brain. *Fast Company*. Retrieved from http://www.fastcompany.com/1463532/intels-mind-reading-chips-replace-your-mouse-your-brain

The Economist. (2010, August 14). Let's hear those ideas; social innovation. *The Economist*. Retrieved from http://www.economist.com/node/16789766

Estelle v. Gamble, 429 U.S. 97 (1976).

Fabelo, T., & Thompson, M. (2015). Reducing incarceration rates: When science meets political realities. *Issues in Science and Technology, 32*(1). Retrieved from http://issues.org/32-1/reducing-incarceration-rates-when-science-meets-political-realities/

Feeley, M. M. (2002). Entrepreneurs of punishment: The legacy of privatization. *Punishment and Society, 4*(3), 321–344.

Horne, L., Bass, V., & Silva, S. (2013). Multisector coalitions build healthier communities through ACHIEVE initiative. *Journal of Public Health Management and Practice, 19*(3), 281–283. doi:10.1097/PHH.0b013e31828e25ff

Kanter, R. M. (1999). From spare change to real change. *Harvard Business Review, 77*(3). Retrieved from https://hbr.org/1999/05/from-spare-change-to-real-change-the-social-sector-as-beta-site-for-business-innovation

Kilgore, J. (2015, January 21). *These five corporations are making millions from mass incarceration*. Moyers & Company. Retrieved from http://billmoyers.com/2015/01/21/five-corporations-youve-never-heard-making-millions-mass-incarceration/

Leventhal, R. (2013). Effecting progress: Using social impact bonds to finance social services: Articles and comments arising from the 2012 fall conference The Law & Finance of Social Enterprise. *New York University Journal of Law and Business, 9,* 511–534.

Petry, R. A., Fadeeva, Z., Fadeeva, O., Hasslöf, H., Hellström, Å., Hermans, J., . . . Sonesson, K. (2011). Educating for sustainable production and consumption and sustainable livelihoods: learning from multi-stakeholder networks. *Sustainability Science, 6,* 83–96. doi:10.1007/s11625-010-0116-y

Plata v. Brown, 01-cv-01351 (N.D. Cal. Apr. 23, 1990).

Quan, L. T., Abarbanel, S., & Mukamal, D. (2014). *Reallocation of responsibility: Changes to the correctional control system in California post-realignment.* Standford Criminal Justice Center. Stanford Law School. Retrieved from http://law.stanford.edu/wp-content/uploads/sites/default/files/child-page/183091/doc/slspublic/CC%20Brief%20Jan%2014.pdf

Raphel, S., & Stoll, M. (2013). *Why are so many people in prison?* New York, NY: Russell Sage Foundation.

Severson, M. (2009). Social policy and the correctional system. In J. Midgley & M. Livermore, (Eds.) *The handbook of social policy* (2nd ed., pp. 463–484). Thousand Oaks, CA: Sage.

Shrimali, B., Luginbuhl, J., Malin, C., Flournoy, R., & Siegel, A. (2014). The building blocks collaborative: Advancing a life course approach to health equity through multi-sector collaboration. *Maternal and Child Health Journal, 18*(2), 373–379. doi:10.1007/s10995-013-1278-x

Solomon, A. L., Osborne, J. W. L., Winterfield, L., Elderbroom, B. L., Burke, P., Stroker, R. P., . . . Burrell, W. D. (2008). *Putting public safety first: Parole supervision strategies to enhance reentry outcomes.* The Urban Institute. Retrieved from http://www.urban.org/sites/default/files/alfresco/publication-pdfs/411791-Putting-Public-Safety-First--Parole-Supervision-Strategies-to-Enhance-Reentry-Outcomes-Paper-.PDF

Sykes, H. (1958). *The Society Of Captives: A Study Of A Maximum Security Prison.* Princeton, NJ: Princeton University Press.

Taxman, F. (2011). The cattle call of reentry. Not all processes are equal. *Criminology and Public Policy, 10*(4), 925–937. doi:10.1111/j.1745-9133.2011.00780.x

Tetrick, J. (2015, July 26). Dear presidential candidates, an open letter. *New York Times.* Retrieved from https://www.hamptoncreek.com/new-york-times/dear-presidential-candidates

Welch, M. (1991). Expansion of jail capacity: Makeshift jails and public policy. In J. A. Thompson and G. L. Mays (Eds.), *American jails: Public policy issues.* Chicago, IL: Nelson-Hall.

The White House. (n.d.). *About SICP: The community solutions agenda.* Retrieved from https://www.whitehouse.gov/administration/eop/sicp/about

Social innovation has made what we think of as human development, progress, and civilization possible. Social innovation has made possible all of the social systems and institutions that we take for granted. Unfortunately not all human social innovations are successful. Arguably, mass incarceration in the United States today is one of those wayward innovations. Humans created mass incarceration, and we have the ability to uncreate it.

MICHAEL SHERRADEN

15

Guideposts for the Smart Decarceration Era

RECOMMENDED STRATEGIES FROM RESEARCHERS, PRACTITIONERS, AND FORMERLY INCARCERATED LEADERS

Carrie Pettus-Davis, Matthew W. Epperson, Samuel Taylor, and Annie Grier

---

BACKGROUND

Reducing the United States' overreliance on incarceration requires a targeted and deliberate framework for action. Proponents of smart decarceration are increasingly recognizing the need for guideposts—clearly articulated areas for targeted intervention—to inform the anticipated stages of criminal justice reform. An important first step in developing a framework for decarceration is to merge the collective goals and strategies of the diverse range of stakeholders.

Despite the expansion of efforts to reduce jail and prison populations and reform criminal justice policy and practice, a comprehensive approach has been largely absent from the conversation. Such an approach is only possible if criminal justice stakeholders agree on the foundational objectives that can generate lasting decarceration. In this chapter, we offer such guideposts and actionable strategies as a directive framework for the era of smart decarceration in America.

Comparative Decarceration in Context

As is well documented, the United States stands out among most industrialized nations in its reliance on incarceration. By international standards, this approach has long been viewed as the de facto means of crime deterrence in America, with little to mixed effects on crime rates (Roeder, Eisen, Bowling, Stiglitz, & Chettiar, 2015). However, this does not mean other Western countries have not wrestled with the issue of decarceration. Indeed, contemporary momentum to reduce U.S. prison and jail populations can be informed by a rich history of prison reduction efforts in other countries. Whereas the decarceration debate in the United States has only recently, if cautiously, taken shape, the topic has been central to criminal justice policy in other countries since the mid- to late-20th century.

Countries such as Canada, the United Kingdom, the Netherlands, Finland, and Sweden have at different times in the last half-century adopted statutory doctrines that treated incarceration as a last resort for myriad nonviolent offenses (Webster & Doob, 2015; Von Hoffer, 2003). Under a principle of *least-restraint*, custodial sentences in many of these penal systems are applied as alternatives only after noncustodial alternatives have been first considered (Cavadino & Dignan, 2006; Doob, 2012). And in many western countries, though politically and culturally diverse, incarceration rates have declined in ways that contrast the United States. In the Scandinavian countries, for instance, a confluence of factors prompted policymakers to begin a gradual process of reform that would drastically reduce prison populations in the mid-20th century (Lappi-Seppälä, 2000, 2007). In Canada, a *decarceration effect* took shape beginning in the 1990s and continuing into the 2000s (Roberts & Gabor, 2004). Although the trends in these countries are not all germane to the United States, they offer important examples of successful criminal justice reform and valuable lessons for developing a strategic framework for decarceration in America.

Decarceration and Reform: One Country's Approach

Compared with other western countries, Canada's incarceration rate is seen as considerably high, and the country's mid-1990s federal prison population experienced an annual growth rate of 10% (Zubrycki, 2002). Between 1985 and 1995, Canada's custodial admission rate for all offenders increased by 30% (Zubrycki, 2002). Rapid, unexpected prison inflation in Canada came at a time when, as in other countries, violent crime rates were steadily decreasing. But 10-year forecasts for the country's federal correctional institutions revealed that the custodial population was likely to double if formidable steps were not taken to thwart its growth, and provincial correctional facilities were experiencing similar challenges in reducing already overcrowded capacities, while protecting public safety (Zubrycki, 2002). Recognizing that such trends would be unsustainable, federal- and provincial-level policy actors promptly seized the opportunity to advance preventative measures to stymie incarceration growth.

To respond to their incarceration crisis, Canada's various provincial and territorial governments began convening in 1995 annually to reach consensus on universal principles and objectives that would form a policy framework for reforming its justice system. The collaborative efforts of all levels of Canada's justice system were laid out in a series of Population Growth Reports offering practicable strategies to reduce incarcerated populations through the use of existing alternatives to incarceration such as community-based corrections or sentencing reforms (Government of Canada, 2000). In 1996, an amendment to the Criminal Code of Canada introduced alternative forms of sanctioning such as "conditional sentences" and provided a foundation for greater court discretion in sentencing nonviolent offenders to community alternatives. Simultaneous to these efforts, recommendations presented to the Canadian government were intended to improve the plight of Canada's Aboriginal and minority populations who represented an increasingly disproportionate share of the incarcerated share population (Government of Canada, 2013). Citing growing overrepresentation of the Aborigines and minorities in Canadian prisons and the unique health, social, and economic needs of vulnerable incarcerated populations, new amendments to the Criminal Code called on courts to consider alternative sanctions, especially in regard to Aboriginal offenders (Jeffries & Stenning, 2014).

Over the period following these reforms, sentencing, conviction, and custodial admissions rates had declined in eight out of the nine provincial correctional jurisdictions (Roberts & Gabor, 2004). By all accounts, the concerted and multifaceted efforts of Canada's jurisdictions, coupled with declining crime rates, compelled the generation of a *decarceration effect* that extended into the mid-2000s. In the decade following Canada's national reforms, crime rates plummeted, and they continue to do so into the present (Government of Canada, 2013). For the better part of the last half-century, the use of imprisonment in Canada has remained relatively stable even as crime trends mirrored those in the United States and other western countries. As some have argued (e.g., Doob & Webster, 2006), the stability of incarceration in Canada and its later decline reflected a coordinated rejection of the more punitive application of criminal sanctions being either considered or implemented in places like the United Kingdom or the United States.

To be sure, the Canadian experience offers many sharp contrasts from the one in the United States, but it is useful to know the decarceration experiences of other countries. A review of multiple countries is beyond the scope of this chapter. We described Canada's decarceration experience because it was spurred by intentional efforts to build consensus on principles and objectives to guide policy and practice reform. The intentionally convened key stakeholders across sectors helped to develop a shared understanding of the causes of overincarceration, and how to remedy these causes, leading to a largely restorative, rehabilitative approach to reforming Canada's criminal code (Roberts & Gabor, 2004; Roberts & Roach, 2003). The principles-based appeal prompted judicial restraint in the sentencing of those convicted of crime, and subsequent legislation targeted the reduction of racial and ethnic disproportionality in the criminal justice system.

As the United States enters into an era of decarceration, there is great need to engage in similar processes to build consensus and articulate targets and principles to guide stakeholders in such efforts. This planful, principles-based approach is integral to ensuring that the ideas and needs of multiple stakeholders are represented, and it will help to create long-term, sustainable framework for decarceration.

METHODS

To develop guideposts and action steps for stakeholders, we used a two-phase approach. During Phase 1, we employed an adapted mixed-method research method known as Concept Mapping. Multistaged and participatory, the concept mapping approach enabled us to collect qualitative information from each respondent and later interpret it. Quantitative analytical techniques are then used to identify, structure, and visually demonstrate core concepts that were organized by respondents. For this work, the concept mapping process was carried out in four stages: (1) identifying key stakeholders to decarceration; (2) generating a strategic focus prompt and respondent brainstorming; (3) respondent sorting and ranking; and (4) analysis for priority area development. Phase Two of the project took place during a workshop with nearly 100 attendees to further refine and generate action steps from the priority areas that were generated during concept mapping in Phase One.

Phase 1: Concept Mapping

Concept mapping involved four steps: (1) identifying stakeholders, (2) focus prompt and respondent brainstorming, (3) respondent sorting and rating, and (4) analysis for priority area development.

Identifying Stakeholders

The first stage in this process was to identify and invite key experts from criminal justice fields, paying special attention to diverse sectors and actors whose voices are considered to be underrepresented in the decarceration movement, including substantial representation from individuals and families who have experienced incarceration. Also, snowball sampling methods were used to identify experts who represented areas of work that were not fully accounted for in our recruitment. In total, we invited 197 expert stakeholders to participate in the concept-mapping project. Prospective participants reflected higher education, healthcare, corrections, nonprofit advocacy, social and legal services, and public sectors, and included academic researchers, practitioners, policymakers, and advocates.

Focus Prompt and Respondent Brainstorming

A focus prompt was developed by the research team to garner the participants' expert knowledge of criminal justice reform to brainstorm sector-specific ways of achieving decarceration. More precisely, the focus prompt nudged participants to consider specific actions, areas of need, policies, or practices from their domain of work—broadly defined here as *ingredients*—that would advance decarceration in America:

> Based on your expertise, the key ingredients for successful decarceration of American prisons and jails is/are . . .

Participants could enter an unlimited number of responses. Ninety-seven respondents (49%) participated in the brainstorming phase altogether, generating a total of 261 completed statements.

Respondent Sorting and Rating

Following respondent brainstorming, a team of three researchers independently reviewed the 261 statements so that the number of concepts could be condensed and synthesized for the sorting and rating stage. Based on consensus among the research team, redundant, vague, or incomplete statements were eliminated to produce a final list of 166 statements for the sorting and rating exercises.

A group of 69 expert stakeholders were invited to participate in the second stage of the concept-mapping process, the sorting and rating stage. These respondents included both expert stakeholders from the brainstorming stage (48), as well as 16 newly identified expert stakeholders. During this stage, participants are presented with the full, synthesized list of responses from the brainstorming exercise and asked to sort, or group, each statement into distinct categories of similar concepts. Participants could then create a title that best reflected the conceptual similarities of each statement grouped into that category.

For instance, if a participant interpreted a statement that addressed mandatory minimum sentences as conceptually similar to a statement that addressed drug sentencing laws, he or she might compile those and other relevant statements and title this group "Sentencing Reforms." Participants were given discretion when sorting, but were asked to ensure that a statement was not sorted in more than one distinct group.

After all statements were sorted, participants completed a survey that asked them to evaluate each individual statement based on its (1) importance for accomplishing long-term decarceration; (2) the degree of *challenge* it would be to accomplish; and (3) the level of *impact* it would have on decarceration. The purpose of this rating exercise is to eventually uncover associations between each idea and scale them based on a certain value relative to the project's central issue.

Analysis for Priority Area Development

The concept mapping software aggregated participant data generated during the sorting and rating stage and developed a visual representation of grouped statements that are similar. The final product was a hierarchy of group statements. The clusters of statements produced 12 priority areas for decarceration (Box 15.1) that best accommodated the conceptual structure of the qualitative data.

Phase 2: In-Person Strategy Development

The in-person strategy development occurred during the Smart Decarceration Initiative Inaugural Conference at Washington University in St. Louis in September of 2015. Conference attendees were organized into working groups that divided up the 12 priority areas and spent an entire morning developing guideposts and strategies for decarceration.

Each of the 12 working groups comprised a representative mix of 93 conference attendees. Each group included diverse stakeholders to limit the possibility that one sector might overly influence the strategies produced from each working group. Two group facilitators were paired with each working group to guide the members through an applied activity to create guideposts and strategies for smart decarceration. Participants were instructed by facilitators to create strategies from their assigned priority area and convert the strategies into actionable interventions that considered the three outcomes of smart decarceration (Box 15.2) and the four guiding concepts of Smart Decarceration Initiative (Box 15.2).

BOX 15.1

PHASE 1: 12 PRIORITY AREAS FOR DECARCERATION

1. Sharing data and resource allocation
2. Incorporating criminogenic risks and needs
3. Implementing evidence-driven innovations
4. Reorienting responses to severity of the crime
5. Resetting norms and narratives
6. Incorporating multiple and new perspectives
7. Responding to behavioral and physical health needs
8. Improving reentry
9. Reducing collateral consequences
10. Building diversionary systems
11. Curtailing sentencing
12. Narrowing the funnel to incarceration

BOX 15.2

THREE INTERRELATED OUTCOMES OF DECARCERATION

1. Substantially reduce the incarcerated population in jails and prisons
2. Redress racial and economic disparities in the criminal justice system
3. Maximize public safety and well-being

While Phase 1 of the study showed *where* to focus decarceration efforts, the working groups of Phase 2 prioritized specific action steps that could be taken to promote decarceration in ways consistent with smart decarceration goals and guiding concepts. To start, groups chose two to three strategies, based on their perceived feasibility and potential impact, that would serve as their top priorities for the remainder of the activity. Then, the group brainstormed actionable steps to address the strategies. At the activity's conclusion, the groups proposed new strategies in line with their assigned cluster and proposed strategies to address decarceration in the adult criminal justice system outside of their assigned cluster. Transcription from audio recordings, pictures of white board notes, notes from a note taker, and individual workbooks were collected and compiled and analyzed for each group. These data were then analyzed and synthesized by the research team. The research team did not create new strategies. All guideposts and strategies described next represent the collective ideas obtained from Phase 1 and Phase 2 of this national study.

GUIDEPOSTS AND STRATEGIES FOR THE ERA
OF SMART DECARCERATION

For the purposes of this chapter, we have organized guideposts and strategies into the four guiding concepts for smart decarceration: (1) changing the narrative on incarceration and the incarcerated; (2) making criminal justice system-wide innovations;

BOX 15.3

THE FOUR GUIDING CONCEPTS FOR DECARCERATION

1. Changing the narrative on incarceration and the incarcerated
2. Making criminal justice system-wide innovations
3. Implementing transdisciplinary policy and practice innovations
4. Employing evidence-driven strategies

(3) implementing transdisciplinary policy and practice innovations; and (4) employing evidence-driven strategies. The guideposts and corresponding strategies presented here are not comprehensive, rather they illustrate how the guiding concepts can be operationalized into action steps. What follows reflects a prioritization of strategies and action steps that had the biggest potential for impact and were deemed to be the most feasible by the conference working groups. We also acknowledge that these categories are not mutually exclusive, but demonstrate overlapping and integrated concepts.

Changing the Narrative on Incarceration and the Incarcerated

There are four guideposts to changing the narrative on incarcereation and the incarcerated: (1) people with incarceration histories in leadership positions, (2) public awareness campaign, (3) forums for genuine and critical dialogue, and (4) decarceration-driven policymaking.

Guidepost 1: People with Incarceration Histories in Leadership Positions

Historically, effective social movements involved persons most directly affected by the social problem being in positions of leadership. People with incarceration histories have direct experience with incarceration and should be at the forefront of the smart decarceration movement. Leadership by formerly incarcerated individuals reduces the imbalance between the decision makers and those who are being decided on. Leadership not only empowers the individual who has become marginalized by incarceration but also brings presence and voice to those the public is currently taught to fear.

Strategies. An intentional effort to recruit racial minority group members, women, and people with low economic status will create opportunities for those disproportionately affected by incarceration to be well represented. Participants offered the following strategies for leadership opportunity development:

1. Organize individuals with incarceration histories to engage in political action.
2. Develop and disseminate a toolkit for individuals with incarceration histories on how to engage in policy change, including testifying to legislators.
3. Permit individuals with incarceration histories to serve in positions throughout the criminal justice system from law enforcement officers to members of parole boards.
4. Use individuals with incarceration histories as peer mentors for those with criminal records and as trainers for those who work in the criminal justice system.

Guidepost 2: Public Awareness Campaign

The need for a public awareness campaign to formally educate decision makers and lay people is urgent. A public awareness campaign will shed light on the impact of current criminal justice practices on individuals, families, and communities. Particular attention must be paid to how current criminal justice practices are both affected by and drive racial and economic disparities in the United States. The purpose of the public awareness campaign is to establish a shared narrative, raise awareness, change practices of decision makers, and open avenues to increase understanding and explore advocacy.

Strategies. Stakeholders prioritized four strategies, into which issues of race and economic disparities are expected to be interwoven:

1. Provide formal education to employees of the criminal justice system (e.g., law enforcement, judges, prosecutors, probation officers) about the barriers caused by incarceration and the counterproductive impacts.

2. Give TED talks and other presentations at prestigious venues on how current practices are affected by and drive racial and economic disparities.

3. Launch media campaigns targeting the general public using the following content area: personal narratives that counteract popular media stigma; direct and indirect costs of current practices to taxpayers; bail reform and its connections to economic disparities; collateral consequences (i.e., civil disability policymaking); and the role of trauma.

4. Create media guides for reporting stories of crime and matters related to the criminal justice system that curb sensationalism and misinformation; rather, provide critical background and context to audiences.

Guidepost 3: Forums for Genuine and Critical Dialogue

For true reform to occur, Americans must rethink, reimagine, and redesign the criminal justice system. Safe spaces for genuine and critical dialogue lead to real shifts in collective narratives. Forums allow for assumptions to be uncovered, beliefs to be challenged, and goals to be articulated, and transfers power over narrative to the public.

Strategies. Stakeholder strategies captured both content and structure of forums:

1. Hold town hall forums (inclusive of community members with incarceration histories) on defining public safety, examining the assumptions behind "tough on crime" policies, dismantling racial assumptions and perceptions of crime, and challenging the purpose of sentencing.

2. Organize law enforcement and community meetings that explore police department culture, "who" truly needs to be incarcerated, how race and class impact the way "crime" is assessed, root causes of crime, trauma, and the role of restorative justice.

3. Arrange truth and reconciliation panels for community healing. Panels occur around the country to bring together victims of crime, offenders, those who are both victims and offenders, criminal justice employees, and other community

members to share their stories about how they have been affected by incarceration and to look toward a different future.

4. Build interdisciplinary decarceration coalitions in two areas: within direct policymaking stakeholder groups where law and practices are negotiated, and with external entities including advocacy groups, think tanks, and practitioners. Create bridges across the coalitions.

Guidepost 4: Decarceration-Driven Policymaking

Policymaking is tone-setting. Stakeholders recognized that a critical aspect of changing the narrative is shifts in policymaking that are consistent with the "new" narrative. Policymaking demonstrates to the public a sense of trust that a social movement's efforts are being realized. Positive changes in policy help to counteract stigma and redress maladaptive assumptions.

Strategies. Participants identified five ways to drive decarceration policy:

1. Include legislative provisions with the input of individuals and families involved with the criminal justice system and community members with high rates of incarceration in decision-making about the reinvestment of money saved from reduced incarceration.
2. Reclassify criminal statutes and dramatic reform of sentencing guidelines.
3. Propose stringent regulations and oversight of private/for-profit correctional industries, including private prisons and private probation.
4. Require jurisdictions that receive federal funding to reduce mandatory and permanent restrictions on housing, education, employment, public assistance, and other civic participation to those that directly threaten public safety.
5. Restore voting rights to all with histories of felony convictions and improve opportunities for expungement.

Making Criminal Justice System-Wide Innovations

There are four guideposts to making criminal justice system-wide innovations: (1) reform contributors to incarceration, (2) change use of incarceration, (3) cross-sector training, and (4) integrate justice and community.

Guidepost 1: Reform Contributors to Incarceration

Many systemic factors beyond criminal behavior drive incarceration rates. A sole focus on individual actions will not produce meaningful reductions in incarceration. Reforms are needed regarding what warrants criminal justice involvement, accountability and oversight of criminal justice system processes, and how a person experiences the system once involved.

Strategies. Participants identified five ways to reform contributors to incarceration:

1. Revise sentencing structures and reduce sentence length for most offense types.
2. Increase accountability and oversight at the early stages of the system. This includes checks and balances in arrest discretion, prosecution (e.g., statement of readiness for speedy trials, misconduct), conditions of confinement in jails, and collateral consequences of pretrial detention.
3. Individualize parole to better respond to needs, obligations, strengths, and goals of parolees to promote successful reintegration versus "catching" a person doing something wrong. Individualized parole would provide more opportunities to review and revise conditions, shorten length of parole supervision, and alter constituent parole violations to match individual risks and needs.
4. Use cost savings from decarceration to increase the capacity of multiple sectors of the criminal justice system to more sufficiently support, supervise, and service those involved in the criminal justice system (e.g., adequately resourced public defenders offices, social workers in public defender/prosecutor offices, build capacity of strengths-focused community corrections).
5. Generate evidence to develop effective alternatives to probation that decrease intensity and length of involvement in the criminal justice system, emphasizing alternatives that exist outside of the criminal justice system.

Guidepost 2: Change Use of Incarceration

Changing the use of incarceration involves reducing who is funneled to incarceration and why. In addition, it involves changing what happens when a person becomes incarcerated. Changing the use of incarceration does not require the abandonment of punishment and deterrence, but rather new approaches that decrease the likelihood of a person's future involvement with the criminal justice system. Such approaches would prevent individuals from being incarcerated to the extent that they cannot participate in employment or other restitution activities. When a person does become incarcerated, the experience would aim to model and foster positive societal participation.

Strategies. Participants identified four ways to change the use of incarceration:

1. Dramatically reduce the use of pretrial detention through the use of alternative forms of bail payment; expedited processes for lowered bail applications; increased use of release-on-own-recognizance for those who do not pose immediate harm to others; decreased racial and economic bias in who is detained; and reformed systems that process individuals more quickly via increased capacity of courts, prosecution, and public defense.

2. Generate a wider range of sanctions for nonviolent crimes (including technical violations) that use incarceration only as a last resort and when the crime threatens the personal safety of others.

3. Adopt evidence-driven alternatives to conviction (e.g., arrest diversion, precharge diversion, deferred prosecution) with expanded eligibility beyond low-level crimes.

4. Institute practices that coordinate release from institutions that prepare individuals for transition such as (1) increase the number of staff who conduct prerelease planning and make such planning mandatory; (2) innovate programmatic-based furloughs; (3) reform conditions of confinement to make them more similar to community-based living; and (4) shift correctional staff roles to include responsibilities focused on postrelease success.

Guidepost 3: Cross-Sector Training

The siloed nature of the criminal justice system sectors is a driving factor in mass incarceration. Interactions with each stage of the criminal justice system affect interactions at later stages; yet, the characteristics of the involved individual rarely change. Therefore, actors in each sector need to have a shared understanding of the individuals moving through the system, the processes the individuals experience, and the circumstances they face before and after a given stage. Cross-sector training provides a bridge for such shared knowledge.

Strategies. Participants identified four ways to increase cross-sector training:

1. Identify common elements and provide standardized training to all sectors of the criminal justice system within a jurisdiction. Such content includes trauma-informed care, risks and needs, behavioral health, de-escalation skills, the impact of power differentials, fairness and safety, resources, and racial and economic disparities.

2. Reform formal judicial education to include decarceration practices.

3. Share trainings between community members and law enforcement, including the development of specialized units/tasks forces within law enforcement.

4. Create social work positions at every stage of the criminal justice system, from booking to parole.

Guidepost 4: Integrate Justice and Community

Criminal justice system components and practices vary by jurisdiction. Involvement of community members at the local level is needed for reforms to be responsive to the structures and needs of that community. To foster reforms driven by social justice, community members within the local jurisdiction must be involved in the decision-making process.

Strategies. Participants who developed this guidepost considered community members to be those who are not employed by the criminal justice system but are impacted by it, such as local residents or service providers. Community members include families of people who are involved in the criminal justice system as well as victims of crime. Participants also noted that sometimes people who are victims of crime are also perpetrators of crime, and that sometimes those who are family members of a person involved in the criminal justice system were once involved themselves. All of these strategies are conceptualized as inclusive of these different perspectives and are thought to occur at the local jurisdiction level:

1. Improve law enforcement relationships with people who are black, brown, or native, using mechanisms that establish mutual trust, respect, and partnership. For example, engage in shared development of policing reforms.
2. Incorporate and increase community member/group involvement at each stage of the criminal justice system. Examples of community group involvement includes decision-making around what constitutes the need for an arrest, detention and sentencing decisions, and reentry/parole support.
3. Encourage community members at the local jurisdiction level to help to bridge multiple sectors of the criminal justice system by (1) pooling local public and private funding to support expansive innovations that span each segment of the criminal justice system; (2) engaging local actors in redesigning their own jobs to support criminal justice reform; and (3) launching public awareness campaigns about how the sectors in the criminal justice system in that jurisdiction interact and influence incarceration.
4. Hold systemwide workshops for criminal justice system employees on the societal, cultural, and individual factors that influence whether a person engages in crime and how a person might respond to interventions. Training would be conducted by local human service providers who will work with trainees to develop ways awareness of these factors could be incorporated into daily criminal justice practice.

Implementing Transdisciplinary Practice and Policy Interventions

There are four guideposts to implementing transdisciplinary practice and policy interventions: (1) develop decarceration talent, (2) create universal reentry/transitional programs, (3) reevaluate and repeal policy-driven collateral consequences, and (4) build community capacity for social innovation.

Guidepost 1: Develop Decarceration Talent

Current professionals and advocates came of age during the era of mass incarceration. During this time, educational and cultural narratives were framed within the context of using incarceration as the default response to not only crime but also public health crises (e.g., the crack-cocaine epidemic, gun violence). As the era of smart decarceration begins, professional and advocacy training must be redesigned.

Strategies. Participants identified three ways to develop decarceration talent:

1. Develop specialized decarceration-based educational and professional products within the fields of social work, law, criminal justice, psychology, criminology, public policy, public health, medicine, and education. Products include textbooks, internships/practicum/fellowships/rotations, coursework, continuing education opportunities, and modified licensure requirements.
2. Development of talent specifically for those who have had criminal justice involvement by increasing postsecondary education opportunities for people with felony convictions, training in policy advocacy, leadership training, and creating more opportunities to guide research.
3. Integrate research and evidence into decarceration-based policy and practice work through new forms of university/community partnerships and educational offerings.

Guidepost 2: Create Universal Reentry/Transitional Programs

Since the turn of the 21st century, more attention has been given to the need for transitional support for people released from prison and jails. Despite increased funding and attention, access to effective reentry/transitional programs remains limited.

Strategies. Participants identified these strategies to call for federal incentives for universal reentry/transitional programs in local, state, and federal jurisdictions:

1. Require all states that receive federal funding for correctional facilities to complete standardized and valid disability, mental health, and substance use disorders assessments on entering and releasing prisoners.
2. Require all states that receive federal funding for correctional facilities to provide evidence-driven transitional services in the following categories: education, employment, disability assistance, housing, mental health, substance use disorders, transportation, and other areas of formal and informal support.
3. Require local and state jurisdictions that receive any criminal justice–based federal funding to connect inmates incarcerated for 45 days or more to community-based social and health services and health and disability insurance.
4. Periodically assess incarcerated individuals' progress and needs throughout an incarceration experience to adequately plan for postincarceration needs.

Guidepost 3: Reevaluate and Repeal Policy-Driven Collateral Consequences

Civil disability policies are commonly referred to as collateral consequences. Civil disability policies are those public policies that permanently or temporarily deny those with histories of criminal justice involvement access to typical civil resources. Civil disabilities ban access to certain types of employment, professional licensure, education and permits, housing, voting rights, and a range of other civic participation. It is uncommon for defendants or legal representatives to be aware of the complex array of collateral consequences a person will be exposed to on plea or conviction. Legal scholars have been unable to identify a consistent rationale or justification for the civil disabilities policies that proliferated during the era of mass incarceration. Smart decarceration will not be achieved without thoughtful examination and reform of civil disability policies.

Strategies. Participants identified four ways to reevaluate and repeal policy-driven collateral consequences:

1. Inform all defendants, preplea, of potential collateral consequences through pre-plea legal consultation and mandatory inclusion of potential collateral consequences in presentencing reports.
2. Reduce public access to criminal records to mitigate discriminatory decisions related to social structures such as education, employment, and housing.
3. Eliminate automatic collateral consequences, such as revocation of voting rights or professional licensure restrictions for persons convicted of a felony.
4. Review collateral consequences by jurisdiction and eliminate those deemed unnecessary for public and personal safety.

Guidepost 4: Build Community Capacity for Social Innovation

The criminal justice system does not operate in isolation from the broader communities from which those involved with the criminal justice system hail. At the same time that criminal justice reforms proceed, the capacity of communities to adequately support their residents must be increased. Enhancing community capacity promotes both prevention and intervention efforts related to criminal justice involvement.

Strategies. Participants identified four strategies to build community capacity for social innovation:

1. Generate a range of housing opportunities for those with incarceration histories through:
   a. Local partnerships for housing those with incarceration histories and high health needs
   b. Correctional housing choice vouchers
   c. Partnerships between criminal justice system stakeholders and housing developers to design and build affordable housing that fosters a successful postrelease environment for people reentering society and their loved ones.
2. Create corporate and government partnerships to increase employment in living-wage jobs for formerly incarcerated individuals, strengthen incentives for

employers to hire formerly incarcerated individuals by making the hiring part of their corporate social responsibility program, and educate the business community in economic and workforce development strategies.

3. Reinvest savings from decarceration efforts into building community capacity for high quality education, stable housing, family-oriented supports, behavioral health services, healthcare, and asset development as determined by community members.

4. Develop neighborhood crisis centers that are equipped to provide emergency short-term care for those who have law enforcement contact and are struggling with behavioral health crises, traumatic events, or urgent financial/housing needs that may lead to low-level criminal involvement (e.g., panhandling, trespassing, loitering charges).

Employing Evidence-Driven Strategies

There are four guideposts to employing evidence-driven strategies: (1) address gaps in knowledge through research, (2) refine research–practice–policy partnerships, (3) maximize measurement and data collection, and (4) package and disseminate information to targeted audiences.

Guidepost 1: Address Gaps in Knowledge Through Research

Though enormous resources have been needed to support mass incarceration, few have been funneled to research on drivers and costs of incarceration.

Strategies. Participants identified five strategies to address gaps in knowledge through research:

1. Research drivers of incarceration, including social determinants (e.g., community factors, concentrated poverty, access to employment) and individual determinants (e.g., criminal thinking). This includes further research on decarceration innovations' impact on social and individual drivers of crime.

2. Conduct cost-benefit analyses on jurisdiction-specific decarceration innovations compared to current incarceration practices on financial and public safety outcomes, drivers and use of incarceration from the local level up to the federal level, and costs of race and economic disproportionality.

3. Close gaps in intervention research by development and widespread use of fidelity tools.

4. Examine racial bias in existing risk-need assessment tools.

5. Develop research to better understand resilience and protective factors of criminal justice–involved adults. This research is prevalent among juveniles but lacking among adults.

Guidepost 2: Refine Research–Practice–Policy Partnerships

Substantial innovation and evaluation is needed to identify effective and sustainable practices to support the era of decarceration. Research–practice–policy partnerships will be required. Effective partnerships will generate feedback loops in which research evidence is informing practice delivery and policy innovations; in turn, practitioners and policymakers will affect future research agendas.

Strategies. Participants identified four ways to refine research–practice–policy partnerships:

1. Work with diverse stakeholders, including formerly incarcerated individuals and their loved ones, to create a range of intermediate outcomes that identify "success" beyond recidivism that is meaningful to researchers, clients, and practitioners.
2. Form research–practice–policy partnerships that use community- and action-based, participatory research to develop a broader array of policy and practice interventions.
3. Facilitate and incentivize research–practice–policy partnerships to enhance the dissemination and implementation of evidence-driven programs into practice—and the continual examination of such practices.
4. Generate evidence-driven, model legislation for decarceration reforms through active collaboration between research, practice, and policy entities.

Guidepost 3: Maximize Measurement and Data Collection

Lack of uniform data measurement and collection limits the ability to fill gaps in knowledge about current and future approaches. This guidepost identifies the type of data to be standardized to increase the availability of such data.

Strategies. Participants identified four strategies to maximize measurement and data collection:

1. Develop standardized measures of recidivism and other key criminal justice and behavioral outcomes as well as race and economic disparities. Create standardized ways of recording and reporting outcomes.
2. Integrate local, state, and national data sources related to criminal justice, human services, and healthcare through centralized data repositories overseen by transdisciplinary leadership.
3. Create mechanisms to expedite the availability of local, state, and national data to researchers.
4. Collect data on criminal justice–involved individuals' experiences as they move through and interact with various aspects of the criminal justice system.

Guidepost 4: Package and Disseminate Information to Targeted Audiences

Despite the increased attention to the problems of mass incarceration and the need for reform, those not directly working with or experiencing the criminal justice system still have little information on its functions and processes. Participants agreed that information needs to be disseminated more frequently and in more consumable formats to various stakeholder groups to support decarceration efforts.

Strategies. Participants identified three strategies to package and disseminate information to targeted audiences:

1. Develop targeted policy and practice briefs in addition to information packets for practitioners and policy stakeholders that highlight decarceration innovations and their successes.
2. Create press packets and media alerts for journalists on decarceration-related research findings and innovations.
3. Disseminate research findings and decarceration innovations to the general public through new avenues (e.g., public service announcements, social medial, phone apps, commercials).

CONCLUSION

This chapter represents the collective thinking of more than 200 experts in criminal justice reform across disciplines and sectors. We organized the guideposts and strategies under four guiding concepts of smart decarceration. We did so to demonstrate the importance of incorporating the guiding concepts into targeted action. Without a grounding in these concepts, individual strategies can become fragmented or lose intended focus, or result in unintended consequences. Imposing the guiding concepts on existing strategies also generates intervention modifications and improvements to meet simultaneous objectives of reduced incarceration use, reversal of disparities, and fostering public safety and well-being.

Though only representative of the range of action steps generated through our online survey and in-person working groups, the guideposts and strategies presented in this chapter highlight the breadth, complexity, and challenge of ushering in an era of smart decarceration. What is needed to advance these and other strategies in a coordinated and cohesive nature is the development of comprehensive and integrated implementation strategies to inform decarceration-focused policies and practices at the local, state, and national level. For example, the potential impact of advancing leadership among formerly incarcerated individuals will only be fully realized when simultaneous effort is aimed at removing unnecessary civic and legal restrictions from people with criminal convictions. And evidence garnered from social innovations must be disseminated to a broad range of stakeholders so that evidence-driven decarceration efforts can be properly implemented.

Who will do the work of developing frameworks to further guide and sustain an era of smart decarceration? Implementing components of these guideposts into meaningful action will require the commitment and engagement of state and local officials, community-based providers and organizations, scholars committed to applied research, and advocates and formerly incarcerated leaders. We hope that this chapter underscores the kinds of synergies that can come about from this type of collective action.

Combined, the guideposts of this final chapter and the collective content of the book demonstrate that smart decarceration will not be successful if reforms are grounded in revising current approaches—entire paradigms will need to be rejected and reconstructed with collective examination. Authors critically questioned current thinking about criminal justice and challenged readers to create a futurescape of justice. Such a futurescape was described as one that views the disenfranchisement and stigmatization of those who have become involved in the criminal justice system as untenable. Chapter contributors challenge reformers to examine factors well beyond individual change to include structural conditions before, during, and after correctional supervision. Finally, it was emphasized throughout the book that the role of public policies in fueling and perpetuating mass incarceration cannot be ignored if true change is to occur. This book compiles the current thinking of leaders at a time in which the United States is on the cusp of decarceration. We hope that this book archives efforts and ideas present at the beginning of a social movement that is likely to lead to a different era of in the experience of justice and safety in America.

REFERENCES

Cavadino, M., & Dignan, J. (2006). *Penal systems: A comparative approach* (4th edition). London, UK: Sage Publications.

Doob, A. N. (2012). Principled sentencing, politics, and restraint in the use of imprisonment: Canada's break with its history. *Champ Pénal, 9*. http://doi.org/10.4000/champpenal.8335

Doob, A. N., & Webster, C. M. (2006). Countering punitiveness: Understanding stability in Canada's imprisonment rate. *Law and Society Review, 40*(2), 325–368. doi:10.1111/j.1540-5893.2006.00266.x

Government of Canada. (2000). *Corrections population report* (4th ed.). Solicitor General Canada. Iqaluit: Government of Canada.

Government of Canada. (2013). *Strategic plan for Aboriginal corrections*. Retrieved February 18, 2016, from http://www.csc-scc.gc.ca/aboriginal/002003-1001-eng.shtml#3

Jeffries, S., & Stenning, P. (2014). Sentencing, Aboriginal offenders: Law, policy, and practice in three countries. *Canadian Journal of Criminology and Criminal Justice, 56*(4), 447–494. doi:10.3138/cjccj.2014.S03

Lappi-Seppälä, T. (2000). The fall of the Finnish prison population. *Journal of Scandinavian Studies in Criminology and Crime Prevention, 1*(1), 27–40. http://doi.org/10.1080/14043850050116246

Lappi-Seppälä, T. (2007). Penal policy in Scandinavia. In M. Tonry (Ed.), *Crime and justice: A review of research* (Vol. 36, pp. 189–211). Chicago, IL: University of Chicago Press.

Roberts, J. V., & Gabor, T. (2004). Living in the shadow of prison lessons from the Canadian experience in decarceration. *British Journal of Criminology, 44*(1), 92–112.

Roberts, J. V., & Roach, K. (2003). Restorative justice in Canada: From sentencing circles to sentencing principles. In A. von Hirsch, J. V. Roberts, A. E. Bottoms, K. Roach, & M. Schiff (Eds.), *Restorative and criminal justice.* Oxford, UK: Hart.

Roeder, O. K., Eisen, L. B., Bowling, J., Stiglitz, J. E., & Chettiar, I. M. (2015). *What caused the crime decline?* Brennan Center for Justice. New York University School of Law.

von Hoffer, H. (2003). Prison populations as political constructs: The case of Finland, Holland, and Sweden. *Journal of Scandinavian Studies in Criminology and Crime Prevention, 4,* 21–38.

Webster, C. M., & Doob, A. N. (2015). US punitiveness "Canadian style"? Cultural values and Canadian punishment policy. *Punishment and Society, 17*(3), 299–321. http://doi.org/10.1177/1462474515590893

Zubrycki, R. M. (2002). Community-based alternatives to incarceration in Canada. *United Nations Asia and Far East Institute for the Prevention of Crime and Treatment of Offenders Japan. Annual Report.* Retrieved from http://www.unafei.or.jp/english/pdf/PDF_rms/no61/ch07.pdf

INDEX

Page numbers followed by *f* indicate figures; page numbers followed by *t* indicate tables; page numbers followed by *b* indicate boxes.

Abercrombie, Neil, 55
accountability
  assessment of, 242
  system, 242–43
actuarial risk assessment, 210, 221–23
  accuracy, 215–17
  challenges of, 211
  criticisms of, 213
  and decarceration, 222–23
  guiding principles of, 214–15
    decarcerative purpose, 214, 220–23
    judicious implementation, 214, 218–19
    maximized accuracy and transparency, 214–18
  from statistical uncertainty to misplaced
    information, 219–20
  from traditional risk assessment to, 211
  transparency, 215, 217–18
actuarial risk assessment tools, 211–12, 214–16,
  218, 221–23
Adoption Safe Families Act of 1997, 171–72
Affordable Care Act of 2010 (ACA), 151, 188,
  190, 197

African Americans, 6, 93–94, 103–4, 165. *See
  also* race
age-crime curve, 145–46, 146*f*
age-graded theory of crime, 163
age group, prison population
  growth by, 149, 149*f*
agency of formerly incarcerated persons,
  normalizing and supporting, 246–47
aging out of crime, 145–47
Albertson, S., 125
Alexander, Amanda, 106
All of Us or None, 48
American Bar Association, on the role of
  prosecutors, 72
Anderson, Elijah, 123
Anti-Drug Abuse Act of 1986, 162
anti-immigration bias, 41–42
apartheid (South Africa), 47
apprehension, certainty of, 148
area under the curve (AUC) statistic, 216
Armstrong, Robert W., 153
Auburn-style prisons, 37

bail reform in New York, 184–85
Ball, Cary, 123
banishment, 33–34
behavioral health disorder disparities of mass
    incarceration, 6–7
behavioral health specialists, collaboration
    with, 83–84
Bennett, Mark, 153
Biko, Steven, 47
bipartisan support for decarceration, 50,
    101–2, 138
"black box" phenomenon, 217
black communities, overpolicing of, 123
blacks. *See* African Americans; race
Blackstone's formulation, 57
Blitz, C. L., 164
blood sanctions, 31–32, 34
Blumstein, Alfred, 140
bootstrapper mentality, 91–93
bootstrapping, 91
Boston Ceasefire model, 122
Braga, Anthony, 123
Britain. *See* England
broadening, 221
broken windows policing, 122, 124, 125
Brown, Michael, 123
Bush, George W., 66

California
    fewer prisoners and less crime in, 144, 145*t*
    life sentences in, 141, 147, 148
Canada
    decarceration and reform, 251–53
    homicide rate and incarceration rate in,
        142–43, 144*f*
capital punishment. *See* death penalty
carceral citizenship, 106, 110
Carson, E. A., 143*f*
Catholic Church. *See* ecclesiastical court system
Cavanagh, Michael, 60
certainty of apprehension, 148
Chamberlain, A. W., 118
childcare, giving people leaving prison money to
    secure, 245–46
Children's Hospital of Wisconsin, 85
Christianity, 67. *See also* ecclesiastical court system
citizenship
    carceral, 106, 110

in the carceral age, 105–6
    violation of, 12, 72
civic engagement, 173*t*
"civil death," 161
civil disabilities, 160. *See also* citizenship;
    collateral consequences
    defined, 160, 161
    forms of relief from, 174
civil disabilities policies, 160
    history and trends, 161–63
    implications for research and reform,
        172, 174–75
    shifts in state-level policy in the era of mass
        incarceration, 165–66
    a tale of two states, 172, 173*t*
    theory and empirical support for
        examination, 163–65
civil disability policies, 263–64. *See also* collateral
    consequences
civil rights. *See also* civil disabilities
    restoring to formerly incarcerated
        individuals, 188–89
Clear, Todd R., 119–21, 128, 231, 233
coercive mobility, defined, 119
coercive mobility thesis, 119–20
cognitive-behavioral framework, 107, 205–6
cognitive restructuring programming, gaps in,
    201, 202*f*
collaborating for system change, 82–84
collaboration. *See also* multisector collaboration;
    person-system synergies; public-private
    collaborations
    a focus on system change through, 236–37
    multidisciplinary, 85–87
    transdisciplinary, 21. *See also* transdisciplinary
        policy and practice interventions,
        implementing
collaborative model offered at Emmaus Road,
    110. *See also* Emmaus Road
collateral consequences, 160. *See also* civil
    disabilities; civil disability policies
    reevaluating and repealing
        policy-driven, 263–64
Collateral Consequences of Conviction Act of
    2009, 174
College & Community Fellowship
    (CCF), 93, 94
Common Justice program, 185

communities
  receiving, 106
  reinvesting in and revitalizing, 86–87
community, 130
  as epicenter of crime and victimization, 117
  as epicenter of punishment, 117–18
  as epicenter of surveillance, 118–19
  integrating justice and, 261–62
  policing and, 122–24
  removal from the, 245
community agency involvement in addressing
    violent crime, 85–86
community-based organizations, engaging and
    sharing information with, 81
community capacity for social innovation,
    building, 264
  strategies for, 264–65
community-centered smart decarceration,
    115–16, 121–28, 130
  the case for place, 116–21
community corrections, 126
community courts, 124–26
community empowerment, 62
community groups, connecting government
    agencies to, 81–82
community identity, promoting a, 126
community interventions for justice-involved
    individuals, 193–94, 205–7, 222. *See
    also* Milwaukee Community Diversion
    Program
  an approach to understanding program-related
      issues, 195–96
    individual-level approach: matching
        individuals to appropriate programs, 196
    jurisdiction-level approach: planning for
        service needs, 197
    program-level approach: implementing
        quality programming, 196–97
community justice, 121, 246
  defined, 121
Community Justice Council (CJC), 83–84
community leadership, models of, 187–88
community prosecution, 78
  defined, 78
Community Prosecution Unit (CPU),
    79–82, 87
community prosecution units
  creating, 78–82

role in decarceration, 82
community prosecutors, being available 24/7, 82
community reconciliation processes, 246
community supervision, 222
  innovations in, 18–19
commutation contracts, 65–66
Commutation Review Boards, 65–66
Comprehensive Crime Control Act of 1984, 162
Convict Criminology (Ross & RIchards), 50
Cooper, A. D., 104, 180
corporal punishment, 32–34, 41
"corporate welfare," 92
"corrections," 14, 18, 39
court, community and the, 124–26
court system, innovations in the, 17–18
crime decisions, why long sentences have a
    limited impact on, 148
crime drop
  global, without mass incarceration, 142–43
  mass incarceration's limited contribution to
      the, 142–44
crime-prevention initiatives. *See also* prevention
  creating, 80
Criminal Code of Canada, 252
criminal justice system. *See also specific topics*
  focus on individual change through
      incarceration, 234–35
  growth, 5
  improving it from within, 47–48
    necessary support, 48–49
  reform movement, 45–46
criminal justice system sectors, multisector social
    innovation, 261
  cross-sector training, 261
  ways to increase, 261
criminal justice system-wide innovations, 4
  making, 16–19, 259
criminal justice transformation, guiding concepts
    for smart incarceration through, 12–23
criminogenic effects of incarceration,
    30, 220–21
criminogenic needs, 164, 166–67
criminogenic risks, 107. *See also*
    criminogenic needs
crisis centers, neighborhood, 265
Crisis Intervention Team (CIT), 83
Culhane, D. ., 170
Cullen, F. T., 12–13, 166

data collection. *See* measurement and data collection

death penalty, 151

debtor prisons, 185

decarceration, xvii. *See also* smart decarceration; *specific topics*
  appetite for, 137–39
  comparative decarceration in context, 250–53
  era of, xviii
  ingredients for successful, 254
  lessons for, 40–42
  priority areas for, 255*b*
  rate of, 139
  reforms have initiated, 138–39
  three interrelated outcomes of, 256*b*

decarceration effect, 251, 252

decarceration movement, evolution and purpose of data in, 77–78

decarceration policy. *See* policy

decarceration talent, developing, 262–63
  strategies for and ways of, 263

decarcerative purpose, principle of, 214, 220–23

decision-making, opportunities for shared, 246

deferred prosecution programs, viii

deinstitutionalization, a lesson from, 10–11

"deserving" and "undeserving" beneficiaries of reform efforts., 96, 99

(de)stabilizers, 195

deterrence, 148
  general deterrence strategies and specific deterrence, 84
  individual vs. collective, 32

dialogue, forums for genuine and critical, 258–59

Dickens, Charles, 37–38

directly affected individuals, 90, 95
  leadership from, 95, 98
  organizing a movement led by, 98–99

disruption, empirical support for, 164–65

District Attorney's Office of New York (DANY), 85

diversion programs, 76–77

Doob, Anthony N., 144*f*

dosage-based probation model, 75, 83–84

Douglass, Frederick, 45

downsizing, 13

drug law reform, 183–84

drug offenders, nonviolent, 64

drug offenses, 140, 162. *See also* substance use

drugs, war on, xvii, 6, 20, 68, 140, 162, 189

drug treatment programs, 187, 200, 201, 201*f*, 204*f*, 205
  expanding, 150–51

Durlauf, S., 147–48

Durose, M. R., 14, 104, 180

early intervention (EI) programs, 75–77, 83

ecclesiastical court system, 33

ecological consequences of disproportionate burdens on particular neighborhoods, 119

economic disparities of mass incarceration, 6, 116

education, 169. *See also* higher education
  packaging and disseminating information to targeted audiences, 267
  transforming prisons and jails to agents of, 186–87

education programs, providing, 81

elderly. *See also* geriatric release; older adults
  high cost of incarcerating the, 149

Ellis, Eddie, 97

Emmaus Road (reentry program), 108–10

employment, 167–69, 173*t*, 264–65
  giving people leaving prison enough money to secure, 245–46

England, 34–36

evidence
  privileging evidence in smart incarceration, 22–23
  the problem with not responding to, 22

evidence-based corrections, 166–72. *See also* *specific topics*

evidence-based programs, 193–94
  defined, 193

evidence-driven strategies, employing, 4, 22–24, 222
  guideposts to, 265–67
  questions to ensure that smart incarceration approaches foster and uphold, 23

Ewald, A., 165

Fagan, J., 120

family, civil disability laws and the, 171–72

Family Peace Center model, 85

family-related consequences of incarceration, 8

Farrington, D., 146*f*

felony murder rule, 59, 60*b*

Flake, Floyd, 91–92

food stamps, denial of, 161

Formerly Incarcerated and Convicted People and Families Movement, 48

formerly incarcerated individual(s)
 amplifying perspectives on, 15
 empowering them to lead, 46
 hearing the voices of, 46–49
 in leadership positions, 257
 myth of the voiceless, 49–51
 normalizing and supporting, 246–47
 a personal testimony, 44–45
 a perspective on decarceration from a, 55–68
 restoring civil and human rights to, 188–89. *See also* civil disabilities
 working with them to implement reform strategies, 49–51
forums for genuine and critical dialogue, 258–59
Francis, Pope, 151
freedom, 47, 246. *See also* civil disabilities
From Mass Incarceration to Effective and Sustainable Decarceration, xviii
future of justice, imagining the, 231–34, 247
 moving forward, 240–41, 247

geographic mobility. *See* coercive mobility
geriatric release. *See also* elderly
 developing a meaningful process of, 152–53
ghettos, 94, 129
Gingrich, Newt, 101
Giuliani, Rudolph W., 124
Good Neighbor Project, 62
 as a proactive program, 62
Gordon, Neil, 58
Grant, Oscar, 123
Graves, Anthony, 57
Gray, Freddy, 123
Growth of Incarceration in the United States: Exploring Causes and Consequences, The (Travis et al.), 5, 12, 72

Hamilton, Z. K., 170
Harding, Reginald, 60*b*
health concerns, 7–8. *See also* public health
health risks and limitations of social reintegration at reentry, 181–82
Helland, E., 148
higher education, 93, 94. *See also* education
 need for, 97–98
high-risk incarceration, rethinking, 221–22
Holder, Eric, 138, 222
Hollan, J., 120
Holsinger, Alexander, 221

homicide rate and incarceration rate in Canada, 142–43, 143*f*, 144*f*
housing, 169–71, 173*t*
 giving people leaving prison enough money to secure, 245–46
Housing First, 238
housing opportunities for those with incarceration histories, generating a range of, 264
housing programs, 170
hulks, 33–35
human and civil rights. *See also* civil disabilities
 restored to formerly incarcerated individuals, 188–89
Hume, David, 214
"hurt people, hurt people," 66–67
hyperincarceration, 7

Illinois, civil disabilities in, 172, 173*t*
Imbler v. Pachtman, 63
immigrants. *See* anti-immigration bias
imprisonment. *See also* incarceration
 without opportunity, 245
incarcerated individuals. *See also* formerly incarcerated individual(s); incarceration and the incarcerated; *specific topics*
 amplifying perspectives on currently, 15
incarcerated population in jails and prisons
 reducing the, 10–11
 setting inmate population caps, 12
incarceration. *See also specific topics*
 a bidirectional relationship between crime and, 119–21
 changing the use of, 260
  ways of, 260–61
 defined, 115n
 reforming contributors to, 259–60
  ways of, 260
 utility of
  assumptions about the, 14–15
  reconsidering the, 14–15
incarceration and the incarcerated, changing the narrative on, 4, 13–16
 guideposts to, 257–59
incarceration rate
 homicide rate and, 142–43, 144*f*
 importance of reducing, 222
 murder rate and, 142, 143*f*
 number of people incarcerated by year, 8–9, 9*t*

individual change through incarceration,
criminal justice system's focus on, 234–35
institutional inertia, overcoming, 219
Intelligence Led Prosecution, 84–85
intervention programs. *See also* community
interventions for justice-involved
individuals; early intervention (EI)
programs; transdisciplinary policy and
practice interventions
developing and applying new data sources and
analytics to inform new, 73–78
isolation of prisoners, 36–37

Jackson, John H., 57
jails. *See also* bail reform in New York; prisons
and jails
early, 31–32
Jim Crow laws, 93–94
Johnson, Lyndon Baines, 94
Jones, Van, 101
judges, selecting proper community court, 126
judicious implementation, principle of,
214, 218–19
justice, 234
language of, 245
types of, 246
justice-involved population (JIP), 194
justice multisector, 237–38. *See also* multisector
social innovation
justice preinvestment, 129
justice pursuits, a working framework for, 234–35
historical context, 234
justice reinvestment, 193, 244. *See also*
reinvesting in and revitalizing communities
defined, 128
rethinking, 128–30
juvenile offenders, 146

Kelly, William R., 213
Kennedy, Anthony M., 66
King, Ryan, 140

labor, prison, 35
lack of intent laws, 59, 60*b*
Laub, J. H., 163
law enforcement. *See also* policing
innovations in, 16–17
Lawrence, S., 95
leadership

capacity to lead among people in reentry, 97–99
community, 187–88
learning to lead in the decarceration
movement, 93. *See also* directly affected
individuals; reentry
true reform requires leadership from directly
affected individuals, 98
leadership positions, people with incarceration
histories in, 257
leading with conviction, 44–46
least restraint, principle of, 251
Legal Action Center (LAC), 165
Levin, Charles, 60
life-course theory, 164
Lifer Review Boards, 65–66
"lifers." *See also* life sentences
recidivism rate, 147
released through mandatory parole
reviews, 64–65
life sentences, 62, 245. *See also* "lifers"
in California, 141, 147–48
depoliticizing and professionalizing the parole
process for, 152
historic rise in, 140–41
lifers released through mandatory parole
reviews, 64–65
Lippman, Jonathan, 184
local knowledge. *See also* community
seeking, 126
Loeber, R., 146*f*
Loeffler, C., 118
Lowenkamp, Christopher T., 221
Lutze, F., 170

Makarios, M., 170
mandatory minimum laws, 20, 101, 138, 153, 162.
See also mandatory sentencing policies
mandatory sentencing policies, 137, 151, 180,
183–84. *See also* mandatory minimum laws;
three-strikes laws
Maricopa County Adult Probation, 127
Maruna, Shadd, 188–89
mass incarceration. *See also specific topics*
alternatives to, xvii
connotations of the term, 10
vs. hyperincarceration, 7
limited contribution to the crime
drop, 142–44
as new kind of epidemic, 181–82

as peculiar institution, 94
primary features, 103
rate of decline of, 139
ripple effects, 3, 7–8
those who profit from, 244
mass incarceration era, 5–10. *See also specific topics*
end of the, 8–10
evidence of the, 9–10
what will follow the, 3–4
mass supervision, 102, 106
reentry in an era of, 106–8
maturity, social controls, and crime, 145–47
Mauer, Marc, 95, 151
maximized accuracy and transparency, principle of, 214–18
McDonald, LaQuan, 123
measurement and data collection, maximizing, 266
strategies for, 266
Metraux, S., 170
Midtown Community Court, 124
Miller, Lisa, 216
Miller, Reuben Jonathan, 106, 118
million dollar blocks, 117, 129
Milwaukee Community District Attorney's Office (MCDA), 74–76, 86
Community Prosecution Unit (CPU), 79–82, 87
Milwaukee Community Diversion Program, 76–77
Milwaukee Community Justice Council (CJC), 83–84
Milwaukee Homicide Review Commission (MHRC), 73–74
mobility. *See* coercive mobility
money given to people leaving jail and prison, 245–46
multidisciplinary collaboration. *See under* collaboration
multisector collaboration, "actuarializing," 239–40
multisector social innovation, 235–43
imagining the possibilities for, 243–47
murder. *See* felony murder rule
murder rate and incarceration rate, 142, 143*f*
My Brother's Keeper, 98

Nagin, D., 147–48
National Institute of Corrections (NIC), 75
Near West Side Partners (NWSP), 86–87

need principle, 212, 213, 222
needs, 195
defined, 195
needs-based factors, 212. *See also* risk-need-responsivity (RNR) model
neighborhood crisis centers, developing, 265
neighborhoods, disproportionate burdens on particular, 119
Nellis, Ashley, 140–41
New Jersey, fewer prisoners and less crime in, 144, 145*t*
New York, fewer prisoners and less crime in, 144, 145*t*
New York City Police, 85
number needed to treat (NNT), 194

Obama, Barack, 45, 101, 138
Obamacare. *See* Affordable Care Act of 2010
offender management, 126, 128
Office of Social Innovation and Civic Participation (OSICP), 235–37
older adults, 149. *See also* aging out of crime; geriatric release
lower recidivism rates of, 147
Operation Ceasefire. *See* Boston Ceasefire model
otherizing, 66
overcriminalization, 59, 60*b*

Padilla v. Kentucky, 166
Pan, K. Y., 164
Parenti, Christian, 95
parole, 126, 141
in California, erosion of, 141
individualizing, 260
parole requirements, 66
parole reviews, mandatory
for individuals incarcerated more than 20 years, 64–66
parsimony (sentencing), 12, 72
Patient Protection and Affordable Care Act. *See* Affordable Care Act of 2010
peculiar institutions, 93–96
penal incarceration, 31
penal labor, 35
penitentiary, the dream of the, 34–35
turned into a nightmare, 36–38
Penitentiary Act of 1779, 34–36
person-system synergies, 241–43. *See also* collaboration

Petersilia, J., 12–13, 166
Piquero, Alex, 146–47
place. *See also* community
  the case for, 116–21
"Places Not Cases: Re-thinking the Probation
  Focus" (Clear), 233
Plague of Prisons, A (Drucker), 180
Pogorzelski, W., 164
polarization. *See* otherizing
police chiefs, 101
police shootings, racial disparities in, 103–4
policing. *See also* law enforcement
  community and, 122–24
policy. *See also specific topics*
  science and, 214–15
  true reform requires leadership from directly
    affected individuals in, 98
  ways to drive, 259
policymaking, decarceration-driven, 259
policy recommendations to achieve
  decarceration, 62–66
political pressures and influences on criminal
  justice system, 63, 152
political support for decarceration, bipartisan,
  50, 101–2, 138
poverty, 168, 185. *See also* childcare; economic
  disparities of mass incarceration;
  employment
prevention, 80, 246
  primary, 182–85
    key task in, 185
  public health principles of, 181. *See also*
    public health
  reallocating investments toward, 150
  secondary, 186
    key task in, 186–87
  tertiary, 187–88
    key tasks for, 188–89
  three stages of, 182
prison cycling/prison migration, 119
prisoner reentry. *See* reentry
prisons and jails, 29–31
  historical perspective on, 30–31, 38–39. *See also*
    penitentiary
    prisons today, 39–40
  innovations in, 18
  in literature, 37
  before the prison, 31–34
  transforming, 186–87

prison sentences. *See* sentences
prison ships. *See* hulks
Proactive Community Supervision (PCS), 127
probability, defined, 216
probation, 126
probation population, risk level distribution of,
  198f, 198–99
probation population needs, general, 199, 199f
probation subpopulation needs, 199, 200f
probation subpopulations
  factors affecting different, 199, 200f
  gaps in cognitive restructuring programming
    among, 201, 202f
Promoting Assets and Reducing Crime (PARC)
  project., 86, 87
proportionality (sentencing), 12, 72
prosecution. *See also* community prosecution
  increasing quality, efficiency, and priorities
    for, 80–81
prosecution practices, reforming, 63
prosecutorial immunity, reduced to qualified
  immunity, 63
prosecutorial misconduct
  the commonplace nature of, 56–57
  decarceration's role in reforming, 56–59, 60b
  definitions, 56–57
  reasons for, 57, 58
prosecutors, 71, 101
  eliminating the election of, 63
  functions and duties, 72n
  line, 71
provable charges, 77
public awareness campaign, 257–58
public health, 7–8, 189–90, 243–44
  decarceration and, 181–82
  from punishment to, 179–81
  transforming prisons and jails to agents of, 186–87
public health framework, 182
public-private collaborations, 238, 240, 246. *See
  also* collaboration
public-private partnerships, 87
public safety
  how to better allocate public resources to
    promote, 148–51
  maximizing, 12
  vs. personal safety, 245
  problems with the term, 245
Public Safety Assessment (PSA) risk-screening
  tool, 77

Public Safety Realignment Act of 2011, 243
Public Safety Realignment Assembly Bill (AB)
109, 198, 201–3, 243
distribution of AB-109 programs, 204, 204*f*
punishment. *See also* sentences
certainty of. *See* certainty of apprehension
transforming prisons and jails from institutions
of, 186–87
punitive sentiment, waning, 137, 138*f*

race. *See also* African Americans
and the problem of punishment, 103–4
racial caste line, 93
racial disparities, 165
of mass incarceration, 6, 116
in police shootings, 103–4
in policing, 123
and prosecutorial misconduct, 58–59
racial justice, reform as hinging on new
understandings of, 96–97
racism, 41–42, 93–94
biopolitical, 97
peculiar institutions and, 93–94
Ramirez, Mark, 137, 138*f*
receiving communities, 106
recidivism, 7, 12, 103
prevention of, 246. *See also* prevention
recidivism rates, 179–80, 183
age and, 147
redemption and second chances to return to
humanity, 66–68
Red Hook Center, 124
Reducing Racial and Ethnic Disparities in Jails
(roundtable discussion), 223
reentry, 39–40, 94, 101–3. *See also* public health
in an era of mass supervision, 102, 106–8
defined, 102
the Emmaus Road way, 108–10
extends penal forms beyond the prison
walls, 95–96
as peculiar institution, 94–96
people in reentry have the capacity to
lead, 97–99
organizing a movement led by those most
affected, 98–99
preparing incarcerated individuals for, 61–62
records, risk, and responsibility, 104–5
a way forward, 110–11
reentry reform efforts, limitations of current, 96

reentry/transitional programs, creating
universal, 263
strategies for, 263
rehabilitation, 12–13, 151, 188–89
civil disabilities and, 160–61, 166–72
commitment to, 166–72
measuring the success of, 236
transforming prisons and jails to agents
of, 186–87
rehabilitation efforts, those who profit from
mass incarceration must invest in, 244
reintegration, evaluating partners for
contributions to successful, 245
reinvesting in and revitalizing communities,
86–87. *See also* justice reinvestment
repeat offending, 222
research, true reform as requiring leadership
from directly affected individuals in, 98
research-practice-policy partnerships,
refining, 266
strategies for and ways of, 266
responsivity principle, 199, 213
restorative justice, application of the principles
of, 246
restorative justice models, 185
restorative justice programs, 68, 186, 187
restoring justice in the prison setting, 61–62
revolving door of incarceration, 39
risk, 194–95. *See also* actuarial risk assessment;
criminogenic risks
defined, 194
predictors of, 194
risk-need-responsivity (RNR) methodology,
195–97, 202–3, 207
risk-need-responsivity (RNR) model, 194–96,
212–13. *See also* system risks, needs, and
responsivity
principles, 212
risk principle, 212
risk reduction, the science and practice of, 221
Rosky, J. W., 170
Rothman, David, 38–39

safety. *See also* public safety
personal vs. public, 245
Sampson, R. J., 118, 163
San Francisco, programming in, 199–200
gap between programming needed and
programming available, 201, 201*f*

San Francisco Adult Probation Department
    (APD), 198–201
    gaps in services, 200–202
    lessons from, 202–3
San Francisco probationers, characteristics
    of, 198–99
Santa Cruz Probation Department, 203–5
screening, universal, 83
Sebesta, Charles, 57
Second Chance Act of 2007, 94n, 101, 105
second chances, 94, 95
    to return to humanity, 66–68
self-determination, 46, 51
sentences
    establishing an upper limit on, 151–52
    limited deterrent value of longer, 147–48
    reducing all, 137
        how to shorten all sentences, 151–53
        meaningful decarceration requires, 139–41
        why it would not harm public safety, 145–48
sentencing, guiding principles of, 12, 72–73
sentencing commissions, 152
Sentencing Project, 74
Sentencing Reform and Corrections Act of
    2015, 101
Sentinel Event review process, 77
shared decision-making, opportunities for, 246
Sherraden, Michael, 250
ships, prison. *See* hulks
Silver, Eric, 216
Simon, David, 101
slavery, 93–94
Small, Deborah, 189
smart decarceration, xviii, 181, 189, 222, 250. *See
    also* decarceration; *specific topics*
    articulating outcomes for, 10–12
    defined, 4
    guideposts and strategies for the era of, 256–68
Smart Decarceration Initiative (SDI), vii, viii,
    66, 120. *See also specific topics*
    driving motivation behind the creation of
        the, xvii
    guiding concepts for, 256b
Smart Decarceration Initiative Inaugural
    Conference, 255
smart decarceration outcomes and guiding
    outcomes, 4–5
smart incarceration

questions for exploring how it can rethink
    incarceration and the incarcerated, 4, 13–16
transforming policies and practices for, 20–21
"smart on crime" vs. "tough on crime," 138. *See
    also* "tough on crime" policies and practices
Snyder, H. N., 104, 180
social assistance, denial of. *See* civil disabilities
social controls, maturity, and crime, 145–47
social disparities
    among the incarcerated, redressing, 11
    of mass incarceration, 6–7, 116
social innovation. *See also* Office of Social
        Innovation and Civic Participation
    building community capacity for, 264
    strategies for, 264–65
social justice, 12, 72
social network analysis, 122
social networks, positive, 105, 173t
social work, viii–ix
Sojourner Family Peace Center (SFPC)
    model, 85
South African freedom struggle, 47
Spohn, Cassia, 221
(de)stabilizers, 195
Starr, S. B., 218
Steinberg, Laurence, 146
Steinberg, R., 125
Steiner, B., 170
substance abuse treatment programs, 200, 201.
        See also drug treatment programs
    gaps in substance dependence programming
        among subpopulations, 200, 201f
substance use, 241–42
substance use disorders, 6, 187, 195, 199. *See also*
    drug treatment programs
substantive success, defined, 236
success stories, investing in creating, 244
supervision. *See also* mass supervision
    from case- to place-based, 233. *See also* place
    community and, 126–28
Sutherland, George, 56–57
synergies. *See also* collaboration
    person-system, 241–43
system accountability, 242–43
system change through collaboration, focus
    on, 236–37
system risks, needs, and responsivity, 239. *See also*
    risk-need-responsivity (RNR) model

Tabarrok, A., 148
Tallahassee, Florida, 120
Taxman, Faye S., 241, 246
Tetrick, Josh, 232
three-strikes laws, 20
    in California, 141
        limited payoff of, 148
tipping point (coercive mobility thesis), 120
Tocqueville, Alexis de, 37
Tonry, Michael, 152, 215
"tough on crime" policies and practices, 9, 20, 50,
        58, 99, 138, 162, 220
training programs, providing, 81
transdisciplinary policy and practice
        interventions, implementing, 4, 19–23
    guideposts to, 262–65
    questions for guiding criminal justice system
        in, 21–22
transdisciplinary strategies, developing, 21
Travis, Jeremy, 5–6, 12–13, 95, 104
Travis, L. F., 170
Tseloni, A., 143

"undeserving." *See* "deserving" and "undeserving"
        beneficiaries of reform efforts.
unemployment. *See* employment
Uniform Law Commission, 174
United States. *See also specific topics*
    first penitentiaries, 36
    spirit of innovation and forward thinking, 36
universal screening, 83

VanNostrand, Marie, 221
Vera Institute of Justice, 74, 152, 165, 185
victim anger, 67
victim-offender mediation, 185, 246
Violence Reduction Strategies, 122–23
violent crime, 142–43
    increased punitiveness toward, 140–41
    law enforcement's response to, 84
    as a public health crisis, focusing on, 84–86
    three models to address, 84–85
Violent Crime Control and Law Enforcement
        Act of 1994, 20
Virginia, civil disabilities in, 172, 173*t*
vulnerable populations, 13
    identifying them and diverting them from
        incarceration, 185

Wacquant, Loic, 93–94
Wallace, D., 118
Walsh, Lynda, 214–15
Webster, Cheryl Marie, 144*f*
welfare benefits, denial of, 161–63
well-being, maximizing public, 12
Weller, Mark, 153
West, V., 120
Willingham, Cameron Todd, 57
Wolff, N., 164
Woodmore, Flozelle, 153
wrongfully convicted allowed to sue for
        monetary relief, 63